THE RIGHT AGAINST RIGHTS IN LATIN AMERICA

For over 100 years the *Proceedings of the British Academy* series has provided a unique record of British scholarship in the humanities and social sciences. These themed volumes drive scholarship forward and are landmarks in their field. For more information about the series and guidance on submitting a proposal for publication, please visit www.thebritishacademy.ac.uk/proceedings.

PROCEEDINGS OF THE BRITISH ACADEMY • 255

THE RIGHT AGAINST RIGHTS IN LATIN AMERICA

Edited by
LEIGH A. PAYNE, JULIA ZULVER,
AND SIMÓN ESCOFFIER

Published for THE BRITISH ACADEMY
by OXFORD UNIVERSITY PRESS

Oxford University Press, Great Clarendon Street, Oxford OX2 6DP

© The British Academy 2023

Database right The British Academy (maker)

First edition published in 2023

All rights reserved. No part of this publication may be reproduced, stored in a retrieval system, or transmitted, in any form or by any means, without the prior permission in writing of the British Academy, or as expressly permitted by law, by licence, or under terms agreed with the appropriate reprographics rights organisation. Enquiries concerning reproduction outside the scope of the above should be sent to the Publications Department, The British Academy, 10–11 Carlton House Terrace, London SW1Y 5AH

You must not circulate this book in any other form and you must impose this same condition on any acquirer

British Library Cataloguing in Publication Data
Data available

Library of Congress Cataloging in Publication Data
Data available

Typeset by Newgen Publishing UK
Printed in Great Britain by TJ Books Ltd, Padstow, Cornwall

ISBN 978-0-19-726739-4
ISSN 0068-1202

Under conditions of tyranny it is far easier to act than to think.

Hannah Arendt, The Human Condition

Freedom is not – and never is – the freedom to do harm. If a free action injures another person or deprives them of freedom, then the first act cannot be regarded as free; it becomes an injurious action.

When violence and hatred become the instruments of religious morality and politics, then democracy is threatened by those who would tear apart the social fabric, punish difference, and undermine the social bonds required to support our co-existence here on earth.

Judith Butler, The Phantom of Gender: Reflections
on Freedom and Violence

Contents

List of Figures and Tables		ix
Notes on Contributors		x
Acknowledgements		xiv

1   Introduction: The Right against Rights in Latin America   1
SIMÓN ESCOFFIER, LEIGH A. PAYNE, AND JULIA ZULVER

2   The Right against Rights in Latin America: An Analytical Framework   29
LEIGH A. PAYNE

3   Families of Perpetrators Mobilising against Human Rights Trials
in Argentina   59
VALENTINA SALVI

4   The Religious Right and Anti-Genderism in Colombia   78
ELIZABETH S. CORREDOR

5   The Transnational Force of Anti-LGBT+ Politics in Latin America   98
SAMUEL RITHOLTZ AND MIGUEL MESQUITA

6   'In the Name of the Family': The Evangelical Caucus and Rights
Rollbacks in Brazil   112
ANDREZA ARUSKA DE SOUZA SANTOS

7   Framejacking Rights Discourse to Undermine Latin American
Multilateral Human Rights Institutions   129
GILLIAN KANE, MIRTA MORAGAS, AND KIRAN STALLONE

8   Why Anti-Abortion Movements Fail: The Case of Chile   141
SIMÓN ESCOFFIER AND LIETA VIVALDI

9   The Violent Rollback of Indigenous and Environmental Rights:
The Emblematic Case of Lenca Leader Berta Cáceres in Honduras   162
NANCY R. TAPIAS TORRADO

viii *Contents*

10 Opposing Affirmative Action: Covert and Coded Challenges
to Racial Equality in Uruguay   181
DEBBIE SHARNAK

11 Resisting Redistribution with Recognition: A Radical Neoliberal
Countermovement in Santa Cruz, Bolivia   205
ANNA KRAUSOVA

12 Righting Rights, Righting Wrongs: Final Reflections   229
JULIA ZULVER AND LEIGH A. PAYNE

Bibliography   248
Index   281

List of Figures and Tables

Figures

6.1	Draft laws on family in Brazil's Congress.	122
8.1	Protests over abortion by type of demand (2009–19). Authors' calculation using data from the Observatory of Conflicts Cumulative Dataset.	149
8.2	Catholics' trust in the Catholic Church (2006–18). Authors' calculation using data from the *Encuesta Nacional Bicentenario*.	150
10.1	Implementation of Ley 19.122: percentage of state vacancies that went to Afro-Uruguayans. Author's calculation based on secondary data.	194
11.1	CPSC attention to indigeneity. Corpus from the CPSC website, elaborated by the author.	218
11.2	CPSC and media attention to indigeneity and the TIPNIS conflict. Corpora from EFE Newswires and the CPSC website, elaborated by the author.	219
11.3	Collocations of *indígena*. Corpus from the CPSC website, elaborated by the author.	220

Table

2.1	Right-against-rights mobilisations: An analytical framework.	30

Notes on Contributors

Elizabeth Corredor is a postdoctoral research fellow in the Department of Politics and Public Administration at Toronto Metropolitan University. She holds a Ph.D. in political science, a certificate in women's, gender, and sexuality studies from Rutgers University, and an M.A. from the University of Chicago in Latin American studies. Her research centres on gender politics in Latin America, with a specific focus on social movements, gender mainstreaming in policy, and conservative resistance to feminist and LGBT+ agendas. Her book project *Gender Justice, Resistance, and the Politics of Peace in Colombia* investigates how and under what conditions gender and sexual rights are incorporated into the 2010–16 peace process between the Colombian Government and the Revolutionary Armed Fores of Colombia (FARC). Her work has appeared in *Signs: Journal of Women in Culture and Society*, *Latin American Politics and Society*, and *International Negotiations: A Journal of Theory and Practice*.

Andreza Aruska de Souza Santos is a lecturer at the Latin American Centre and the Director of the Brazilian Studies Programme at the University of Oxford. She is the author of *The Politics of Memory: Urban Cultural Heritage in Brazil*, published in 2019. Andreza's research agenda focuses on grassroots politics and inequality in Brazil. She received her Ph.D. in social anthropology from the University of St Andrews, and her M.A. in social sciences was jointly awarded by the University of Freiburg (Germany), the University of KwaZulu Natal (South Africa), and Jawaharal Nehru University (India). In addition to research and teaching she also has policy experience, and worked as a political adviser for the United Nations Office on Drugs and Crime in Vienna, the Indian Embassy in Brazil, the Brazilian Confederation of Municipalities, and the Brazilian Ministry of Social Development.

Simón Escoffier is an assistant professor at the School of Social Work at Pontificia Universidad Católica de Chile. He is the author of the book *Mobilising at the Urban Margins: Citizenship and Patronage Politics in Post-Dictatorial Chile* (forthcoming, 2023). He holds a doctorate from the Sociology Department and St Antony's College at the University of Oxford. His research sits at the intersection of social movements, citizenship, urban marginality, local governance, democracy, and Latin American studies. He teaches on sociological theory, politics, and social movements.

Gillian Kane is a recognised researcher and writer on global movements against sexual and reproductive rights, and LGBT+ rights. She is Senior Technical Lead for Policy and Advocacy at Ipas, an international organisation focused on expanding access to safe abortion and contraception. Gillian has a B.A. from the University of Wisconsin-Madison, and a master's degree in Latin American and Caribbean studies from New York University. She has spent the last two decades advocating for women's human rights, and has authored numerous articles and reports highlighting risks and harms to women's access to their health and human rights.

Anna Krausova is an ESRC postdoctoral fellow in the Department of Sociology at the University of Oxford. Her research focuses on the consequences of social movements in general, and protest in particular. She connects sociological theories of protest and framing to political theories of recognition and authenticity, and analyses empirical cases ranging from Indigenous protest in Chile to refugee rights activism in the UK. She holds a doctorate in sociology from the University of Oxford. She is passionate about mixed-methods and interdisciplinary research, and about building a North–South dialogue between Latin American and northern scholarship.

Miguel Mesquita is a human rights specialist at the Inter-American Commission on Human Rights, part of the Organization of American States. He oversees themes related to LGBTI, women, afro-descendants, and Indigenous people's rights. For over 11 years, he has worked on human rights issues in different positions and organisations in civil society, academia. and governance. Miguel holds an LL.B. and an M.Phil. from the Federal University of Rio de Janeiro in Brazil, and is a Chevening Alumnus with an LL.M. in human rights from Birkbeck, University of London.

Mirta Moraga is a Paraguayan lawyer, feminist activist, and human rights advocate. She has an LL.M. in international legal studies from American University Washington College of Law with a specialisation in human rights and gender. She has investigated hate crimes against trans people in Paraguay, the impact of criminalisation of abortion in the human rights of women in Paraguay, and the offensive of anti-rights groups within the Organization of American States.

Leigh A. Payne is Professor of Sociology and Latin America at St Antony's College, Oxford. She works broadly on responses to past atrocity. Together with Gabriel Pereira and Laura Bernal Bermúdez she has published *Transitional Justice and Corporate Accountability: Deploying Archimedes' Lever* (2020) and a follow-up edited volume on *Economic Actors and the Limits of Transitional Justice* (2022). With Karina Ansolabehere and Barbara Frey she has also edited *Disappearances in the Post-Transition Era in Latin America* (2021), and with Juan Espindola she edited *Collaboration in Authoritarian and Armed Conflict Settings* (2022). In addition to the Newton Fund–British Academy, she gratefully acknowledges the support for these projects from the University of Minnesota Human Rights Program (where she is a senior researcher), National Science Foundation, ESRC, AHRC, Leverhulme, and the Open Society Foundation.

Samuel Ritholtz is a Max Weber Fellow in the Department of Political and Social Sciences at the European University Institute and a D.Phil. candidate in the Department of International Development at the University of Oxford. Their research interests include LGBT+ experiences of conflict, crisis, and displacement, as well as political theories of brutality, cruelty, and violence. They are the co-author of *Toward a Queer Theory of Refuge* (forthcoming, 2023) and co-editor of *Queer Conflict Research* (forthcoming, 2023). Samuel has an M.Sc. in refugee and forced migration studies from the University of Oxford and a B.Sc. in international agriculture and rural development from Cornell University.

Valentina Salvi is a sociologist who obtained her Ph.D. in social sciences at Universidad Estadual de Campinas, Brazil. She is a researcher at the National Council of Scientific Research (CONICET) and a member of the editorial board of *Clepsidra: Revista interdisciplinario de estudios sobre memoria social*. Until 2021, she was the director of Núcleo de Estudios sobre Memoria (Memory Studies Programme) at the Centro de Investigaciones Sociales/Institute of Economic and Social Development (CIS-IDES). Her research deals with memory, responsibility, perpetrators, and the armed forces in post-dictatorship Argentina. She has published various articles, and the monographs *De vencedores a víctimas: Memorias militares sobre el pasado reciente en la Argentina* (2012) and *Las voces de la represión: Las declaraciones de los perpetradores de la dictadura argentina* (2019) with Claudia Feld.

Debbie Sharnak is an assistant professor of history and international relations at Rowan University. Her research examines the history of human rights, transnational advocacy networks, Latin America, and foreign policy. In *Of Light and Struggle: Social Justice, Human Rights, and Accountability in Uruguay* (2023) she explores the evolution of human rights discourse in and about Uruguay, particularly during the country's transition back to democratic rule. Her work has been published in the *Journal of Iberian and Latin American Studies*, *Diplomacy & Statecraft*, *Taller*, the *Washington Post*, and several edited volumes. She received her M.A. and Ph.D. in history from the University of Wisconsin-Madison.

Kiran Stallone is a Ph.D. candidate in sociology at the University of California, Berkeley. She writes about civilian agency and gender-based violence in war, with a focus on the Colombian armed conflict. She has published on these topics for academic journals and news outlets such as the *Washington Post*, the *Guardian*, and the BBC. Kiran has a master's degree in Latin American studies from the University of Oxford, and a bachelor's in political science from Barnard College, Columbia University. She currently lives in Bogotá, Colombia.

Nancy R. Tapias Torrado is a Postdoctoral Fellow in the Faculté de Science Politique et de Droit at the Université du Québec à Montréal (UQAM). She holds a Ph.D. in sociology from the University of Oxford, an LL.M. in international

Notes on Contributors   xiii

human rights law from the University of Essex, and an M.Phil. and an LL.B. from the Pontificia Universidad Javeriana in Colombia. Her postdoctoral investigation explores the impact of Indigenous women-led mobilisations on the practice of corporations involved in human rights abuses in connection to mega-projects in Canada. Her research comes out of over a decade of experience working with and for neglected communities and human rights defenders in the Americas and several previous years working in Colombia on gender, human rights, and armed conflict. She is a former regional researcher with Amnesty International and has consulted for the United Nations, Oxfam, and the Centre for Justice and International Law (CEJIL), among others.

Lieta Vivaldi is a faculty member in the Law Department at Universidad Alberto Hurtado, Chile. She is also a research fellow in the Centre for Applied Ethics (CEDEA) at Universidad de Chile and an associate researcher in the Faculty of Law at Universidad Diego Portales. Lieta has a Ph.D. in sociology from Goldsmiths, University of London and a master's in sociology from the London School of Economics and Political Science; she is a lawyer, with a diploma in gender and violence from Universidad de Chile. She has published journal articles and book chapters on human rights, reproductive rights, feminist movements, and Latin America.

Julia Zulver is a Marie Skłodowska-Curie research fellow at the Oxford School of Global and Area Studies. She is currently based at the Instituto de Investigaciones Jurídicas at the Universidad Nacional Autónoma de México. Her project 'High-Risk Leadership in Latin America' focuses on women's leadership in the pursuit of social justice in various violent contexts. She earned her D.Phil. in Sociology at the University of Oxford in 2018, where she studied how and why women's organisations mobilise in high-risk contexts – actions that expose them to further danger. Her book *High-Risk Feminism in Colombia: Women's Mobilization in Violent Contexts* was published in 2022.

Acknowledgements

THE IDEA FOR this edited volume began years ago, when Leigh Payne was asked to summarise and update the approach taken in her book *Uncivil Movements* (2000) for an entry in *The Oxford Handbook of Latin American Social Movements*. Leigh contacted her current and former doctoral students to seek their advice: 'If you were writing about right-wing movements in Latin America today, what would you write about?' A flood of ideas came in: more than could possibly be included in a short entry in the *Handbook*. And, thus, *The Right against Rights in Latin America* took off.

The volume extended beyond Leigh's students. A lively Latin American Studies Association (LASA) meeting in Barcelona in May 2019 packed a room, further confirming for the authors and the editors that this was an important project that added a new perspective on the right wing in Latin America and right-wing movements elsewhere. The volume evolved; its framework became ever more solid, strengthened by incisive comments from the LASA discussant Sonia Alvarez, two manuscript reviewers – Lindsay Mayka and Cristobal Rovira Kaltwasser – and the ever careful and critical reader Stephen Meili.

We extend our deep gratitude to the contributors of this volume's chapters, who shared their important and exciting research with us. They have worked with us over years to edit their chapters and put them into conversation with each other. They waited patiently as we experienced delays resulting from the pandemic and other professional and personal life events. They had faith in this final volume and a commitment to the study of the impact of the right against rights. We appreciate their creativity and generosity. Perhaps most importantly, we wish to underscore that each of them, in their own way, is contributing academic and policy research to make the world a fairer place. This is no easy task, and one that merits our recognition, and indeed gratitude.

To the British Academy, we are thankful for the funds provided for an earlier iteration of this study. We also acknowledge Portia Taylor and the editorial staff at Oxford University Press and Newgen Publishing (especially Helen Flitton and Robert Whitelock) for the care and attention they have given our volume. We are grateful for their willingness to engage with our project, to move it forward and over a few unexpected bumps along the way. We further appreciate the anonymous reviewers, whose suggestions were thorough, thoughtful, and deeply generous. The final version of this volume has been greatly improved by incorporating their edits and additions. Many thanks also to Dorian Singh for the creation of the index for this book.

Leigh wishes to add her thanks to her former and current students. They continue to inspire projects – indeed, more projects than seem humanly possible at

Acknowledgements

times. But they compensate for that excessive work with an equal measure of love, care, and laughter. Just as we were finishing up the manuscript and these acknowledgements, I learned that my very first doctoral student – Jeff Cason – had passed away suddenly, leaving an enormous hole in my heart. Jeff began my journey as a doctoral supervisor. He taught me how to listen, to think creatively about ways to guide students through the emotional wreckage and professional disenchantment that are a seemingly intrinsic characteristic of our academic pathways, and to survive, embrace life, and even have some fun. I will miss him terribly. In losing Jeff, I acknowledge how deeply my students have touched my life. You too, Finn; I miss you. To my two kids – Zack and Abbe – now grown up, and the new members of our family – Lily and Jimmi – thank you for always reminding me of what is important in life. Steve, your picky edits are all over this book, as usual, but so too is your enduring belief in me and your hard work at living life to its fullest, including a shared commitment to righting wrongs.

Julia wishes to thank her mother, Geraldine, who, when the world was entering the panicked first weeks of the pandemic, and international borders were shutting, let her take up residence in her childhood home, where part of this book was written. Though there were difficult moments, we weathered them together; the months we spent together are the most precious silver lining I could have imagined. Thanks also to Kiran Stallone and Samuel Ritholtz, both for agreeing to contribute to this volume, and for the academic engagement, debate, and camaraderie. Finally, in the context of both this project and my adjacent research projects focusing on women's resilience in the face of backlash, I have had the privilege of meeting activists who dedicate their lives to the defence of women's, LGBT+, Indigenous, Afro, and migrant rights, often with minimal or no resources to support them. Their work positions them at the heart of protests, campaigns, and struggles for change, which means that they assume personal risks of violence and retribution. They inspire me, and I hope that my academic work serves as a contribution to the frontline battles they fight every day.

Simón wishes to thank his colleagues in the Latin American Centre at the University of Oxford. They have supported this project since its inception in 2018. Diego Sanchez-Ancochea and Eduardo Posada warmly hosted me as a postdoctoral visitor when they acted as directors at the Centre. While I was there, Francesca Lessa and Markus Hochmüller became terrific friends. They discussed this project with me on many occasions and gave me encouraging feedback. I am also grateful to my friends, Marti Rovira and Aino Jarvelin, who were an emotional rock to hold on to as I worked on this book during the pandemic. I owe much of my inspiration for this book to my family. They gave me the motivation and unconditional love I needed to persevere in this project. I also thank Hugo Rojas, my colleague and dear friend, who provided Lieta Vivaldi and me with excellent help for our chapter in the volume. Additionally, we received critical research assistance from Juan Pablo Miranda and Anna Clemente. My participation in this project obtained financial support from different sources. The Chilean National Agency for Research and Development supported me through its Becas Chile postdoctoral fellowship.

xvi *Acknowledgements*

Since this book project began in 2018, the world has undergone many changes: a global pandemic, the storming of the US Capitol, the reversal of *Roe v. Wade*, the Russian invasion of Ukraine, the school shooting in Uvalde. The media we consume impress on us the ubiquitous threats of violence, illness, and death that many around the world face on a daily basis. To be sure, during this time there have also been progressive gains; however, sometimes the rise of the right against rights feels like an oppressive and depressing force that we witness not only in the United States but also in the Latin American countries where we live and work. In a small way, however, coming together in academic community to compile these chapters has felt like a reprieve and an act of resistance. Across the miles, we communicated over Zoom, via WhatsApp messages, and through phone calls to create a volume that documents how the right against rights functions and, by extension, how we can continue to struggle for a more just world for those whose rights are under attack.

The cover image – a photograph of Colombian artist Doris Salcedo's *Shibboleth* project for the Unilever Series at Tate Modern, London – depicts our world: the deep fissure in society; the rupture in the foundation of rights. The title of the piece further evokes division in societies. The word 'shibboleth' is derived from the bible (Book of Judges, Chapter 12), the story of villagers who determined who belonged or not based on how they pronounced the word. Incorrect pronunciation met with violent retaliation. We believe that Salcedo shares with us a hope that deep and harmful schisms can be closed, that acceptance of difference will bring societies together and not divide them. We thank her for all she has done toward that aim. And we thank her for allowing us to use her work to represent our own hope for the future.

1

Introduction: The Right against Rights in Latin America

SIMÓN ESCOFFIER, LEIGH A. PAYNE, AND JULIA ZULVER

SINCE THE FALL of the dictatorships and the end of the armed conflicts in Latin America, the struggle for rights has made impressive gains. The region boasts some of the most extensive rights for the LGBT+ (lesbian, gay, bisexual, transgender, queer, and intersex) community, including hate crime legislation, equal marriage, and anti-discrimination laws. Indigenous rights achieved in international law and regional bodies gained constitutional status. The environment has similarly made its way into certain constitutions through the rights of nature. Communal land, and cultural language and practice rights, have been won – at least on the books – by Afro-Indigenous movements. Afro-Latinx groups have seen legislative gains against employment and other forms of discrimination. Quota laws and affirmative action legislation have advanced the rights to political representation for women, and ethnic and racial groups. Abortion rights have also been won in some countries, an impressive achievement in a region dominated by Catholicism and conservative Evangelicals. Victims' rights have advanced through efforts to hold state and non-state actors accountable for human rights violations during dictatorships and armed conflicts. A veritable 'rights revolution' (Epp 1998) – on issues of gender and sexuality, ethnicity and the environment, and accountability for crimes against humanity – has occurred, in which the region is not just catching up with rights gains in the Global North, but even surpassing them in some cases. These achievements are noteworthy in a region with a legacy of violently entrenched colonialism, authoritarianism, and cultural, political, and economic conservatism.

Where such a politically, socially, and economically powerful right wing prevails, it may seem unsurprising that efforts on the right would emerge to check, roll back, or reverse the rights gains of previously marginalised and excluded groups. Yet there are some surprises in that mobilisation. First, the mobilisation of these forces in the region challenges what is generally assumed about the right wing. For example, the right's need to mobilise collectively at this moment suggests

Proceedings of the British Academy, **255**, 1–28, © The British Academy 2023.

that its traditional bases of power in politics, economics, and society have proved insufficient to stem the rights revolution before it gained traction. Second, the composition of this right against rights is distinct from the privileged and elite forces that have historically formed the alliances that controlled political, economic, and social life in the region. Indeed, the right against rights includes sectors of Latin American society whose socio-economic profile is less like the traditional right elite and more like the once marginalised and excluded groups behind the rights revolution. Third, the right against rights mobilises differently than in the past by taking to the streets, collective action that the traditional right-wing powerholders did not need to influence political outcomes. Fourth, existing analytical frameworks for understanding other right-wing groups in the region (e.g. parties, populism, lobbies, interest groups, and policy-makers) do not fit the right against rights. However – and fifth – frameworks to analyse right-wing movements that developed in Europe and the United States have tended to exclude Latin America from comparison, thereby requiring a broader analytical lens to consider similarities and differences in the right's mobilisation across regions. Sixth, the right against rights has had an impact in Latin America, but not always; it has succeeded in rolling back rights gains and in threatening and harming rights-seekers, violating their fundamental and universal rights, but sometimes it fails in those objectives.

There is both a dearth of empirical information about these groups, and a lack of a framework for how to best analyse them. Indeed, there is little analytical grappling with what we might call a *new* tide of anti-rights mobilisation in the region. Those mobilised against progressive rights in Latin America have ties to right-wing political parties, religious groups, business associations, the military and police, and other institutional and informal organisations, but also work outside those institutional frameworks. Even the transnational advocacy networks that provided in past decades the leverage to advance progressive reforms (Keck and Sikkink 1998) have been hijacked by the global right to roll back those advances. Whereas the boomerang effect was meant to amplify the silenced voices demanding rights in the Global South, it now also amplifies the voices of those groups attempting to roll back those rights. This study aims to make visible the threats to newly established rights in the region and to those who have advanced them. It also examines when the right against rights fails to achieve its goals, providing insights for policy-makers and rights advocates to resist rollback efforts.

This introduction begins to develop the volume's contributions. It first sets out concepts and definitions of right-against-rights mobilisations. This includes making distinctions between the right against rights and other right-wing forces in the region and abroad. The notion of 'rights' and competition over them is examined. Mobilisation as opposed to movements is also discussed as relevant to understanding the right against rights. The chapter's second section explores the regional context in which the right-against-rights mobilisations have grown in the past decades and their impact on Latin American democracies. The chapter then concludes with a summary of the case-study chapters included in the volume.

INTRODUCTION 3

Defining Right-against-Rights Mobilisations

We define the 'right against rights' as *collective extra-institutional and institutional mobilisation to check, roll back, or reverse specific rights promoted by previously marginalised groups and communities (i.e. gender and sexuality, ethnic, race, environment, accountability for crimes against humanity) and to restore, promote, or advance a status quo ante of traditional political, social, economic, and cultural rights.* This definition clearly specifies a particular subset of right-wing political forces and movements; it does not intend to define the entire spectrum of the right, even if the right against rights may strategically join forces with other right-wing groups for electoral, legislative, or judicial gains. The definition is also broad enough to encompass different types of mobilisations within the right against rights that may act independently or join forces behind specific mobilisations or causes. Payne (Chapter 2) distinguishes three sometimes overlapping categories of right-against-rights mobilisations: countermovements, uncivil movements, and radical neoliberal mobilisations. Countermovements mobilise specifically to 'counter' or oppose specific social movements' efforts to promote rights for LGBT+ and BIPOC (black, Indigenous, and people of colour) communities, women, the environment, and victims of past crimes against humanity. Uncivil movements aim to eliminate, through uncivil or violent acts, the rights-seekers included in the rights revolution whom they perceive as threats to the social, economic, and cultural status quo. Radical neoliberal mobilisations focus specifically on rolling back the promotion of rights that they perceive as impinging on property rights and business freedoms. This definition and typology of mobilisations offers clarity and parsimony around a specific phenomenon within the political right that involves a distinct cause (roll back rights), target (social, economic, and cultural rights adversaries), and form of action (extra-institutional mobilisation in the streets and outside the political system, even if they also operate within the system). It is a definition that travels across time and geographic borders. It separates defining characteristics of such mobilisations from explanations for their emergence and success in achieving their political objectives. It avoids conceptual blurring by calling all these groups 'right-wing movements', or assuming that the right against rights is encompassed by existing studies of right-wing movements. As a distinct category, the right-against-rights mobilisation warrants discussion of what is meant by 'the right' in relationship to 'rights' and differences in the organisation of some right-wing groups into mobilisations rather than movements.

Defining Rights

The existing literature on the right in Latin America or right-wing movements in Europe and the United States has not analysed a crucial aspect of a contemporary right that has emerged around the world in response to the rights revolution. Castro Rea's

(2018) definition of the right, in contrast, offers a notion of the right that focuses on its conception of rights. Payne (2023) summarises Castro Rea's definition of that right as oriented toward 'those who deserve or prove their worthiness as rights-seekers. The left, in contrast, recognises rights based on the intrinsic equality of individuals and groups, their worth as humans.' Legal scholars would describe this notion as 'human dignity'. Despite its contested nature, the idea of dignity refers to the inherent freedom and equality that all humans enjoy in their moral and legal existence (Adler 2020; McCrudden 2008). This definition allows for an understanding of why the right ideologically rejects the value of certain 'new' rights – LGBT+, gender, sexual, and reproductive, environmental, BIPOC, distributional accountability for victims of dictatorships – over traditional rights and the worthiness of the rights-seekers promoting them. The left, in contrast, considers these rights intrinsic to the struggle for equality in social democracies.

As Castro Rea's definition shows, the right against rights does not oppose the expansion of rights per se, but rather the expansion of those rights promoted by the 'undeserving'. An event in September 2020 captures this contention over rights. United States Secretary of State Mike Pompeo used the United Nations General Assembly to drum up support for his Commission on Unalienable Rights, a policy promoting a vision of human rights that prioritises religious freedom and property rights (Verma 2020). Although Pompeo used the language of rights promotion, a law professor quoted in the *New York Times* identified the initiative as an effort at a rollback of rights, stating: 'It's shorthand for erasing subsequent rights guarantees for LGBT+ persons and rights guarantees for sexual and reproductive health' (Verma 2020). We do not argue that Pompeo, or the broader right-against-rights mobilisation, is insincere in its protection and expansion of certain rights or cynical in its use of rights language. Rather, this event illustrates that the language of rights can be a double-edged sword. Anti-rights mobilisations are adept at using a moralistic and traditional language of rights to undermine the rights of the historically excluded and to justify, validate, and promote their own rights claims: rights to free speech, rights of the family, rights of the innocent, right to life, rights of religious freedom, property rights, and due process and penal rights of perpetrators of past human rights violations. As we will see in this volume's chapters, right-wing groups often adopt the language of rights that their adversaries engage. Thus, when we speak about anti-rights groups or an anti-progressive backlash, we are talking about mobilisations aiming to prevent or roll back a specific set of rights linked to social justice and equalities around gender, race, ethnicity, sexuality, ability, geography, environment, and class.

Anti-rights groups are also rights-oriented, therefore, in the sense that they hope to defend and expand rights they perceive as under attack. They defend, for example, the right of each family to decide freely the content of their children's education. This right clashes with school systems advancing more inclusive content and procedures to recognise the rights and equality of LGBT+ pupils and protection from bullying (see the Colombian example in Corredor (Chapter 4)). These mobilisations thus do not oppose rights themselves, since they attempt to restore

INTRODUCTION

traditional rights. Nor do they defend only the exclusive rights of the privileged or the elite; in many cases, right-against-rights groups recruit from the same socioeconomic sectors as their social movement adversaries. Right-against-rights groups often express the same sense of marginalisation and exclusion as those adversaries, even when such a loss of power and influence is often exaggerated. Their stated aims are similar – to give voice to the silenced, to speak truth to power – even when they often possess ready access to media outlets, where they are frequently accused of promoting 'fake news campaigns' and untruths about their adversaries.

What the analysis of the right against rights emphasises is the politics of contention over rights. The authors in this volume are in line with Castro Rea's understanding of a rights orientation on the left that emphasises the intrinsic equality of individuals and groups, their worth as humans rather than their proof of worthiness. The attempts to roll back rights of individuals or groups because of who they are – their worth – undermines basic concepts of universality. To use or threaten violence against those rights-seekers denies them their intrinsic equality. Thus, how the right against rights mobilises to roll back some, and advance other, rights is critical to the analysis.

Mobilisation by the Right against Rights

Some scholars consider right-wing movements to be 'social movements'. Caiani and della Porta (2018, 329), for example, identify a set of 'right-wing social movements' that they define as 'networks of more or less formal groups ... [in which] the structure of these networks defines their mobilising capacity ... [and] these networks use a broad repertoire of collective action'. Diani (1992, 5) also emphasises that social movements emerge when 'excluded interests try to get access to the established polity', thereby suggesting that the right-against-rights mobilisations that perceive their rights/interests as excluded, particularly during the rights revolution, would fit a social movement definition.

Yet other scholars reject the notion that right-wing mobilisations could be defined as social movements. Blee and Creasap (2010, 271), for example, argue: 'Rightist movements fit awkwardly into the theoretical templates of social movements that were largely developed in studies of feminism, the New Left, and civil rights. Such progressive movements ... are poor models for movements of privileged groups.' Although right-against-rights mobilisations do not always represent 'privileged groups', we share the reluctance to extend the category of social movements to encompass groups that aim to roll back the rights of the historically marginalised and excluded. Social movements fundamentally aim to bring about social change, and not to halt change and return to the traditional status quo ante.

How the right against rights mobilises also questions the application of a social movement label. Tilly (1984, 306), for example, defines social movements as 'sustained series of interactions between power holders and persons successfully claiming to speak on behalf of a constituency lacking formal representation, in the course of which those persons make publicly visible demands for changes in the distribution or exercise of power, and back those demands with public demonstrations of support'. Right-against-rights mobilisations are often oriented toward power holders. They also tend to possess formal representation, although we contend that they mobilise when they perceive a loss in traditional sources of power (see e.g. McVeigh 2009). Indeed, right-against-rights mobilisations often seek to restore power to groups upholding conservative values or traditional bases of economic, social, and political power. In this effort, they are not distant from power. Thus, they do not demand change in the distribution or exercise of power, since they are still very much part of a traditional political power structure in their countries – whose right-wing political parties rely on them for support – even if they operate outside it. While they may feel that the rights revolution has shifted political power in the country, or threatens to do so, they aim to restore or preserve that traditional power structure, not challenge it.

While, by definition, right-against-rights groups *mobilise*, they do not all form movements. Some do, however. Some right-against-rights groups fit the social movement concept of 'countermovements'. Scott and Marshall (2015) define countermovements or backlash movements as reactionary, designed to oppose and roll back the advances made by progressive movements. Thus, even those right-against-rights groups that *could* be considered movements (rather than mobilisations) fail to meet the criteria generally used to define social movements in terms of advancing transformation; their orientation is to reverse and expand an earlier set of traditional rights protections against the changes promoted by previously marginalised and excluded groups.

Not all right-against-rights groups form 'countermovements', however. Accordingly, our conceptual framework prefers the broader term 'mobilisation' to 'movement'. By referring to mobilisations, the right-against-rights concept encompasses those groups that never establish, or even aim to establish, a sustained and coherent movement structure. Some may coalesce and act in unison sporadically, to defend specific shared goals at only one moment in time. They mobilise this collective action without forming an organised movement. It is important to note, however, that not all social movements have enjoyed a sustained or coherent movement structure either. Thus, the traditional and status quo orientation toward rolling back transformative rights, rather than organisational structure alone, distinguishes the right-against-rights mobilisations from social movements.

O'Brien and Walsh (2020) assert that an 'entrenched opposition' has emerged in Latin America, oriented by an ideological and tactical rivalry against progressive civil society organisations in matters of public policy, political opportunities, and recognition. This opposition sometimes engages in 'backlash' efforts to prevent gains by progressive groups. It is that mobilisation to block rights that is the focus of this volume. In that effort, some right-against-rights groups mobilise as movements; some mobilise as less sustained, less organised, less coherent groups, but still form small, if temporary, strategic alliances. More often than not, the right

INTRODUCTION

against rights consists of ephemeral mobilisations oriented toward a particular aim. Once that aim is achieved, they will tend to divide, merge, morph, or disband altogether. While the term 'mobilisation' better captures the type of groups analysed here than 'social movement', the social movement literature offers a framework for understanding how such groups nonetheless forge their identity, constituency, strategies, and tactics to achieve their objectives to check, roll back, or reverse rights gains.

Defining the Right against Rights as a Distinct Phenomenon

This volume contends that the right against rights is distinct from other groups on the right. As right-wing mobilisations outside the political system, these groups differ from right-wing parties, interest groups, and lobbies. While they may, and often do, ally with such institutionalised entities, they maintain sufficient autonomy to act outside the system. This is as true in Europe and the United States as it is in Latin America. On the other hand, right-wing political institutions depend to a large extent on the mobilisational power of the right against rights. Clifford Bob (2011, 9–11) asserts, for example, that right-wing parties depend on extremists for votes; these 'extremists' include the mobilisations analysed in this volume. Yet the purpose of this study is not to analyse right-wing voting constituencies or behaviour. On the contrary, it explores how right-wing mobilisations amass power without necessarily electing their representatives to political office or assuming an institutional role.

We suggest, then, that existing frameworks for analysing the right within Latin America and outside the region are not adequate for understanding the right against rights. We set this out below by looking at distinctions between the right against rights and existing right-wing studies in Latin America. We then explore similar distinctions between the right against rights in Latin America and in European and US studies of right-wing movements.

Latin American Approaches to the Right: Bringing in the Right against Rights

Most studies of the right in Latin America have focused on right-wing political forces within the institutional system. The institutional right wing in the region draws on historic political patterns, but also cultural approaches, specifically the role of the Catholic Church in the past (Middlebrook 2000) and evangelical Protestantism more recently (Pérez Guadalupe 2019). Other studies have considered the role that business has played in strengthening the political power of the right, most specifically the authoritarian coups and regimes between the 1960s and the 1980s (O'Donnell 1973; Payne 1994; Dreifuss 1981). As such, the right wing in Latin America is perceived typically as an alliance of traditional political, social, cultural, and economic elites with power from the agricultural, extractive, and industrial sectors, politicians, legislatures, and judiciaries, the Church, and the military.

Three key scholarly approaches to the contemporary right in Latin America can be highlighted. First, researchers have analysed the institutional right. The studies under this approach focus mainly on right-wing political parties and on other manifestations of elite institutional political power on the right (Cannon 2016; Middlebrook 2000; Gibson 1992; Power 2000; Alenda 2020; Roberts 2014). One group of scholars analyses the factors underlying those parties' electoral success, as well as the reasons for their failures (Loxton 2021; Luna and Rovira Kaltwasser 2014). Luna and Rovira Kaltwasser (2014), for example, examine the right wing's effort to regain electoral power in a region that became widely dominated by the left in the first decade of the 2000s. Their work incorporates non-electoral, elite initiatives, such as the use of military power to reach the state, the influence of certain right-wing groups over mass media outlets, and the alliances that the Latin American right has used with business partners to bolster electoral campaigns.

Studies on the institutional right also include those looking at the right's impact on Latin American democracies (Middlebrook 2000; Loxton 2021; Power 2000; Goldstein 2019). This work regularly points to the controversial interaction of the Latin American right-wing with pluralist, inclusive political regimes. It shows how the right strongly benefits from its allegiance with dictatorships (Loxton 2021; Power 2000). It also discusses how the right's staunch defence of market-oriented policies and property rights sustains elite dominance at the expense of the lower classes' full access to political rights (Cannon 2016). In his study of the right wing in post-dictatorial Brazil, Power (2000), for instance, uses data on the parliament, political party members, and elections to show how the conservative elite undermined democratic development by clinging to political power. The Brazilian democratic transition, he argues, gave the right wing the ability to exercise disproportionate political influence and hold to entrenched positions of power. Hence, instead of a full democracy, the Brazilian conservative elite created 'a perverse situation in which, instead of the right accommodating itself to the rules of the new democracy, the rules of the new democracy must accommodate the right' (Power 2000, 239; see also Hunter 1997).

A second approach explores the institutional and elite political dynamics leading to the rise of a populist right (Soares 2020; Rennó 2020; Barrenechea and Dargent 2020; Rovira Kaltwasser and Van Hauwaert 2020). This included the appeal of the 1990s governments of Alberto Fujimori in Peru, Fernando Collor in Brazil, and Carlos Menem in Argentina, which combined populist tactics with market liberalisation policies (Rovira Kaltwasser 2014). Studies of right-wing populism shifted following the left-wing administrations of the so-called 'pink tide' to consider the support for right-wing presidents in Peru, Brazil, Chile, Argentina, and Ecuador. The case of Jair Bolsonaro's government in Brazil received special attention: a paramount example of far-right populists' capacity to capitalise on economic recession,

INTRODUCTION 9

the erosion of party systems, and heightened disappointment with democracy during the 2000s (Borges 2021; Hunter and Power 2019).

A third approach emerged only recently to consider new origins and tactics of right-wing grassroots mobilisation (Mayka and Smith, 2021a; Vaggione, 2005; O'Brien and Walsh, 2020; Payne 2000, 2020, 2023). These studies examine the triggers of contemporary right-wing mobilisation by pointing to their perception of intensified threats to conservative values from increasing secularisation, economic instability, globalisation, and immigration crises. They highlight the rise of evangelical churches' political power, right-wing networks, and international collaborations among the origins of contemporary mobilisation on the right (Reuterswärd 2021; Pérez Guadalupe 2019). When it comes to tactics, some studies have examined the right against rights' increasing employment of strategic litigation to limit LGBT+ and women's rights in domestic courts (Peñas and Morán 2014) as well as in the Inter-American System (Urueña 2019). Argentine conservative groups, for instance, fought against abortion rights by repeatedly filing cases under the collective writ of *amparo*, which allows them to represent the rights of abstract groups, such as Argentine women as a whole, or unborn children (Peñas and Morán 2014; Balaguer *et al.* 2021). More frequently, this new approach to the right focuses on framing and rhetorical devices. Framing includes family values, or the family as the backbone of society (O'Brien and Walsh 2020), patriarchy, neoliberalism, and anti-communism (Payne and de Souza Santos 2020) to appeal to a broad constituency. The spreading of manipulative rhetoric is identified as a tactic, with 'gender ideology' as key. A rhetorical device used within Catholic and evangelical communities and by their political allies, this notion arose in Vatican texts between 2001 and 2003; right-wing groups have adapted it to counter feminist and LGBT+ advocacy (Corredor 2019; Chapter 4). Right-wing social media activity has also proliferated on Facebook, WhatsApp, and Twitter (Davis and Straubhaar 2020; Gold and Peña 2021). Calling it 'populist communication', Davis and Straubhaar (2020) argue that nationalist movements used internet platforms to successfully tap into the multiple grievances behind Brazil's 2013 protests in order to foster opposition to and resentment of the Workers' Party (PT). Additionally, this research shows how right-wing activists often draw on frames and actions that proved successful to the left. Organisers on the right have, for example, appropriated the human rights discourse for their own purposes (Morgan 2014; Salvi (Chapter 3)). These arguments often include a veneer of scientific support to conceal a moral and religious orientation (Morán 2015; Vaggione 2005; Kane *et al.* (Chapter 7)).

This last approach comes closest to the aims of this book to develop a framework to examine Latin America's right-wing extra-institutional mobilisations. The introduction to the 2021 special issue of *Latin American Politics and Society* (*LAPS*) by Lindsay Mayka and Amy Erica Smith is an exception in looking at right-wing mobilisations that move beyond an institutional analysis. After highlighting the dearth of focus on what they refer to as the 'grassroots right', they address the nature, origins, causes, strategies, and impact of these groups. Their definition of the right includes 'a diverse set of individuals and organisations aiming to maintain social hierarchies that are perceived as traditional or natural', and to further 'refer to civil society groups that engage in activism to support rightist issues and identities' (Mayka and Smith 2021b, 3, 4). This definition addresses Scott and Marshall's emphasis on countermovements as reactionary and backlash mobilisations. Nonetheless, Mayka and Smith focus only on 'grassroots movements'. The authors concede that a grassroots right defies certain definitions of social movements, but highlight the right's use of social movement tactics (e.g. social media, street mobilisations, and visibility). What they leave out of their study are non-grassroots right-wing movements, such as radical neoliberals, analysed in our volume (Tapias Torrado (Chapter 9); Sharnak (Chapter 10); and Krausova (Chapter 11)). Moreover, Mayka and Smith are more optimistic about the democratic nature of grassroots right-wing movements, particularly by distinguishing them from authoritarian populism in the region and even suggesting that such movements might provide a stabilising and democratising force (2021, 5). We disagree; the chapters in this volume illustrate tactics used by the right against rights that undermine equal rights, human rights, and other basic rights fundamental to democracy, sometimes using violence to do so. In this volume, we attempt to take the process begun by the *LAPS* special issue a step further to develop a comprehensive framework and empirical analysis of a broader set of right-against-rights mobilisations.

The volume also overcomes the limitations of Leigh A. Payne's 2000 book, *Uncivil Movements*. That study provided a framework to understand certain types of right-wing mobilisations at an early phase of the democratic transition in the region, but is limited in its application to the full panoply of contemporary right-wing movements, the context in which they emerge, and the grievances behind their mobilisation. Payne analyses a traditional right in the region – the military, landholders, and paramilitary forces – a *dramatis personae* of *uncivil movements* that uses extra-institutional violence and democratic institutional participation to influence political outcomes in the early years after the democratic transition in the region (2000, xviii). She makes the case that 'uncivil movements ... employ the same mobilisational strategies used by social movements within civil society: like social movements, they claim to identify and empower a new political constituency, conscious of its identity while struggling to overcome its marginal status in the political system' (xix). The book's definition of uncivil movements finds uncomfortable parallels to pro-rights or democratic social movements insofar as they are 'movements'. They engage in similar strategies (identity and symbolic politics, oppositional politics, unconventional political action), and double-militancy tactics (maintaining movement autonomy while also participating in the political system through litigation, lobbies, parties, and representation in government) (3). Our volume updates and incorporates some of Payne's work on uncivil movements within a broader analytical framework of right-against-rights mobilisations.

INTRODUCTION

The task of our book, then, is to fill the ongoing gap in the literature on the region by developing a conceptual and empirical study on the phenomenon. In doing so, this volume will highlight not only the breadth and diversity of these movements in Latin America, but also why they are fundamentally different from previous movements, and – perhaps more importantly – why it is of vital importance that we study, analyse, and understand them in global context.

Right-Wing Movements in Comparative Perspective: Bringing Latin America In

Analyses of right-wing movements in Europe and the United States have a longer history than the recent studies in Latin America. Kopecky and Mudde (2003) show that these movements are particularly talented at using structures of political opportunity broadly. The more moderate anti-rights movements are often well-incorporated into an intricate web of political influence that extends within and outside the state, including right-wing political parties, think tanks, and NGOs. They use strategic litigation to push conservative rulings in court against progressive-issue networks seeking to advance rights concerning LGBT+ people and women, and rights linked to education, euthanasia, and other issues that they see as matters of moral contention (Heinz *et al.* 2003). According to McCrudden (2015), these moderate factions of the right against rights are so well equipped in legal activism that they operate transnationally to engage in litigation 'culture wars'.

Right-wing movements on the far right face a more hostile context (Caiani and Borri, 2012). They experience legal constraints in some European countries that ban extremism, hate speech, and discrimination. They also have limited support in the wider population and may face state repression. Consequently, movements on the far right tend to develop their work underground, create safe spaces of interaction (e.g. online sites), and produce leaderless organisations or 'lone wolf' types of actions (Cunningham 2004; Daniels 2009; Simi and Futrell 2011). Recent studies of the radical right in Europe and the United States, however, note bold departures from these earlier underground tactics; in emerging in public they have provided the base of support for far-right political leaders (Mudde 2022). These European mobilisations resemble their counterparts in Latin America, suggesting that similar types of right-against-rights mobilisation are emerging around the world.

The vast enterprise of studies on right-wing movements in Europe and the United States, however, only rarely travels outside those two geographic boundaries and tends to ignore the parallels with the Latin American right. Sometimes the reason for excluding Latin America is expressly stated, such as the region's distinct political history of dictatorships and civil conflict. Such a history envisions Latin America's right-wing movements as trapped in the authoritarian past and inconsequential to contemporary social and political life, and therein incomparable with European and US mobilisations. Roger Griffin, for example, dismisses the relevance of comparisons between Latin America's right-wing mobilisations and European ones, stating 'Considerations of traditionalist forces operating outside Europeanised societies in a non-parliamentary context, such as Islamic fundamentalism, or of ideologically vacuous dictatorships, whether military or personal [such as those in Latin America] … need not detain us' (Griffin 2017, 16). Meyer and Staggenborg (1996, 630) describe a process in Latin America in which right-wing mobilisations have little to offer to comparisons with Europe: 'In Central America, movements of the left and right often engage in combat in which the state is at most a marginal player.' Camus and Lebourg (2017, 2) lament the exclusion of Latin America's '"caudillist", reactionary, and clerical parties' from studies of the far right. These statements not only show that Latin America has been excluded from right-wing studies, but also reflect a surprising ignorance about the contemporary right in the region, a gap in knowledge that this book aims to fill.

The decades since Latin America's transitions from authoritarian rule and armed conflict have generated right-wing mobilisations that are not unlike those in Europe and the United States. Indeed, these mobilisations are at times directly linked through financial, cultural-ideological, and tactical alliances. In other words, not only *are* right-against-rights mobilisations in Latin America comparable to those in other parts of the world, but this volume contends that the comparison *should* be made. A comparison of similar groups to the Latin American right against rights adds breadth and depth to scholarship on right-wing mobilisations. The current volume has the ambition to use the Latin American cases to develop a better analytical framework for comparison that is capable of travelling across world regions. It suggests that the phenomenon of the right against rights has emerged around the globe with a powerful impact, sometimes with clear financial and organisational linkages, which demand a distinct analytical framework that can move out of the parochial approaches developed in Europe and extended to the United States.

Thus, we contend that the problem of comparison is not the distinctiveness or irrelevance of Latin America's right-wing mobilisations, but the poverty and parochialism of the existing analytical frameworks. A great deal of variation exists among right-wing movements on the European continent without inhibiting scholars from attempting comparison. As Blee and Creasap (2010, 270) note, there is a lack of uniformity in definitions of 'the right' in Europe and the United States. They highlight the nomenclatural distinctions among conservative movements, the radical right, the extreme right, and the far right, adding the further caveat that these take on different meanings in different country contexts. Such variations in understandings of the right have not prevented comparison across Europe and the United States and, similarly, should not prevent finding comparison with Latin American right-wing mobilisations. Yet, the right against rights does not fit easily into the existing categories. It is not a 'conservative movement', since the right against rights goes beyond 'conserving' and into 'expanding' some rights and 'rolling back' others. It is not necessarily 'radical', 'extreme', or 'far' right, since the mainstream right wing in some countries agrees with the views of the right against rights. Moreover, not all of the right against rights engages in radical or violent action.

INTRODUCTION 13

A central challenge for comparison, therefore, is situating the right against rights within the existing frameworks for understanding right-wing movements elsewhere. European and US scholarship has struggled with creating a coherent concept that includes the array of groups. Indeed, Cas Mudde (2017, 3–4) refers to this endeavour as a 'terminological quagmire', owing to the abundance of defining characteristics associated with right-wing movements in Europe and the United States. He attempts to overcome this problem by suggesting three core unifying features: nativism, authoritarianism, and populism. These characteristics are not as compelling when applied to Latin American right-against-rights mobilisations. Radical neoliberal groups, for example, comprise new generations who distance themselves from nativism, authoritarianism, and populism at times, even if at other times they strategically ally with such right-wing groups. As economically privileged groups, they do attempt to preserve their historic – authoritarian and nativist – rights, but also aim to radically expand business rights to compete internationally, thus lacking a populist orientation. Certain countermovements and uncivil movements, however, resemble Mudde's nativist, authoritarian, and populist classification. Within these mobilisations there is a nostalgic right that idealises authoritarian pasts and strong state security systems, but the same groups attempt to appeal to younger generations and to moderates uncomfortable with authoritarian and populist tendencies in the region. The effort to build dynamism at the bases involves rhetorical strategies that simultaneously unite traditional and conservative (nativist, authoritarian, and populist) forces with those who do not wish to be seen as a throw-back to an authoritarian past. There is, thus, a modern language of rights protection used by the right against rights that does not fit Mudde's classification.

In other words, the aims of the right against rights, its mobilisational tactics, and its composition, suggest that this is a new category of right-wing movement. It is not unique to Latin America, but the existing frameworks do not adequately capture how these mobilisations are similar or different across world regions.

Political Context and Backlash

It may be tempting to situate the rise of the right against rights as a backlash against the progressive rights implemented by the left-of-centre governments in office during Latin America's so-called 'pink tide' beginning in 2000. Certain leaders associated with the pink tide did indeed rhetorically challenge neoliberalism in the region and promote more egalitarian distribution to address deep structural inequalities, such as Evo Morales in Bolivia, Rafael Correa in Ecuador, and Lula da Silva in Brazil. There are several reasons why the pink tide context behind right-against-rights mobilisations does not provide a complete picture of right-against-rights mobilisation, however. First, the right against rights has grown in recent decades in several Latin American countries that did not experience a pink tide, including Honduras, Colombia, and Chile. In addition, pink tide governments did not deliver as much as anticipated in terms of advancing the rights of the marginalised or translating those rights into policy (Grugel and Fontana 2019; Friedman and Tabbush 2018; Biroli and Caminotti 2020; Blofield *et al.* 2017). Indeed, as some of the chapters in this volume show, LGBT+, Indigenous, and Afro-Latinx communities, feminists, and environmental and human-rights defenders expanded legal rights and jurisprudence that promoted equality without the support of pink tide governments. Moreover, social movements often mobilised outside their own pink tide or other countries to achieve rights at the regional or international level (see Kane *et al.* (Chapter 7)). In sum, the struggle for these rights began before, during, and after pink tide governments' terms in office, and in countries without left-of-centre governments.

For this reason, we consider the rights revolution that began to sweep the region after the end of the dictatorships and armed conflicts as a more compelling explanation for the rise of the right against rights. That rights revolution depended on mobilisation from below. Dramatic gains were made – at least on paper – by social movements, sometimes but not always during pink tide governments. Where these rights exist, access to them has not always proved possible, creating a disconnect between rights on the books and rights in practice (see Lemaitre 2009). The point we make in this volume is that the right against rights mobilises when there is a perception that marginalised groups have made advances that threaten them. That perception existed during pink tide governments whether the rights gains were realised or not. But that perception also existed without pink tide governments and at the regional level because of the visibility politics used by social movements.

The Rights Revolution in Latin America

Led by national and transnational feminist movements, for example, abortion has been made more available in countries around the region. Restrictions on abortion have been removed in Argentina, Colombia, Cuba, Uruguay, and Mexico City. It nonetheless continues to be completely prohibited or criminalised in the Dominican Republic, El Salvador, Guatemala, and Nicaragua (HRP 2022; Center for Reproductive Rights 2022). In the past couple of decades, activists have coordinated actions within and outside states to support pro-abortion legislation, promote the use of international law in abortion trials, and draft healthcare protocols that protect women's reproductive rights. For example, as Escoffier and Vivaldi (Chapter 8) highlight, in 2017 lawmakers in Chile changed legislation from complete prohibition to allowing abortion in the case of rape, to save the pregnant woman's life, or in the case of fetal unviability.

The LGBT+ community has also made great advances throughout the region,[1] including when it comes to issues of legal same-sex marriage (in Argentina, Brazil,

---

[1] Although the Caribbean continues to take a conservative stance toward LGBT+ rights. For example, in nine Caribbean countries, 'buggery' faces criminal punishment.

INTRODUCTION   15

Uruguay, Colombia, Ecuador, Costa Rica, and Mexico). Moreover, the Inter-American Court of Human Rights ruled in 2018 that same-sex marriage is a human right. Colombia provides a strong example of a country that has seen a vast expansion of rights for the LGBT+ population, even during conservative governments. Article 13 of the 1991 Constitution makes guarantees of equality for marginalised and discriminated groups, which the Constitutional Court has liberally interpreted to include protections for sexual and gender minorities (Lemaitre 2009). These court rulings – in conjunction with strong pressure from social movements – have paved the way for gay marriage and adoption, amongst other rights (Ritholtz and Mesquita (Chapter 5)).

Indigenous peoples in Latin America have proved more successful at winning collective rights than in the past (Tapias Torrado (Chapter 9)). They have used the advances made in national, regional, and international law to promote their rights against the environmental degradation of their lands and health consequences for their communities. As an outcome, environmental protections have been entrenched in several countries around the region, including through the passage of International Labour Organization (ILO) Convention 169 on Indigenous and Tribal Peoples (ILO 1989). This Convention includes special protections for the environments where Indigenous people live, as well as obliging governments to take into account the environmental impacts of any development activities they undertake. Ecuador's 2008 Constitution goes a step further, to include guarantees for the rights of nature, whereby the *Pacha Mama* (Mother Earth) has the right to exist, maintain, and regenerate vital cycles. Citizens have the ability to demand that authorities uphold and protect the rights of nature, and the state is obliged to create protective measures to restrict activities that could lead to the extinction of a species, the destruction of ecosystems, or the alteration of natural cycles (Asamblea Nacional Constituyente de Ecuador 2008, Chapter 7). Similar constitutional provisions exist in Bolivia and Colombia.

Afro-Latinxs' historical struggle for recognition in the region (Hooker 2005) has also experienced a recent series of successes around affirmative action in Colombia (Ng'weno 2007), Brazil (Htun 2004), and Uruguay (Sharnak (Chapter 10)), among others. Constitutional and legislative changes have challenged and addressed these countries' histories of discrimination by admitting to racism, furthering the rights of Afro-Latinx populations via the teaching of history, and implementing affirmative action policies and quotas in government, higher education, and other job vacancies. Quota laws have also been useful in expanding access for other groups in the region. For example, all countries in Latin America (except Guatemala and Venezuela) now have quotas for women in parliament (although this does not necessarily guarantee that women's rights are promoted) (Piscopo 2020). Countries including Bolivia, Colombia, Venezuela, Peru, and Mexico have mandated multicultural and/or plurinational provisions for Indigenous peoples' participation in formal politics (Htun 2016; Krausova (Chapter 11)). Many Brazilian universities now use race and class quotas in their admissions processes.

Victims of human rights violations carried out during authoritarian regimes and armed conflicts have also begun to advance international rights to truth, justice, reparations, and guarantees of non-repetition throughout the region. Indeed countries in this region were the first to hold state perpetrators criminally accountable for those violations. In some cases, these trials extended to non-state actors, such as doctors and priests. Even more recently, members of the business community have been held responsible for crimes against humanity during dictatorships and armed conflicts. These processes of accountability in the region have gone farther than any other region in the world, suggesting that there is a 'Latin American transitional justice' that advances victims' rights (Salvi (Chapter 3)).

These impressive rights advances for groups previously marginalised and excluded in the region explain the context in which the right against rights emerges. Such advances signal to the right that its traditional forms of power have not worked to maintain the social, economic, and cultural status quo ante. They see the erosion of their traditional values around the family, marriage, gender, sexuality, land, property, religion, and racial hierarchy. Where this sense of a loss of traditional power and values prevailed, mobilisation in the streets, at the base, seems to be the only appropriate tactic to win back power, that is, to reverse the rights revolution. Dramatic and unprecedented mobilisation on the right has ensued.

Backlash against Rights in Latin America

We know from collective action research that grievances alone are rarely enough to mobilise groups. There is no doubt that grievances have emerged in reaction against the rights revolution. But certain opportunities to mobilise have also presented themselves in a way that allows for right-against-rights movement leaders to tap into a general sense of malaise as ideological adversaries appear to be winning the rights revolution.

In October 2016, the right against rights seized on the Colombian peace plebiscite as a way to roll back rights. The plebiscite gave the Colombian people the chance to vote for a peace deal that would end a 52-year armed conflict with the Revolutionary Armed Forces of Colombia (Fuerzas Armadas Revolucionarias de Colombia; FARC). This vote would bring an end to the western hemisphere's longest-running armed conflict, one that had led to the deaths of hundreds of thousands and the displacement of millions of people. Yet in the days leading up to the plebiscite, religious leaders and their allies began to mobilise in communities, publicly speaking out against the deal's inclusion of a so-called 'gender ideology', a term that was never actually mentioned in the text of the proposed accords themselves. This 'gender ideology' was presented as a threat to families, to innocent children, and to morality through gay indoctrination. Against nearly all predictions, on 2 October, the 'No' campaign was successful. The razor-thin margin of votes against peace is explained in part by the mobilisation of religious groups and their allies

INTRODUCTION 17

on the 'gender ideology' issue, an example of countermovements motivated to act by the threat to traditional values and an opportunity to reassert them (Corredor (Chapter 4); Ritholtz and Mesquita (Chapter 5); Krystalli and Theidon 2016).

Latin America is seen as the leader of transitional justice protagonism, or advancing accountability for past human rights violations, in the world. It is thus something of a shock to see the backlash against human rights trials in the region, and particularly in one country that has been seen as progressive on social justice issues: Uruguay. In September 2015, retired Uruguayan General Pedro Barneix took his own life while on trial for crimes committed during the dictatorship from 1973 to 1985. In January 2017, an open letter from the group known as 'Comando General Pedro Barneix' was circulated in the country, threatening a group of thirteen lawyers, public servants, and human rights researchers with death if they continued their ongoing investigations into the human rights abuses committed during the country's military dictatorship. The email was clear: in the case of any additional suicides, the authors would kill three people on the list. To date, and despite involvement from the Inter-American Commission on Human Rights, the intellectual authors of the email have not been identified, and no measures of protection have been issued for those included in the death threat. The use of uncivil, violent threats against the advocates of accountability for past human rights violations seems to reflect the loss of influence the military once enjoyed in the country. This mobilisation is explained by the desire to overpower the human rights community, roll back their rights, and restore the right's power, the status quo ante. When new transnational trials (Condor Trials; Lessa (2022)) began to intensify around past abuses, an opportunity emerged around which anti-rights groups mobilized to roll back human rights accountability.

The election of far-right populist leaders also relies on the mobilisation of the right against rights. In backing extreme candidates, right-against-rights mobilisations seize opportunities to roll back the rights won by groups perceived as threatening. One example can be seen in Brazil. In October 2018, Jair Bolsonaro won 55.1 per cent of the vote in the second round of Brazil's general election. He entered office on 1 January 2019. His campaign is known to have rallied anti-rights sentiments, particularly among the Pentecostal community. He used rhetoric that tapped into threats to traditional values. He also evoked violent sexist language, for example when he stated that a female lawmaker was 'too ugly to be raped', thereby challenging feminism. In June 2019, he spoke out against a Supreme Court decision to ban homophobia. This was not a surprise, given his previous homophobic statements, such as his claim that he would 'be incapable of loving a homosexual son'. In the wake of the Supreme Court decision he expressed his desire to appoint an evangelical judge to the bench in the interest of 'balance'. Buoyed by right-wing mobilisations, including the neoliberal Movimento Brasil Livre (MBL), Bolsonaro promised a vision of 'saving the country [that] meant denying LGBT and feminist groups their rights while protecting the rights of others (heterosexuals, neoliberals, and Christian religious groups)' (Payne and de Souza Santos 2020, 36).

18   Simón Escoffier, Leigh A. Payne, and Julia Zulver

In recent years, the region has witnessed the political killing of Berta Cáceres in Honduras for her Indigenous environmental activism, and of city councillor and Afro-Brazilian bisexual activist Marielle Franco in Brazil after her open criticism of police brutality in Rio de Janeiro. It is clear that these murders are political in nature. Regarding Honduras, journalist Nina Lakhani's (2020) book – *Who Killed Berta Cáceres?* – reveals a Gordian knot of culpability: the US-trained men who pulled the trigger, the multinational corporations and institutions funding the dam that Berta Cáceres opposed, the elite families maintaining their political vice-grip on Honduran politics. The homophobic violence in Brazil that has impacted Marielle Franco and other political leaders has reached such proportions that gay activists refer to it as the 'homocaust' (Encarnación 2016).

These are not isolated incidents. Moreover, with the shift away from left-of-centre governments to those reliant on a right-wing base, the right against rights has found a set of electoral, legislative, and policy opportunities around which to mobilise. And they are mobilising not only in the political institutions them-selves, but also in the streets. These mobilisations are not unique to the region. The United States, especially during Donald Trump's presidency, and various countries in Europe have also witnessed political moments that the right against rights has exploited. Moreover, evidence supports the claim that right-wing mobilisations in Europe and the United States are, in fact, funding and otherwise supporting these mobilisations in Latin America. Yet, to date, there have been few scholarly attempts to theorise on the growing mobilisation of Latin America's right against rights, their global connections to counterparts in other areas of the world, and their impact. This volume attempts to fill that gap.

Impact of the Right against Rights

Most social movement research and literature in Latin America focuses on pro-rights movements. Indeed, a variety of scholars have shown the myriad legal and judicial reforms that have expanded rights for marginalised groups across the region. A kind of optimism, born of the rights revolution, pervades scholarship. Kathryn Sikkink's work on the 'justice cascade' (2011, 5) advances forward-looking arguments that imply a linear or unidirectional shift when it comes to progressive gains. How does such an approach based on the human rights trials in Latin America understand the reactions against such trials in Uruguay and Argentina (Salvi (Chapter 3))? Writing more globally, Steven Pinker (2011) writes in *The Better Angels of Our Nature* that violence has declined over the march of human history, painting an optimistic pic-ture of an increasingly empathetic world. While this may be true in the aggregate, it may not feel like a better world for LGBT+, feminists, Indigenous, and environ-mental, and human rights activists in Latin America today.

This form of optimism may relegate the right against rights to the position of a minority extremist fringe without influence. It may see the focus on the right against rights as alarmist and paranoid. The focus on putting laws on the books ignores the problems of extra-institutional violent mobilisations against those who promote those laws. Latin America, after all, is identified as the most dangerous place for human rights activists, and for journalists also (Front Line Defenders 2021). The right against rights, and particularly uncivil movements, attempt not only to roll back rights, but also to violently eliminate rights-seekers. This questions whether continued optimism around the rights revolution is warranted.

What is the evidence of the impact of these right-against-rights groups? First, they are mushrooming. They have emerged in a variety of countries around a number of rights issues. They also seem to receive support from foreign groups attempting to roll back rights in their own countries. In Latin America, they have legitimised a set of previously discredited hegemonic and masculinist norms of law and order that are a throw-back to an authoritarian era. They have also become a powerful bloc behind certain electoral victories of far-right candidates such as Bolsonaro in Brazil, Sebastián Piñera in Chile, Iván Duque in Colombia, and Jimmy Morales in Guatemala. They have shifted national discourses away from inclusiveness and the expansion of progressive rights and toward traditional exclusionary values, law and order, national sovereignty, and neoliberal economic policies. They threaten the lives of rights advocates.

Although right-against-rights movements have widely proliferated across the world in the past decade, studies on them are still scarce in relative terms. This is because academics largely understand social mobilisation as a progressive force advancing freedom and citizenship rights. This issue is even more acute in the Latin American context.

Chapter Outlines

The set of chapters presented in this book provide in-depth analysis of mobilisations that work to limit or roll back access to rights, including LGBT+ rights, reproductive rights, Indigenous rights, environmental rights, and women's rights, among others. Given the lack of existing research about right-wing movements in this region, the book facilitates a comparative conversation with scholars who focus on far-right movements in Europe and North America.

In Chapter 2, Leigh A. Payne fills the aforementioned analytical gaps by theorising anti-rights movements in Latin America, updating her work on *Uncivil Movements*. The chapter lays out three sets of right-against-rights movements. Payne's typology in the chapter includes sometimes overlapping sets of countermovements, uncivil movements, and radical neoliberal mobilisations. The three types of movements and the analytical framework address key questions further developed in the case study chapters: *who* constitutes the right against rights, *when* and *why* do these mobilisations occur, *how* do they operate (their tactics), and *what* impact do they have on advancing rights in the region?

The first section of the book includes chapters by Valentina Salvi on the anti-human rights accountability countermovement in Argentina; Elizabeth Corredor on the uses of 'gender ideology' by Colombian countermovements; Samuel Ritholtz and Miguel Mesquita on anti-LGBT+ countermovements; Andreza Aruska de Souza Santos on the evangelical countermovement against threats to the family in Brazil; and Gillian Kane, Mirta Moragas, and Kiran Stallone on the global countermovement mobilisation to roll back rights in the Inter-American system. Simón Escoffier and Lieta Vivaldi examine the failure of an anti-abortion countermovement in Chile.

Valentina Salvi's Chapter 3 looks at mobilisation against human rights trials in Argentina, a country seen as a global protagonist of human rights trials. The Argentine countermovement examined in the chapter aimed to block or reverse the trials and reduce the sentences of the dictatorship's security forces held accountable for past human rights violations. Over the last 15 years, more than 1,000 perpetrators – including military officers, policemen, and civilians – have been sent to prison for human rights violations committed during the country's dictatorship (1976–83). Worryingly, however, as these actors go to prison, the families of the convicted perpetrators have begun to mobilise on the national stage. Among them are groups of perpetrators' wives, sons and daughters, and grandchildren, who draw on the global paradigm of human rights and the universal humanitarian narrative to publicly transform the image of the perpetrator into a victim, engender compassion, and emphasise familial connections to legitimise their authority in demanding justice. This right-against-rights countermovement addressed by Salvi emulated the tactics of their opponents; they adopted the human rights movements' language of 'never again' and organised marches around the Plaza de Mayo. They lost each one of their battles in the highly unfavourable scenario in which they protested.

Elizabeth Corredor, in Chapter 4, examines the responses by conservative religious groups to two separate gender and sexual equality initiatives in Colombia in 2016: an anti-bullying programme that sought greater tolerance for gender-variant identities in schools, and a peace agreement that included the most comprehensive gender perspective to date and, for the first time in global history, provisions addressing the needs of LGBT+ groups. Religious, political, and civil sectors on the right saw these events as opportunities to create and strengthen a mobilising alliance. Their framing devices involved heightening the sense of moral panic through fake news and exaggeration of the threats to children and to traditional family and national values. Other tactics they used included street mobilisation in mass rallies, social media campaigns, and traditional media coverage, as well as working within the political system through connections to leaders. The movement succeeded in eliminating the anti-bullying program from public schools. They were not, however, successful in eliminating LGBT+ rights from the peace agreement. In fact, their campaign backfired in that it provided additional time for women's and LGBT+ groups to clarify and, in some respects, strengthen the gender perspective (Corredor, 2021).

Transnational advocacy networks can also serve as forces for right-against-rights groups, as Samuel Ritholtz and Miguel Mesquita explore in Chapter 5. Building off

INTRODUCTION

literatures on political homophobia and uncivil movements, the authors examine the coordinated transnational counterrights backlash of organised groups against feminist and queer-inclusive state practices. The movement that these groups created brought together a remarkably diverse range of actors, i.e. Catholic and evangelical groups, elites and non-elites, and the urban and rural right wing – many of them for the first time under the same umbrella. These actors have coalesced behind frames that claim to protect innocent children, traditional notions of the family, and the nation. Originally organised around local issues and funded by religious groups, this movement has received political support throughout the region and now operates with great efficiency at the international level.

Andreza Aruska de Souza Santos's Chapter 6 focuses on the rise of the Evangelical Caucus in Brazil and considers the political opportunity of the rights revolution as a key to its success. The year 2013, she argues, was a turning point for the countermovement opposing LGBT+ and abortion rights. In that year, this countermovement consolidated its framing around the moral threat to Brazilian families from the minority interests of the LGBT+ community and feminists, allied with the left-wing PT political party. It located charismatic leaders and movement entrepreneurs using the evangelical church's pyramidical structure, working within and outside the formal political arena. This double militancy, framing, and tactics succeeded in consolidating a powerful bloc within parliament, which attempted to halt progressive legislation, and eventually elected right-wing president Jair Bolsonaro in 2019. The chapter analyses draft laws proposed by evangelical Brazilian politicians related to 'defence of the family'. Additionally, by examining one particular church structure common amongst evangelical denominations in Brazil (church-in-cells, where the congregation is organised in smaller units), de Souza Santos contends that this model of church offers a structure of leadership and obedience that can support the advancement of divisive topics such as family protection.

Chapter 7, by Gillian Kane, Mirta Moragas, and Kiran Stallone, considers the impact that right-against-rights countermobilisations can have for transnational institutions seeking to advance rights of the historically marginalised, democracy, and human rights at the regional and global levels. They specifically focus on these movements' impact on the Organization of American States (OAS) and its Inter-American Human Rights System (IAS). Since 2013, right-against-rights movements have maximised their international influence by coalescing in an international conservative network that includes civil society organisations, think tanks, individual activists and academics, and right-wing politicians across Latin America and the United States. Their framing tactics include demands over the protection of religious freedom, the protection of women, and children's rights to life. Additionally, however, this network has managed to translate and tailor those discourses to attack the OAS with impressive gains. By reframing the OAS's work as cultural imperialism and a threat to national sovereignty, the network has succeeded in reducing funding to the OAS by working with influential Republican politicians in the United States.

While the OAS has always been limited in its ability to advance its basic founding principles – both for financial reasons and owing to certain constraints on its mandate – in the last decade, emerging challenges to the legitimacy of the IAS call into question the genuine survival of this institution.

In Chapter 8, Simón Escoffier and Lieta Vivaldi investigate a right-wing network mobilising against abortion in Chile. They consider why, despite its access to powerful allies and a great deal of resources, the Chilean anti-abortion movement failed to block the abortion bill passed by Congress between 2015 and 2017. The network included far-right civil society organisers and think tanks, as well as conservative medical doctors, social scientists, and lawyers from some of the most prestigious institutions in the country. The authors explain this movement's failure as a result of a shifting, unfavourable political scenario, which included an increasingly powerful pro-choice opposition. This opposition was ready to use highly strategic framing and to publicly denounce the right-against-rights discourse in its insistent defamations, contradictions, and manipulations. The conservative movement used extremely aggressive framing that had worked elsewhere – including Colombia and El Salvador – linking abortion to genocide and the dictatorship's human rights violations. They rhetorically and symbolically equated abortion with the torture, killing, and disappearances at the National Soccer Stadium during the Pinochet dictatorship. They appropriated feminist terminology to refer to abortion as *machista*, and called for the defence of women. Ultimately, they failed, the authors argue, because of their extremism. They did not create the legitimating myths that might have won them crucial support from moderate right-wing forces.

The second type of right-against-rights mobilisation – uncivil movements – is reflected in Chapter 9, by Nancy R. Tapias Torrado. This chapter on violence against Indigenous women human rights defenders offers a unique reflection on a rollback of rights that does not fall neatly into existing definitions. To illustrate a different kind of anti-rights movement, the chapter uses the case of an organised coalition of violent actors defending the Agua Zarca hydroelectric dam project and mobilising against Berta Cáceres, the aforementioned Indigenous human rights defender in Honduras. This powerful uncivil movement included radical neoliberals: a coalition of political, business, and military elites united behind efforts to secure rights to development through megaprojects, and to roll back the rights-on-the-books gains of the Indigenous peoples. It further used its substantial political power to advance legislative gains of its own to allow development projects in protected Indigenous lands. Its strategy of double militancy also meant propagating lies on social media to denigrate Berta Cáceres and her movement. The chapter shows how the resulting conflict escalated. Ultimately, the perceived threat posed by the Indigenous mobilisation under Berta Cáceres to the multinational dam project did not generate a civil countermovement. Instead, it motivated this coalition to eliminate the rights-seekers. Tapias Torrado explains that despite the success of the uncivil movement in intimidating, threatening, undermining, and eventually killing Indigenous leaders, the Indigenous movement has refused to cede power to it.

INTRODUCTION

The struggle continues against future megaprojects, to protect the Bertas of today and the future, and to seek justice for wrongdoing.

A third type of mobilisation – radical neoliberalism – is analysed in Debbie Sharnak's work on the Uruguayan group attempting to thwart the passage of anti-affirmative action legislation and Anna Krausova's study of anti-multiculturalism in Bolivia.

Debbie Sharnak's Chapter 10 explores the opposition to Uruguay's 2013 affirmative action law. No right-wing movement emerged to roll back the law aimed at addressing historic social, political, and economic discrimination against the Afro-Uruguayan community. Instead, a coalition of forces operating both within and outside the legislative system – in double militancy – chipped away at the law, mobilising against the measures that would have restricted private employers' freedoms. The tactics used outside the political system, moreover, did not involve street action, massive rallies, symbols, or vitriol against rights or rights-bearers. The mobilisation Sharnak describes took a much more subtle form. Like the other cases examined in this book, it did involve subverting a rights language. The mobilisation in parliament and in the media raised concerns about 'reverse discrimination', about undermining universal rights in favour of specialised and minority rights, and about poor white Uruguayans' unequal access to employment and education. This rights language, however, denied the historic patterns of discrimination behind Afro-Uruguayans' need and demand for redistribution. Instead, this right-against-rights mobilisation attempted to weaken the law, remove any of the restrictions it might pose on hiring practices for the private sector, and block its implementation. In this way, the mobilisation could appear to favour intrinsic democratic values of equality and inclusion, but it used a coded language to hide the racist practices allowed by unfettered business employment practices.

Anna Krausova investigates anti-Indigenous rights in Bolivia in Chapter 11. The political opportunity for the mobilisation occurred with the election of President Evo Morales, an Indigenous social movement leader who advocated Indigenous rights and redistribution policies. His election confronted traditional economic elites in the Santa Cruz region with their inability to control political and policy outcomes. Consequently, they adopted new strategies to maintain their political and economic power, thus creating a mix of radical neoliberal and countermovement mobilisation. They did so in part by appropriating but reinterpreting a notion of multiculturalism that included a historical narrative (legitimating myth) of racial harmony and shared mestizo (mixed race) identity. Their opposition to Morales's redistributive policies included massive rallies and the adoption of Indigenous symbols that aimed at altering the elites' image. By embracing and using Morales's multicultural, plurinational language and concepts of nation building, this Cruceño elite legitimised cultural recognition as an inclusive concept of which they were also a part through the cultural dress, music, and food of the region. This thinly disguised racist rhetoric suggested that no Indigenous people – only mestizos – remain in Santa Cruz. At the same time, a coded language evolved that cast the demands for land redistribution to

Indigenous communities as 'inauthentic' claims that violated historical legal rights to the land held by these elites. A violent youth uncivil movement further reflected a willingness to use force against Indigenous leaders within and outside government. Despite this movement's efforts to reverse the redistributive gains under the Morales government, it failed to achieve sufficient popular support to advance its objectives beyond the region. Morales's political party returned to power.

The concluding Chapter 12, written by Julia Zulver and Leigh A. Payne, reflects on the contributions the book makes to understanding the right against rights. It summarises, first, the assessment from each chapter regarding the impact of the right against rights. That section of the conclusion, called 'Righting Rights', explores the skills used by right-wing mobilisations in the region to adapt a rights language to roll back, reverse, or block rights. In the next section, however, the chapter explores 'righting wrongs', or the different methods identified in the volume for rights-seekers to check the power on the right. The third section of the conclusion explores these two concepts of 'righting rights' and 'righting wrongs' in comparative perspective. In the discussion, the conclusion explores how the study of countermovements, uncivil movements, and radical neoliberal mobilisations provides a framework for examining similar processes in other Global South contexts to roll back, reverse, or block rights. It also considers how uncivil movements and radical neoliberalism have emerged in the Global North, thereby advocating broader comparative analysis across the North–South divide. The conclusion also discusses processes that have been used in the Global North to monitor right-against-rights mobilisations and how such efforts could be adapted in other world regions. The conclusion ends with reflections on future directions of research.

References

Adler, J. (2020), 'The Genealogy of "Human Dignity": A New Perspective', *Publications of the English Goethe Society*, 89:1, 17–59.

Alenda, S. (2020), *Anatomía de la derecha chilena: Nuevos y viejos protagonistas* (Santiago, Fondo de Cultura Económica Chile).

Asamblea Nacional Constituyente de Ecuador (2008), 'Constitución de la República del Ecuador', https://www.oas.org/juridico/pdfs/mesicic4_ecu_const.pdf.

Balaguer, M. I., M. L. Baretta, and A. B. Copetti (2021), 'El litigio conservador y su repercusión sobre los derechos sexuales y (no reproductivos desde Córdoba, Argentina', *Derecho y ciencias sociales*, 26, 9–25.

Barrenechea, R. and E. Dargent (2020), 'Populists and Technocrats in Latin America: Conflict, Cohabitation, and Cooperation', *Politics and Governance*, 8:4, 509–519.

Biroli, F. and M. Caminotti (2020), 'The Conservative Backlash against Gender in Latin America', *Politics & Gender*, 16, 1–38.

Blee, K. M. and K. A. Creasap (2010), 'Conservative and Right-Wing Movements', *Annual Review of Sociology*, 36, 269–86.

Blofield, M., C. Ewig, and J. M. Piscopo (2017), 'The Reactive Left: Gender Equality and the Latin American Pink Tide', *Social Politics*, 24:4, 345–69.

INTRODUCTION

Bob, C. (2011), *The Global Right Wing and the Clash of World Politics* (Cambridge, Cambridge University Press).

Borges, A. (2021), 'The Illusion of Electoral Stability: From Party System Erosion to Right-Wing Populism in Brazil', *Journal of Politics in Latin America*, 13:2, 166–91.

Caiani, M. and R. Borri (2012), 'Between Violent and Non-Violent Action Strategies: A Study on Extreme-Right Organizations in Italy and Spain', *22nd IPSA World Congress of Political Science*, July, http://aei.pitt.edu/39280/1/pw_130.pdf.

Caiani, M. and D. della Porta (2018), 'The Radical Right as Social Movement Organizations', in *Oxford Handbook of the Radical Right*, ed. J. Rydgren (Oxford, Oxford University Press), pp. 327–47.

Camus, J.-Y. and N. Lebourg (2017), *Far Right Politics in Europe* (Cambridge, MA, Belknap Press of Harvard University).

Cannon, B. (2016), *The Right in Latin America: Elite Power, Hegemony and the Struggle for the State* (Abingdon, Routledge).

Castro Rea, J. (2018), 'Right-Wing Think Tank Networks in Latin America: The Mexican Connection', *Perspectives on Global Development and Technology*, 17:1–2, 89–102.

Center for Reproductive Rights (2022), *Center for Reproductive Rights*, https://reproductiv erights.org.

Corredor, E. S. (2019), 'Unpacking "Gender Ideology" and the Global Right's Antigender Countermovement', *Signs: Journal of Women in Culture and Society*, 44:3, 613–38.

Corredor, E. S. (2021), 'On the Strategic Uses of Women's Rights: Backlash, Rights-based Framing, and Anti-Gender Campaigns in Colombia's 2016 Peace Agreement', *Latin American Politics and Society*, 63:3, 46–68.

Cunningham, D. (2004), *There's Something Happening Here: The New Left, the Klan, and FBI Counterintelligence* (London, California University Press).

Daniels, J. (2009), *Cyber Racism: White Supremacy Online and the New Attack on Civil Rights* (New York, Rowman & Littlefield).

Davis, S. and J. Straubhaar (2020), 'Producing Antipetismo: Media Activism and the Rise of the Radical, Nationalist Right in Contemporary Brazil', *International Communication Gazette*, 82:1, 82–100.

Diani, M. (1992), 'The Concept of Social Movement', *Sociological Review*, 40:1, 1–25.

Dreifuss, R. A. (1981), *1964: A conquista do estado: Ação política, poder e golpe de classe* (Petrópolis, Vozes), https://docero.com.br/doc/nec00vc.

Encarnación, O. G. (2016), *Out in the Periphery: Latin America's Gay Rights Revolution* (Oxford, Oxford University Press).

Epp, C. R. (1998), *The Rights Revolution: Lawyers, Activists, and Supreme Courts in Comparative Perspective* (Chicago, University of Chicago Press).

Friedman, E. J. and C. Tabbush (2018), 'Contesting the Pink Tide', in *Seeking Rights from the Left*, ed. E. J. Friedman (Durham, NC, Duke University Press), 1–47.

Front Line Defenders (2021), 'Global Analysis', https://www.frontlinedefenders.org/sites/default/files/2021_global_analysis_-_final.pdf.

Gibson, E. (1992), 'Conservative Electoral Movements and Democratic Politics: Core Constituencies, Coalition-Building, and the Latin American Electoral Right', in *The Right and Democracy in Latin America*, ed. D. A. Chalmers, M. do C. C. de Souza, and A. A. Boron (New York, Praeger-Greenwood), pp. 13–42.

Gold, T. and A. M. Peña (2021), 'The Rise of the Contentious Right: Digitally Intermediated Linkage Strategies in Argentina and Brazil', *Latin American Politics and Society*, 63:3, 93–118.

Goldstein, A. A. (2019), 'The New Far-Right in Brazil and the Construction of a Right-Wing Order', *Latin American Perspectives*, 46:4, 245–62.

Griffin, R. (2017), 'Interregnum or Endgame? The Radical Right in the "Post-Fascist" Era', in *The Populist Radical Right: A Reader*, ed. C. Mudde (New York, Routledge), pp. 15–27.

Grugel, J. and L. B. Fontana (2019), 'Human Rights and the Pink Tide in Latin America: Which Rights Matter?', *Development and Change*, 50:3, 707–34.

Heinz, J. P., A. Paik, and A. Southworth (2003), 'Lawyers for Conservative Causes: Clients, Ideology, and Social Distance', *Law and Society Review*, 37:1, 5–50.

Hooker, J. (2005), 'Indigenous Inclusion/Black Exclusion: Race, Ethnicity and Multicultural Citizenship in Latin America', *Journal of Latin American Studies*, 37, 285–310.

HRP [UNDP/UNFPA/UNICEF/WHO/World Bank Special Programme of Research, Development and Research Training in Human Reproduction] (2022), *Global Abortion Policies Database*, https://abortion-policies.srhr.org.

Htun, M. (2004), 'From "Racial Democracy" to Affirmative Action: Changing State Policy on Race in Brazil', *Latin American Research Review*, 39:1, 60–89.

Htun, M. (2016), *Inclusion without Representation: Gender Quotas and Ethnic Reservations in Latin America* (Cambridge, Cambridge University Press).

Hunter, W. (1997), *Eroding Military Influence in Brazil: Politicians against Soldiers* (Chapel Hill, University of North Carolina Press).

Hunter, W. and T. J. Power (2019), 'Bolsonaro and Brazil's Illiberal Backlash', *Journal of Democracy*, 30:1, 68–82.

ILO [International Labour Organization] (1989), 'C169: Indigenous and Tribal Peoples Convention', https://www.ilo.org/dyn/normlex/en/f?p=NORMLEXPUB:55:0::NO::P55_TYPE,P55_LANG,P55_DOCUMENT,P55_NODE:REV,en,C169,/Document.

Keck, M. and K. Sikkink (1998), *Activists beyond Borders: Advocacy Networks in International Politics* (Ithaca, Cornell University Press).

Kopecky, P. and C. Mudde (2003), *Uncivil Society? Contentious Politics in Post-Communist Europe* (London, Routledge).

Krystalli, R. and K. Theidon (2016), 'Here's How Attention to Gender Affected Colombia's Peace Process', *Washington Post*, 9 October, https://www.washingtonpost.com/news/monkey-cage/wp/2016/10/09/heres-how-attention-to-gender-affected-colombias-peace-process/.

Lakhani, N. (2020), *Who Killed Berta Cáceres? Dams, Death Squads, and an Indigenous Defender's Battle for the Planet* (New York, Verso).

Lemaitre, J. (2009), 'Love in the Time of Cholera: LGBT Rights in Colombia', *Sur: International Journal on Human Rights*, 6:11, 73–90.

Lessa, F. (2022), *The Condor Trials: Transnational Repression and Human Rights in South America* (New Haven, Yale University Press).

Loxton, J. (2021), *Conservative Party-Building in Latin America: Authoritarian Inheritance and Counterrevolutionary Struggle* (Oxford, Oxford University Press).

Luna, J. P. and C. Rovira Kaltwasser (2014), *The Resilience of the Latin American Right* (Baltimore, Johns Hopkins University Press).

Mayka, L. and A. E. Smith (2021), 'The Grassroots Right in Latin America: Patterns, Causes, and Consequences', *Latin American Politics and Society*, 63:3, 1–31.

McCrudden, C. (2008), 'Human Dignity and Judicial Interpretation of Human Rights', *European Journal of International Law*, 19:4, 655–724.

McCrudden, C. (2015), 'Transnational Culture Wars', *International Journal of Constitutional Law*, 13:2, 434–62.

McVeigh, R. (2009), *The Rise of the Ku Klux Klan: Right-Wing Movements and National Politics* (London, University of Minnesota Press).

INTRODUCTION

Meyer, D. S. and S. Staggenborg (1996). 'Movements, Countermovements, and the Structure of Political Opportunity', *American Journal of Sociology*, 101:6, 1628–60.

Middlebrook, K. J. (2000), *Conservative Parties, the Right, and Democracy in Latin America* (London, Johns Hopkins University Press).

Morán, J. M. (2015), 'El desarrollo del activismo autodenominado "pro-vida" en Argentina, 1980–2014', *Revista mexicana de sociología*, 77:3, 407–36.

Morgan, L. M. (2014), 'Claiming Rosa Parks: Conservative Catholic Bids for "Rights" in Contemporary Latin America', *Culture, Health and Sexuality*, 16:10, 1245–59.

Mudde, C. (2017), *The Populist Radical Right: A Reader* (New York, Routledge).

Mudde, C. (2022), 'The Far-Right Threat in the United States: A European Perspective', *Annals of the American Academy of Political and Social Science*, 699:1, 101–15.

Ng'weno, B. (2007), 'Can Ethnicity Replace Race? Afro-Colombians, Indigeneity and the Colombian Multicultural State', *Journal of Latin American and Caribbean Anthropology*, 12:2, 414–40.

O'Brien, C. and S. D. Walsh (2020), 'Women's Rights and Opposition: Explaining the Stunted Rise and Sudden Reversals of Progressive Violence against Women Policies in Contentious Contexts', *Journal of Latin American Studies*, 52:1, 107–31.

O'Donnell, G. (1973), *Modernization and Bureaucratic-Authoritarianism: Studies in South American Politics* (Berkeley, Institute of International Studies, University of California).

Payne, L. A. (1994), *Brazilian Industrialists and Democratic Change* (Baltimore, Johns Hopkins University Press).

Payne, L. A. (2000), *Uncivil Movements: The Armed Right Wing and Democracy in Latin America* (Baltimore, Johns Hopkins University Press).

Payne, L. A. (2023), 'Right-Wing Movements in Latin America', in *The Oxford Handbook of Latin American Social Movements*, ed. F. M. Rossi (Oxford, Oxford University Press), Chapter 32.

Payne, L. A. and A. A. de Souza Santos (2020), 'The Right-Wing Backlash in Brazil and Beyond', *Politics and Gender*, 16:1 (*Special Symposium on Women's Parties*), 32–8.

Peñas, M. A. and J. M. Morán (2014), 'Conservative Litigation against Sexual and Reproductive Health Policies in Argentina', *Reproductive Health Matters*, 22:44, 82–90.

Pérez Guadalupe, J. L. (2019), *Evangelicals and Political Power in Latin America* (Lima, Konrad Adenauer Stiftung; Instituto de Estudios Sociales Cristianos de Perú).

Pinker, S. (2011), *The Better Angels of Our Nature: Why Violence Has Declined* (London, Penguin Random House).

Piscopo, J. M. (2020), 'Women Leaders and Pandemic Performance: A Spurious Correlation', *Politics and Gender*, 16:4, 951–9.

Power, T. J. (2000), *The Political Right in Postauthoritarian Brazil: Elites, Institutions, and Democratization* (University Park, Pennsylvania State University Press).

Rennó, L. R. (2020), 'The Bolsonaro Voter: Issue Positions and Vote Choice in the 2018 Brazilian Presidential Elections', *Latin American Politics and Society*, 62:4, 1–23.

Reuterswärd, C. (2021), 'Pro-Life and Feminist Mobilization in the Struggle over Abortion in Mexico: Church Networks, Elite Alliances, and Partisan Context', *Latin American Politics and Society*, 63:3, 21–45.

Roberts, K. M. (2014), 'Democracy, Free Markets, and the Rightist Dilemma in Latin America', in *The Resilience of the Latin American Right*, ed. J. P. Luna and C. Rovira Kaltwasser (Durham and London, Johns Hopkins University Press).

Rovira Kaltwasser, C. (2014), 'From Right Populism in the 1990s to Left Populism in the 2000s – and Back Again?', in *The Resilience of the Latin American Right*, ed. J. P. Luna and C. Rovira Kaltwasser (Baltimore, Johns Hopkins University Press), pp. 143–66.

Rovira Kaltwasser, C. and S. M. Van Hauwaert (2020), 'The Populist Citizen: Empirical Evidence from Europe and Latin America', *European Political Science Review*, 12:1, 1–18.

Scott, J. and G. Marshall (2015), *A Dictionary of Sociology* (Oxford, Oxford University Press).

Sikkink, K. (2011), *The Justice Cascade: How Human Rights Prosecutions Are Changing World Politics* (London, W. W. Norton).

Simi, P. and R. Futrell (2011), *American Swastika: Inside the White Power Movement's Hidden Spaces of Hate* (Toronto, Rowman & Littlefield).

Soares, F. B. (2020), 'As estratégias de argumentação e as formas de desinformação nas mensagens de Jair Bolsonaro no Twitter durante o segundo turno das eleições presidenciais de 2018', *Mediação*, 22:30, 8–22, http://revista.fumec.br/index.php/mediacao/article/view/7424.

Tilly, C. (1984), *Big Structures, Large Processes, Huge Comparisons* (New York, Russell Sage Foundation Publications).

Urueña, R. (2019), 'Evangelicals at the Inter-American Court of Human Rights', *AJIL Unbound*, 113, 360–4.

Vaggione, J. M. (2005), 'Reactive Politicization and Religious Dissidence: The Political Mutations of the Religious', *Social Theory and Practice*, 31:2, 233–55.

Verma, P. (2020), 'Pompeo's Quest to Redefine Human Rights Draws Concern at UN', *New York Times*, 22 September.

2

The Right against Rights in Latin America: An Analytical Framework*

LEIGH A. PAYNE

A NEW KIND of right wing – a right against rights – is mobilising in Latin America. *Who* on the right is mobilising against rights, *when* and *why*, *how*, and with *what* impact, set these contemporary mobilisations apart from other types of right-wing movements in the region and elsewhere.

This chapter examines three distinct types of right-against-rights mobilisations: countermovements, uncivil movements, and radical neoliberal mobilisations. They include elite and non-elite adherents, in urban centres and rural areas within and across Latin America and abroad. They mobilise to roll back the rights gains of previously marginalised groups; undermine those rights-seekers; and reassert their traditionally held social, economic, cultural, and political rights. In these efforts they use mainstream and social media, and street mobilisation tactics, while also working within political institutions. Their incendiary rhetoric and symbols capture attention and strengthen their support among some extremist sectors of society (Gold and Peña 2021), while parallel moderate messages attempt to appeal to a broader constituency (Bale and Rovira Kaltwasser 2021; Feldman 2019). Their organisational framework does not always, or even often, create formal or sustainable movements. Loose connections behind charismatic leaders and movement entrepreneurs, funded by international or local right-wing forces, unite a fragmented network of adherents who mobilise in response to rallying cries. These networks seize moments – policy changes, lawmaking, and elections – to assert traditional rights claims. Their effective adaptation of framing and mobilisation tactics from their social movement adversaries sometimes, but not always, pays off in rights reversals.

---

* This chapter is based on two shorter pieces on right-wing movements in Latin America: Payne (2023); and Payne (forthcoming).

Proceedings of the British Academy, **255**, 29–58, © The British Academy 2023.

30 _Leigh A. Payne_

Table 2.1 Right-against-rights mobilisations: An analytical framework

	Countermovements	Uncivil movements	Radical neoliberals
Anti-rights orientation	Against rights gains by social movements	Against rights-seekers	Against business rights infringements
Composition	Wide-ranging	Anti-establishment elite	Elite
Rights orientation	Rights of the family Right to life Rights of the child Rights of the innocent Rights of religion Rights of the accused Rights of victims	Against rights-seekers: Environmentalists Women BIPOC LGBT+ Human Rights	Property rights Business rights Land rights Employment rights
Emergence	Perception of rights gains by adversaries and loss of traditional rights	Perception of public visibility and legitimacy of previously marginalised rights-seekers	Perception of threats to business prerogatives from previously marginalised groups
Tactics: Framing Leadership and organisation Double militancy Visibility and disruption	Rights framejacking Moral panic Movement entrepreneur Double-militancy Street mobilisation Transnational advocacy networks	Demonising rights-seekers Charismatic leaders Movement entrepreneurs Extra-legal violence Double militancy	National economic development framing Movement entrepreneur Double militancy
Intended impact	Halt or reverse rights of adversaries; legal protection of traditional rights	Eliminate rights-seekers	Promote and protect business rights and freedoms

The framework set out in this chapter analyses that process: the mobilisation, tactics, and outcomes of the right against rights. It overcomes the institutional focus of studies on the right in the region and develops an analytical framework for understanding a contemporary right against rights in Latin America linked to similar types of mobilisations in Europe, the United States, and elsewhere.

Types of Right-against-Rights Mobilisations: Who Mobilises?

The typology developed here recognises three distinct types of right-against-rights mobilisations that sometimes work together. The first category –

AN ANALYTICAL FRAMEWORK

countermovements – has been analysed in Europe and the United States, but has received surprisingly little attention in Latin America.[1] Uncivil movements (Payne 2000) are a category of right-wing movements developed for Latin America that adds analytical precision for understanding types of radical or extreme groups studied in Europe and the United States. Radical neoliberals also exist around the world, but have not yet been analysed as a distinct mobilisation within the right. The typology of right-against-rights mobilisations aims to provide a comparative framework that could be used within and outside Latin America for understanding *who* is mobilising today against the rights of the previously marginalised.

Countermovements

Countermovements are defined as 'an organised response to a social movement, with the purpose of blocking the movement's activities, resisting change, and presenting alternative points of view' (Encyclopedia.com 2018; see also Meyer and Staggenborg 1996; Mottl 1980). Certain right-against-rights groups fit countermovement categorisation when they emerge to block social movements' rights advances and to restore and protect traditional rights in new ways, specifically through street mobilisations rather than institutional politics. Right-against-rights countermovements in Latin America resemble those in the United States by countering social movement demands for abortion, LGBT+, and women's rights. Consistent with Castro Rea's (2018) definition of the right, they aim to roll back, reverse or block social movements' 'undeserving' gains, and to promote an alternative set of rights that they believe to be fundamental and 'worthy', such as the right to life, rights of the family, and religious rights.

The emphasis on elite or middle-class countermovements and right-wing movements in Europe and the United States (Creasap and Blee 2010, 271; Hirsch-Hoefler and Mudde 2013) overlooks the broad constituencies behind contemporary right-against-rights mobilisations. In the United States and Latin America, cross-class alliances have formed that link working-class and poor sectors with middle-class and elite groups, largely through Catholic and evangelical churches, to roll back reproductive, LGBT+, and women's rights. That Catholic and evangelical churches unite behind a shared goal to restore traditional rights marks a dramatic – and previously unthinkable – shift within right-wing mobilisations and their class composition (Vaggione and das Dores Campos Machado 2020). Elites also play a significant role in countermovements, particularly through funding, media coverage, and right-wing think tanks that advance platforms and strategies.

---

[1] One exception is Teichman (2019).

Uncivil Movements

Uncivil movements include right-against-rights groups that advance exclusionary attitudes, language, and violent practices aimed at eliminating rights-seekers. They differ from countermovements in their use of violence or the threat of violence to eliminate social movements and other rights-seekers. Uncivil movements mobilise to eliminate those advocating for the intrinsic equality of specific groups: women, members of the LGBT+ community, the BIPOC rights community, environmentalists, and human rights defenders. They fit Castro Rea's (2018) definition of the right by seeing those individuals and groups as lacking 'intrinsic equality' or 'worth'.

Like countermovements, uncivil movements are not elitist. Indeed, they tend to express anti-elite, anti-establishment, anti-intellectual views (Wodak 2015). They present themselves as the authentic voice of the marginalised and against a cosmopolitan elitist view. They see the institutional right as too willing to compromise or sell out. Their rejection of the institutional right has characterised them as 'radical', 'far right', or 'extreme' by scholars of European and US right-wing movements, though debates abound over the appropriateness and application of those labels (Ignazi 2003). Like those mobilisations, uncivil movements' views are not necessarily radical or extreme; their racist, sexist, homophobic, and anti-communist views are consistent with long-standing discriminatory attitudes and practices in the countries in which they emerge. What differentiates them is not their radical or extreme attitudes, but their uncivil behaviour – their use of violence, or the threat of violence, to eliminate rights-seekers.

Their behaviour and anti-establishment views have not precluded their participation in the institutional system; they have formed alliances with mainstream right-wing parties, political figures, countermovements, and radical neoliberals. Indeed, such groups often depend on uncivil movements to build and mobilise broad grassroots support, even if they sometimes attempt to distance themselves from the movements' use of violence. Uncivil movements similarly rely on their alliances with the political mainstream for legitimacy and protection, while simultaneously criticising those groups as political cowards. Working within and violently outside the democratic system has led to some impressive victories for uncivil movements, most notably the election of Jair Bolsonaro and the endurance of *uribismo* in Colombia and *fujimorismo* in Peru.

The anti-LGBT+ mobilisation in Brazil provides an example of the power of uncivil movements. A relatively fringe group gained power, taking advantage of a particular political and economic moment, and uniting a loose coalition of forces, to win the presidency. Without the use of violence against the LGBT+ community, this group would fit the countermovement category. The mobilisation was not limited to rolling back gains in anti-discrimination, marriage equality, and family rights; rather, it aimed to eliminate rights-seekers. Former president Jair Bolsonaro, known as the 'Far-Right Trump of the Tropics', became the charismatic leader and embodiment of this anti-LGBT+ uncivil movement. He was presented as a maverick leader, outside the political establishment, despite his 27 years in the legislature (Nemer 2021; Power and Hunter 2019) spouting right-wing, authoritarian, and anti-LGBT+ rhetoric. The anti-LGBT+ uncivil movement played a key role in winning the presidency for its charismatic leader, allowing acts of violence to continue with impunity. From 2019, such violence led gay-rights activist Beto de Jesus to warn: 'the gates of hell have been opened ... [it's] as if hunting season has been declared' (Phillips 2018). The violence against the LGBT+ community most notably led gay activist and parliamentarian Jean Wyllys to flee the country.

Existence of uncivil movements outside Latin America is also evident, even if these groups have not (yet) been labelled as such. The violent storming of the US Capitol on 6 January 2021 by the Proud Boys, other white supremacists, and religious-oriented moral warriors suggests a link between an uncivil movement and the mainstream right. The violent mobilisation on that day, and in earlier episodes, targeted women in politics (such as Nancy Pelosi, Alexandria Ocasio-Cortez, and Ilhan Omar) and members of Black Lives Matter, who were advancing gender and BIPOC rights. Similar violent targeting of female and BIPOC political leaders in Europe has captured media attention (Spring and Webster 2019). The US shootings in Black churches, in synagogues, in mosques, in Latinx schools, and the killing of abortion doctors and violence at abortion clinics identifies right-against-rights mobilisations that do not fit existing categories of countermovements or 'extreme', 'far right', radical, or populist right-wing movements. Uncivil movements provide a better way to understand the violent rollback of rights occurring around the world. Their actions are coordinated, if loosely, by a powerful communication network – including social media – to mobilise forces quickly and to act violently, to attempt to eliminate rights-seekers. Adherents share an opposition to rights-seekers from previously marginalised groups, and a commitment to a way of doing politics, outside the mainstream. They seem to lack interest in, or perhaps capacity for, developing a sustained and organised structure, leadership, membership, and action over time. But that scepticism of formal and institutional politics is also what unites the group.

Radical Neoliberal Mobilisations

Radical neoliberals mobilise within and outside political institutions to defend elite economic interests from rights advancements for previously marginalised groups. They are distinct from uncivil movements and countermovements in their elite composition and their specific economic rights focus. They are also distinct from a mainstream neoliberal elite in their engagement in extra-institutional political action. They are part of a 'power elite' (Mills 1956) that is assumed to possess sufficient social, economic, and political resources on their own – without collective action – to influence outcomes affecting them. What is distinctive about radical neoliberals, therefore, is their mobilisation within and outside the political system to roll back workers, Indigenous, and environmental rights that they perceive as threatening their business interests.

Radical neoliberals defend a free trade economic philosophy over the rights claims made by the historically excluded, repudiating their 'intrinsic equality' (Castro Rea 2018). Radical neoliberals consider the demand for greater social and economic equality, greater redistribution of resources, protection of the environment, affirmative action, and other forms of state intervention in the economy, as not only 'undeserving', but as also threatening to liberal economic logic. To advance the set of economic rights, and to roll back threats to them, radical neoliberals lobby government officials and engage in legal action in the courts to advance private property rights, contract rights, and the rights to development. They defend private land rights (even when questionably acquired), megaprojects, mining and other natural resource extraction, and sweatshops, among other business interests. In this regard, radical neoliberals fight threats to business regardless of whether they originate with states, social movements, or other rights-seekers.

Radical neoliberals thus share with countermovements and uncivil movements a perception of threats to traditional rights, but they focus exclusively on economic rights. Their elitist and economic orientation does not preclude them from strategic alliances with other right-against-rights mobilisations. Countermovements sometimes benefit from radical neoliberal participation in street events, social and mainstream media campaigns, and their right-wing think tanks, as the Free Brazil Movement (MBL) shows – a group of economic elites first mobilising against corruption and then extending their work to oppose women's, reproductive, and LGBT+ rights (Payne and de Souza Santos 2020; Payne 2023; Payne, forthcoming). Such alliances broaden out an otherwise narrow economic constituency behind radical neoliberal mobilisation.

Alliances between radical neoliberals and uncivil movements also exist. Sara Motta (2014) identifies a form of 'militarised neoliberalism' in Colombia, reflecting such an alliance. Comprising cattle ranchers, regional elites, landed estate owners, right-wing politicians, paramilitaries, and the armed forces, this alliance formed to eliminate the armed left in Colombia's 50-year conflict. Neoliberal economic projects – such as resource extraction, land seizures and forced displacement, and control over rural labour – also united the group. The undisputed leader of this alliance is businessman and former president Álvaro Uribe Vélez (2002–6, 2006–10). Uribe's landed elite background; strong links within the business community; connection to paramilitaries, and to military policies toward the guerrilla; and social conservatism solidified his leadership of radical neoliberals allied with uncivil movements (Kajsiu 2019; Wills-Otero 2014). A strategic alliance of radical neoliberals and uncivil movements, working within and outside the state, is also evident in the business involvement in the murder of Honduran environmentalist and Indigenous activist Berta Cáceres (Tapias Torrado (Chapter 9)).

At times, radical neoliberals work without right-against-rights alliances. The affirmative action campaign for Afro-Uruguayans, for example, relied less on engagement with countermovements than on mainstream political groups to

AN ANALYTICAL FRAMEWORK   35

roll back the perceived threats to business (Sharnak (Chapter 10)). The mobil-isation of Cruceño elites in Bolivia against the perceived threats of multicultur-alism is also evidence of the choice of collective action by radical neoliberals working within and outside mainstream institutional politics largely on their own (Krausova (Chapter 11)).

Radical neoliberal mobilisations exist outside Latin America, even if they have not been labelled as such. 'Anti-environmentalism' and the 'Green Backlash' involve a coalition of businesses and others on the right in the United States and elsewhere that formed an alliance and mobilised outside the main-stream right when they determined that their former strategies for influencing government and policies no longer secured their interests (Beder 1997; Rowell 1996; Switzer 1997). 'Rich people's movements' (Martin 2013, 2) or 'movements of the rich and by the rich, but ... especially, and categorically movements *for* the rich' mobilise collectively when they perceive threats to economic rights and privileges, including personal security (Davis 2006). At these moments, they per-ceive that they cannot rely on their traditional power resources to lobby individu-ally, finance politicians, or carry out legal action to protect their interests. They do not abandon institutional politics, but supplement it with extra-institutional collective action: mobilisation.

Martin (2013, 26–7) suggests that 'rich people's movements', like radical neoliberals, often mobilise against 'small changes in their economic standing as signals that larger losses are yet to come ... You do not have to be one of the have-nots to protest. Nor do you have to believe that the odds are on your side. You just have to believe that you might lose what you have if you sit idle.' The 'rich people's movements' Martin analyses in the United States are aimed at policy threats, and target policy-makers. Radical neoliberal mobilisations as part of the right against rights are equally concerned with policy and practice. Their targets, their alliances, and their tactics vary depending on their perception of strategies most likely to advance the rollback of threats to their economic rights.

When the Right against Rights Mobilises

Existing scholarship explains social movement emergence as a combination of resources and political opportunities during contexts of political instability and economic downturn (McAdam 1982; Caiani and della Porta 2011; Caiani *et al.* 2012). Because the right against rights mobilise in response to perceived threats, these would probably coincide with political instability and economic downturn. I argue that even without dramatic political instability and economic downturn, the right against rights will react to perceived threats, particularly in key moments around elections, referenda, or legislative debates. In other words, the perceived threat – more than the context – motivates the right against rights to mobilise.

36 *Leigh A. Payne*

Moreover, that perception of threat can generate the resources – leadership, numbers, networks, funding, organisational structure – necessary to mobilise.

Concurring with Simmons (2014) and others (Gould 2009; Jaspers 1997), how the right against rights makes meaning from the rights revolution is critical to understanding its emergence, the mobilisational structures that evolve, and the framing devices used. Moghadam (2018, 296) reinforces the idea that 'people mobilize on the basis of feelings and images, not facts or policies'. Rather than assuming that threats, resources, and opportunities exist prior to right-against-rights mobilisation (Smith 2019), my argument is that the right against rights transforms the perception of threats from the rights revolution into mobilisational resources and opportunities.

The rights revolution marked a dramatic shift, challenging the dominance of traditional religious morality; business prerogatives; and the economic, social, cultural, and political exclusion of marginalised groups in society. Returning to Castro Rea (2018), the right against rights mobilises when it perceives that rights are advancing based on the 'intrinsic equality' of groups, rewarding the undeserving, and threatening traditional rights of 'worthy' rights-holders on the right.

These perceptions do not require material or definitive evidence of a shift in policies or practices; the mere hint of legal or legislative gains triggers perceptions of threat and mobilises the right against rights. As Martin (2013, 25) contends, threats mobilise because

> Threats make it rational to engage in protest by reducing the opportunity cost of mobilization: If people weigh the expected costs and benefits of protest before deciding on a course of action, then the threat of adversity can alter their calculations by increasing the perceived cost of doing nothing ... even apparently small threats sometimes motivate people to protest more than this sort of rational decision calculus would lead us to expect.

Gains in the rights revolution are sometimes only rhetorical, rather than material; are never fully implemented and enforced; and are highly limited. Traditional rights are not eroded by advancing new rights in law or practice; the right wing has continued to hold on to – and has sometimes even expanded – its political, social, cultural, and economic rights, even when rights claims by previously excluded groups began to be heard. The work of the right against rights is to transform even small threats into catalysts for mobilisation.

This does not happen overnight. One of the world's oldest gay rights associations, Grupo Gay da Bahia, attributes the rise of an anti-gay uncivil movement to legislative gains for civil unions and same-sex marriage in Brazil during the Workers' Party government, but homophobic violence predated those legislative gains. The movement's power depended on instilling 'moral panic' (Cohen 2011), and a zero-sum calculation in which LGBT+ legislative wins cancelled out the rights and protections for traditional heterosexual families. The right against rights tapped into fears leading to widespread support behind the 2019 election of Jair Bolsonaro and his legitimation of homophobic violence.

AN ANALYTICAL FRAMEWORK

Similarly, the 1995 liberalisation of abortion under the left-wing (former guerrilla) Farabundo Martí Liberation Front (FMLN) did not alone catalyse the anti-abortion countermovement in El Salvador (Viterna 2012, 250). Because the country's previous abortion ban had not been enforced, its liberalisation did not change abortion practice dramatically. Nonetheless, the new legislation by a left-wing government allowed the right against rights to inflame a sense of threat to, and loss of, the traditional right's political and economic influence. This threat forged a broad coalition of economic forces and political elites, alongside a moral religious right, in a countermovement allied with radical neoliberals.

Such mobilisations prevailed even where the right held on to power, as Colombia shows (Corredor (Chapter 4)). The referendum on the peace process offered an opportunity to reassert the traditional power and privilege on the right. A countermovement against 'gender ideology' and its threats to the family already existed, but the peace referendum united Catholic and evangelical moral forces, rural and urban business elites, and the military.

The capacity to translate rights advanced by previously marginalised groups into threats to traditional rights and privileges – to make the rights revolution a political opportunity and to derive organisational resources from it – explains right-against-rights mobilisation. The rights revolution in the region is propitious for such mobilisations, regardless of the conservative, moderate, or progressive nature of the governments. How to tap into fears and mobilise is thus critical to understanding the power of the right against rights.

How the Right against Rights Mobilises: Tactics

To roll back, reverse, or check social movements' rights gains, the right against rights borrows, adapts, or appropriates the same set of mobilisation tactics used by their rights adversaries. These include the framing devices, leadership and organisation, double militancy, transnational advocacy networks, and visibility and disruptive actions discussed below.

Framing

Framing (Benford and Snow 2000) is key to right-against-rights mobilisations to expand their appeal and support. Effective framing can mobilise support even when the threat to the traditional right is small and its political, economic, social, and cultural influence remains powerful. Framing creates the sense of urgency to act. In contrast,

> even very dramatic shifts can fail to produce political movements if agents prove incapable of framing them in ways that generate collective action. [Yet] very moderate proposals for political reform can generate dramatic political movements if agents frame these reforms in ways that mobilise groups. Successful framing involves depicting contemporary events in ways that resonate with individuals' personal experiences or their perspectives on the world (Payne 2000, 22).

38 Leigh A. Payne

Threat, Historical Symbols, and Cultural Cues

Framing by right-wing mobilisations, not unlike their social movement adversaries, involves naming, blaming, aiming, and claiming (Payne 2000, 22–4). Naming the grievance, using a vernacular of threat or crisis, unites a broad constituency behind political action. Blaming a clear set of actors for that threat or crisis provides an identifiable culprit for the problems. In addition, right-wing mobilisations take aim at a political system that has excluded them from power or decision-making. Together, naming, blaming, and aiming could be seen as constituting Dias *et al.*'s (2021) notion of the 'framing of antagonism'. In addition to antagonism, effective right-against-rights framing involves claiming a likely victory over adversaries, representing the mobilisation as a viable alternative to living with threat.

Jocelyn Viterna has described Salvadoran anti-abortionists' framing as moral panic, 'a kind of collective hysteria … [over threats] to transform traditional power relations. Moral panics work to reimpose a traditional social order by targeting as "villains" or "folk devils" the very marginalized group that appears to be gaining power' (quoted in Nicholasen (2018)). Abortion and LGBT+ rights activists are named as evil, and are blamed for threatening national social and religious values. Naming and blaming thus legitimise the effort to roll back rights and eliminate rights-seekers. Cataclysms are not necessary to mobilise against threat; effective framing is.

Not all naming and blaming involves moral panic, but extreme language is common. Wodak (2019, 67, 75) refers to 'post-shame', in which the right's 'shamelessness, the humiliation of other participants, defamation, lies, and ad hominem attacks dominate', adding that 'bad manners also play an outsized role, as do deliberate rudeness, lies, insults, destructive (eristic) argumentation, and intentional breaches of taboos on racist, sexist, homophobic, or antisemitic remarks. Norms of political correctness are not merely violated, but explicitly challenged as restricting free speech, thus offering identification with an anti-elitist politics.'

To name and blame effectively, the right against rights sometimes 'draw[s] on a stock of cultural symbols that "cue up" the movement with recognisable movements from the past, either domestic or foreign' (Payne 2000, 24). In their effort at naming the problem, these mobilisations evoke the memory of past threats and the necessity of mobilising to prevent them. They demonise their opponents as 'cultural villains', using 'vitriolic language and symbols' to provoke rage (Payne 2000, 24–7). They do not faithfully adhere to past languages, symbols, or mobilisations, and instead adapt them to current needs (Tilly 1978, 154–6). In this way, right-wing mobilisations play out 'old ideas in new ways, but also new ideas in old ways' (Payne 2000, 27).

Culture constitutes 'usefully manipulatable tools' (Lancaster 1992, 90). Stories from the past can be used in different ways for different audiences. The right against rights may sometimes represent itself as part of the legacy of the heroic and patriotic authoritarian or armed-conflict past (Loxton 2014), but at other times attempt to downplay past violence or the movement's association with it (Zavatti

AN ANALYTICAL FRAMEWORK 39

2021). The Salvadoran anti-abortion movement demonised the FMLN government, associating it with its 'terrorist' guerrilla past, which would logically lead it to 'legalise the slaughter of innocent unborn children' (Viterna, 2012, 252). The Colombian right against rights similarly warned that casting a 'Yes' vote in the peace referendum would legalise the armed guerrilla FARC Party and unleash 'gender ideology' and LGBT+ indoctrination in schools, thereby threatening traditional families (Corredor (Chapter 4)).

The Chilean anti-abortion movement took the opposite approach, equating abortion with the Pinochet dictatorship's torture, disappearance, and killing of innocents (Escoffier and Vivaldi (Chapter 8)). The right-against-rights mobilisations in Argentina paradoxically adapt the language of human rights used to hold the dictatorship's perpetrators accountable, so as subsequently to defend those perpetrators. They 'framejacked' (Bob 2011) rights language: universal human rights principles, victims' rights to truth and justice, family members' dignity, and 'never again' (Salvi (Chapter 3)).

Tapping into cultural cues, evoking specific types of demons, naming and blaming them for threats, can resonate deeply (Busby 2010). In this way, the right against rights can take aim at the target – the source of the threat – and make sense of collective action to fight it (Simmons 2014). They can also claim to be the alternative, the way to roll back rights threats and reinstate traditional rights protections.

Framing devices do not always produce the desired outcome for the right against rights, however. Sometimes they backfire when they are perceived as inherently contradictory, as the Argentina case shows; or illogical, as the Colombian case illustrates; or simply too extreme for the right, as the Chilean case suggests. Legitimating myths sometimes allow right-against-rights mobilisations to overcome these contradictions, leaps in logic, and extremism.

Legitimating Myths

Framing efforts reveal contradictions. For example, right-against-rights groups might condemn foreign intervention, ideas, or financing, while accepting such support for their own mobilisation. Or a mobilisation may claim to be oriented toward values such as pro-life, while failing to condemn feminicide. The notion of 'legitimating myths' behind right-against-rights mobilisations attempts to overcome these potential barriers to mobilisation by trading on 'conflicting, and even contradictory, understandings of the movement and its goals' (Payne 2000, 30). Right-against-rights mobilisations generate images and stories that can appeal to different constituencies. Pragmatic, economically oriented members, for example, may endorse uncivil movements, disregarding evidence of violence in favour of ambiguous and contradictory statements by the movement about its use of violence. 'Anti-politics' stances allow right-against-rights mobilisations to 'present themselves as political mavericks, unbeholden to any "special interest group" and thus able to find non-political solutions to national problems. They portray themselves as the authentic and "democratic" representatives of excluded voices' (Payne 2000, 33), while also – by definition – advancing an exclusionary agenda.

Legitimating myths provide ways to disassociate from stigmatised and violent pasts and discredited political figures when that is necessary (Feldman 2019). They allow the right against rights to play both sides: as responsible institutional actors while also excusing certain violent acts. The contradiction between civil and uncivil political action can be exploited by movements to their advantage to sustain support among militant and pragmatic constituencies. They deny wrongdoing – blaming enemies for lies about them – to appeal to pragmatic constituencies, while at the same time sending clear cues to maintain support from extremist constituencies. These seemingly contradictory messages involve particular uses of language such as relative-weight defence of uncivil acts (e.g. violence to end greater violence), civil disobedience (e.g. opposing unjust policies or practices), bad apples (e.g. blaming some unrepresentative members for uncivil acts), just-war analogies (e.g. 'soldiers sacrificing their personal security to fight a brutal and demonic enemy for the greater good of the nation' (Payne 2000, 34)), and traditional gendered ideals (e.g. hypermasculinity in defence of endangered women and children). Right-against-rights mobilisations construct 'these myths largely by drawing on cultural symbols but transforming them to fit a contemporary context' (Payne 2000, 36).

Framejacking also provides a means of tempering extremism. Gendered framing is particularly relevant in this regard. Using traditional notions of gender, right-against-rights mobilisations claim to defend the family and innocent women and children from threat. Graff *et al.* (2019, 6) argue that, paradoxically, 'the concept of women's empowerment has ... [also] been successfully hijacked by right-wing movements and ideologies and has drawn many women to the Right'. Mason (2019, 665) identifies a way in which the right framejacks women's empowerment, 'deploying pro-women stances strategically'. She describes a shift away from the image of 'a scolding male zealot' and 'right-wing misogynists' toward a pro-women and women's equality discourse and action, such as promoting women to leadership positions within the movement. In addition, anti-LGBT+ mobilisations exploit the debate between some feminists and the trans community over trans claims of discrimination. They mobilise against certain laws as discriminatory, attempting to roll back women's and LGBT+ rights. Moreover, claiming 'equality under the law', right-against-rights groups have mobilised to replace the language of 'gender violence' with 'family violence' (Norris 2019; Rousseau 2020). Biroli and Caminotti (2020, 3) contend that in defence of the family, the right against rights portrays 'human rights, feminism, and LGBTQ activists [as] "neocolonial" actors, advocating ideas that the majority of citizens do not share'.

Religious groups have also employed legitimating myths to appeal to a broader secular pro-life community, a tactic Vaggione refers to as 'strategic secularism'. These strategies include moving beyond perceived moral and religious threats of abortion and LGBT+ rights to cast such rights as secular and scientific (e.g. biological, psychological, and bioethics) threats to the public (Reuterswärd 2021, 24).

AN ANALYTICAL FRAMEWORK

Secular arguments have the potential to reach non-religious adherents without losing support from the devout.

Judith Butler (2017) probes whether these legitimating myths may also attempt to shield religious groups from criticism. After she was attacked in Brazil for her critical gender theory, she wrote an essay about the experience:

> At the Congonhas airport, one of the women confronting me started to yell about pedophilia. Why is this? It may be that she believed that gay men are pedophiles, and that the movement for LGBT+ rights was propaganda for pedophilia. But I found myself wondering why a movement for sexual dignity and rights and against sexual violence and exploitation is blamed for pedophilia when it is surely the Catholic Church in the last years that has been exposed to harbor pedophiles, protecting them from discipline and prosecution while not protecting their hundreds of victims. Could it be that 'gender ideology' has become a phantasm of sexual chaos and predation precisely in order to deflect from the sexual exploitation and moral corruption within the Catholic Church, a situation that has profoundly shaken its moral authority?

Presenting 'two more-or-less contradictory meanings, oriented towards at least two different audiences ... not only increases the overall audience, but also enables the speaker or writer to deny responsibility ... [to claim] "it wasn't meant that way"' (Wodak 2019, 75), or plausible deniability. To avoid accusations of racism and to build support from moderates, radical neoliberals carefully constructed coded language in their effort to defeat the Afro-Uruguayan affirmative action law. Using framejacking, they emphasised equality and opposition to discrimination in hiring. They further challenged the left-wing government's commitment to universal rights and anti-discrimination when the law would exclude poor whites from employment opportunities. Framejacking appealed to extremists who understood the coded language and the traditional right-wing sectors who needed it to support the cause (Sharnak (Chapter 10)).

The white elites in Santa Cruz appropriated and reinterpreted multiculturalism and plurinationalism to promote their own cultural rights and contribution to nation-building in Bolivia. They embraced cultural recognition as a uniting concept that encompassed Santa Cruz's traditional cultural dress, music, and food. They spun a historical foundational (legitimating) myth of a shared mestizo identity in the region manifested in racial harmony and inclusion (Krausova (Chapter 11)).

The notion of dog whistles probably best describes the coded language used by the right against rights in Honduras. Referring to Berta Cáceres and the Indigenous movement that she led as 'deceptive' and 'manipulative', it cued up prevalent racist views without making them explicit. Extremists heard, understood, and agreed with the slurs; moderates took the language at face value (Tapias Torrado (Chapter 9)).

Legitimating myths developed by the right against rights take the form of contradictory narratives and coded racist, sexist, or homophobic language. They include framejacking, appropriating and utilising instrumentally a rights language used by their adversaries to roll back the rights those adversaries have long defended. Moderates who eschew extremist views overlook the underlying

Leigh A. Payne

racism behind these expressions. Extremists decode the rhetoric and recognise and support the movement for what it is. Legitimating myths allow the potential for the right against rights to maintain unity despite contradictions, deep divisions, and conflicting rights perspectives within the mobilisation.

Leadership and Organisation

Leadership can also unite otherwise disparate forces on the right. When charismatic leaders emerge, they become the identifiable face of the movement. They play a crucial role in its appeal and expansion, and the embodiment of the movement's message, contradictions and all. Movement entrepreneurs, in contrast, are often unknown figures preferring to work behind the scenes rather than on the front lines. They do not become household names. 'They package that movement, using the frames and cuing discussed above. They create both the movement-product and consumer demand for that product' (Payne 2000, 31).

As an example, the leader of El Salvador's high-profile anti-abortion movement maintains a relatively low profile. Rather than using inflammatory language and vitriol, Sara Larín is professional, youthful, reasonable, and unemotional. She seems to embody the Vida SV ('Si a la Vida' (Yes to Life)) movement's claim to political neutrality, religious pluralism, and a secular (science and health) and women's rights approach to opposing abortion. There are obvious contradictions, however. Larín and Vida SV promote a total abortion ban, and criminalisation of abortion doctors and women who abort. The movement's strong and unequivocal support from the archbishop of El Salvador and the far-right ARENA Party further contradicts the religious and political neutrality claims. Larín's leadership, the movement's website (vidasv.org), and its Facebook page (Escúchanos SV) advances on one hand a modern image that appeals to the moderate right wing and a younger generation, but simultaneously maintains links to ARENA and other far-right extremists.

Movement entrepreneurs, whether charismatic or not, thus generate the legitimating myths that

> allow constituents to deny, filter out, or justify aspects of the movement that they do not want to acknowledge or interrogate too thoroughly. They provide the means to bring together different individuals who share some, but not necessarily all, of the movement's tactics and ideas. They provide justification for individuals who might not otherwise join an overtly armed, right-wing, movement [or an elitist neoliberal movement]. They build on the vulnerability felt by certain sectors of the population, urging them to engage in collective action to end an urgent threat. They propose a possible solution to that threat that is recognisably similar to, but also distinct from, past ... solutions. They create a new identity that unites individuals with different views. And they broaden the appeal of the movement by casting it in terms of democratic, collective, and national goals rather than authoritarian, self-, or class interests (Payne 2000, 36).

While movement entrepreneurs generate these myths, those who join the mobilisation 'make sense' of them. Anthony Cohen describes this process as people finding 'common currency in behaviour whilst still tailoring it subjectively (and interpretively) to their *own* needs' (Cohen 1985, 17).

The face of the movement thus becomes part of the legitimating myths, the cultural cues, the very symbols that expand the mobilisation from a small fringe group to a broader constituency, that overcome individuals' reluctance to join. In some sense, entrepreneurs – whether charismatic or not – can transform objectively insignificant threats into an urgent need for collective action.

The tendency toward loose organisational structures may facilitate the process of uniting extremists and moderates in mobilisable networks. Legitimating myths, in contrast to formal political platforms and structures, absorb contradictions and facilitate the design and implementation of tactics to roll back rights: double militancy, linking up with right-wing transnational advocacy networks, and visibility and disruption.

Double Militancy

Right-against-rights movements and their leaders vary in terms of double militancy, or the degree to which they work autonomously from or closely within political or legal institutions (Alvarez 1990; Alenda 2020). The mobilisational aspects of the right against rights usually involve disruptive street tactics challenging their rights adversaries, but sometimes they equally target the government. In other cases, they move fluidly between street mobilisations and working within the government, as a block within legislatures, to fight or pass laws, and to reverse rights and return to the status quo ante.

Right-against-rights mobilisations, like their social movement adversaries, use standard tactics of engaging with like-minded political parties, lobbying, campaigning, and running for elected office, as ways to influence political outcomes within the system. But, also like social movements, they retain their autonomy from institutional politics, mobilising outside formal political structures. Indeed, this is one of the contradictions within the right-against-rights mobilisations, but is not necessarily unique to it: the desire to appear as untainted outsiders while simultaneously working within the political system to affect change.

Working within judicial institutions while also carrying out street mobilisations is a strategic form of double militancy. A key actor in legal mobilisation within the right against rights is the Catholic Church. This so-called 'juridification of religion' (Crumper and Lewis 2019) aims to roll back sexual and reproductive rights, seen by Church leaders as a 'tragic caricature of legality' (Vaggione 2018, 25). The Vatican has encouraged local legal activism, arguing that 'when states fail to respect "objective moral order", the Church and its members should oppose secular laws' (Vaggione 2018, 24). Vaggione cites Pope John Paul II's 1995 declaration that 'no circumstance, no purpose, no law whatsoever can ever make licit an act which is intrinsically illicit since it is contrary to the Law of God which is written in every human heart, knowable by reason itself, and proclaimed by the Church' (25).

44 *Leigh A. Payne*

Vaggione refers to the 'NGO-isation' of religious groups and their reliance on lawyers to advance three primary legal claims: the defence of conscientious objection (to refuse on religious grounds to perform abortion, marry same sex couples, or teach tolerance), the rights of parents to raise their children, and the need to protect religious freedom (27).

Pérez and Rocha-Carpiuc (2020) have tracked the Chilean anti-abortion countermovement's legal mobilisation comprising right-wing political parties and social organisations linked to the Catholic Church. Rousseau (2020) has analysed the anti-gender ideology countermovement in Peru that allies Catholic and evangelical groups in street mobilisation (by the group #ConMisHijosNoTeMetas) and legal mobilisation in the courts (by its ally Padres en Acción). Lemaitre (2012), analysing the Colombian context, concurs that legal mobilisation by religious groups has been a key strategy alongside mobilisation in the streets. That mobilisation claims to advance an objective and universal moral order, not a religious one, that holds at its core religious freedom; the right to life in its essence, and not existence (brain function); and the exclusive recognition of and protection for heterosexual marriages.

The move to the courts may result in part from certain political institutions proving closed to extremist groups (Wiesehomeier and Doyle 2014; Bowen 2014). Yet the right against rights continues to engage parliaments and executives through lobbying and other strategies to influence policy and legislative outcomes. In this endeavour, right-against-rights mobilisations may engage legitimating myths to disguise or soften extreme attitudes or behaviour.

On a double militancy spectrum, with exclusive street mobilisation on one end, and work primarily within the institutional political system on the other, most of the cases in this volume fall in the middle. The relatives of convicted Argentine human rights violators (Salvi (Chapter 3)) faced more difficulty gaining support within political parties, and thus combined street mobilisation with legal mobilisation. The anti-affirmative action mobilisation in Uruguay, in contrast, eschewed street action in favour of mobilisation in the halls of parliament and in the media. Despite its privileged position within the right-wing political party of former president Álvaro Uribe, the Colombian right against rights still worked outside the political system, launching legal and policy battles, street mobilisations, and social media and mainstream campaigns (Corredor (Chapter 4)). The evangelical right against rights formed a parliamentary bloc that combined street mobilisation with legislative, executive, and legal tactics (de Souza Santos (Chapter 6)).

Transnational Advocacy Networks on the Right

An additional tactic is forming a right-wing transnational advocacy network (Keck and Sikkink 1998; Bülow 2018; Mayka and Smith 2021), or R-TAN. Bob (2011, 74–6) shows that right-against-rights mobilisations build such networks across borders to amplify their demands and enhance their power and influence.

AN ANALYTICAL FRAMEWORK 45

Sutton and Borland (2013, 200, 232n21) suggest, moreover, that Latin American countermovements may flourish because of financing and ideological linkages in international networks. The US Human Life International is believed to have stimulated and sustained pro-life anti-reproductive rights movements in Argentina and El Salvador. The Madrid-based CitizenGo has provided funding, training, and a 'bus of freedom' to travel to the region and elsewhere to build anti-LGBT+ movements (Whyte 2017; Parke 2018; see also WikiLeaks n.d.). Graff *et al.* (2019, 1) refer to a new global anti-feminist right in which 'antagonism toward feminism is both a sentiment at the heart of the Right's value system and a political strategy, a platform for organising and for recruiting massive support' around the world.

It may be tempting to see right-against-rights mobilisations as imposed from powerful forces abroad. Such a view ignores the deeply religious, moral, and ideological orientation within the region that gives rise to these countermovements. It seems unlikely, however, that the Latin American right would have had the same level of visibility, organisational structure, communicative power, and financial support without R-TANs. Right-wing think tanks in Latin America, moreover, are sustained by substantial financial support from think tanks abroad, as well as foreign corporations and governments (Fang 2017; Cannon 2016). Some of the posters in street actions are in English, rather than Spanish or Portuguese, further hinting at strong connections across borders.

These foreign linkages also constitute right-against-rights contradictions. Despite building their own international networks, right-against-rights mobilisations have cast women's, LGBT+, and abortion rights as foreign imports, cultural imperialism, 'gaymony', and neocolonialism. Contradictions are overlooked when anti-LGBT+ mobilisations attempt to build a strong transnational network on one hand and mobilise against the threats to national values from foreign-inspired LGBT+ activism (Ritholtz and Mesquita (Chapter 5)) or anti-gender ideology (Kane *et al.* (Chapter 7)) on the other. Moreover, although the Latin American right against rights and its international network have demonised the IAS, attempting to defund it because of perceived foreign and cultural imperialism (Kane *et al.* (Chapter 7)), this has not prevented the right against rights from advancing their rights claims in that system (Salvi (Chapter 3)).

Visibility and Disruption

Right-against-rights mobilisations use the common anti-system tactic of visibility and disruption. Taking to the streets to protest with provocative signs, banners, and slogans indicates that these mobilisations are not part of a staid political elite, but represent the popular sector. Unconventional street politics also capture media attention. That attention can make the mobilisation appear much stronger, more representative and powerful, belying its actual low level of support.

Examples of right-against-rights visibility and disruptive tactics abound. El Salvador's anti-abortion movement used highly visible street protests, with dramatic language and images, especially posters of bloody babies. In Argentina, the anti-human-rights trials mobilisation is in the streets with provocative banners and graffiti, employing disruptive tactics within courtrooms, engaging in weekly marches around the May Pyramid, replacing the iconic white headscarves of the Madres de la Plaza de Mayo with black ribbons, and chaining themselves to military installations (Salvi (Chapter 3)). The Bolivian right against rights held massive rallies and appropriated Indigenous symbols as their own, while a violent youth uncivil movement formed, threatening Indigenous leaders within and outside government (Krausova (Chapter 11)). The Colombian alliance of right-wing Catholic and evangelical groups carried out street protests against curricular reforms to end bullying of gay students in schools. It also mobilised during the peace referendum, sending 'intimidating text messages, threatening pamphlets and ominous posts on social media' (Idler 2016; Corredor (Chapter 4)).

'Information politics' has also advanced right-against-rights visibility in the media (Alenda *et al.* 2019; Castro Rea 2018). These are often referred to by the right's opponents as 'misinformation campaigns' and the production of 'fake news'. Links to right-wing think tanks and the mainstream media have facilitated the promotion of these views in the public sphere (Cannon 2016). Such seemingly scientific and pseudo-academic studies give an air of legitimacy and disguise fear-mongering. As one report stated, these right-wing think tanks are 'oriented less on developing genuinely new policy proposals [their typical role], and more on establishing political organisations that carry the credibility of academic institutions, making them an effective organ for winning hearts and minds' (Fang 2017).

High-visibility tactics in the streets suggest that the right against rights prefers such action, despite its high costs, over passively waiting for elected officials and judiciaries to fight their battles. It seems to suggest that the right against rights does not trust representatives in the branches of government to defend right-wing interests effectively. Yet very few exclusively use one – street action or mainstream institutional – form of mobilisation. The combination may improve the right-against-rights influence, but it does not always win outcomes.

Impact of Right-against-Rights Mobilisations

To summarise, right-against-rights mobilisations have proliferated throughout the region to roll back rights of previously excluded groups. Countermovements have attempted to roll back rights advances spearheaded by social movements representing women, the LGBT+ community, Indigenous and BIPOC peoples, the environment, labour, and victims of human rights abuses. Uncivil movements have mobilised against the rights-bearers themselves. Radical neoliberals have attempted to advance the rights and freedoms of the private sector in response to perceived economic threats. To achieve their goals, the right against rights have

AN ANALYTICAL FRAMEWORK

tended to use double militancy: institutional forms of right-wing political participation, combined with autonomous mobilisation, often engaging in visible and
disruptive street actions. They have framed their goals by appropriating the language of rights used by their adversaries. They have generated legitimating myths
to expand their appeal to include extremists and moderates on the right, elitists
and non-elite groups. Charismatic leaders and movement entrepreneurs have held
fragile coalitions together to strengthen right-against-rights mobilisations, even in
the face of deep contradictions. Despite this array of tactics, right-against-rights
mobilisations are not always successful. This section of the chapter analyses the
impact the right against rights has had in Latin America.

Right-against-Rights Successes

The very visibility and disruptive capacity of the right against rights already
indicates a level of success in contesting the rights gains of previously excluded
groups. Even higher levels of success by the right against rights include
rolling back laws, legislation, and policies aimed to advance the rights of the
marginalised.

Sometimes the right against rights use violent – anti-democratic – strategies
alongside democratic ones to roll back rights or to promote exclusionary ones. These
groups have intimidated, threatened, harmed, and killed rights-seekers, such as
women, abortion rights advocates, members of the LGBT+ community, Indigenous
human rights defenders, and environmentalists. They have advanced extreme legislation to criminalise those seeking certain rights, such as reproductive rights. They
have watered down legislation so that rights gains, such as anti-discrimination
and pro-affirmative action, are checked, thereby perpetuating social and economic
inequalities. They have elected extreme-right political representatives and leaders.
They can influence political outcomes for the rights of victims in peace and other
transitional justice processes.

An example is the Salvadoran anti-abortion countermovement, which won a
total ban on abortion in 1997,[2] and a constitutional amendment to protect life from
the moment of conception in 1999. The most stringently enforced anti-abortion ban
in the world followed (BBC 2018; Malkin 2018). El Salvador criminalises abortion
with a prison sentence of two-to-eight years for the woman and six-to-12 years
for abortion practitioners, with 'accomplices' facing sentences of between two and
five years. If a viable foetus is terminated, the abortion penalty can be converted

---

[2] In an interview, Jocelyn Viterna added the detail of the 1994 United Nations International Conference
on Population and Development in Cairo. The Vatican responded negatively to the conference focus
on advancing global education and family planning, and improving reproductive health. It highlighted
those countries –such as El Salvador – that banned abortion, thereby further stimulating the movement
against abortion in the country (Nicholasen 2018).

48 *Leigh A. Payne*

to aggravated homicide, with a sentence of 30-to-50 years.[3] The mobilisation's success particularly impacts poor young women vulnerable to sexual assault.

The Uruguayan anti-affirmative-action mobilisation (Sharnak (Chapter 10)) also succeeded. Although the affirmative action law passed, radical neoliberals had managed to remove all sanctions for failing to comply with law. It thus protected the very hiring rights and freedoms that businesses had promoted, at the expense of advancing the social, political, and economic rights and redress of the Afro-Uruguayan community.

The right against rights also succeeded in Brazil (de Souza Santos (Chapter 6)). The strategy involved finding charismatic leaders and movement entrepreneurs through the pyramidical evangelical church structure, working within and outside the formal political arena, and developing effective framing and action tactics, consolidating a powerful bloc within parliament. The bloc has checked rights legislation promoted by social movements. Its primary success may be the election of former president Jair Bolsonaro. Also effective in Brazil is an uncivil movement that succeeded in intimidating, threatening, harming, killing, and exiling rights-seekers.

The global right against rights has also achieved some success. It has weakened the IAS by reducing funding, challenging its legitimacy, shifting its rights agenda, and heightened right-wing representation. The alliance against the IAS has also strengthened and emboldened a regional right against rights. Nonetheless, the right against rights cannot claim full victory against the IAS's promotion of LGBT+, women's, or reproductive rights (Kane *et al.* (Chapter 7)).

Failed Right-against-Rights Mobilisations

Internal factors, such as ineffective framing, and external factors, such as the strength of their adversaries, explain the weakness of right-against-rights mobilisations. But these factors are not always predictable. Despite using the same tactics of other anti-abortion movements – taking advantage of the rights revolution context, rights framing, and double militancy – the Chilean countermovement failed. In this case, the countermovement may have used such extreme tactics that it could not build broad support from the moderate right in society or in Congress. The use of radical language and symbols that had worked in the Salvadoran context instead prompted a public outcry against the anti-abortion group from feminists, human rights groups, and others on the left that further alienated moderate support. Even the supporters of the dictatorship may have opposed the movement, given that it linked the regime to human rights atrocities (Escoffier and Vivaldi (Chapter 8)). The failure to build legitimating myths coupled with social movement adversaries who used framing

---

[3] Viterna documented 20 cases of women facing criminal sentences for abortion, and 51 cases of aggravated homicide, including when proof of a miscarriage or stillbirth existed (Nicholasen 2018).

AN ANALYTICAL FRAMEWORK

to gain support from moderates within Congress and Chilean society ultimately undermined the movement's success.

In Argentina the relatives of convicted human rights violators failed to win concessions in the courts during a favourable government under Mauricio Macri. Authoritarian regime supporters never achieved the legitimacy and support they needed to roll back efforts to hold human rights trials and sentence violators. In this case, the human rights movement was too deeply entrenched in the country and too embedded in social and political institutions to be undermined (Salvi (Chapter 3)). Trying to roll back social movements' control over the human rights agenda via leaders, symbols, and framing that appear neutral and appeal to moderates seemed impossible in this context.

The Bolivian right against rights also failed. Elite forces in the most economically and politically powerful subregion of the country could not achieve the popular support necessary to block the return to power of Evo Morales's political party. They lacked the capacity to build legitimating myths or the sense of urgency and threat that more successful movements developed.

Initial wins by the right against rights may turn into eventual losses. In Honduras, for example, the uncivil-radical neoliberal alliance has historically used intimidation, threats, and murder to gain power over Indigenous and environmental rights defenders. The alliance seemed to win again with the killing of Berta Cáceres. Yet rights defenders refused to back down. Indeed, killing Cáceres redoubled efforts against megaproject elites' power within the state, the economy, and the courts. Those involved – including a top executive – eventually faced criminal convictions and imprisonment (Tapias Torrado (Chapter 9)). This indicates that even relatively weak social movements may sometimes defeat the right against rights, a topic picked up in the next section.

Reducing the Impact of the Right against Rights

As the discussion and cases above show, the success of the right against rights depends on designing and implementing effective mobilisation tactics. But the failures also point to the obstacles that the right against rights face in achieving aims. There are both internal and external dynamics that potentially weaken right-against-rights movements.

Inherent Dynamics

The right against rights tend to form minority movements that are unlikely to win mass support, or even substantial support from elite political groups. These mobilisations are deeply fragmented and comprise a variety of groups with conflicting interests. Indeed, one of the greatest inherent weaknesses of the right against rights is that of internal differences and disunity. Reducing the impact of the right against rights, therefore, depends in part on exploiting internal fragmentation over past violence, leadership crises, and corruption.

Where right-against-rights mobilisations are associated with historically violent right-wing actors, they confront unique challenges. Past right-wing ideology may continue to hold appeal for extremists, but right-against-rights mobilisations struggle with how to reframe their message to appeal to supporters of the old authoritarian/armed conflict right while also attracting new generations, or those on the right intolerant of past human rights violations. In these cases, right-against-rights mobilisations 'do not break with past patterns but adopt and adapt them' to the current situation (Payne 2000, xxiv). Avoiding authoritarian or armed conflict legacies and appealing to contemporary worries and new generations – creating legitimating myths – provides one way to overcome that weakness.

While charismatic leaders have the potential to overcome this weakness and form an emotional bond with a full range of constituents, they also have the tendency to plant the seeds of their own destruction. A host of events – succession crises, power-seeking leaders and competitors, instability, moderation, and contradictions – undermine the long-term capacity of movements to sustain themselves over time. These internal and leadership weaknesses often emerge with efforts to institutionalise the movement and transform it into a coherent political party. Because these movements derive much of their support from their anti-politics, anti-system, and anti-elite positions, becoming part of the mainstream can lead to a loss of support from those who view the shift as selling out the movement (Payne 2000, 44).

Yet even when the right against rights survives institutionalisation – such as the Evangelical Bloc in the Brazilian Congress – other forms of internal weaknesses can result. The leadership of the movement became linked to some of the corruption scandals in the country. Given that the movement gained traction particularly by charging Workers' Party leaders with corruption, hypocrisy and the scandals themselves tainted the movement (de Souza Santos (Chapter 6)). The Honduran right against rights engaged in the violence against Indigenous environmental and human rights activists has also been exposed for corruption. Such revelations raise doubts about the right's commitment to morality, law and order, and good governance.

To reduce the power of the right against rights involves denouncing contradictions in the mobilisations' rhetoric and behaviour on rights and responsibilities, making visible the immoral behaviour of moral leaders, and condemning extremist positions on rights. Such activities are unlikely to eliminate such mobilisations. Indeed, the right-against-rights development of a loose, mobilisable coalition has the agility to garner massive support at protest events, attracting substantial media attention, even without a firm foundation. Enduring networks respond to siren calls to action. Nonetheless, fewer moderates are likely to turn out for such events if the image of the network is tarnished, thereby weakening the broad coalition that enhances the power of the right against rights.

AN ANALYTICAL FRAMEWORK

External Dynamics

External dynamics also potentially weaken the effectiveness and impact of the right against rights. 'Information politics' reduces not only its internal strength, but also its appeal outside the organisation from potential constituents, political and economic leaders, and transnational forces. Paradoxically, institutional success may also reduce the mobilisation's power, as anti-politics and anti-elite constituencies withdraw. One of the key checks on right-against-rights mobilisations, however, is the strength and ability of its rights adversaries.

Outside investigations into wrongful acts such as corruption, extralegal violence, and misinformation may undermine the already fragile alliances within the mobilisations themselves. Similarly, investigative journalists and widespread campaigns in the media could play a role in exposing misinformation, 'fake news', exaggerated moral panic, and fear-mongering tactics by the right against rights. These counterinformation campaigns from external forces may help fragment the movement, separating moderates from the militant hardcore (Payne 2000, 45–9). Yet, as studies of 'fake news' show, objective facts and science fail to shift the emotional appeal of right-wing mobilisations. Such resistance to factual truths is evident in Brazil: 'The accusations made by Bolsonaro and believed by evangelicals need not correspond to the truth: it is enough that such themes fit the Brazilian evangelical understanding of evil – an evil that, in a hidden and satanic way, seeks to pervert believers' (Kibuuka 2020; see also Romancini 2018). Yet sometimes very small shifts away from the mobilisation by moderate forces is an outcome. The hearings on the 6 January 2021 attack on the US Capitol suggest, for example, a very slight change in views about those events, most probably among moderates, while also indicating entrenchment among the militant hardcore (Galston 2022).

Context matters for shifting views on the right. In the killing of Berta Cáceres, for example, the courts have put the killers, the masterminds, and the financiers on trial (Tapias Torrado (Chapter 9)). In such a conservative country and judiciary, efforts by the right to reframe the trials as biased or politically motivated have not held. That violent acts were investigated and the perpetrators held accountable might also explain why the Argentine right-against-rights claims have difficulty gaining broad appeal (Salvi (Chapter 3)).

Policy outcomes, legislative decisions, and legal rulings – whether positive or negative for the mobilisation – can weaken it. Rational-choice scholars explain that individuals are less likely to join unsuccessful political movements if they perceive that the cost of action outweighs the benefits. The stigma attached to right-wing mobilisations, particularly extremist ones, is likely to limit potential membership and alliances within mainstream institutions. This is the case with negative outcomes that mean that the high cost of an alliance outweighs the benefits. The extremism of the Chilean anti-abortion movement and the more compelling arguments by the pro-reproductive-rights social movement and the public (Escoffier and Vivaldi

(Chapter 8)) – cost the movement its necessary support from within the mainstream political system. Victory, however, may also result in demobilisation for different reasons. Success may transform the mobilisation into a political party, thus reducing its appeal among anti-system members. It may also result in burn-out, a desire to return to 'normal life' after high-intensity mobilisation. If victory is achieved, the movement may become 'latent', part of the cultural stock or collective action repertoire upon which future movements may rely.

Reliance on external support is thus a key weakness for the right against rights. Zaremberg (2020) notes that it is usually only with such support that the right against rights can overpower their typically more coherent and consolidated rights adversaries. Yet this strategic alliance, Zaremberg notes, between right-wing movements and economic and political allies – each needing the other to bolster the rollback of rights – is fraught with tensions, as discussed above. The right against rights may rely on R-TANs' support to hold together weak and fragmented movements. As Corrales (2022, 42) states: 'Transnationalism makes it harder for local actors to contain [backlash] on their own.' Yet perhaps visibility of the reliance of the right against rights on external support for financing, framing ideas, and tactics is another way to expose the limited appeal of the mobilisation within the country and its hypocrisy around patriotism and anti-imperialism, thereby weakening it.

Perhaps the greatest challenge to right-against-rights mobilisation is the strength of social movements in defending rights gains. The Chilean pro-choice movement used tactics to link legal, free, and safe abortion to women's life and health, and inequality against the anti-abortion movement's depiction of such decisions as torture, killing, and genocide. The LGBT+ movement in Brazil has highlighted the 'homocaust' carried out by the right against rights. The international prize awarded to Berta Cáceres recognised the legitimacy of the environmental and Indigenous struggle against those promoting violence to end it.

This balance of forces between the right against rights and their adversaries resembles Archimedes' Lever (Payne *et al.* 2020). Social movements, rights-seekers, and communities attempt to use the correct tool (lever) – social movement mobilisational tactics – to lift up the weight of rights from under the pressure of the right-against-rights veto players. In a favourable context – where the fulcrum is closer to the weight – rights groups need to apply less pressure to lift up the rights' weight. This may be best explained by Argentina, where the context has been favourable to human rights advocates since the dictatorship. A less propitious context is Brazil, where human rights protections and practices have proved less consolidated. In that context, the right against rights has more power to resist the weight of rights. The right against rights in Brazil, moreover, has benefited from powerful international forces on their side of the balance, making it even more difficult for the historically marginalised to lift up the rights weight. In cases where international forces are on the marginalised communities' side of the balance, they can gain that leverage to lift up rights. Thus, external forces in the role of transnational advocacy networks (TANs) can also play an important role in bolstering the demands of the marginalised, as a counterweight to the

AN ANALYTICAL FRAMEWORK 53

right's power domestically and the support they receive from R-TANs to weigh rights down.

Conclusion

The analytical framework presented in this chapter reveals three types of right-against-rights mobilisations: countermovements, uncivil movements, and radical neoliberal mobilisations. They share the defining characteristics of engaging in institutional and extra-institutional collective action to check, roll back, and reverse certain rights, replacing them with a set of traditional rights supported by moral, political, and economic groups. In this sense, they form a kind of veto power over the rights of the historically marginalised.

Analysing right-against-rights mobilisations fills a gap in understanding. Existing approaches to right-wing movements in Europe and the United States do not capture the way in which the right against rights has risen in response to the rights revolution, creating the political opportunity to mobilise that is more specific than economic downturn or political instability. The analytical framework offered in this chapter distinguishes the types of mobilisation, moving beyond vague categories of countermovements, populist, extreme, or far-right movements. In contrast to the literature on right-wing movements, the right-against-rights mobilisations include elites (radical neoliberals), anti-elites (uncivil movements), and cross-class alliances (countermovements). They are also distinguished by their use of 'moral panic' (countermovements), perceived threats from rights-seekers to traditional rights (uncivil movements), and the perception of losses to business privileges (radical neoliberal mobilisations).

These types of mobilisations exist around the world. Analysing Latin American mobilisations provides the basis for a comparative framework to look across country- and regional boundaries at the phenomenon of the right against rights. Such a framework allows us to consider: who mobilises in the right against rights; when, where, why and how; and with what impact on the struggle for rights of the historically marginalised. The analysis of Latin America illustrates that these mobilisations transcend borders not only in one region but also internationally. A global right against rights that acts within countries and in regional and international bodies is evident.

This study also shows that the right against rights presents life-and-death issues. These include the lives of LGBT+ and Indigenous human rights defenders; the lives of women forced to have illegal abortions; and the lives of people of colour, those in minority religions, or immigrants. These are fundamental democratic rights to equality and for safe environments for all people standing up to the rights of powerful businesses. The studies in this book show that at key moments, with appropriate rights framing devices, the right against rights can have a powerful impact that reverses the rights gains for those who have struggled against violent oppression and exploitation. Understanding the mobilisation and threat of right-against-rights movements, as well as their vulnerabilities, provides the means to reduce their power.

References

Alenda, S. (ed.) (2020), *Anatomía de la centro-derecha chilena: Nuevos y viejos protagonistas* (Santiago, Fondo de Cultura Económica Chile).

Alenda, S., A. Gartenlaub, and K. Fischer (2019), 'Ganar la batalla de ideas: El rol de los think tanks en la reconfiguración de la centro-derecha chilena', in *Anatomía de la centro-derecha chilena: Nuevos y viejos protagonistas*, ed. S. Alenda (Santiago, Fondo de Cultura Económica Chile), pp. 119–56.

Alvarez, S. (1990), *Engendering Democracy in Brazil: Women's Movements in Transition Politics* (Princeton, Princeton University Press).

Bale, T. and C. Rovira Kaltwasser (2021), 'The Mainstream Right in Western Europe: Caught between the Silent Revolution and Silent Counter-Revolution', in *Riding the Populist Wave: Europe's Mainstream Right in Crisis*, ed. T. Bale and C. Rovira Kaltwasser (Cambridge, Cambridge University Press).

BBC [British Broadcasting Corporation] (2018), 'El Salvador Court Frees Woman Jailed under Anti-Abortion Laws', *BBC News*, 18 December.

Beder, S. (1997), *Global Spin: The Corporate Assault on Environmentalism* (Dartington, Green Books).

Benford, R. D. and D. A. Snow (2000), 'Framing Processes and Social Movements: An Overview and Assessment', *Annual Review of Sociology*, 26 (August), 611–39.

Biroli, F. and M. Caminotti (2020), 'The Conservative Backlash against Gender in Latin America', *Politics & Gender*, 16, 1–38.

Blee, K. M. and K. A. Creasap (2010), 'Conservative and Right-Wing Movements', *Annual Review of Sociology*, 36, 269–86.

Bob, C. (2011), *The Global Right Wing and the Clash of World Politics* (Cambridge, Cambridge University Press).

Bowen, J. D. (2014), 'The Right and Nonparty Forms of Representation and Participation: Bolivia and Ecuador Compared', in *The Resilience of the Latin American Right*, ed. J. P. Luna and C. Rovira Kaltwasser (Baltimore, Johns Hopkins University Press), pp. 94–116.

Bülow, M. von (2018), 'The Empowerment of Conservative Civil Society in Brazil', in *The Mobilization of Conservative Civil Society*, ed. R. Youngs (Washington, DC, Carnegie Endowment for International Peace), pp. 13–18.

Busby, J. W. (2010), *Moral Movements and Foreign Policy* (Cambridge, Cambridge University Press).

Butler, J. (2017), 'The Phantom of Gender: Reflections on Freedom and Violence', *Folha de São Paulo*, https://www1.folha.uol.com.br/internacional/en/culture/2017/11/1936921-the-phantom-of-gender-reflections-on-freedom-and-violence.shtml.

Caiani, M. and D. della Porta (2011), 'The Elitist Populism of the Extreme Right: A Frame Analysis of Extreme Right-Wing Discourses in Italy and Germany', *Acta politica*, 46:2, 180–202.

Caiani, M., D. della Porta, and C. Wagemann (2012), *Mobilizing on the Extreme Right: Germany, Italy, and the United States* (Oxford, Oxford University Press).

Cannon, B. (2016), *The Right in Latin America: Elite Power, Hegemony and the Struggle for the State* (Abingdon, Routledge).

Castro Rea, J. (2018), 'Right-Wing Think Tank Networks in Latin America: The Mexican Connection', *Perspectives on Global Development and Technology*, 17:1–2, 89–102.

Cohen, A. P. (1985), *The Symbolic Construction of Community* (London, Routledge).

AN ANALYTICAL FRAMEWORK

Cohen, S. (2011), *Folk Devils and Moral Panics* (London, Routledge).

Corrales, J. (2022), *The Politics of LGBT Rights Expansion in Latin America and the Caribbean* (Cambridge, Cambridge University Press).

Crumper, P. and T. Lewis (2019), 'Human Rights and Religious Litigation: Faith in the Law?', *Oxford Journal of Law and Religion*, 8, 121–50.

Davis, M. (2006), *City of Quartz: Excavating the Future in Los Angeles* (London, Verso).

Dias, T., M. von Bülow, and D. Gobbi (2021), 'Populist Framing Mechanisms and the Rise of Right-Wing Activism in Brazil', *Latin American Politics and Society*, 63:3, 69–92.

Dreifuss, R. A. (1981), *1964: A conquista do estado* (Petrópolis, Vozes), https://docero.com.br/doc/nec00vc.

Encarnación, O. G. (2016), *Out in the Periphery: Latin America's Gay Rights Revolution* (Oxford, Oxford University Press).

Encyclopedia.com (2018), 'Counter-Movement' (Oxford University Press), https://www.encyclopedia.com/social-sciences/dictionaries-thesauruses-pictures-and-press-relea ses/counter-movement#:~:text=counter%2Dmovement%20An%20organized%20r esponse,or%20fronts%20for%20interest%20groups.

Epp, C. R. (1998), *The Rights Revolution: Lawyers, Activists, and Supreme Courts in Comparative Perspective* (Chicago, University of Chicago Press).

Fang, L. (2017), 'Sphere of Influence: How American Libertarians are Remaking Latin American Politics', *The Intercept*, August.

Feldman, M. (2019), 'On Radical Right Mainstreaming in Europe and the US', in *Europe at the Crossroads: Confronting Populist, Nationalist, and Global Challenges*, ed. P. Bevelander and Ruth Wodak (Lund, Nordic Academic Press).

Galston, W. A. (2022), 'What Are Americans Thinking about the January 6 Hearings?', *FixGov* (Brookings Institution), 23 June, https://www.brookings.edu/blog/fixgov/2022/06/23/what-are-americans-thinking-about-the-january-6-hearings/.

Gold, T. and A. M. Peña (2021), 'The Rise of the Contentious Right: Digitally Intermediated Linkage Strategies in Argentina and Brazil', *Latin American Politics and Society*, 63:3, 93–118.

Gould, D. B. (2009), *Moving Politics: Emotion and ACT UP's Fight against AIDS* (Chicago, University of Chicago Press).

Graff, A., R. Kapur, and S. D. Walters (2019), 'Introduction: Gender and the Rise of the Global Right', *Signs*, 44:3, 1–22.

Griffin, R. (2017), 'Interregnum or Endgame? The Radical Right in the "Post-Fascist" Era', in *The Populist Radical Right: A Reader*, ed. C. Mudde (London, Routledge), pp. 15–27.

Hirsch-Hoefler, S. and C. Mudde (2013), 'Right-Wing Movements', in *The Wiley-Blackwell Encyclopedia of Social and Political Movements*, ed. D. Snow, D. della Porta, B. Klandermans, and D. McAdam (Hoboken, NJ, Wiley-Blackwell), pp. 1–8.

Idler, A. (2016), 'Why the Real Test for Colombia's Peace Process Begins after the Demobilisation Process', *Monkey Cage*, 8 September.

Ignazi, P. (2003), *Extreme Right Parties in Western Europe* (Oxford, Oxford University Press).

Jaspers, J. M. (1997), *The Art of Moral Protest: Culture, Biography, and Creativity in Social Movements* (Chicago, University of Chicago Press).

Kajsiu, B. (2019), 'The Colombian Right: The Political Ideology and Mobilization of Uribismo', *Canadian Journal of Latin American and Caribbean Studies*, 44:2, 204–24.

Keck, M. E. and K. Sikkink (1998), *Activists beyond Borders: Advocacy Networks in International Politics* (Ithaca, Cornell University Press).

Kibuuka, B. G. L. (2020), 'Complicity and Synergy between Bolsonaro and Brazilian Evangelicals in COVID-19 Times: Adherence to Scientific Negationism for Political Religious Reasons', *International Journal of Latin American Religions*, 4, 288–317.

Lancaster, R. N. (1992), *Life Is Hard: Machismo, Danger and the Intimacy of Power in Nicaragua* (Berkeley, University of California Press).

Lemaitre, J. (2012), 'By Reason Alone: Catholicism, Constitutions, and Sex in the Americas', *International Journal of Constitutional Law*, 10:2, 493–511.

Loxton, J. (2014), 'The Authoritarian Roots of New Right Party Success in Latin America', in *The Resilience of the Latin American Right*, ed. J. P. Luna and C. Rovira Kaltwasser (Baltimore, Johns Hopkins University Press), pp. 117–40.

Luna, J. P. and C. Rovira Kaltwasser (2014), *The Resilience of the Latin American Right* (Baltimore, Johns Hopkins University Press).

Luxton, J. (2014), 'The Authoritarian Roots of New Right Party Success in Latin America' in *The Resilience of the Latin American Right*, ed. J. P. Luna and C. Rovira Kaltwasser (Baltimore, Johns Hopkins University Press), pp. 117–40.

Malkin, E. (2018), 'They Were Jailed for Miscarriages: Now Campaign Aims to End Abortion Ban', *New York Times*, 9 April.

Martin, L. (2013), *Rich People's Movements: Grassroots Campaigns to Untax the One Percent* (Oxford and New York, Oxford University Press).

Mason, C. (2019), 'Opposing Abortion to Protect Women: Transnational Strategy since the 1990s', *Signs*, 44:3, 665–92.

Mayka, L. and A. E. Smith (2021), 'The Grassroots Right in Latin America: Patterns, Causes, and Consequences', *Latin American Politics and Society*, 63:3, 1–31.

McAdam, D. (1982), *Political Process and the Development of Black Insurgency, 1930–1970* (Chicago, University of Chicago Press).

Meyer, D. S. and S. Staggenborg (1996), 'Movements, Countermovements, and the Structure of Political Opportunity', *American Journal of Sociology*, 101:6, 1628–60.

Mills, C. W. (1956), *The Power Elite* (Oxford and New York, Oxford University Press).

Moghadam, V. (2018), 'Gendering the New Right-Wing Populisms: A Research Note', *Journal of World Systems Research*, 24:2, 293–303.

Motta, S. C. (2014), 'Militarized Neoliberalism in Colombia: Disarticulating Dissent and Articulating Consent to Neoliberal Epistemologies, Pedagogies, and Ways of Life', in *Constructing Twenty-First Century Socialism in Latin America*, ed. S. C. Motta and M. Cole (Basingstoke, Palgrave Macmillan)

Mottl, T. L. (1980), 'The Analysis of Countermovements', *Social Problems*, 27:5, 620–35.

Nemer, D. (2021), 'The Human Infrastructure of Fake News in Brazil', *Item*, 6 July, https://items.ssrc.org/extremism-online/the-human-infrastructure-of-fake-news-in-brazil/.

Nicholasen, M. (2018), 'Mothers of Stillborns Face Prison in El Salvador', *Harvard Gazette*, 31 October, https://news.harvard.edu/gazette/story/2018/10/how-the-pro-life-movement-became-entrenched-in-el-salvador/.

Norris, S. (2019), 'International Anti-Feminist Network Organises Rally in Spain', *Open Democracy*, 8 March, https://www.opendemocracy.net/en/5050/international-anti-feminist-network-organises-rally-spain/.

Parke, C. (2018), 'The Right's "Gender Ideology" Menace Rolls to Africa', *Political Research Associates*, 4 May, https://politicalresearch.org/2018/05/04/the-rights-gender-ideology-menace-rolls-to-africa.

Payne, L. A. (2000), *Uncivil Movements: The Armed Right Wing and Democracy in Latin America* (Baltimore, Johns Hopkins University Press).

Payne, L. A. (2023), 'Right-Wing Movements in Latin America', in *The Oxford Handbook of Latin American Social Movements*, ed. F. M. Rossi (Oxford, Oxford University Press), Chapter 32.

Payne, L. A. (Forthcoming) 'Right-Wing Movements (Latin America)', in *The Wiley-Blackwell Encyclopedia of Social and Political Movements*, ed. D. Snow, D. della Porta, B. Klandermans, and D. McAdam (Hoboken, NJ, Wiley-Blackwell).

Payne, L. A. and A. Aruska de Souza Santos (2020), 'The Right-Wing Backlash in Brazil and Beyond', *Politics and Gender*, 16:1 (*Special Symposium on Women's Parties*), 32–8.

Payne, L. A., G. Pereira, and L. Bernal Bermúdez (2020), *Transitional Justice and Corporate Accountability: Deploying Archimedes' Lever* (Cambridge, Cambridge University Press).

Pérez Bentacur, V. and C. Rocha-Carpiuc (2020), 'The Postreform Stage: Understanding Backlash against Sexual Policies in Latin America', *Politics and Gender*, 16:1, 11–18.

Phillips, T. (2018), 'Brazil's Fearful LGBT Community Prepares for a 'Proud Homophobe', *Guardian*, 27 October.

Power, T. J. and W. Hunter (2019), 'Bolsonaro and Brazil's Illiberal Backlash', *Journal of Democracy*, 30:1, 68–82.

Reuterswärd, C. (2021), 'Pro-Life and Feminist Mobilization in the Struggle over Abortion in Mexico: Church Networks, Elite Alliances, and Partisan Context', *Latin American Politics and Society*, 63:3, 21–45.

Romancini, R. (2018) 'From "Gay Kit" to "Indoctrination Monitor": The Conservative Reaction in Brazil', *Contracampo*, 37:2, 85–106.

Rousseau, S. (2020), 'Antigender Activism in Peru and Its Impact on State Policy', *Politics and Gender*, 16:1, 25–32.

Rowell, A. (1996), *Green Backlash: Global Subversion of the Environmental Movement* (London, Routledge).

Simmons, E. (2014), 'Grievances Do Matter in Mobilization', *Theory and Society*, 43, 513–46.

Smith, A. E. (2019), *Religion and Brazilian Democracy: Mobilizing the People of God* (Cambridge, Cambridge University Press).

Spring, M. and L. Webster (2019), 'A Web of Abuse: How the Far Right Disproportionately Targets Female Politicians', *BBC Newsnight*, 15 July, https://www.bbc.com/news/blogs-trending-48871400.

Sutton, B. and E. Borland (2013), 'Framing Abortion Rights in Argentina's Encuentros Nacionales de Mujeres', *Feminist Studies*, 39:1, 194–234.

Switzer, J. V. (1997), *Green Backlash: The History and Politics of the Environmental Opposition in the US* (Boulder, CO, Lynn Rienner).

Teichman, J. (2019), 'Inequality in Twentieth-Century Latin America: Path Dependence, Countermovements, and Reactive Sequences', *Social Science History*, 43:1, 131–57.

Tilly, C. (1978), *From Mobilization to Revolution* (Reading, MA, Addison-Wesley).

Vaggione, J. M. (2018) 'Sexuality, Law and Religion in Latin America: Frameworks in Tension', *Religion and Gender*, 8:1, 14–31.

Vaggione, J. M. and M. das Dores Campos Machado (2020), 'Religious Patterns of Neoconservatism in Latin America', *Politics and Gender*, 16:1, 6–10.

Viterna, J. (2012), 'The Left and "Life" in El Salvador', *Politics and Gender*, 8:2, 248–54.

Whyte, L. (2017), '"They are coming for your children": The Rise of CitizenGo', *Open Democracy*, 9 August, https://www.opendemocracy.net/en/5050/the-rise-of-citizengo/.

Wiesehomeier, N. and D. Doyle (2014), 'Profiling the Electorate: Ideology and Attitudes of Right Wing Voters', in *The Resilience of the Latin American Right*, ed. J. P. Luna and C. Rovira Kaltwasser (Baltimore, Johns Hopkins University Press), pp. 48–72.

WikiLeaks (n.d.), 'The Intolerance Network', https://wikileaks.org/intolerancenetwork/press-release?fbclid=IwAR3DjUVwoFTMrzqMtEz1P1o2A7hzfUCTd893xdhGqik6yf6I5k7Prs70ChA.

Wills-Otero, L. (2014), 'Colombia: Analyzing the Strategies for Political Action of Álvaro Uribe's Government, 2002–10', in *The Resilience of the Latin American Right*, ed. J. P. Luna and C. Rovira Kaltwasser (Baltimore, Johns Hopkins University Press), pp. 194–215.

Wodak, R. (2015), *The Politics of Fear: What Right-Wing Populist Discourses Mean* (London, Sage Publications).

Wodak, R. (2019), 'Analysing the Micropolitics of the Populist Far Right in the "Post-Shame Era"', in *Europe at the Crossroads: Confronting Populist, Nationalist, and Global Challenges*, ed. P. Bevelander and R. Wodak (Lund, Nordic Academic Press), pp. 63–92.

Zaremberg, G. (2020), 'Feminism and Conservatism in Mexico', *Politics and Gender*, 16:1, 19–25.

Zavatti, F. (2021), 'Making and Contesting Far Right Sites of Memory: A Case Study on Romania', *Memory Studies*, 14:5, 949–70.

3

Families of Perpetrators Mobilising against Human Rights Trials in Argentina*

VALENTINA SALVI

ARGENTINA IS SEEN by many as a global leader when it comes to trials for human rights violations. As Sikkink and Booth Walling argue, 'the Argentina example is very influential for other experiences of transitional justice' (2006, 321). In 2006, a new round of trials against military officers, members of the police force, and others who violated human rights during the dictatorship (1976–83)[1] was initiated under the legal concept of crimes against humanity.[2] Over the course of the last 15 years, more than 1,000 perpetrators have been imprisoned. [3] The families of these convicted perpetrators reacted by protesting the trials in the public arena. The perpetrators' wives, children, and grandchildren paradoxically employed a global language of human rights, a humanitarian narrative, and the figure of victim – the same discourse used against their convicted family member – to make their demands for clemency visible.

---

* A previous draft of this chapter was published in Spanish in *Papeles del CEIC: International Journal on Collective Identity Research*, 2 (2019).

[1] The dictatorship was called the National Reorganisation Process. It began with the coup on 24 March 1976 and ended in December 1983 after the defeat by the British in the Malvinas (Falkland Islands) War. During this period, the ruling armed forces executed a repressive plan that involved the forced disappearance of persons, systematic torture, abduction to clandestine detention centres, and appropriation of children, among other forms of violence.

[2] In June 2005, the Supreme Court of Justice of the Nation declared the Superior Orders Act (*Obediencia debida*), Full Stop Law (*Punto final*), and the pardons unconstitutional, and endorsed Law 25.779, by which the National Congress had annulled the rules of impunity in 2003. These laws, which limited the prosecution of military and police officers accused of violations against human rights, were passed, owing to the powerful lobbying of the armed forces.

[3] From 2006 to time of writing, there have been judgment procedures for approximately 200 sentences, where more than 800 people have been condemned,100 were absolved, and another 750 are pending and ongoing cases; https://www.cels.org.ar/web/estadisticas-delitos-de-lesa-humanidad/.

Proceedings of the British Academy, **255**, 59–77, © The British Academy 2023.

60   *Valentina Salvi*

This chapter examines the strategies and arguments used by mobilisations of the right against rights in Argentina: perpetrators' relatives challenging the legitimacy of Argentina's trials for crimes against humanity. These family members mobilise against the adverse conditions of the perpetrators' prosecution and the criminal charges made against them.[4] The analysis aims to identify how these groups (1) try to reverse the success of the human rights movement with regard to access to justice for the victims of the dictatorship (Castro Rea 2018); (2) adapt the global paradigm of human rights and the universal humanitarian narrative (i.e. universality, equal treatment under the law, fair prison conditions, due process, and the language of suffering); (3) construct an image of the victim through the appropriation of the language used by human rights defenders, focusing on age, health problems, trauma, and suffering to generate compassion as a moralistic language of suffering; and (4) resort to biological ties to legitimise their demands for justice, in the same way as the historic Argentine grandmothers, mothers, and children of the disappeared. Finally, the chapter addresses the tensions generated by the presence of these groups, which want to restore privileges and inequities in the post-dictatorship political life in Argentina, as Payne discusses (Chapter 2).

Brief Background

During the last dictatorship (1976–83), thousands of Argentinians were kidnapped, tortured, assassinated, and disappeared. In addition, hundreds of children born in the clandestine detention centres set up by the regime were appropriated by the families of the armed forces. Although members of the Military Junta were tried for human rights abuses and condemned to prison sentences,[5] two impunity laws protected the armed and police forces against prosecution for decades.[6] Thus, most of the crimes remained unpunished. Armed forces exerted pressure on the executive power to maintain this impunity. Nonetheless, human rights organisations, in particular the Madres de la Plaza de Mayo (hereafter 'Madres'), persisted in their call for justice and truth. The situation changed at the beginning of the 2000s with the derogation of the impunity laws and the reinitiation of thousands of prosecutions

---

[4] In recent years, intellectuals, lawyers, journalists, and politicians have advocated for meanings similar to those upheld by these family organisations, allowing their arguments to gain greater status in the public arena. These procedures are not analysed in this chapter.

[5] As soon as President Alfonsín came to power in 1983, he formed a commission that would be in charge of investigating the disappearance of people during the dictatorship. This commission prepared a report that was used by the Executive as part of the indictment for the Trial of the Military Juntas. This trial took place between April and December 1985.

[6] Enacted in December 1986, the Full Stop Law (*Ley de Punto final*) set a statute of limitations on crimes committed during the dictatorship. It was followed by the Superior Orders Act (*Ley de Obediencia debida*), which similarly exempted middle- and low-ranking military and police officers under the argument that they were simply following orders.

FAMILIES OF PERPETRATORS MOBILISING IN ARGENTINA 61

for crimes against humanity.[7] Since that time, military officers and their families have asserted that 'the civilian justice system was corrupted by the human rights policies of the new left-wing government led by Néstor Kirchner that initiated a nationwide debate on memory and accountability of the state repression' (Van Roeckel and Salvi 2019, 116).

In 2015, Mauricio Macri, a candidate from the so-called 'new right' Alianza Cambiemos Party, came to power at a moment when dozens of trials were under way of a broad set of individuals responsible for state terrorism. In a context of marked political polarisation against Kirchnerism, this new-right party publicly expressed its desire for change with regard to this legacy. At the beginning, the Macri administration served as a channel for mobilisation by organisations of perpetrators' relatives. Over time, however, the Macri government demonstrated less resolve and leadership in the field of memory and justice. Its efforts sparked a strong reaction within Argentine society, forcing the administration to – pragmatically – backpedal on certain initiatives in this area.[8] This chapter thus analyses the efforts by the right against rights: the framing strategies used, but also how the mobilisation has been checked by a powerful social mobilisation on behalf of victims of the dictatorship.

Perpetrators' Families Enter the Public Arena

In 2006, after a period of inactivity, during the years when impunity for the perpetrators was guaranteed,[9] different organisations emerged with the purpose of defending members of the military and police forces, among them the Asociación de Familiares y Amigos de Presos Políticos en Argentina (Association of Friends and Family of Political Prisoners in Argentina; AFyAPPA), and Hijos y Nietos de Presos Políticos (Children and Grandchildren of Political Prisoners; HNPP), which now bears the name Puentes para la Legalidad (Bridges to Legality). The first is mostly made up by wives and friends of perpetrators, and maintains a confrontational position vis-à-vis the human rights movement.[10] The second is less confrontational, especially after its name change in 2015; it is made up of exclusively of

---

[7] In June 2005, the Argentine Supreme Court overruled the Full Stop Law and the Superior Orders Act, determining them unconstitutional. With this decision, the court confirmed the constitutionality of Law 25.779, which Congress had employed in 2003 to abolish the laws granting impunity.

[8] In the current era, organisations of perpetrators' relatives have relied on linkages to right-wing mobilisations within and outside the government.

[9] L. A. Payne, 'Right-Wing Movements in Latin America' (2023), in *The Oxford Handbook of Latin American Social Movements*, ed. F. M. Rossi (Oxford, Oxford University Press), Chapter 32.

[10] Since its foundation, the human rights movement has been made up of a heterogeneous mix of people and groups, and includes its share of internal conflicts. It comprises organisations traditionally linked to the advocacy of human rights, and others made up of people directly affected by repression, ecumenical groups, and associations of lawyers.

the children and grandchildren of political prisoners and focuses on legal discourse and mobilisation (Goldentul 2016).[11]

AFyAPPA and HNPP emerged as civil society organisations in 2006, when they sought to transcend the military institutional framework and enter the public arena.[12] This shift was brought about not only because of the convictions of their relatives, but also because of the refusal of the heads of the armed forces and the state (during the presidencies of Néstor and Cristina Kirchner (2003–15)) to endorse their claims and demands.[13] The loss of alliances within the political structure, and their limited lobbying success within the government, forced them to shift strategies to 'win the fight in the streets', seeking greater visibility to gain recognition within civil society. To that end, they sought to discredit and challenge their opponents in the political arena, specifically the human rights organisations and advocates for the trials for crimes against humanity. Paradoxically, over time, the organisations formed by the perpetrators' families adopted the language and mirrored the actions of their human rights organisation adversaries. For three years, between 2006 and 2009, the AFyAPPA and HNPP marched around the Pirámide de Mayo on the first Tuesday of each month, imitating the Madres' Thursday afternoon marches in the same place. They also painted black ribbons over the white headscarves of the Madres, to cover them up, and in commemoration of the military officers killed by armed left-wing organisations during the 1970s.[14] The loss of institutional channels within the armed forces (see note 13) became publicly clear in 2011, when a group of 15 women – spouses of military officers – chained themselves to the main entrance of the Ministry of Defence and Joint Chiefs of Staff, intending to shame military authorities and convince them to stand up for their prosecuted comrades. Indeed, the public nature of their actions shows the deterioration of ties with the military authorities, and a weakened capacity to apply political pressure to the government in office, a pressure that the military related to the dictatorship had historically been able to exert in order to resolve the political and/or criminal conflicts that emerged as by-products of their active involvement

---

[11] The change of name was due to a new strategy toward the visibility of their demands and to the key role played by Anibal Guevara in the organisation. Guevara sought to soften the organisation's politically contentious statements, allowing for a practice of greater dialogue and communication (Goldentul 2016).

[12] From 1983 to time of writing, the pro-military groups went beyond military circles to enter the public scene only when an active justice became a real threat to their impunity. That happened twice: during the 1980s, when Familiares y Amigos de los Muertos por la Subversión (Family and Friends of those Killed by Subversives; FAMUS) objected to the sentences handed down to the commanders of the armed forces in the Trial of the Military Juntas (1985), and in 2000, which is the focus of analysis in this chapter (see also Salvi 2012).

[13] During the Kirchner administrations (2003–15), the heads of the armed forces adhered to the trial-based policy, refusing legal counsel and financial support to the accused military officers, penalising those who engaged in public demonstrations of support for their comrades with imprisonment or discharge from service, and even providing secret military documents to justice institutions (Salvi 2012).

[14] Because of this, the president of AFyAPPA, Cecilia Pando, was sentenced to community work for damaging a public asset (*La Voz*, 7 March 2013).

in state terrorism.[15] In sum, they aim, as Payne (Chapter 2) argues, to restore lost privileged positions that guarantee impunity, as well as to block access to justice for the victims of the dictatorship.

The mobilisation by perpetrators' families seeks to contest and delegitimise the trials for crimes against humanity through actions that are not necessarily well-received by Argentine civil society. The members of AFyPPA regularly attend oral hearings, joining the families of the victims of the dictatorship; displaying banners with their claims; and sometimes adopting provocative and intimidating actions toward the prosecuting lawyers, the victims, and the relatives of the disappeared.[16] In this way, the groups mobilise a backlash against, and rollback of, the justice gains made by victims and human rights organisations in Argentina, thereby constituting them as a rights-against-rights group, as identified in the introduction to this volume.

AFyAPPA and NHPP are both part of a larger group of organisations that gather family members, as well as comrades of military and police officers killed by armed organisations during the 1970s, under the slogan 'Memoria Completa' (Complete Memory) (Salvi 2012).[17] The Memoria Completa groups emerged with the revival of trials for crimes against humanity, and construe their legitimacy in being the 'other' victims of political violence.[18] In their condition as wives, children, nephews and nieces, and parents of the officers allegedly murdered by the armed left-wing movements, they seek to position themselves as victims and play a prominent role in the battle for remembrance. Aiming to compete with the discourse of human rights organisations, they strategically position their memories of the recent past in public opinion in order to achieve social and state recognition for their deceased, and to defend the officers who were convicted of crimes against humanity. These Memoria Completa groups strive – as I will outline in the following section – to

---

[15] In April 1987, the government of Raúl Alfonsín suffered a disruptive revolt on the part of the mid-level army officers who resisted criminal prosecution. They mobilised against the understanding at the local level of state terrorism, or the systematic and planned violation of citizens' fundamental rights on the part of the state during the civil-military dictatorship.

[16] In 2008, during the reading of the sentence of a case in Corrientes City, Cecilia Pando made a menacing gesture to the then Secretary of Human Rights, Eduardo Luis Duhalde, who was present in the courtroom. She said to him 'I'm going to kill you with my own hands' (*La capital*, 7 August 2008). In Cordoba City, in 2010, members of AFyAPPA used negative terms in referring to the former Spanish judge Baltazar Garzón in the first hearing of the La Perla case (*Clarín*, 11 August 2010).

[17] The name 'Memoria Completa' constructs a narrative that reflects, while being opposed to, the memory of the disappeared. Based on the resignification of the figures and speech typical of the human rights organisations – particularly the slogan 'Memoria, verdad, y justicia' (Memory, truth, and justice), Memoria Completa accounts for the shift in the memory of the figure of combatants and victors in the 'fight against subversion' – that is, in support of the performance of generals and commanders – to the figure of 'victims of terrorism': i.e. of the officers murdered by the armed organisations in the first half of the 1970s (Salvi 2011)

[18] In a context of resistance to the dictatorship named the 'Argentine Revolution' (1966–73) and the banning of Peronism, a political process emerged with strong left-wing leanings and the onset of an armed struggle with revolutionary intentions.

64 *Valentina Salvi*

resignify the meanings of the recent past based on the memory of the 'victims of the guerrilla' (Salvi 2011).

New Forms of Contention in the Human Rights Arena

When life sentences and imprisonment in the Federal Prison Services began to take place,[19] family organisations, especially those comprising children and grandchildren, began to strengthen their presence in the national media (TV, radio, and newspapers), with a new public discourse focused on human rights.[20] Overall, the arguments they used to defend their relatives drew on two paradigms that held both symbolic and political weight in public debates about Argentina's recent past: on the one hand, the human rights ethos that emerged in the country towards the end of the 1970s, through the political engagement of human rights movements and with the restoration of the Rule of Law in 1983, and on the other hand, the standards of international humanitarian law to which Argentina subscribed via the reform of the National Constitution in the mid-1990s. Beyond these processes of high impact at the local level, the repositioning of family organisations should also be interpreted as part of an international phenomenon in which humanitarian rationale and the language of human rights form the core of a new moral economy of suffering, and the hegemonic retrospective treatment of violence on a global scale (Fassin 2016,19).

In terms of the first paradigm, the remarkable interest that the human rights ethos achieved in Argentina can be closely linked to the way in which human rights organisations expressed and made visible their complaints during the dictatorship. Moreover, the ethical grounds of the new Rule of Law created in 1983 supported the political values and demands expressed by these organisations (Jelin and Azcárate 1991, 32).[21] In that transitional context, the link between the human rights paradigm, a democratic regime, and an 'obligation to remember' are consolidated in the motto 'Nunca Más' (Never Again). According to this political imaginary, human rights need a democratic government to evolve; the democratic government must abide by the Rule of Law (legality); and, finally, the Rule of Law must be safeguarded by a duty to remember that guarantees non-repetition. Three decades later, this relationship among human rights, democracy (as justice), and public memory has paradoxically become the position and discourse of an actor that previously and ferociously rejected that claim: that of convicted officers' families. This

---

[19] During the 1980s, the military served their sentences in army units that offered certain privileges. This led the human rights movements to demand that sentences be carried out in regular jails.

[20] Until their access to the national media, these groups usually distributed books, magazines, documents, and reports on recent history; held conferences; launched websites; and organised discussion forums using counterinsurgent language.

[21] The circulation of the human rights paradigm is a product of worldwide impact that grew significantly after the end of the Second World War and managed to establish humanity as a moral reference at a global level (Gatti 2011, 524).

FAMILIES OF PERPETRATORS MOBILISING IN ARGENTINA

rapprochement of the human rights discourse and of Nunca Más also reinforces the idea that the military officers brought to justice would be excluded from these democratic principles (Payne 2000, 5). Indeed, the organisations of family members, especially children, build on the symbolic and socially widespread significance of Nunca Más as a civic category. An HNPP militant expressed this view with regard to his father's imprisonment: 'Unfortunately, we were excluded from Nunca Más. So we are talking once again about human rights violations, state power abuses, and due process violations.'[22]

However, herein lies the paradox: through the usage of this common language in the public sphere, these organisations exhibit what seem to be shared meanings with broad public opinion in Argentina. The use of this rights language is instrumental, however, and directly contradicts the perpetrators' relatives' identity, values, and ideological stance (Benford and Snow 2000).

Regarding the second paradigm, it is noteworthy that these family organisations rely on international humanitarian law and customary international law adopted by human rights organisations and judicial officials to initiate the trials for crimes against humanity.[23] Family associations and their sponsors draw on the terminology and interpretations of international treatises and agreements in order to make claims before the legal system and civil society (Cowan 2006, 10). In so doing, they challenge the legal framework of those who conduct the trials for crimes against humanity, but simultaneously seek to apply it to improve conditions for their convicted relatives.

Human Rights in Dispute

What are the arguments and strategies used by families to reduce the sentences or improve the procedural situation of their relatives? Or, in other words, how do they adjust their language to the normative framework of human rights and humanitarian law? This section analyses the shift of these associations toward a human rights discourse, with a focus on the different meanings that the humanitarian narrative acquires (Según Skinner cited in Guilhot 2011, 222). In line with the work of Didier Fassin (2016, 21), the purpose here is to examine the way in which suffering and vulnerability are presented as a vivid and naturalised reality that must serve to arouse moral indignation and social empathy *to the benefit of* the military and police officers in prison.

Initially, the goal of family organisations was to prevent the trials for crimes against humanity from advancing. To that end, they tried – unsuccessfully – to

---

[22] https://www.youtube.com/watch?v=Gjcjsk7UBV8.

[23] The Supreme Court's verdict in the 'Simón case' in 2005, declaring the laws of *Obediencia debida* and *Punto final* unconstitutional, was grounded on the constitutional nature of international law, effective since the constitutional amendment of 1994.

question the legitimacy of the criminal proceedings and the imprescriptible nature of the cases that were to be tried in court. Once the cases materialised and the sentences became effective, however, the family organisations then sought both to reduce the sentences issued by federal courts (by presenting second- and third-instance appeals) and to modify the system of penal enforcement applied to their relatives by requesting house arrest and transfers to military units instead of common jails. In order to implement changes in the penal enforcement system, their claims focused on two aspects: first, the lawfulness of trials for crimes against humanity and observance of due process guarantees, and second, the conditions of detention in Federal Penitentiary Service jails. In this regard, in a meeting with the Inter-American Commission of Human Rights in 2017, Aníbal Guevara, Chair of Puentes para la Legalidad, claimed that

> The accused are denied the principle of innocence reversing the burden of proof, forcing them to prove their innocence 40 years after the events for which they are being charged, extending pre-trial detention beyond the maximum period provided by law … they are denied the right to be tried within a reasonable timeframe … home imprisonment is denied to the sick, and the penalties imposed prevent their resocialisation.[24]

By questioning the legitimacy of these trials, the family groups played an active role in the struggle to define the 'human rights' category. In this way, they enter the arena of symbolic and political debates – the same ones that the military officers had historically resisted and belittled (Cowan 2006, 9). For decades, the military viewed the public commitment of human rights organisations – the Madres among them – as a campaign led by 'militarily defeated enemies' intentionally created by the media to discredit armed institutions. Although these kinds of allegations and direct confrontations within the armed forces have become more nuanced over the years, they are still evident in the speeches of those accused during the oral hearings in federal courts.[25] In this sense, the ethos of human rights has been resisted by an entire generation of military and police officers involved in the repressive apparatus during the dictatorship. Importantly, though, this ethos has *not* been rejected by their children and grandchildren – many of whom were born in democratic times, and have adopted the same language to legitimise their own course of action (Vecchioli 2013, 7). The adoption of a human rights framework by the families of perpetrators is less related to the use of judicial language than to a political and symbolic practice. The families do not limit themselves to petitioning the courts and presenting the perpetrators as victims; they also react against the classification of 'crime against humanity' and the implication it has for the acts committed by their relatives. They try to frame this classification as a contradictory and instrumentalising use of human rights discourse.

---

[24] https://www.youtube.com/watch?time_continue=5&v=M3vRHMG2Oxw&feature=emb_title.

[25] Although in the context of oral hearings for crimes against humanity the defendants speak with different purposes in mind, they mostly try to denigrate the families of victims and the human rights organisations, and vilify their struggle, branding them as liars, corrupt, terrorists, etc. (Salvi 2020).

In order to gain empathy and support for their cause, this new generation attempts to shape a new type of model-victim, in line with the standards socially acknowledged by a humanitarian culture that was born with the figure of the disappeared in the transitional context. They frame prison detentions as traumatic experiences equal to those experienced by victims of the dictatorship in clandestine detention centres. In public speeches, these groups refer to their relatives using the generic image of 'human beings', thereby erasing their repressive behaviour during state terrorism (Goldentul 2016). For example, they talk about the 'Argentine citizen' or 'victims of Argentinian state', instead of 'armed forces', 'heroes', or 'combatants', as their parents or grandparents did in the 1980s and 1990s. This shift toward a humanitarian narrative relies on an abstraction of the legal, political, and historically exceptional nature of the prosecuted. From a legal point of view, their families overlook the gravity of the crimes they committed, which were proven in trials; from a political perspective, they downplay the social condemnation weighing against the perpetrators; and, in terms of historical significance, they conceal their relatives' involvement in or responsibility for state terrorism. In sum, as Goldentul (2016) argues, the humanitarian discourse neutralises the historical repressive action of the prosecuted by using abstract and judicial descriptions, in which perpetrators are presented not as perpetrators of atrocious crimes, but as rights-bearing subjects. An example of this tactic is expressed on the institutional website of Puentes para la Legalidad: 'Our association strives to achieve full respect of the constitutional guarantees of rule of law and, consequently, the rights that must be guaranteed to any defendant in any penal case, with no discrimination of any kind.'[26]

A Language of Suffering

Why do these families resort to the humanitarian narrative? What benefits do they obtain from doing so? To answer these questions, I focus on the language of suffering used by families to support their claims in public debate. Fassin and Rechtman (2009, 20) established a very important point: before the memory boom, suffering caused by violent experiences was considered dishonest, fake, and self-serving, instead of traumatic and true. In contrast, in the global context today, victims are viewed as bearers of moral qualities, and their suffering is regarded as proof of an uncontested traumatic fact. The humanitarian rhetoric that focuses on the human condition of victims as pure bearers of rights nowadays represents a traumatic figure that can be reflected in public opinion, inasmuch as that abstract humanisation overshadows the historical and political condition of the victim, that is, effacing their most controversial aspects. In Argentina, this process of abstraction was made in a transitional context to construct the disappeared as victims.

---

[26] http://www.puentesparalalegalidad.org/denuncia.html.

68 *Valentina Salvi*

The humanitarian rhetoric emerged among groups who opposed the dictatorship in the mid-1970s. The Madres tried to obtain support and empathy from different segments of civil society through references to the extreme experience of the victims: the disappeared (Crenzel 2008). Complaints about disappearances at the beginning of the dictatorship were expressed by the Madres in historical-political terms, referring to the disappeared as militants. As an effect of the transnationalisation of the human rights organisations (Markarian 2004),[27] they switched to a humanitarian narrative, emphasising the factual description of the violations, focusing on the physical and mental integrity of the victims in their condition as individuals.

Relatives of convicted military officers seek to do the same. That is, they attempt to gain support from civil society. These family groups describe suffering using terms in line with the language employed in human rights paradigms. They try to achieve a balance between two dimensions: particularity (i.e. the arbitrariness of suffering) and universality (i.e. the reference to violated rights) on the one hand, and literalism (the factual description of each case) and exemplariness (its construction as an asset to preserve) on the other. Several 'leading cases' on the Puentes para la Legalidad website are used as examples of their claims:

> Omar Antonio Ferreyra, born on 23 June 1950, graduated from the Escuela Sargento Cabral of the Argentine Army. He worked as a police motorcyclist during his entire career. He was arrested ... on 16 June 2009. The oral trial did not take place until mid-2014. This alone is a clear violation of the right to personal freedom ... During the trial, in Olavarría, he fell seriously ill and was transferred to the city hospital ... It was discovered that he suffered bodily injury with active bleeding. This was later confirmed by another test that revealed an adenocarcinoma grade G3 with mucinous areas ... This account shows that no authority, legal or penal, had bothered to determine if Ferreyra was physically and mentally fit to face an oral trial and fully exercise his guarantees, especially the right to defense during trial ... He underwent chemotherapy while still on trial. This implied attending court sessions which, in these cases, tend to be very lengthy ... In addition, he was submitted to an esophagectomy, a bloody and high-risk surgery that involves removing part of the esophagus. Overall, Ferreyra has been subject to cruel, inhuman, and degrading treatment, which has compromised his personal integrity as well as the recognition of his legal identity ... On 5 July 2015, thanks to his family's efforts, Ferreyra was finally granted house arrest in his home in Olavarría. Less than two months after the change in his imprisonment status, Ferreyra died on 23 August 2015.[28]

According to Laqueur (1989, 177), the use of the literal and the particular dimensions when referring to the situation of convicted military and police officers, and the description of corporeal suffering using a medical and realistic language is

---

[27] In order to understand how this paradigm arrived in Argentina, one must consider the transnationalisation processes that took place in the Southern Cone at the end of the 1970s as a result of the contact that Argentine political exiles had with human rights activists in Europe (Sikkink 1997; Markarian 2004).

[28] http://www.puentesparalalegalidad.org/casostestigo.html.

FAMILIES OF PERPETRATORS MOBILISING IN ARGENTINA   69

a symbol of 'truth'. It is a biographical account of sickness and disease, as well as the deaths of the convicted during their time in pre-trial detention or deprivation of liberty. In this respect, the account aims to be included in a truth regimen that provides legitimacy to traumatic experiences (Fassin and Rechtman 2009, 110). In turn, it obliterates any other kind of information referring to procedural status, sentences, or crimes proven by justice. In addition, these arguments ignore the fact that during the trials the defendants had all the guarantees of criminal procedural law, and the rulings handed down in the trials included both convictions and acquittals (Crenzel 2020, 9).

Family members often tend to minimise the repressive actions of their relatives when interviewed in public. When questioned about the responsibility of their parents during state terrorism, they mention procedural arbitrariness, such as sentences 'without evidence' or prison sentences with 'only one testimony against them'. They also seek to downplay their responsibility, with arguments such as 'he was very young during the dictatorship', and 'he was only following orders as a low-rank soldier', or 'he had been found guilty just for being in a given place at a given time'.[29]

As for the universal dimension, family organisations resort to national laws and international treatises protecting convicted military and police officers to build their complaints against the trials for crimes against humanity. With regard to exemplariness, they resort to a notion of universal human rights as natural rights that extend beyond the political sphere and certain historical contingencies, in order to legitimise their strategies and courses of action. The paradox or 'apparent contradiction' here is that the discourse of equality-as-natural functions as a means to obliterate the status of crimes against humanity and to re-establish privileges and impunity lost by perpetrators.[30] In the passage from the literal to the exemplary (Todorov 2000), the discourse of specific suffering (perpetrators with names and identities), gave way to a more neutral and abstract legal rhetoric. Both the principle of equality before the law in the treatment of the convicted officers, and the acknowledgement of human dignity, present these claims as by-products of objective and normative statements, and not as subjective and particular appreciations or biased points of view excluded from historical and political controversy (Vecchioli 2013, 23).

The family members of the accused value certain court decisions that are beneficial to their cause as 'acts of justice' and consider others to be harmful. From their point of view, the beneficial rulings separate legal, political, and

---

[29] See https://www.youtube.com/watch?time_continue=5&v=M3vRHMG2Oxw&feature=emb_title. There is another group of children of military officers, however, who are in favour of criminal prosecution and publicly denounce their fathers. They have even provided information at the trials. See 'Historias desobedientes: Hijos, hijas y familiares de genocidas. Por memoria, verdad y justicia', http://historiasde sobedientes.com/index.php.

[30] A similar recource to equality-for-all is also observed in the criticism that radical neoliberal groups make against social policies that benefit precarious social sectors in Argentina.

humanitarian arguments from ideological ones, and acknowledge human rights as an abstract notion divorced from perpetrators' conditions as individuals convicted of crimes against humanity. The rulings that they oppose are categorised as ideological and biased.

The language of suffering is accompanied by claims of arbitrariness, injustice, and abuse supposedly experienced by the military and police officers during criminal proceedings and their imprisonment. This switch from 'personal' to 'political' becomes clearer when using the category of 'political prisoner', with which they seek to underscore the bias they believe is implicit in trials for crimes against humanity. The summons to an event 'in defence of political prisoners' in May 2017 organised by AFyAPPA sought to stress these biases: 'Demonstration against the lack of guarantees in this unjust persecution against members of the Armed Forces. During the event, a claim will be read out and handed to the Minister of Justice, demanding the immediate restitution of judicial independence and Rule of Law. Demonstration for liberation of political prisoners.'[31]

If the humanitarian language aims to bring the convicted military and police officers into the realm of victims, the notion of 'political prisoner' (used to refer to their relatives) seeks to differentiate the performance of these groups from their adversaries in the judicial field. Indeed, family organisations intend to show that their standards of legality are less ideological and political and, therefore, more universal and impartial than those advocated by human rights organisations and implemented by federal courts. To support this argument, family members of convicted officers label and decry the legal actions carried out by judicial officers and human rights organisations as a policy of revenge. Some of the expressions used to point out both the arbitrariness and the bias of criminal prosecutions of their relatives include: 'It's not about justice, but revenge', 'Political prisoners exist due to official revenge', 'They seek revenge, not justice.'[32]

Despite their efforts, the actions taken by these family associations have had little political impact overall. Even though they have gained some advocates in specific media sectors and among political opponents to the Kirchner administration, their demands – broadly speaking – have met strong social and political opposition. This became evident at a mass protest in May 2017, during the Macri administration, in the Plaza de Mayo, against a verdict issued by the Supreme Court of Justice granting a reduction of penalties in favour of a convicted perpetrator. This mass rally was organised under the slogan 'Nunca Más un Genocida Suelto' (Never Again a Free Genocidaire). The slogan clearly brought to the public arena the historical and political roles of the perpetrators. This social and political response against reducing the sentences of military perpetrators highlighted the difficulties that family groups face when attempting to set up a humanitarian

---

[31] http://afyappa.blogspot.com/2017/.
[32] http://afyappa.blogspot.com.

FAMILIES OF PERPETRATORS MOBILISING IN ARGENTINA 71

narrative that separates the human condition of the military officers from their repressive activities.[33]

The Figure of the Victim

All things considered, it is important to examine how these family groups build legitimate authority to channel their claims. First, they prioritise family ties in order to make their claims visible: the love of a son, daughter, or grandchild born after the acts were committed can be presented as transcending all political and ideological struggles. The notion of family is the key element that can distinguish love from politics, and suffering from self-interest. To this end, the accounts about the suffering of prisoners and their close relatives function as bearers of 'truth'. Effectively, this ensures that what is said by a son or a daughter is at least socially *heard*, especially in Argentina, where family language is particularly powerful in the public arena (Jelin 2010). Direct experience resulting from family ties becomes a source of legitimacy for family groups.[34] These groups thus become a mirror image of the human rights organisations, which prioritise family ties over the political identities of the disappeared, and also make their claims and demands based on notions of kinship. Children and grandchildren in particular stress family ties based on love, drawing on the image of the 'good father' and family life as 'normal'. In sum, family relationships play a crucial role in showcasing action as legitimate, and naturalising family groups' interests. Accordingly, the claims made by these organisations are represented as by-products of blood ties, and not as a result of their standpoint within a broader scenario of conflicting views and definitions of the figure of the victim as the bearer of human rights (Vecchioli 2005, 244). For example, Puentes para la Legalidad describes itself on its website in the following way: 'We are a group of relatives of defendants in cases involving crimes against humanity. In 2015, we formed the civil association Puentes para la Legalidad, and since 2008, as Children and Grandchildren of Political Prisoners, we have been reporting the different irregularities and violations of human rights that our parents have suffered during judicial procedures.'[35]

---

[33] Militants of human rights organisations often use the prefix 'ex-' to refer to places or persons that bear the traces of state violence but whose identity or function exceeds that condition: for example the ex-clandestine detention centres, or the ex-detainees-disappeared, among others. However, its usage is questioned when naming those responsible for state terrorism – repressor (perpetrator), torturer, genocidaire, or dictator – because, seen from an activist perspective, it is a condition that does not disappear or change with time.

[34] According to Jelin (2010, 227), the directly affected parties, especially close relatives of victims of state repression, became the authorised voice and source of 'truth', able to determine the human rights agenda in Argentina. The leading group was the Madres de Plaza de Mayo (and, later, HNPP).

[35] http://puentesparalalegalidad.org/quienes_somos.html.

72 *Valentina Salvi*

Secondly, family groups, especially children and grandchildren, aim to shape a legitimate authority based on having been born after the events in question took place. Even though their age frees them from suspicion of involvement in criminal activities, they are still liable for taking political responsibilities as citizens, and moral responsibilities in relation to what they know about criminal acts committed by their parents (Arendt 2007). In fact, in public debates they are often asked about their opinions regarding the military dictatorship, or the uncertain situation of the children of the disappeared whose true identity is still ignored.[36] The generation factor enables another way of legitimising the family members' position, as children and grandchildren present themselves as victims of the violence in the 1970s. The descendants of officers serving prison terms aim to equate their experiences with those of the children of the disappeared. From their point of view, drawing these comparisons is possible because they regard themselves as passive victims of a violence that they did not create. This argument produces an effect of relativising children of convicted military officers and children of disappeared, militants of armed organisations and business people murdered by the guerrilla, and the disappeared and convicted military officers.

Finally, from the perspective of family organisations, the suffering endured by both the children of convicted military and police officers and the children of the disappeared will persist as long as conflicts keep dividing 'both sides': the armed forces against the guerrilla during the 1970s. This levelling of suffering on 'both sides' is built on an existing trope in the battlefield of public memory in Argentina: 'the theory of the two demons'. According to this theory, state violence is equal to the violence used by armed organisations in the context of insurgent actions. Thus, these types of violence – the political processes that encouraged each of them, as well as the responsibilities that supported them – become de-historicised and de-differentiated around a recurring figure in the discourse of family organisations: that of 'the tragedy of the 1970s'.[37]

That said, what other meanings are involved in the positioning of these groups that endow their political performance with moral justification and generate positive feelings regarding the judicial situation of their relatives? How is it possible that the children of military and police officers who were prosecuted and convicted for atrocious crimes seek to position themselves publicly as victims of the 1970s? The use that the groups of relatives of convicted military and police officers make of the humanitarian narrative can be attributed to the centrality that the figure of the victim has acquired in the memories of the military in Argentina since the 2000s, as shown in the following paragraphs.

---

[36] In Argentina, it is estimated that there are around 500 children who were appropriated by military families during the captivity of their mothers. More than 100 of them had their identity restored, but the fate of the majority is still unknown.

[37] This appeal to the tragic 1970s is a recurring topic in the military discourse since the 1980s (Salvi 2012). It is not the discourse alone but also the activism of these groups that accounts for political processes whereby the victim and suffering take centre stage.

As mentioned earlier, family groups are part of the Memoria Completa association, which became a new 'actor of memory' in Argentina in 2006. These associations define themselves through their ability to retell the recent past both in tension with and by reflecting the narratives of human rights organisations. The narrative of Memoria Completa aims to provide social existence to the victims of the guerrilla. They shape the image of 'victims of the guerrilla' like the socially legitimated image of 'victims of state terrorism'. The efforts made by the Memoria Completa associations to draw social attention and obtain political recognition of the 'victims of the guerrilla' show that there is not an immediate and natural connection between a person's death and his or her description as a victim (Vecchioli 2001, 85). On the contrary, the social existence of the figure of the victim is the result of a complex process, whose construction involves memory-engaged agents, tensions, and contentions.

What are the criteria that define the figure of 'victim of the guerrilla'? There is a clear meaning from which the Memoria Completa associations recall and build this social category. Even if civilians *and* military officers who died in attacks, assaults to headquarters, and armed confrontations are already considered victims by Memoria Completa, the paradigmatic figure of the 'victim of the guerrilla' remains the officer who was killed months after being kidnapped by armed organisations during the first half of the 1970s. Focusing on the kidnapped military officers is not accidental, and responds to the antagonism with the figure of the disappeared, as well as the need to sanctify the military officers' image. The figure of the 'victim of the guerrilla' relies on both the redefining of the dramatic events and the personality of the military officers who were kidnapped and assassinated by the armed organisations during the first half of the 1970s. In fact, the figure of the 'victim of the guerrilla' is built without political and moral ambiguities and purified in order to replace the image of immoral and antidemocratic generals of the dictatorship with 'innocent victims' in military memory.

Conclusion

In 2006, as trials for crimes against humanity were resumed in Argentina, new groups of relatives of convicted military and police officers appeared on the scene. In view of the loss of institutional ties with the armed forces during the Kirchner administration (2003–15), these groups promoted actions in the public arena to improve the procedural status of their relatives and to delegitimate their trials. Ironically, the loss of their relatives' privileges that had guaranteed impunity for more than 20 years encouraged the members of the so-called 'military family' to become politically active. They thus formed a right-against-rights mobilisation consistent with this volume's discussion in Chapters 1 and 2 when they perceived a loss of their previously held power in the political system.

The case analysed in this chapter shows how conflicts over the recent past are a particular topic for understanding right-against-rights mobilisations in Argentina.

The groups analysed reacted in opposition to human rights organisations' gains in their struggle for justice. No longer able to advance their interests within political institutions, they took to unconventional actions in the streets to oppose and roll back the advances made by their adversaries.

The strategies and arguments used by the Argentine right-against-rights mobilisations discussed in this chapter further reflect the adaptation and appropriation of their adversaries' methods. They employed the paradigm of human rights and humanitarian rhetoric in a local field of contention around the definition of its scope, meanings, and potential beneficiaries. They emphasised universality and normative approaches. They also drew on a global process in which violence has been increasingly negotiated through a moral economy of suffering. This scenario, where memories of the military are woven around the narrative of 'victims of the guerrilla' – which is created in imitation of and in tension with the 'victims of state terrorism' – is used by the relatives of military and police officers convicted for crimes against humanity as an image that a society embued with an understanding of victimhood might relate to (Vecchioli 2005, 250).

For this right-against-rights mobilisation, the use, reinterpretation, and adaptation of the paradigm of human rights; the humanitarian rhetoric; and the figure of the victim work at different levels. On the judicial front, they hope to appeal the sentences of military and police officers within a legal framework to guarantee impunity and benefits. On the ideological front, they pushed for the universalisation of particular claims through the use of meanings that became normalised in the democratic transition, as was the case with the concept of human rights. On the political front, they make their claims known publicly by using a language and set of symbols and actions highly valued by their own interlocutors and adversaries. On the moral front, they aim to win civil society empathy and solidarity through a discourse of suffering.

To spread their claims and demands, these family organisations also sought to recreate a mythical scene in which, on the one hand, the paradigm of human rights dehistoricises and depoliticises the repressive past of their family members, and, on the other, the suffering of their children and grandchildren naturalises their stance as simply familial love. In this manner, the families of imprisoned military officers paradoxically present themselves as part of an extended community of victims, those of the 1970s, bound together as they grieve the disappeared and the departed. This extended community also includes the mothers, children, grandchildren, grandparents, and siblings 'on both sides', confronted by past violence and by dissenting political ideologies. From their point of view, it is possible to form a national community of victims, insofar as the blood ties among 'victims of the guerrilla' are extended to the 'other' victims and their relatives: the disappeared. They recognise the suffering of the 'other' victims, aiming for their own suffering to be recognised in turn. In this large community of victims of the 1970s, they frame all victims as one and the same, including the relatives of military and police officers convicted of crimes against humanity. In so doing, and over time, they have attempted to move away from an adversarial relationship with the victims of state terrorism and instead to build bridges through shared victimhood.

Despite the minor impact of actions carried out by AFFyAPPA, HNPP, and Puentes para la Legalidad, and beyond the interest they sparked in certain political circles and among journalists opposed to Kirchnerism, the presence of these groups in the public arena creates tensions, rather than harmony. The first tension expresses itself in how these groups resist the advance of trials for crimes against humanity, which put an end to impunity, by publicly using human rights discourse and the principle of equality before the law.[38] In other words, they react to the process of justice that recognised the rights of the victims, and appeal to values of equality to contest meanings and gain empathy for their cause in the public arena. The second tension lies in the use by these groups of collective actions, narratives, and symbols that are historically linked to the civic engagement of families of the disappeared, thus contesting the latter's meaning and significance. The third tension surfaces in the ways that they use the signs and symbols that emerged out of democratic process in Argentina, and aim to break away from the social disapproval of their relatives that resulted from their violations of human rights during the dictatorship.

In sum, the performance of family groups of perpetrators reveals a paradox wtih regard to the relation between memory, human rights, and democracy as core values of post-dictatorship life in Argentina. On the one hand, these groups use and resignify the human rights paradigm as a normative principle that is both abstract and universal. But on the other hand, according to Barros (2017, 55), this concept of human rights as a global ideology produces a disconnect between human rights as signifier, and the specific experience suffered during state terrorism in Argentina. This division between human rights and memories of state terrorism – memories that condemn those human rights abuses – brought about by the political agency of these family groups has the potential to destabilise the agreements, meanings, and social representations that narrate the past and built the democracy following the en dof the dictatorship in Argentina

References

Arendt, H. (2007), 'Responsabilidad personal bajo una dictadura', in *Responsabilidad y juicio* (Barcelona, Paidós), pp. 49–74.

Barros, M. (2017), 'Cambiemos pasado por futuro: Los derechos humanos bajo el gobierno de Mauricio Macri', in *Tensiones en la democracia argentina: Rupturas y continuidades en torno al neoliberalismo*, ed. M. T. Piñero and M. S. Bonetto (Córdoba, Editorial CEA), pp. 47–64.

Benford, R. D. and D. A. Snow (2000), 'Framing Processes and Social Movements: An Overview and Assessment', *Annual Review of Sociology*, 26 (August), 611–39.

---

[38] Payne, 'Right-Wing Movements in Latin America'.

76 *Valentina Salvi*

Castro Rea, J. (2018), 'Right-Wing Think Tank Networks in Latin America: The Mexican Connection', *Perspectives on Global Development and Technology*, 17:1–2, 89–102.

Cowan, J. K. (2006), 'Culture and Rights after "Culture and Rights"', *American Anthropologist*, 108:1, 9–24.

Crenzel, E. (2008), *La historia política del Nunca Más: La memoria de los desaparecidos en la Argentina* (Buenos Aires, Siglo Veintiuno).

Crenzel, E. (2020), 'Four Cases under Examination: Human Rights and Justice in Argentina under the Macri Administration', *Modern Languages Open*, 26:1, 1–13.

Fassin, D. (2016), *La razón humanitaria: Una historia moral en el tiempo presente* (Buenos Aires, Prometeo).

Fassin, D. and R. Rechtman (2009), *The Empire of Trauma: An Inquiry into the Condition of Victimhood* (Princeton, Princeton University Press).

Gatti, G. (2011), 'De un continente al otro: El desaparecido transnacional, la cultura humanitaria y las víctimas totales en tiempos de guerra global', *Política y sociedad*, 3, 519–36.

Goldentul, A. (2016), 'De "hijos y nietos de presos políticos" a "puentes para la legalidad": La conformación de una nueva agrupación de familiares de agentes de represión en Argentina (2008–2016)', paper presented at the seminar on *La investigación en proceso*, GESHAL, 24 November.

Guilhot, N. (2011), '¿Limitando la soberanía o produciendo gubernamentalidad? Dos modelos de derechos humanos en el discurso político de Estados Unidos', *Revista política*, 49:1, 219–41.

Jelin, E. (2010), '¿Victimas, familiares o ciudadanos/as? Las luchas por la legitimidad de la palabra', in *Los desaparecidos en la Argentina: Memorias, representaciones e ideas (1983–2008)*, ed. E. Crenzel (Buenos Aires, Editorial Biblos), pp. 227–49.

Jelin, E. and P. de Azcárate (1991), 'Memoria y política: Movimientos de derechos humanos y construcción democrática', *América Latina hoy*, 1, 29–38.

Laqueur, T. (1989), 'Bodies, Details, and the Humanitarian Narrative', in *The New Cultural History*, ed. L. Hunt (Berkeley, University of California Press), pp. 176–204.

Markarian, V. (2004), 'De la lógica revolucionaria a las razones humanitarias: La izquierda uruguaya en el exilio y las redes transnacionales de derechos humanos (1972–1976)', *Cuadernos del CLAEH*, 89:2, 85–108.

Payne, L. A. (2000), *Uncivil Movements: The Armed Right Wing and Democracy in Latin America* (Baltimore, Johns Hopkins University Press).

Salvi, V. (2011), 'The Slogan "Complete Memory": A Reactive (Re)Signification of the Memory of the Disappeared in Argentina', in *The Memory of State Terrorism in the Southern Cone*, ed. F. Lessa and V. Druliolle (New York, Palgrave Macmillan), pp. 43–61.

Salvi, V. (2012), *De vencedores a víctimas: Memorias militares sobre el pasado reciente en la Argentina* (Buenos Aires, Biblos).

Salvi, V. (2020), 'Tayectoria, capital e ideología: Las declaraciones de los perpetradores en los juicios por crímenes de lesa humanidad en Argentina', *Kamchatka revista de análisis cultural*, 15, 193–215.

Sikkink, K. (1997), 'The Emergence, Evolution, and Effectiveness of the Latin American Human Rights Network', in *Constructing Democracy: Human Rights, Citizenship and Society in Latin America*, ed. E. Jelin and E. Hershberg (Boulder, Westview), pp. 59–84.

Sikkink, K. and Booth Walling, C. (2006), 'Argentina's Contribution to Global Trends in Transitional Justice', in *Transitional Justice in the Twenty-First Century: Beyond*

Truth and Justice, ed. N. Roht-Arriaza and J. Mariezcurrena (New York, Cambridge University Press).

Todorov, T. (2000), *Los abusos de la memoria* (Buenos Aires, Paidós Asterisco).

Van Roeckel, E. and V. Salvi (2019), 'Unbecoming Veteranship: Convicted Military Officers in Post-Authoritarian Argentina', *Conflict and Society*, 5, 115–31.

Vecchioli, V. (2001), 'Políticas de la memoria y formas de clasificación social: ¿Quiénes son las "víctimas del terrorismo de estado" en la Argentina?', in *La imposibilidad del olvido*, ed. B. Groppo and P. Flier (La Plata, Ediciones Al Margen).

Vecchioli, V. (2005), 'La nación como familia: Metáforas políticas del movimiento argentino de derechos humanos', in *Cultura y política en etnografías sobre la Argentina* (Quilmes, Universidad Nacional de Quilmes), pp. 241–69.

Vecchioli, V. (2013), 'Las víctimas del terrorismo de Estado y la gestión del pasado reciente en la Argentina', *Papeles del CEIC: International Journal on Collective Identity Research*, 90, 1–26.

4

The Religious Right and Anti-Genderism in Colombia

ELIZABETH S. CORREDOR

RIGHT-AGAINST-RIGHTS MOBILISATIONS ARE becoming increasingly visible around the globe and are adding anti-gender campaigns to their political arsenal. Anti-genderism is a global phenomenon that seeks to roll back, reverse, or block expanding gender and LGBT+ rights. It is both an epistemological response to emancipatory claims with regard to sex, gender, and sexuality, and a political mechanism to thwart feminist and queer agendas (Corredor 2019). Anti-genderism has grown in Latin America as in other parts of the world, but without a corresponding level of attention by scholars. Most of what we have come to understand about anti-gender countermovements to date comes from the European context, where the Catholic Church undoubtedly has been leading the charge.[1] In Latin America, however, anti-genderism presents a more unique arrangement of religious right activity, whereby conservative evangelical churches, in addition to the Catholic Church, are major leaders (Corrales 2020). With a more complex constellation of religious engagement in anti-genderism come new dynamics of the right against rights that warrant investigation.

This chapter examines two anti-gender campaigns in Colombia that took place in 2016, one that targeted a school programme, and the other a major peace process. The first campaign, which occurred in August 2016, targeted a national anti-bullying programme that sought greater tolerance in schools for gender-variant identities and children struggling with their sexuality. This initiative was met with open resistance from the Catholic Church, conservative evangelical churches, right-wing politicians, and certain factions within civil society – all of whom claimed that the programme spread a form of 'gender ideology' that attacked the nuclear family and threatened 'educational autonomy, religious liberty, and the right of

---

[1] See Anić (2015); Case (2011); Corredor (2021); Fassin (2016); Graff (2014); Korolczuk and Graff (2018); Kováts and Pető (2017); and Paternotte and Kuhar (2017).

Proceedings of the British Academy, **255**, 78–97, © The British Academy 2023.

THE RELIGIOUS RIGHT AND ANTI-GENDERISM IN COLOMBIA   79

parents to determine the education of their children' (Urbina Ortega 2016). Their campaign was successful. Just weeks after its announcement, the programme was scrapped, and the Minister of Education stepped down.

As the first anti-gender campaign was winding down, a second one emerged, this time around a landmark peace agreement that sought to end 52 years of violent civil war between the Colombian government and the Revolutionary Armed Forces of Colombia – People's Army (Fuerzas Armadas Revolucionarias de Colombia – Ejército del Pueblo; FARC-EP), Colombia's largest guerrilla group. This second anti-gender campaign targeted the peace agreement's gender perspective, or *enfoque de género*, which sought 'the inclusion and exercise of equal rights and conditions for all of society, specifically for women and the LGBT+ population' (FARC-EP 2016, 2). Religious and political conservatives argued that language pertaining to sexual diversity and diverse gender identity threatened Colombia's legal system, traditional marriage, and the nuclear family, as well as the right to life and religious freedom (*Semana* 2016b). Unlike the first campaign, however, this anti-gender mobilisation was ultimately unsuccessful in eliminating the peace agreement's gender perspective.

This chapter takes a deep dive into these two anti-gender countermovements, showing that each was marked by loose and informal coalitions of religious leaders, civil society, and conservative politicians, who coalesced around a particular aim but did not, in the end, establish a long-standing, consolidated movement beyond these two mobilisations. The temporary nature of these countermovements, as discussed in the introduction to this volume, is characteristic of right-against-rights groups. As I will show in this chapter, however, the ephemeral style of anti-gender countermovements does not imply that their effects are minimal. In Colombia, the short-lived anti-gender mobilisations had substantial impacts on the outcomes of the anti-bullying programme and the 2016 peace agreement.

The loose and informal nature of anti-gender countermovements is also important because, as Escoffier, Payne, and Zulver (Chapter 1) note, historically Latin America's military, political, and economic elite have dominated the region's 'right wing'. As a result, much of their influence has taken place either behind the scenes or within party politics. Yet, anti-gender movements are largely dependent on the support of the masses, and thus, to influence their political worlds, they engage in mobilisation tactics that include street protests, as well as digital and social media campaigns, while also participating in formal politics. As I will show, Colombia's anti-gender campaigns were neither entirely a grassroots effort, nor staunchly operating within the realm of party politics, thus demonstrating how today's political polarisation is 'not simply a form of contentious politics driven by political parties', but is also caused by 'social conflict driven by non-institutionalised groups, grassroots movements and ordinary citizens' (Brändle *et al.* 2022, 234). These countermovements were short-lived, albeit impactful.

This chapter is organised into five parts. I begin by explaining anti-genderism, followed by a discussion of how it has manifested to date in Latin America. I then delve into the two cases of anti-gender countermovements in Colombia, where

80 *Elizabeth S. Corredor*

I conduct an in-depth analysis of the actors involved, their mobilisation strategies, framing tactics, and the final outcomes. For each case study, I rely on qualitative data gathered through print and social media, as well as press releases and other public statements made available by leaders from Catholic and conservative evangelical organisations. I conclude with a discussion of how these right-against-rights groups seek to roll back the rights of women and LGBT+ groups in the name of parental rights, religious freedom, and the Colombian family. In this final section, I further discuss the implications of these anti-gender countermovements for the region at large.

Anti-Genderism: An Overview

In the last two decades there has been a global rise of a specific type of opposition against progressive women's and LGBT+ rights, often referred to as anti-genderism. The first seeds of organised anti-gender countermovement were planted at the 1995 United Nations World Conference on Women in Beijing, where feminists and lesbian activists sought to include a definition of gender in the conference's Platform for Action that recognised gender as a social and cultural construction. The Holy See, however, was quick to respond, issuing its 'Statement of Interpretation of the Term "Gender"', where it reinforced its understanding of gender 'as grounded in biological-sexual identity, male or female', and 'thus exclud[ing] dubious interpretations based on widespread conceptions, which affirm that sexual identity can adapt indefinitely, to accommodate new and different purposes' (Glendon 1995).[2] Rallying support from Islamic and other conservative nations, the Vatican successfully prevented feminist definitions of gender from being incorporated into the final Platform for Action.[3]

Since 1995, the Catholic Church has waged anti-gender counterattacks around the globe, challenging policy that acknowledges the socially and culturally constructed notions of gender. At the heart of these movements is a rejection of queer and progressive feminist assertions that gender, sexuality, and biological sex are social, political, and cultural constructs. For Catholics, gender, sex, and sexuality are predictably correlated and 'harmoniously woven together' (Burggraf 2003, 402). As seen in Beijing, the Catholic Church does not act alone. These campaigns are driven by complex systems of conservative religious networks and socially conservative civil organisations who come together to resist the actual or perceived policy promoting women's bodily autonomy and sexual diversity (Tabbush and Caminotti 2020).

Together they tackle a wide range of policy issues, including but not limited to marriage equality; adoption for same-sex couples; domestic violence prevention;

---

[2] Unless otherwise noted, all translations are my own.

[3] For more on the Vatican's oppositional campaigns at the Beijing conference see Bayes and Tohidi (2001); Buss (1998); Case (2019); Friedman (2003); and Garbagnoli (2016).

sex education; reproductive health; and, as seen in this case study, peace processes. The spectrum of issues that it challenges allows anti-gender camps to garner support from multiple sites of resistance. They also demonstrate immense transnational organisational and discursive power.

Anti-gender campaigns are emotionally charged, often using fear and panic that capitalise on exaggerated but credible threats to fundamental religious values (Cespedes-Baez 2016; Domínguez Blanco 2020; Rodríguez Rondón 2017; Korolczuk and Graff 2018). They espouse oversimplified and deceptive adversarial framing to delegitimise LGBT+ groups and progressive feminists in their quest for social and political emancipation. Vague terms such as 'gender ideology', 'genderism', and 'gender theory' (herein referred to as 'gender ideology') are regularly employed by these camps to promote a perceived threat. 'Gender ideology', according to these groups, incites gender confusion by allowing people to 'freely determine whether they want to be men or women and freely choose their sexual orientation' (Graff 2014, 433). It is said to be an 'ideological aggression against girls and women' (Rice Hasson 2019) that is rooted in the 'rejection of the family' and motherhood (Alzamora Revoredo 2003, 475), and promotes 'abortion ... homosexuality, lesbianism and all the other forms of sexuality outside of marriage' (Alzamora Revoredo 2003, 465). By using ambiguous and sweeping language, these countermovements aim to capture a wide range of complex theories on gender, biological sex, and sexuality and distil them into a single, fabricated ideology/theory that threatens the family, children, and ultimately the nation. In other words, these frames serve as 'symbolic glue' (Brustier 2015) for a whole host of issues culled from a diverse constellation of social and political theories and policy agendas.

Anti-gender countermovements also employ a fear-based, oversimplified 'symbolic glue' approach when naming those responsible for promoting 'gender ideology'. Pointing to a contrived group of 'gender feminists' (Alzamora Revoredo 2003), 'feminazis' (Angulo 2019), or 'fundamental feminists' (Blabbeando 2013), anti-gender campaigns have seemingly collapsed two distinct and complex social movements – those of feminists and of LGBT+ rights – and all of their diverse subgroups into a single unit. This serves to create a single enemy that is easy to digest for the masses (Garbagnoli 2016). Campaign leaders have also shrewdly connected 'gender ideology' to distinct political cleavages that resonate with varying highly controversial national histories, such as communism, colonialism, and imperialism. Pope Francis has likened 'gender ideology' to 'ideological colonization' (McPhate 2016); Polish Bishop Tadeusz Pieronek stated that 'gender ideology is worse than Communism and Nazism put together' (Graff and Korolczuk 2017); and Guinean Cardinal Robert Sarah argued that the world is navigating 'two radicalizations' in which 'we find ourselves between gender ideology and ISIS ... What Nazi-Fascism and Communism were in the 20th century, Western homosexual and abortion ideologies and Islamic Fanaticism are today' (Pentin 2015). These analogies shrewdly incite fear around political anxieties and the role of the nuclear family; exaggerate the potency of the enemy, who are radical feminists and LGBT+ communities; and connect anti-genderism to potent, nationalist rhetoric.

Anti-Genderism in Latin America: New Religious Right-against-Rights Formations

While anti-gender mobilisations were mostly contained within Europe in the first decade of the 2000s, more recently we have seen a rise of anti-genderism in other regions of the world. In Latin America, specifically anti-gender mobilisations have organised against abortion, same-sex marriage, and sex education programmes. In September 2016, tens of thousands of protestors mobilised in Mexico to oppose same-sex marriage and the inclusion of gender ideology in sex education curriculums in public schools. Right-wing populist parties have also used gender ideology rhetoric as a political platform, and joined forces with anti-gender groups, as seen in the presidential campaigns of Costa Rica's Alvarado Muñoz and Brazil's Jair Bolsonaro in 2018. What sets these movements apart from their European counterparts, however, is the involvement of conservative evangelical churches alongside the Catholic Church: historically considered competitors in the political arena. In a region where Catholicism has long dominated, evangelical protestants have challenged Catholic hegemony and now make up almost 20 per cent of Latin America's population (Sahgal 2017). Moreover, the majority of evangelicals self-identify as Pentecostal or neo-Pentecostal, the most socially and politically conservative factions of Protestantism (Masci 2014). Across the region, conservative evangelicals have been leaders in anti-gender mobilisations and, as a result, they are proving to be effective at grassroots organisation among the group's faithful, as well as reliable allies for other political heavyweights who share core conservative values around the social issues of gender and sexuality.

The rise of evangelicalism in Latin America is just one component of a larger regional shift toward social and political conservatism (Fassin 2020; Biroli 2020). Colombia is no exception. President Iván Duque, like other leaders in the region, represents a return to a set of conservative policies following eight years of centrist rule. Duque is a member of the right-wing Democratic Centre Party and is known for his close relationship with former president and radical-right firebrand Álvaro Uribe. As in neighbouring countries, evangelicalism in Colombia is also on the rise. In 1970, roughly 95 per cent of Colombians identified as Catholic (Pérez Guadalupe 2019). In 2018, 73 per cent identified as Catholics and 16 per cent as evangelical and/or Protestant.[4] While evangelical Protestants remain a minority in Colombia, their emergence has greatly aided the nation's conservative political base, as conservative evangelicals bring a renewed enthusiasm for touting traditional values such as protection of the heterosexual, nuclear family. For example, in Colombia, evangelicals are more likely to reject LGBT+ rights than members of other religious and non-religious groups (Corrales and Sagarzazu 2019). Such conditions provide fertile ground for anti-genderism.

---

[4] Data retrieved from the Latinobárometro database, 30 June 2020, https://www.latinobarometro.org/latOnline.jsp.

THE RELIGIOUS RIGHT AND ANTI-GENDERISM IN COLOMBIA   83

The First Anti-Gender Campaign: Sexual Diversity Education in Schools

In the summer of 2016, an anti-gender campaign emerged to protest an educational manual entitled *School Environments Free from Discrimination*. The education manual was developed in response to a Constitutional Court ruling on an incident where a 16-year-old boy took his own life after being bullied by school administrators because of his sexual orientation. Together with the United Nations Children's Fund (UNICEF), United Nations Population Fund (UNFPA), and the United Nations Development Programme (UNDP), the Ministry of Education created a 97-page manual to educate teachers about the distinctions and relationships among the terms sex, gender, sexuality, and gender identity. This manual sought to accomplish two goals. First, it promoted freedom from discrimination based on sexual orientation and gender identity (*Tiempo* 2016a), and second, it sought to explain the complex nature of embodiment and identity in ways that could help teachers support and foster the development of children who identify as LGBT+ (Ministerio de Educación de Colombia *et al.* 2016). These manuals, popularly known as *las cartillas*, were set to be distributed to school administrators in August 2016.

At the time of the manuals' development and release, Gina Parody, an openly gay politician, was serving as the Minister of Education for the moderate U Party. On 4 August 2016, just days before its release, a fake manual depicting a cartoon of two men having sex went viral on the internet and was rumoured to be part of the new sex education curriculum (Marcos 2016). The religious right against rights, primarily Catholic and conservative evangelicals, with the support of conservative politicians, responded with fury. For the first time in Colombian public discourse, accusations surfaced around 'gender ideology'. Together these groups organised mass demonstrations throughout the country, making claims that the educational manuals violated constitutional rights to freedom of religion, belief, dignity, and the right for parents to educate their children (Marcos 2016; *Espectador* 2016).

Mobilising Leaders, Forms of Protest, and Framing

The Catholic Church and conservative evangelicals led the resistance and were supported by government representatives with varying party affiliations. Calling upon its people to 'support initiatives ... [that] protect the guiding principles of humanity, especially in defense of life, children, and the family' (Jaramilo Monsalve in Cháchara (2016)), the Catholic Church was extremely vocal. In an interview with *El Tiempo* (2016c), a leading Colombian newspaper, the then archbishop of Bogotá, Rubén Salazar Gómez, stated: 'We reject the implementation of gender ideology in Colombia's education system, because it is a destructive ideology, it destroys the human person ... It takes away from him the fundamental content of the complementarity between men and women.' Additionally, Archbishop Oscar

84   *Elizabeth S. Corredor*

Urbina Ortega (2016), the vice-president of the Colombian Episcopal Conference, stated on behalf of all bishops in Colombia:

> We lament that the Constitutional Court and now the Ministry of Education are abusing the law to promote gender ideology in the most diverse areas of our society ... [it is an] attack against the family as an essential institution of society, against the educational autonomy, religious liberty, and the right of parents to determine the education of their children, liberty of conscience, freedom of association, and the right of children to receive an education in accord with the ethics and morals of their parents.

On 10 August 2016, mass protests broke out across Colombia; they were organised by Abanderados por la Familia, or Champions of the Family, a civil society movement with a mission of defending traditional, Christian-based family values. The marches were attended by civil society, including community individuals, Christian-based organisations, private education advocacy organisations, and prominent Catholic and conservative evangelical leaders. In addition, the marches were attended by conservative government representatives from an array of political parties, including the Democratic Centre, the U Party, the Liberal Party, the Conservative Party, and the newly formed evangelical party Justa Libres.

Hundreds of thousands of people marched through the streets in more than 35 cities around the country, chanting 'We are alive; we are present; families are here' ('Se vive, se siente, la familia está presente'). They held signs with biblical passages, as well as individually crafted messages that connected the rejection of gender ideology to familial and educational rights, such as:

> In defence of children, the family, and education. No to gender ideology! (Cobos 2016)

> I am in favour of divine creation. Long live the family! Resurrect family principles! (PCCMM 2016)

> We reject gender ideology in schools. (*Semana* 2016a)

> It is the right of parents to educate our children. (PCCMM 2016)

As demonstration organisers, Champions of the Family also provided people with protest signs stating 'Family comes first.' The protests offered a platform for Catholic and conservative evangelical leaders, as well as politicians, to give speeches and interviews in which they made statements connecting nationhood with family values. Archbishop Ismael Rueda Sierra of Bucaramanga bellowed from the stage at his local march: 'Respect the people, respect the nation, respect the Colombian family!' (Radio Católica Metropolitana 1450AM 2016). Ricardo Rodríguez, founder and leader of the Centro Mundial de Avivamiento, or World Revival Centre Church, the largest evangelical church in Latin America, stated that 'it is a tremendous victory that all of the country came out to say that the Colombian family is based in principles and values and that our children are educated by [the parents]' (Detrás de Cámaras DTC 2016).

At the forefront of government opposition was Conservative Party member Alejandro Ordoñez, who at the time was serving as Attorney General of Colombia. A staunch Catholic, Ordoñez stated that the Ministry of Education manuals were

THE RELIGIOUS RIGHT AND ANTI-GENDERISM IN COLOMBIA   85

'being used to indoctrinate our children and our grandchildren in gender ideology … to dissolve the family and erase childhood by taking away innocence and purity from children and young people' (*Heraldo* 2016). Ángela Hernández, an evangelical state representative and a member of Gina Parody's own moderate U Party, made claims that the Minister of Education was seeking 'colonisation of her customs and ideas' and was 'try[ing] to impose [Parody's] way of life' upon the Colombian people (*Tiempo* 2016b). In a call to action, Yolanda Vargas, state representative of the far-right Democratic Centre Party, whose husband heads the neo-Pentecostal International Charismatic Mission Church of Barrancabermeja, stated 'the cause that unites us is the family, because we believe in a society where the parents have the right to educate and raise their children' (Rodriguez 2016).

On 16 August, less than a week after the mass protests, government officials convened a senate debate to challenge the legality and the context of the school manuals. The session was initiated by María del Rosario Guerra, a senator from the far-right Democratic Centre Party and a practising Catholic, along with Jimmy Chamorro, another member of Gina Parody's party and a prominent evangelical. As a result of the debate, the anti-bullying manuals were scrapped (Las2orillas 2016), and on 30 August 2016, Gina Parody announced that she would take a sabbatical from her position as Minster of Education to work on the peace process's 'Yes' campaign. On 4 October, just two days after the peace agreement failed in a national plebiscite, Parody officially resigned.

While conservative politicians played a role in the termination of the manuals, it was the religious right against rights who led the public campaign against the educational programme. Through a grassroots, populist style of organisation, these religious networks – comprising the Catholic and conservative evangelical churches – used social media, traditional media, and street protests to send out their message. They packaged and disseminated so-called gender ideology as a hostile form of left-wing ideological colonisation and an unwanted imposition that threatened traditional families and children. They capitalised on rights-based language by employing parental and educational rights rhetoric, regularly claiming that parents have the sole right to sex- and other value-based education.[5] Finally, they promoted the traditional Christian family as a symbol of Colombian nationhood and citizenship.

The Second Anti-Gender Campaign: The 2016 Peace Agreement Referendum

Background to the 2016 Peace Agreement

In the early months of 2016, prior to the first anti-gender campaign, right-wing politicians organised in opposition to the highly anticipated peace agreement,

---

[5] For more information on Colombia's history with human rights rhetoric see Corredor (2021).

which was set to end 52 years of violent civil war between the government and Colombia's largest guerrilla group, the FARC. Former president Álvaro Uribe, the political nemesis of then President Juan Manuel Santos, led the charge against the peace efforts. Prior to the start of the peace process, Santos and Uribe were both members of the centrist U Party and were allies. In fact, during Uribe's presidency, Santos had served as Minister of Defence from 2006 to 2009. Uribe has long been suspected of having deep ties with right-wing paramilitary groups and, during his presidency, preferred to use military might over negotiation in attempts to end the war. When Santos was elected president in 2010, he took a different approach, opting to initiate peace talks with the FARC. Uribe vehemently rejected the peace negotiations with the rebels from the start. He repeatedly attacked Santos for being weak on issues related to terrorism, and in 2012 broke with the U Party and formed the neoconservative Democratic Centre Party. Together with members from his newly formed party, Uribe launched what would come to be known as the 'No' campaign against the Santos-led peace efforts with the FARC.

Political polarisation in Colombia is not a new phenomenon; in fact, intense polarity between contending elites has plagued the nation since its independence from Spain in 1810. The bitter rivalry between Santos and Uribe is thus relatively characteristic of Colombian politics. Furthermore, it is not uncommon for peace agreement processes to ignite intense political battles, as such agreements can significantly threaten the power, interests, and ideologies of political leaders and parties (Stedman 1997, 5). Thus, while the opposition to this agreement was not unforeseen, the eventual makeup of the opposition and their mobilisation strategies were less expected.

Initially, the 'No' campaign rejected the accords for reasons that are typical in such peace agreement debates. Central to their grievances were concerns regarding land rights, impunity, and political opportunities for those they considered war criminals and drug traffickers. They further claimed that the agreement did not go far enough to protect victims (Oficina del Alto Comisionado para la Paz 2016b; Feldmann 2019). Despite the growing momentum of the 'No' campaign between March and June 2016, multiple opinion polls showed significant support among the Colombian people for the peace agreement (Ideaspaz 2016). Nonetheless, the 'No' campaign charged forward and garnered the backing of former president Andrés Pastrana, the Association of Retired Officers of the Military Forces, the Colombian Federation of Victims of the FARC, and a number of former Supreme Court Justices.

On 24 June, the government and the FARC signed a monumental ceasefire agreement, signalling that a peace agreement was imminent. However, political tensions continued to rise, and in response, religious leaders from across the country organised to cull support for the ongoing negotiations. On 4 July, more than 115 Catholic and evangelical religious leaders signed a decree in the presence of President Santos expressing their hope for peace. At the signing, Colombian Episcopal Conference president Archbishop Luis Castro Quiroga publicly stated that the Catholic Church supported the ongoing negotiations and that it would call on its people to participate in the plebiscite. Nevertheless, he stopped short of telling his parishioners how to vote on whether or not to endorse the anticipated peace agreement (Sistema Informativo del Gobierno 2016). Also at the signing was Hector Pardo, a prominent charismatic evangelical, founder of the evangelical-based political party Justa Libres, and president of the Colombian Confederation for Freedom of Religion, Conscience, and Faith (Confedirec). Pardo stated that should peace come, the churches would continue to serve as peacemakers by facilitating reconciliation, principles of non-repetition of violence, and 'peace, freedom, order and justice for all' (Sistema Informativo del Gobierno 2016). A few months later, Pardo would emerge as a leading figure in the anti-gender campaign against the peace agreement's gender perspective.

On the same day, the Colombian Episcopal Conference convened its 101st Plenary Assembly, which was dedicated to discussing issues of peace and post-conflict reconciliation (*Nuevo Siglo* 2016), two issues the Catholic Church had consistently endorsed over the course of the negotiations. On the last day of the four-day summit – 8 July – Archbishop Castro Quiroga reiterated the continued need to find peace and called on people to eradicate violence and seek reconciliation and good will. In the session, the archbishop cited numerous causes for the violence in Colombia over the previous several decades, including the disintegration of the family, loss of values, and an ethics of relativism. He also stated that the family was an important site of reconciliation and peace, and a 'sanctuary where human life and creation are protected' (Castro Quiroga 2016, 4). The Catholic Church called on politicians not to politicise the agreement and to make sure that it did not serve as a source of division. Once again, instead of taking an official position for or against the forthcoming peace agreement, the archbishop made the following statement: 'We call on the Colombian people to participate in the discussion of the [peace agreement] responsibly, with an informed and conscientious vote, freely expressing their opinion, as an effective exercise of democracy and with due respect for what the majority ultimately determines' (Castro Quiroga 2016, 5).

This declaration neither publicly to endorse nor to reject the peace agreement was not simply a decision to stay outside the political fray; it also aligns with Catholic doctrine, which states that it is not in the Church's interest to tell people how to vote and that its leadership is not directly to intervene in politics and elections (Keane 2020; Congregation for the Doctrine of the Faith 2002). Thus, despite its integral involvement in the negotiations over the prior four years, the Catholic Church deferred to its tradition of staying out of national elections and kept the Church on the side-lines of the second anti-gender campaign.

On 24 July 2016, the Colombian government announced the inclusion of an innovative gender perspective, or *enfoque de género*, in the forthcoming peace agreement, which would guarantee 'the inclusion and exercise of equal rights and conditions for all of society, specifically for women and the LGBT+ population' (FARC-EP 2016, 2). In a press release, the government acknowledged the fundamental need for the peace agreement to 'create conditions so that women and people with diverse sexual identities can access the benefits of living in a country without armed conflict' (2). At a ceremony celebrating the work of the Gender Subcommission, the chief negotiator for the government delegation, Humberto de la Calle, gave a speech endorsing the gender perspective. In his talk, de la Calle stressed that gender is a socially constructed concept that 'evokes roles of domination [and] discrimination, especially against women and different forms of sexual identity'. He cited Simone de Beauvoir's famous quote: 'One is not born a woman, but rather becomes, a woman' and followed it up by saying 'And today we could also add: "you are not born a man, you become one"'. He also emphasised the progress that women have made in becoming more than just a marker of motherhood in society, and how the Colombian Constitution recognises 'diverse forms of configuration of the family'. Finally, he emphasised his support for the LGBT+ rights within the constitution, stating that 'the multiplicity of identities and orientations broadens the democratic spectrum' (Oficina del Alto Comisionado para la Paz 2016a). On 24 August, the Colombian government announced that it had reached a peace deal with the FARC. The two parties would sign the agreement on 26 September, and on 2 October the Colombian people would be asked to vote on whether or not to accept the agreement in a national plebiscite.

While the gender perspective was praised internationally by the United Nations and transnational feminist networks, it did, nevertheless, lead to the rise of Colombia's second anti-gender campaign. Capitalising on the massive mobilisation that had recently been galvanised around the educational manuals, factions of the religious right against rights joined the 'No' campaign, arguing that the gender perspective in the peace agreement constituted another attempt to impose gender ideology upon the Colombian people. They argued that language pertaining to sexual diversity and diverse gender identity threatened Colombia's legal system and its rights to marriage and family, as well as the right to life and religious freedom (*Semana* 2016b). Uribe, the leader of the 'No' campaign, reiterated 'the need to stimulate family values without putting [the family] at risk. These family values are defended by our religious leaders and moral pastors/guides' (Uribe Vélez 2016).

Mobilising Leaders, Forms of Protest, and Framing

Although the 'No' campaign involved a strategic partnership among conservative political groups to advance their diverse agendas, the attack on the gender- and sexual-equality provisions in the peace agreement were championed by the most conservative factions of the evangelical movement with the support of far-right Catholic politicians. While the Catholic Church was at the forefront of the first anti-gender campaign – and has been the primary mobilising leader for anti-gender campaigns around the globe – it was not officially involved in opposing the peace agreement or its gender inclusions. As already noted, the Catholic Church had publicly announced that it would not tell its parishioners how to vote, but rather would

THE RELIGIOUS RIGHT AND ANTI-GENDERISM IN COLOMBIA   89

simply encourage them to read the agreement and vote with their conscience, as is its regular practice around issues of domestic elections (Rojas Herrera 2016). Thus, conservative Catholic leaders within Colombia who may have been against the agreement personally had their hands tied when it came to denouncing the peace agreement publicly as a form of gender ideology.

Thus, it was conservative evangelical churches who mobilised and denounced gender ideology in the peace agreement. Right-wing evangelical leaders included the Christian Pact for Peace, a coalition of high profile evangelical church leaders; the World Centre of Revival, a megachurch whose leaders have held political office and who currently maintain strong ties to the Democratic Centre Party; megachurch Ríos de Vida; the evangelical Confederation of Colombia; the Charismatic International Church, led by Cesar and Claudia Castellanos, founders of the Charismatic International megachurch and the National Christian Party (PNC), one of the first evangelical political parties; Pastor Marco Fidel Ramírez, a city councillor of Bogotá; the evangelical-based political party Justa Libres; and evangelical government officials, including Senator Viviane Morales and state representative Ángela Hernández. It is important to note that a significant evangelical minority favoured the agreement and its gender perspective, and did not actively participate in this campaign.[6] Examples of churches that did support the agreement include the Mennonite and Baptist Churches, as well as a handful of Pentecostal megachurches and the Pentecostal-based MIRA Party (*Semana* 2016c).

While the Catholic Church did not take a position on the agreement, key conservative politicians who are practising Catholics and known for their religious conservatism – specifically former Attorney General Alejandro Ordoñez and former Undersecretary for the Family Ilva Myriam Hoyos – publicly opposed the gender perspective on religious and moral grounds. However, they were speaking not as official representatives of the Catholic Church but rather as elite politicians, unlike their evangelical counterparts, who were speaking as politicians, political hopefuls, and church representatives.

While some public marches against the agreement transpired, they did not occur to the same extent or at the same scale as those against the education manual. Instead, mobilisation strategies focused on getting people out to vote 'No' in the referendum. To do this, movement leaders spoke from the pulpit and leveraged social media to reach the masses (Beltrán and Creely 2018). Leaders used Twitter, Facebook, YouTube, and WhatsApp to spread their message, which was simple: the peace accord's gender perspective is synonymous with the same gender ideology that permeated the educational manuals. State representative Ángela Hernández

---

[6] Much of the literature on the political involvement of evangelicals focuses on conservative groups; however, evangelicals are a diverse group with varying political leanings, and thus there are many evangelical groups in Colombia who do not identify with the political agendas of those involved in the anti-gender movements. For a more in-depth explanation of which evangelical churches supported and opposed the 2016 Colombian peace agreement see Moreno (2016).

(2016) tweeted: 'They wanted to impose the GENDER IDEOLOGY in schools. Now we are concerned that they intend to include it in the Constitution with the plebiscite.' Attorney General Alejandro Ordoñez (2016) professed in a YouTube video: 'Colombia marched a month ago when the government intended to implement a manual about gender ideology in schools ... now in the [peace agreement], it appears once again with infinite intensity ... and they call it *un enfoque de género*.' Instead of framing their arguments in terms of parental rights, in this instance the right against rights forces used fear-based language rooted in conspiracy theories about a hostile takeover by far-left ideologies. Marco Fidel Ramírez (2016), city council member of Bogotá, tweeted: 'I just voted No in the FARC-Santos plebiscite because I do not want a Colombia in the claws of atheism, communism, and the homosexual agenda.'

On 2 October 2016, the country narrowly rejected the peace agreement. Reasons for rejecting the agreement went beyond the gender inclusions; nonetheless, there is a general consensus among media, government leaders from all sides, religious organisations, and academics that the anti-gender campaign against the gender perspective served as a tipping point for rejection of the peace agreement (Beltrán and Creely 2018). In the days following the unexpected loss, President Santos met with religious and civil society leaders, as well as members of government, to discuss revisions to the peace accord, including but not limited to those pertaining to the gender perspective. In various proposals to the government, conservative evangelical leaders and Catholic politicians argued their concerns and articulated their demands. As in the lead-up to the referendum, grievances centred on anxieties about conspiracy, and the destruction of Colombian institutions and the traditional family. However, the written proposals were far more explicit. The evangelical Confederation of Colombia (CEDECOL) issued a statement declaring that the gender perspective '[e]xceed[s] a guaranteed application of women's rights and [instead] generat[es] ambiguity and confusion ... the so-called "*Enfoque de Género*" has absorbed "Gender Ideology", whose scope promotes a new anthropology of being, which ignores sexual distinction and denies the difference and reciprocity between men and women' (Castaño Díaz, Palacios, and Moreno 2016, 1). Former Undersecretary for the Family Ilva Myriam Hoyos (Hoyos Castañeda 2016, 24–5) stated that the peace agreement 'recognises the LGBTI population as the architect and beneficiary of public policies', and that 'Institutions that are essential to society will have to be modified, such as marriage, family, adoption, kinship, civil status, all of which will not only have constitutional recognition, but will also be reinterpreted through ... diverse sexual orientations and gender identities'. Attorney General Alejandro Ordoñez (Ordoñez Maldonado 2016a) argued that the gender perspective intended to 'redesign our legal system, the family, marriage, the right to life and religious freedom'.

In addition to their grievances, opposition leaders also demanded the elimination of all mentions of gender and other phrases that alluded to sexuality and identity. Furthermore, they sought to replace the term 'gender perspective' with a 'women's rights approach', which would in effect remove LGBT+ protections

THE RELIGIOUS RIGHT AND ANTI-GENDERISM IN COLOMBIA   91

but retain rights for heterosexual, cis-gendered women. Finally, they demanded that the traditional family be recognised as the principal institution of Colombian society, around which all other social and legal institutions should be structured (Rodríguez *et al.* 2016; Hoyos Castañeda 2016; Castaño Díaz 2016; Oficina del Alto Comisionado para la Paz 2016b).

After reviewing religious opponents' concerns over the gender perspective 'with extreme care' (Santos 2016a), the president announced a series of changes to the language of the peace accord that he hoped would satisfy conservative activists (Santos 2016b). On 30 November 2016, Congress approved the revised peace accords, officially ending the civil war between the FARC and the Colombian government. Much to the disappointment of the religious right against rights, much of the gender perspective was preserved and, to date, still stands as the only peace agreement in the world that offers protections for LGBT+ communities.[7]

Analysis and Conclusion

While conservative politicians played a supportive role in the termination of the sexual diversity educational manual, it was a broad range of the religious conservatives who led the public right-against-rights campaign. Through grassroots, populist styles of organisation, Catholic and conservative evangelical churches used social media, traditional media, and street protests to send out their message. They packaged and disseminated so-called gender ideology as a hostile form of left-wing ideological colonisation and an unwanted imposition that threatened traditional families and children. They capitalised on rights-based language by employing parental and educational rights rhetoric, regularly claiming that parents have the sole right to sex- and other value-based education. Finally, they promoted the traditional Christian family as a symbol of Colombian nationhood and citizenship.

While there was less unity among the religious right against right in its opposition to the gender perspective included in the peace accord (when compared to the case of the education manuals) – particularly given that the Catholic Church did not actively oppose the peace agreement – the critiques of gender ideology were more sweeping, going beyond the threat to the family and parental rights. In this case, framing strategies employed fear-based messaging of a nefarious LGBT+ takeover, enabling the religious right against rights to position themselves as the victim in the process, as well as the true defender of women's rights.[8] Nonetheless, these grievances align with Catholic-led anti-gender mobilisations not only in Colombia, but across the globe.

---

[7] For an in-depth comparison of the gender perspective within the original and final peace agreement see Corredor (2021).
[8] For a more comprehensive framing analysis of anti-gender opposition to the 2016 Colombian peace agreement see Corredor (2021).

92   *Elizabeth S. Corredor*

As Escoffier, Payne, and Zulver (Chapter 1) discuss, recent backlash to progressive rights in Latin America often emerges in the form of loosely knit and temporary coalitions or countermovements that coalesce around a particular aim, but never exactly establish a sustained movement beyond the immediate issue. Anti-gender campaigns throughout Latin America illustrate precisely this. In Colombia, strategic yet brief right-against-rights alliances were formed among right-wing politicians; conservative evangelical church leaders; civil society groups; and, in the first campaign, the Catholic Church. These mobilisations, however, did not result in a fully fledged, consolidated, and long-standing countermovement. Indeed, since the writing of this chapter (in 2022), Colombia has not yet experienced another anti-gender campaign to the same degree. Their temporality, however, does not mean they are not impactful. As the two anti-gender countermovements in Colombia show, whether or not they were successful in the end, these short-lived campaigns had demonstrable effects on gender- and sexual-equality policy.

The Colombian case also demonstrates how these right-against-right mobilisations operate predominantly in civil society with the aid of strategic alliances within party politics. This phenomenon is a break from the past, whereby control over right-wing politics was primarily concentrated in the hands of the political, economic, and military elite. Furthermore, these mobilisations draw attention to the changing religious landscape in Colombia and within the region at large. Colombia's anti-gender campaigns demonstrate how Latin America's religious right against rights, once dominated by the Catholic Church, is fast adapting to the surge of evangelicalism and leveraging these new alliances to assert control over gendered policy in the region. This is particularly apparent in the first anti-gender campaign against the sexual diversity education programme, where evangelicals and the Catholic Church campaigned together, which led to the termination of the programme before it even got started. Evangelicals and the Catholic Church also united in their response to the ceasefire between the FARC and the government, where together they announced their support for continued efforts to reach a peace deal. While the Catholic Church would take a step back with regard to the referendum, some evangelical leaders initially in favour of supporting peace would eventually switch to the 'No' campaign because of the gendered inclusions. In other words, evangelical leaders were able to carry the proverbial torch in the second anti-gender campaign when the Catholic Church was unable to participate (although certain prominent Catholic figures did participate in their positions as politicians). In short, their united front – albeit temporarily – shows that these forces, who have historically been politically at odds with each other, are finding new ways of coming together when their political agendas align.

These cases shed light not only on the changing religious landscape in Latin America, but also on the greater bandwidth that anti-genderism can have in the region. With the inclusion of conservative evangelicals – who operate without the same structural coherency as the Catholic Church – there is greater potential to promote anti-genderism in times that the Church is unable to mobilise. Research on

THE RELIGIOUS RIGHT AND ANTI-GENDERISM IN COLOMBIA   93

anti-genderism in Latin America is still in its infancy, and thus greater attention to evangelical-led anti-gender mobilisations promises greater insight into how right-against-rights rhetoric and ideas spread among competing groups and across geo-political and cultural borders.

References

Alzamora Revoredo, B. O. (2003), 'An Ideology of Gender: Dangers and Scope', in *Lexicon: Ambiguous and Debatable Terms Regarding Family Life and Ethical Questions*, ed. Pontifical Council for the Family (Front Royal, VA, Human Life International).

Angulo, Y. (2019), 'Fabricio Alvarado califica de "feminazis" a las mujeres que promueven el aborto', *El Mundo, Costa Rica*, 30 November, https://www.elmundo.cr/costa-rica/fabricio-alvarado-califica-de-feminazis-a-las-mujeres-que-promueven-el-aborto/.

Anić, J. R. (2015), 'Gender, Gender "Ideology" and Cultural War: Local Consequences of a Global Idea – Croatian Example', *Feminist Theology*, 24:1, 7–22.

Bayes, J. and N. Tohidi (2001), 'Introduction', in *Globalization, Gender, and Religion: The Politics of Women's Rights in Catholic and Muslim Contexts*, ed. J. Bayes and N. Tohidi (New York, Palgrave), pp. 1–16.

Beltrán, W. M. and S. Creely (2018), 'Pentecostals, Gender Ideology and the Peace Plebiscite: Colombia 2016', *Religions*, 8, 1–19.

Biroli, F. (2020), 'The Backlash against Gender Equality in Latin America: Temporality, Religious Patterns, and the Erosion of Democracy', *LASA Forum: The Quarterly Newsletter of the Latin American Studies Association*, 51:2, 22–6.

Blabbeando (2013), 'Ecuador: President Rafael Correa Says "Gender Ideology" Threatens Traditional Families', YouTube, 29 December, https://www.youtube.com/watch?v=4J7QMXpUt00&lc=z13hhnjbcsmzi5xtn22viz3b5qqyslzcy.

Brändle, V. K., C. Galpin, and H.-J. Trenz (2022), 'Brexit as "Politics of Division": Social Media Campaigning after the Referendum', *Social Movement Studies*, 21:1–2, 234–53.

Brustier, G. (2015), 'France', in *Gender as Symbolic Glue: The Position and Role of Conservative and Far Right Parties in the Anti-Gender Mobilization in Europe*, ed. E. Kováts and M. Põim (Brussels, Foundation for European Progressive Studies), pp. 19–39.

Burggraf, J. (2003), 'Gender', in *Lexicon: Ambiguous and Debatable Terms Regarding Family Life and Ethical Questions*, ed. Pontifical Council for the Family (Front Royal, VA, Human Life International), pp. 399–408.

Buss, D. E. (1998), 'Robes, Relics and Rights: The Vatican and the Beijing Conference on Women', *Social & Legal Studies*, 7:3, 339–63.

Case, M. A. (2011), 'After Gender the Destruction of Man? The Vatican's Nightmare Vision of the "Gender Agenda" for Law', *Pace Law Review*, 31:2, 802–17.

Case, M. A. (2019), 'Trans Formations in the Vatican's War on "Gender Ideology"', *Signs: Journal of Women in Culture and Society*, 44:3, 639–64.

Castaño Díaz, E., S. L. Palacios, and P. Moreno (2016), 'Propuesta de ajuste de los Acuerdos de Paz entre el Gobierno Nacional y las FARC-EP por parte de la Iglesia Evangélica de Colombia', 13 October, https://docplayer.es/74076357-Ref-propuesta-de-ajuste-de-los-acuerdos-de-paz-entre-el-gobierno-nacional-y-las-farc-ep-por-parte-de-la-iglesia-evangelica-de-colombia.html.

Castro Quiroga, L. A. (2016), 'Mensaje de la 101a Asamblea Plenaria de los Obispos de Colombia: Artesanos de la paz "Bienaventurados los que trabajan por la paz" (MT 5, 9)', https://www.cec.org.co/sites/default/files/Comunicado.pdf.

Cespedes-Baez, L. M. (2016), 'Gender Panic and the Failure of a Peace Agreement', *AJIL Unbound*, 110, 183–7.

Cháchara (2016), 'The Archidoces of Barranquilla Joins the Rally for the Family', La Cháchara, 8 August, https://lachachara.org/arquidiocesis-de-barranquilla-se-une-a-la-concentracion-por-la-familia/.

Cobos, J. J. (ed.) (2016), 'Marcha abanderados por la familia Bucaramanga', YouTube, 12 August, https://www.youtube.com/watch?v=l3tMzk872rw.

Congregation for the Doctrine of the Faith (2002), *Doctrinal Note on Some Questions Regarding the Participation of Catholics in Political Life: Vatican City November 24, 2002* (Vatican, Libreria Editrice Vaticana).

Corrales, J. (2020), 'The Expansion of LGBT Rights in Latin America and the Backlash', in *The Oxford Handbook of Global LGBT and Sexual Diversity Politics*, ed. M. J. Bosia, S. M. McEvoy, and M. Rahman (Oxford, Oxford University Press), pp. 184–200.

Corrales, J. and I. Sagarzazu (2019), 'Not All "Sins" Are Rejected Equally: Resistance to LGBT Rights across Religions in Colombia', *Political Science and Religion Journal*, 12:2, 351–77.

Corredor, E. S. (2019), 'Unpacking "Gender Ideology" and the Global Right's Antigender Countermovement', *Signs: Journal of Women in Culture and Society*, 44:3, 613–38.

Corredor, E. S. (2021), 'On the Strategic Uses of Women's Rights: Backlash, Rights-Based Framing, and Anti-Gender Campaigns in Colombia's 2016 Peace Agreement', *Latin American Politics and Society*, 63:3, 46–68.

Detrás de Cámaras DTC (2016), 'Marcha 10/08/16 – Abanderados por la Familia', YouTube, 18 August, https://www.youtube.com/watch?v=iOqlLTfp2uI.

Domínguez Blanco, M. A. (2020), '"Nosotros también": Sentimientos queer y políticas de odio amoroso hacia la adopción igualitaria en Colombia', *Latin American Studies Association Forum*, 52:1, 37–41.

Espectador (2016), 'La carta con la que colegios e iglesias se oponen a la Corte por temas LGBTI', *El Espectador*, 5 August, https://www.elespectador.com/colombia/mas-regio nes/la-carta-con-la-que-colegios-e-iglesias-se-oponen-a-la-corte-por-temas-lgbti-arti cle-647547/.

FARC-EP [Fuerzas Armadas Revolucionarias de Colombia – Ejército del Pueblo] (2016), 'Comunicado conjunto #82', 24 July, https://www.cancilleria.gov.co/sites/default/files/comunicadoconjunto82.pdf.

Fassin, E. (2016), 'Gender and the Problem of Universals: Catholic Mobilizations and Sexual Democracy in France' *Religion & Gender*, 6:2, 173–86.

Fassin, E. (2020), 'Anti-Gender Campaigns, Populism, and Neoliberalism in Europe and Latin America', *LASA Forum: The Quarterly Newsletter of the Latin American Studies Association*, 51:2, 67–71.

Feldmann, A. E. (2019), 'Colombia's Polarizing Peace Efforts', in *Democracies Divided: The Global Challenge of Political Polarization*, ed. T. Carothers and A. O'Donehue (Washington, DC, Brookings Institute).

Friedman, E. J. (2003), 'Gendering the Agenda: The Impact of the Transnational Women's Rights Movement at the UN Conferences of the 1990s', *Women's Studies International Forum*, 26:4, 313–31.

Garbagnoli, S. (2016), 'Against the Heresy of Immanence: Vatican's "Gender" as a New Rhetorical Device against the Denaturalization of the Sexual Order', *Religion & Gender*, 6:2, 187–204.

Glendon, M. A. (1995), 'Declaración de interpretación del término "género" por la santa sede', *L'Osservatore Romano*, 38, 1.

Graff, A. (2014), 'Report from the Gender Trenches: War against "Genderism" in Poland', *European Journal of Women's Studies*, 21:4, 431–6.

Graff, A. and E. Korolczuk (2017), ' "Worse than Communism and Nazism Put Together": War on Gender in Poland', in *Anti-Gender Campaigns in Europe: Mobilizing against Equality*, ed. R. Kuhar and D. Paternotte (London, Rowman & Littlefield), pp. 175–94.

Heraldo (2016), '"La ministra Parody miente", dice Alejandro Ordóñez', *El Heraldo*, 9 August, https://www.elheraldo.co/nacional/la-ministra-parody-miente-dice-alejandro-ordonez-277191.

Hernández, Á. ['@AngelaHer'] (2016), 'Nos querian imponer la IDEOLOGIA DE GENERO en los colegios', Twitter, 27 August, https://twitter.com/angelaher/status/76963876949 4491136.

Hoyos Castañeda, I. M. (2016), 'El "Enfoque de género" en el acuerdo final para la terminación del conflicto y la construcción de una paz estable y duradera', https://www.las2orillas. co/wp-content/uploads/2016/10/ENFOQUE-DE-GE%CC%81NERO-EN-ACUERDO-FINAL-LA-HABANA.pdf.

Ideaspaz (2016), 'El termómetro de la paz', http://www.ideaspaz.org/especiales/termometro/.

Keane, J. T. (2020), 'Explainer: Can a Priest or a Member of a Religious Order Publicly Endorse a Political Candidate?', *America: The Jesuit Review*, 3 September.

Korolczuk, E. and A. Graff (2018), 'Gender as "Ebola from Brussels": The Anticolonial Frame and the Rise of Illiberal Populism', *Signs: Journal of Women in Culture and Society*, 43:4, 797–821.

Kováts, E. and A. Pető (2017), 'Anti-Gender Discourse in Hungary: A Discourse without a Movement?', in *Anti-Gender Campaigns in Europe*, ed. D. Paternotte and R. Kuhar (London, Rowman & Littlefield), pp. 117–31.

Las2orillas (2016), 'Las cartillas de orientación sexual que Parody le sacó en la cara a Uribe', 16 August, https://www.las2orillas.co/las-cartillas-de-orientacion-sexual-que-parody-le-saco-en-la-cara-a-uribe/#.

Marcos, A. (2016), 'Unas falsas cartillas sobre educación sexual culminan en marchas en defensa de la familia en Colombia', *El Pais*, 10 August, https://elpais.com/internacio nal/2016/08/10/colombia/1470835286_954924.html.

Masci, D. (2014), 'Why Has Pentecostalism Grown So Dramatically in Latin America?', Pew Research Center, 14 November, https://www.pewresearch.org/fact-tank/2014/11/ 14/why-has-pentecostalism-grown-so-dramatically-in-latin-america/#:~:text=In%20 the%20early%2020th%20century,which%20resonated%20with%20many%20people.

McPhate, M. (2016), 'Pope Francis' Remarks Disappoint Gay and Transgender Groups', *New York Times*, 3 August, https://nyti.ms/2aNN0uR.

Ministerio de Educación de Colombia, Fondo de Población de las Naciones Unidas, Programa de las Naciones Unidas para el Desarrollo, and Fondo para la Infancia de las Naciones Unidas (2016), *Ambientes escolares libres de discriminación: 1. Orientaciones sexuales e identidades de género no hegemónicas en la escuela. Aspectos para la reflexión* (Bogotá, Ministerio de Educación Nacional).

Moreno, P. (2016), 'Colombian Evangelicals and the Debate after the Peace Agreement', Evangelical Focus, 4 November, https://evangelicalfocus.com/features/2055/pablo-moreno-colombian-evangelicals-and-the-debate-after-the-peace-agreement.

Nuevo Siglo (2016), 'Iglesia pide al Gobierno despejar dudas sobre acuerdos de paz', 4 July, https://www.elnuevosiglo.com.co/articulos/7-2016-iglesia-pide-al-gobierno-despejar-dudas-sobre-acuerdos-de-paz.

Oficina del Alto Comisionado para la Paz (2016a), 'Humberto de la Calle habla sobre la inclusión del enfoque de género en los acuerdos de paz', YouTube, 24 July, https:// www.youtube.com/watch?v=SG8X50uyz2w.

Oficina del Alto Comisionado para la Paz (2016b), *Sistematización opciones y propuestas voceros del No y lo acordado en el nuevo acuerdo*, 29 November, Bogotá, https://www.jep.gov.co/Sala-de-Prensa/Documents/tomo-8-proceso-paz-farc-refrendacion-plebiscito-.pdf.

Ordóñez Maldonado, A. (2016), ' "Acuerdo Santos/Timochenko es una imposición de la ideología de género": Alejandro Ordóñez', YouTube, 24 September, https://www.youtube.com/watch?v=gh3Gd4gv0mM&t=86s.

Paternotte, D. and R. Kuhar (2017), ' "Gender Ideology" in Movement: Introduction', in *Anti-Gender Campaigns in Europe*, ed. D. Paternotte and R. Kuhar (London, Rowman & Littlefield), pp. 1–22.

PCCMM [Predicadores Católicos Comunidad María Mediadora] (2016), 'Abanderados por la Familia – Marcha en Manizales', YouTube, 10 August, https://www.youtube.com/watch?v=t1Vxjon7M7k.

Pentin, E. (2015), 'Cardinal Sarah: ISIS and Gender Ideology Are like "Apocalyptic Beasts" ', *National Catholic Register*, http://www.ncregister.com/blog/edward-pentin/cardinal-sarahs-intervention-isis-and-gender-ideology-are-like-apocalyptic-.

Pérez Guadalupe, J. L. (2019), *Evangelicals and Political Power in Latin America* (Lima, Konrad Adenauer Stiftung; Instituto de Estudios Social Cristianos de Perú).

Radio Católica Metropolitana 1450AM (2016), 'Marcha Abanderados por la Familia, Iglesia Católica presente', YouTube, 11 August, https://www.youtube.com/watch?v=5S0xonjxl7Q.

Ramírez, M. F. ['@7MarcoFidelR'] (2016), 'Acabo de votar NO en plebescito de Farc-Santos', Twitter, 2 October, https://twitter.com/7MarcoFidelR/status/782607295125549056.

Rice Hasson, M. (2019), 'Gender Ideology: Ideological Aggression against Women and Girls', Commission on the Status of Women 2019, New York, 20 March, http://webtv.un.org/search/gender-equality-and-gender-ideology-protecting-women-and-girls-csw63-side-event/6016177611001/?term=Gender%20ideology&sort=date&page=2.

Rodríguez, C., E. Canas, H. Pardo, and J. M. Rodríguez (2016), 'Peace Agreement', YouTube, 21 November, https://misionpaz.org/acuerdo-de-paz/?lang=en.

Rodriguez, D. (2016), 'Abanderados por la familia', https://www.youtube.com/watch?v=O8SG-LWDlKc.

Rodríguez Rondón, M. A. (2017), 'La ideología de género como exceso: Pánico moral y decisión ética en la política colombiana', *Sexualidad, salud y sociedad*, 27, 128–48.

Rojas Herrera, J. E. (2016), 'Comunicado de prensa', https://www.cec.org.co/sites/default/files/Comunicado%20de%20prensa.pdf.

Sahgal, N. (2017), '500 Years after the Reformation, 5 Facts about Protestants around the world', Pew Research Center, 27 October, https://www.pewresearch.org/fact-tank/2017/10/27/500-years-after-the-reformation-5-facts-about-protestants-around-the-world/.

Santos, J. M. (2016a), 'Alocución del Presidente Juan Manuel Santos sobre nuevo acuerdo de paz', 12 November, https://www.cancilleria.gov.co/en/newsroom/news/alocucion-presidente-juan-manuel-santos-nuevo-acuerdo-paz.

Santos, J. M. (2016b), 'Declaración sobre el nuevo Acuerdo de Paz tras reunirse con el Jefe del Equipo Negociador y con el Ministro del Interior', in *Biblioteca del proceso de paz entre el Gobierno Nacional y las FARC-EP*, ed. Oficina del Alto Comisionado para la Paz (Bogotá, Presidencia de la República de Colombia), pp. 204–6.

Semana (2016a), 'Ideología de género: Una estrategia para ganar adeptos por el "No" al plebiscito', https://www.semana.com/nacion/articulo/ideologia-de-genero-una-estrategia-para-ganar-adeptos-por-el-no-al-plebiscito/488260/.

THE RELIGIOUS RIGHT AND ANTI-GENDERISM IN COLOMBIA   97

Semana (2016b), ' "Lo que he tratado es de abrirles los ojos a los colombianos": Alejandro Ordóñez', 25 September, https://www.semana.com/nacion/articulo/alejandro-ordonez-habla-del-proceso-de-paz-el-gobierno-santos-la-ideologia-de-genero-y-el-plebiscito/495287/.

Semana (2016c), 'Plebiscito por la paz: El decisivo voto de los evangélicos', 17 September, https://www.semana.com/nacion/articulo/plebiscito-por-la-paz-el-voto-de-los-evangeli cos-es-decisivo-para-la-campana/494042.

Sistema Informativo del Gobierno (2016), 'Más de 100 líderes religiosos de todo el país le dicen sí a la paz', 4 July, http://es.presidencia.gov.co/noticia/160704-Mas-de-100-lide res-religiosos-de-todo-el-pais-le-dicen-si-a-la-paz.

Stedman, S. J. (1997), 'Spoiler Problems in Peace Processes', *International Security*, 22:2, 5–53.

Tabbush, C. and M. Caminotti (2020), 'Más allá del sexo: La ampliación de la oposición conservadora a las políticas de igualdad de género en América Latin', *LASA Forum: The Quarterly Newsletter of the Latin American Studies Association*, 51:2, 27–31.

Tiempo (2016a), 'Cartilla sobre discriminación sexual en colegios dividió al país', *El Tiempo*, 14 August, https://www.eltiempo.com/vida/educacion/cartillas-sobre-diversi dad-sexual-en-colegios-genera-debate-en-colombia-39931.

Tiempo (2016b), ' "Gina Parody trata de imponer sus creencias en la educación": Diputada', *El Tiempo*, 20 August, http://www.eltiempo.com/colombia/otras-ciudades/debate-entre-diputada-angela-hernandez-y-gina-parody-por-educacion-lgbt-31465.

Tiempo (2016c), 'Iglesia apoya rechazo a ideología de género en manuales de convivencia', *El Tiempo*, 9 August, https://www.eltiempo.com/archivo/documento/CMS-16668897.

Urbina Ortega, O. (2016), 'Comunicado sobre las orientaciones del ministerio de educación respecto a los manuales de convivencia de los colegios', 8 August, https://diocesisd ecucuta.com/diocesis2/comunicado-sobre-las-orientaciones-del-ministerio-de-educac ion-respecto-a-los-manuales-de-convivencia-de-los-colegios/.

Uribe Vélez, A. (2016), 'Frente al resultado del Plebiscito: Expresidente Álvaro Uribe Vélez', 3 October, https://alvarouribevelez.com.co/uribe-hoy/frente-al-resultado-del-plebiscito-expresidente-alvaro-uribe-velez/.

5

The Transnational Force of Anti-LGBT+ Politics in Latin America

SAMUEL RITHOLTZ AND MIGUEL MESQUITA

WALTER BENJAMIN FAMOUSLY conceptualised the winds of progress as a chain of events that does not necessarily follow a linear path toward peace, but instead brings new action that can represent even more destruction (Benjamin 2020). As Chapter 1 of this volume discusses, the rights of LGBT+ people in Latin America have been advancing in the last years; however, these gains are at risk. The emergence of a new transnational, far-right political order threatens to erase these guarantees and subject LGBT+ people to new and old forms of violence and discrimination. The rise of a right against rights that aims to stop and reverse LGBT+ equality throughout the region echoes Benjamin's warnings.

This chapter explores the actions through which anti-rights groups in Latin America have recently mobilised against queer- and gender-inclusive state practices. It looks at the genesis of this mobilisation and considers key inflection points in its history. In exploring this history, it seeks to explain an interesting puzzle: why has this movement produced such extreme action in response to seemingly benign efforts, such as national anti-bullying and 'homotolerant' education campaigns, in countries including Brazil, Colombia, Paraguay, and Peru?

To consider the role of LGBT+-inclusive politics in the consolidation of a right-against-rights mobilisation in the region, we examine how queer-inclusive efforts have been politicised by far-right actors. We identify a range of cases within the region to illustrate the various dynamics present within these anti-rights movements.[1] We start by reviewing Leigh A. Payne's (2000) analytical

---

[1] Not discussed in our examples but of potential interest to readers is the growing 'religious litigaton' literature where scholars document how religio-political groups engage in political debates that challenge their moral positions through strategic litigation. This phenomenon has been seen in the United States with recent Supreme Court decisions (e.g. *Dobbs v. Jackson Women's Health Organization*), as well in Latin American countries. In Argentina, several court cases were identified that attempted to criminalise abortion (Monte and Vaggione 2019). In Brazil, the attempted judicialisation against same-sex

Proceedings of the British Academy, **255**, 98–111, © The British Academy 2023.

THE TRANSNATIONAL FORCE OF ANTI-LGBT+ POLITICS   99

framework for uncivil movements – and how the framework has been adapted in Chapter 2 of this volume – to understand how these anti-rights movements framed and mobilised around queer and trans subjects. We use Payne's analytical approach to identify the unique political opportunities produced by social constructions associated with LGBT+ progress. In the first section on naming, we identify how LGBT+ advancements produced the opportunity for political entrepreneurs to activate grievances. Here we explore the situation in Brazil to show how naming a grievance became an effective political tool for anti-LGBT+ rights mobilisation. In the section on blaming, we explore how political homophobia had a productive capacity to produce new social coalitions in a variety of Latin American contexts. In the following section on aiming, we consider the case of a controversy against gender-inclusive education in Colombia to show how the right against rights mobilised a large social contingency to protect the 'innocent'. In this section, we introduce the construction of *childfamilynation* to reinforce how the figure of the child or the family signifies a nation's body politic within these movements. And finally, in the section on claiming, we consider how the success of these movements facilitates their transfer to other contexts. With these constructions better understood, we connect how the questions of progress for LGBT+ people can be escalated to broader debates on the future of the nation.

Countermovements, Uncivil Movements, and LGBT+ Subjects

In Chapter 2 of this volume, Payne updates her theoretical approach to uncivil movements (2000) to include a broader set of right-against-rights mobilisations in Latin America. Using the updated framework, the majority of the right-against-rights mobilisations discussed in this chapter would be considered countermovements, as they mobilise wide coalitions in response to real or perceived social progress at the local or national level. For our analysis of anti-LGBT+ countermovements, Payne's original formulation (which is expanded upon in Chapter 2) continues to provide a compelling analytical framework, nonetheless. The movements she describes are political groups that employ 'both civil and uncivil political action to promote exclusionary policies' (2000, 1). They are 'uncivil' because they resemble authoritarian movements from Latin America's past. At the same time, however, they 'mimic social movements by mobilizing around identity, exclusion and marginalization, and unconventional political actions', and in so doing create new cultural

---

marriage can be seen in the court case *ADIN n. 4.966*, put forward by the Social Christian Party against the decision of the Supreme Court to legalise unions between same-sex partners. Nevertheless, the courts in countries more connected to liberal and human rights traditions have been playing an important role in guaranteeing rights relating to sexual orientation, gender identity, gender expression, and sex characteristics (SOGIESC) and reproductive rights, as opposed to being a venue to limit these rights.

and value-laden identities – including narratives around being a ' "disenfranchised" constituency' (2000, 17–18) that attract and mobilise new members to join them (2).

Payne's theoretical approach explores 'how uncivil movements manipulate democratic symbols, discourse, practices, and institutions to gain power within democratic societies and governments' (2000, 19). To do so she explores how 'they frame political threats, use those threats to justify uncivil political action, and generate myths to counteract their own violent image' (21). Uncivil movements 'generate political threats and opportunities out of fairly banal sets of events' (21), which they present as a grave threat. They 'effectively frame the political threat' by drawing on cultural cues associated with a violent or authoritarian past that can legitimise their purported uncivil action. Framing is a four-part process of naming a grievance, blaming a source of the grievance, aiming at a target to lobby, and claiming a win to justify their uncivil action. To frame these political threats, uncivil actors draw on recognisable movements from the past, including cultural cues, to create a foundational threat that establishes the need for a group identity or unity. Uncivil movements reference 'cultural villains' of the past and identify shared '[symbols] of evil', then blame them for contemporary threats, 'feelings of insecurity, betrayal, and discrimination' (2000, 25). And finally, they create narratives that deny or ignore the movement's uncivilness, facilitating legitimating myths that 'provide a "civil" justification for pragmatic supporters to join uncivil movements' (2000, 30).

Contemporary anti-rights backlash in the region can be effectively analysed using the original uncivil movement theoretical framework identified by Payne. The right-against-rights mobilisation around LGBT+ efforts at achieving equality is more than a 'countermovement' because it intends not only to block or reverse movement gains, but also to eliminate LGBT+ rights-seekers, as Payne shows in Chapter 2. For example, the case could be made that some of the more violent anti-LGBT+ mobilisation in Brazil, which was bolstered by the election of Jair Bolsonaro and referred to as a 'homocaust' by activists, could be considered an uncivil movement. But, as Payne notes, uncivil movements can exist within countermovements.

In this chapter, we consider the role that LGBT+ inclusion plays in the framing, cultural cues, and mythmaking of this anti-rights movement. We continue to draw on cases throughout the region, all tied to the so-called 'gender ideology' moral panic to illustrate the precarity of LGBT+-inclusive interventions in the country. The organisers of the moment frame their movement against the grievance of 'gender ideology'. They blame either the governments in power or opposition parties for promoting this ideology, and then target a seemingly benign effort as an opportunity to produce a referendum on this fake threat.

The success of these efforts throughout the region has become a legitimisation tool for anti-rights movements as a means to access power. These efforts are notable for their transnational characteristics and successes. Actors throughout the region replicate the same cultural cues that associate queer and trans advancement as a threat to the child/family, and the conflation of respect for sexual and gender

THE TRANSNATIONAL FORCE OF ANTI-LGBT+ POLITICS   101

diversity with *castrochavismo* and Marxism – political projects associated with the leftist rebel groups in the region, as well as the perceived 'enemy' states of Venezuela and Cuba (Gómez-Suárez 2016). These framings and cues, combined with disinformation tactics, were able to modify the tenor of debate in countries through the region and produce new myths in different societies that framed social progress as a direct threat to children, the future of any nation, and the family, the foundation of any nation.

The contribution of this chapter is thus to identify and analyse the unique role that LGBT+ inclusion played in inflaming these movements and facilitating the transition from changing social order to existential threat. In this sense, we build on Payne's framing to argue that LGBT+ progress can produce opportunities for actors to use political homophobia as a broad coalition-building mechanism that fuels anti-rights backlash in polarised societies.[2] In what follows, we work through the steps of Payne's uncivil movements framework in order to trace the process of how LGBT+ efforts become targets of anti-rights mobilisation, as well as the impacts of this process.

Naming: The Production of the Perfect Storm

This section demonstrates how LGBT+ advancements on the national as well as international level served as a scapegoat for a broader socioeconomic discontent in the Americas as articulated by anti-rights groups. We propose that these groups took advantage of moments of discontent, distrust, and disenchantment with traditional political parties and the politicisation of culture in the region (Žižek 2008). These moments are produced not only by social conditions but also by economic and political conditions and can easily be replicated in other countries confronted by similar contexts. In this sense, LGBT+ rights have served as a political kindling for these movements. To explore properly how LGBT+ advances can be 'named' as a grievance, we examine the conditions that produce this effective framing. These advancements activate grievances that conservative actors manipulate in order to reproduce discontent (Žižek 2008). This new cleavage produces a unique symbiosis between the goals of conservative religious groups and the rhetoric of political actors in their joint efforts to identify the new 'enemy'. To flesh out these dynamics further, we draw on examples from Brazil, Colombia, and Peru.

At the turn of the 21st century, many countries in Latin America experienced a 'pink tide'. Brazil, Uruguay, Chile, Venezuela, Ecuador, Mexico, and Bolivia elected leftist national governments who promised to deliver economic growth, enhance social development, and decrease inequality (Castañeda 2006). To accomplish these tasks, many countries advanced on legal and juridical frameworks that

---

[2] Here we use Bosia and Weiss's (2013) definition of political homophobia as the instrumentalisation of homophobia for political goals. We understand polarisation to mean a spread of attitudes that cleave to binary positions perceived to be opposite.

sought to protect and promote recognition of human rights, including those based on sexual orientation, gender identity and/or expression, and sex characteristics (IACHR 2018). Nevertheless, many of these governments struggled to deliver on – or at least were not able to accomplish in a short timeframe – promises to redress the impacts of neoliberalism and conservative attitudes about rights.

During this period of leftist rule, the Brazilian government sharply reduced the number of people living in extreme poverty (Tabosa *et al.* 2016). In addition, its Ministry of Health introduced effective instructions to guarantee gender-affirming surgeries for trans people through its public national health system, and the Supreme Court ruled in favour of same sex-marriage recognition (Calixtre and Vaz 2015; IACHR 2018). As a result, these advances became the source of politicisation and 'boundary activation' by political actors in the country who were able to 'name' growing social inclusion as a threat to the country's established middle class. During this time, an article published in a national Brazilian newspaper criticised the 'popularisation' of international tourism, which now could be enjoyed by the new middle class, specifically citing doormen and housekeepers (Leão 2012). The subtle discriminatory tone of the article connected to a broader cultural critique of a government that cared more about building a new middle class than meeting the needs of the existing one (Žižek 2008). This commentary revealed a disconnect between a government and its people: tolerance developed in government institutions occurred without corresponding social or cultural change in attitudes among the broader population.

Frustrations in Brazil were exacerbated by the 2008 global economic crisis, which greatly impacted the region's middle class. This worsened the discontent with and distrust of elected representatives, and fuelled a combustible crisis of democratic representation in the country. The 'wind of progress' then became a storm. These two big factors – a government-led push for progressive social change and an economic crisis – deeply polarised Brazilian society. During the 2018 presidential elections, certain politicians warned of the deterioration of traditional family values as a scapegoat for the situation that was afflicting a great portion of the society (Agamben *et al.* 2011). As reported by UN Women, 'the family is a key to the economic and the moral dimensions connecting the erosion of the public, the backlash against gender and democracy' (Biroli 2019, 3). These tensions created the perfect opportunity for extreme political actors to manipulate the construction of the 'other' as the 'enemy'. Chantal Mouffe labels this Schmittian conception of using politics to identify an enemy in a changing society as 'antagonistic pluralism' (Mouffe 2004; Schmitt 2008).

The denial of pluralism, or adoption of antagonistic pluralism, in Brazilian society made it more susceptible to co-option by extreme politics (Mouffe 2004). During Brazil's 2018 presidential elections, candidate Jair Bolsonaro attacked the PT government for its gender-inclusion programme in schools as undermining traditional Brazilian family values. He evoked the 'gay kit' label for this gender-inclusive programme (see de Souza Santos (Chapter 6)). The campaign became polarised. Language and labels became important instruments in the discourse

THE TRANSNATIONAL FORCE OF ANTI-LGBT+ POLITICS 103

of the far-right candidate, as they allowed him to politicise culture and unite conservatives in a movement called 'Escola sem Partido' (School without Party), which sought to strip any kind of 'ideological education' from schools (IACHR 2018). Unfortunately, social progress became a target through which political actors with the support of conservative groups could name a new 'self' and 'other' in Brazilian society.

This antagonistic pluralism whereby anti-right mobilisations targeted 'gender ideology' as the enemy was not unique to Brazil, but occurred throughout the region during this time period. In 2016, the Minister of Education in Colombia was forced to resign after a controversy that ensued after she promoted an anti-discrimination curriculum – at the order of the Constitutional Court – in public schools (see Corredor (Chapter 4)). As in Brazil, Colombian religious groups, supported by key politicians, framed the policy as an attempt by the state to promote homosexuality in schools, and to 'turn children gay'. This incident had a knock-on effect. In a shock to the international community, the 2016 plebiscite to approve the Colombian peace accords with the FARC rebels was rejected by citizens. An important element of the 'No' vote included the same coalition of actors united against the peace deal on the grounds that its gender-sensitive ('gender ideology') approach threatened the family. That the document did not include such language was ignored. Anti-rights framing became a powerful tool of political mobilisation against a specific target, whether an education minister or a historic peace accord.

These events in Colombia mirrored similar events that took place in Peru in opposition to a new basic education curriculum, which included LGBT+-inclusive education. Groups related to religious institutions connected with politicians in the country and launched several protests in 2016 and 2017 that united people in the streets against the teaching of inclusive pedagogy. Named 'Con Mis Hijos No Te Metas' (Don't Mess with My Kids), the group used money from evangelical groups to promote media campaigns against alleged 'gender ideology', arguing that such an education would make their children question their 'natural gender' (Meneses 2019). This coalition between religious groups and politicians expanded throughout the region, helping to elect politicians who sought to deepen the polarisation as a political strategy. In Peru, members of these right-against-rights coalitions mobilised in the run-up to the general election of 2020 and the presidential election of 2021. Similar events transpired in Paraguay, where the government, with support from a range of politicians, ultimately issued a regulation banning 'gender ideology' and any inclusive pedagogy from use in the schools (IACHR 2017).

During the 2017–18 Costa Rican presidential election, and even after the release of an Inter-American Court on Human Rights Advisory Opinion calling for states to ensure the rights of LGBT+ people, almost all political parties participating in the election adopted the rhetorical strategies opposing 'gender ideology' in an attempt to win the election. During the election, the neo-Pentecostal National Restoration Party (PRN) won the first round with a candidate who was openly conservative and used religious, anti-feminist, homophobic, xenophobic discourse. This candidate ultimately lost the presidential election, however, because of a cultural clash with

Catholic faith groups, as well as the political mobilisation of civil society around LGBT+ rights (Arguedas-Ramírez 2018). This defeat of the PRN in Costa Rica by a broad coalition of actors highlights that counterprogress and backlash are also not linear. Still, this practice of naming a grievance associated with gender-inclusive programming continues in other countries throughout the region, particularly in election years, with both Paraguay (IACHR 2017) and Guatemala (IACHR 2022) serving as other examples.

Blaming: The Formative Potential of Political Homophobia

As evident in these anti-rights mobilisations in Brazil, Colombia, Peru, and Costa Rica, blaming queer- and trans-inclusive social efforts for political or socio-economic ills produces a unique opportunity for anti-rights groups to mobilise to advance broader uncivil political goals in diverse coalitions within Latin America. This section underscores how the activation of grievances produced by 21st-century political homophobia has created a new constellation of actors never seen before in Latin America, especially the creation of a broad religious right that includes both Catholics and evangelicals. We outline the growing unification of certain political and religious interest groups that seek to activate grievances by blaming or scapegoating LGBT+ progress.

The reactionary mobilisation against LGBT+ progress in Latin America is a result of the region's history of progress. Javier Corrales suggests that the success of LGBT+ movements in securing rights is a function of their ability to force political debates, which, in turn, positively impacts public opinion. He cites a study that shows that between 2010 and 2014, people's tolerance for homosexuality improved by 12.3 percentage points, which he attributes to the expansion of public debate on the subject during this time (Corrales 2017). The potential for success on LGBT+ rights, he argues, is heightened in a context of 'competitive political parties, federalism, and independent and progressive courts' (76). Rafael de la Dehesa (2010) has documented how LGBT+ activists in Mexico and Brazil have worked with health agencies and legislators to advance progress. In line with this institutional approach, much progress in the region has also occurred through court rulings inspired by impact litigation strategies. But this public debate and alliance with government institutions has left progress open to the risk of countermobilisation (IACHR 2018). As Chapters 1 and 2 of this book show, right-against-rights mobilisations in the region have catalysed behind even slight gains in LGBT+ rights to heighten 'moral panic' in society.

These anti-LGBT+ countermovements have taken moments of top-down, government-mandated inclusion to produce a securitisation framing that positions LGBT+ progress as a threat, which they refer to as 'gender ideology'. Fernando Serrano-Amaya (2017) argues that this anti-gender-ideology movement has three components: a political strategy, a rhetorical/expressive approach, and an organised reaction/resistance to a changing social order. The concept of gender ideology was productive as a mobilisation tool for countermovements because the resulting political homophobia, as Serrano-Amaya (2017) notes, 'has a formative dimension'. This anti-rights movement has demonstrated the capacity to unite disparate social sectors around a consensus on social issues, creating a new, broader mobilisation category that could manifest as backlash. Corrales (2015) notes that this movement has been uniquely able to unite disparate religious and faith-based groups, who in the past have clashed around other social issues. Alliance between Catholics and evangelicals, two of the largest religious groups in the region, are notable because this type of coalition was once rare and has far-reaching implications because of how much of society it includes. Though these groups may disagree on a range of other issues, they unite in their rejection of queer- and gender-inclusive social progress.

This group's mobilisation around the frames of 'family', 'child', and 'nation' is not unique to the region. As Kristopher Velasco (forthcoming) notes, these three frames appear regularly as part of a global transnational effort to curb LGBT+ rights. Gender-ideology right-against-rights mobilisations have successfully created (or reinvigorated) a major cleavage in Latin American societies: placing LGBT+/feminist activists on one side and the 'believer-citizen' on the other (Vaggione 2017). This cleavage could be understood as what Charles Tilly calls a boundary, or a social fault line between two groups, that could be activated by political entrepreneurs (Tilly 2003). The leaders of this anti-rights movement, often prominent politicians, activate this boundary through the assertion of a moral panic that cleaves society between two poles: those who consider themselves in support of LGBT+ rights and those who consider themselves in support of family values (Rodríguez Rondón 2017). Present in these comments is the latent threat to the constitutional order of the nation, understood by these actors to be linked to the heterosexual family unit (Curiel 2013). Thus, this changing social order is repurposed by anti-gender ideology countermovements as an existential threat produced by LGBT+ people and their allies.

Aiming: *childfamilynation*

It is no coincidence that many of the mobilising instances of anti-rights backlash happen as a result of state-sponsored inclusion in education settings. The position of schools as unique sites of social cleavages is not only tied to their nationalist role in 'educating future citizens of a nation', but is also due to their most prominent residents: children. Judith Butler has recognised the child as the 'martyred figure of an ostensibly selfish or dogged social progressivism' (2002, 21) in these cultural debates around inclusion. She notes that 'these arguments are not only fueled by homophobic sentiment but often focus on fears about reproductive relations, whether they are natural or "artificial", and what happens to the child'. As such, these debates become 'sites of intense displacement for other political fears, fears about technology, about new demographics, and about the very unity and transmissibility of the nation' (21).

Cindy Johana Quintero Garzón (2019) has identified three constructions of the child represented in the Colombian media: the vulnerable child; the child in need of intervention; and the happy, apolitical, redeemer child. These different representations all demonstrate how, according to Butler (2002, 22), 'one can see that the child figures in the debate as a dense site for the transfer and reproduction of culture'. Thus, with this transfer the child becomes a signifier of a broader societal anxiety as a result of a changing social order. Butler articulates that debates surrounding the rights of a child are often stand-ins for a bigger conversation on the future composition of a nation. She notes that the debate on gay marriage in France '[c]onverg[ed] with debates taking place on issues of immigration, of what Europe is, and implicitly and explicitly, of what is truly French, the basis of its culture, which becomes, through an imperial logic, the basis of culture itself, its universal and invariable conditions' (22).

In Colombia, these debates also emerged during a period of both political and social transition. As the then president, Juan Manuel Santos, engaged on an ambitious peace deal that sought to demobilise guerrillas and reintegrate them into the body politic, an opportunity arose for the political opposition to question who constitutes 'the nation'? While there may not be explicit conversations of racial purity when it comes to conceptualising the body politic, there are the old Cold War spectres of ideological purity and its many associations, which haunt this public debate (Corrales 2015). Public commentary from countermovement anti-rights campaigners associated gender ideology with an acceptance of deviancy or subversion that served as a threat to the 'true' body politic and nation.

These constructions set up a moral panic, which Roger Lancaster (2011) identifies as a response to a false, exaggerated, or poorly defined moral danger in society. Lancaster revisits 20th-century American society to see how the construction of certain 'public enemies', such as the sexual aggressor, the paedophile, and the Satanist, legitimizes punitive state action to purge society of these actors, as well as other minority populations associated with deviancy. In 'aiming' to punish state actors, such as the then Colombian Minister of Education, anti-rights groups can legitimise themselves as protectors of the innocent. Previously in Colombia, conservatives mobilised against feminist and LGBT+-inclusive thought by seeking to defend 'life' or the 'family', and this time around it had been extended to include the protection of the child (Mujica 2010; Rodríguez Rondón 2017). Waves of Colombian Constitutional Court decisions extending the legal definition of the family to include homosexual parents (for example, to allow for gay adoption) encouraged this transference of moral panic to the child (Rodríguez Rondón 2017). In Colombia, progressive thought on sexuality and gender – which was linked by countermovements to ideas of queer pedagogy in the case of the anti-discrimination curriculum scandal and so-called 'gender ideology' in the case of the peace accords – has thus become framed as a moral danger to youth in order to mobilise fear and produce a 'subtle synchronization of emotions' reacting to the existential threat of radical ideologies of inclusion (Rodríguez Rondón 2017, 138).

It is from these associations of the child as the future of a nation with the family as its bedrock that a new cleavage is formed (or an old cleavage reinforced) with its locus as the classroom. Similar to how Cynthia Enloe (1991) identifies the joint construction of *womenandchildren* as a central concept in the legitimisation of war in western discourse, anti-rights movements produce the construction of *childfamilynation* when framing opposition to LGBT+ and feminist causes. In this framing, LGBT+ inclusion becomes a placeholder for a new progressive ideology that threatens the fundamental, conservative conception of Colombian society, and the school-age child becomes a representation of the social body of the nation.

It is through this lens that framing can be made to create a new threat, where the Colombian state, as identified by ex-president Álvaro Uribe, is 'an abusive parent' and, as argued by ex-Attorney General Alejandro Ordoñez, 'is usurping the legitimate right of families to educate their children according to their values' (Rodríguez Rondón 2016, 2017). In their selective targeting of LGBT+-inclusive policies, right-against-rights mobilisations can rearticulate themselves from reactionary conservatives to proactive defenders. In their persuasive framing of their advocacy as in defence of children's rights, these groups absolve themselves of any public deliberation of harm caused by their efforts. The appropriation of a rights framing (framejacking) throughout the region has solidified this tactic as a means to roll back or block social progress for previously marginalised groups, mobilise a new base of actors, and produce new persuasive narratives of legitimisation (Payne, Chapter 2).

Claiming: The Transnational Nature of Backlash

In this section, we underscore the growing interconnectedness and success of the anti-LGBT+ rights mobilisation, highlighting its transnational elements of anti-LGBT+ countermovements. We provide a general mapping of this uncivil movement's expansion and highlight some of the growing strategies these movements employ to organise successfully at the regional and international level. We consider cases in Central America to show how the role of religious groups has produced opportunities for cross-border expansion once a success can be claimed.

Social progress on LGBT+ rights throughout much of Latin America is threatened by a growing transregional discourse by politicians, buoyed by the support and growing influence of religious groups, particularly evangelicals (Cordero *et al.* 2021). While politicians have used this polarisation to gain more power, evangelical churches have been enhancing their capacity to influence politics through the production of organisations, arguments, resources, and alliances in opposition to gender and LGBT+ rights (Corrales 2020). This entangled situation between politics and religion sets a new challenge for many Latin American states. According to Corrales, evangelicals are playing an important role in electoral politics. Álvaro Uribe in Colombia, Keiko Fujimori in Peru, and Jair Bolsonaro in Brazil relied on these groups to increase support for their governments and score

108 *Samuel Ritholtz and Miguel Mesquita*

political wins. And the development of the 'gender ideology' argument has been the leitmotif of a unifying process among different religious groups (Corrales 2020; Zilla 2018).

The success of the right against rights in the Latin American Catholic and evangelical churches has a transnational dimension. These religious groups maintain an extensive network in different countries that serves their interests. They are backed by organisations in the United States that train their personnel and provide them with extensive funding to support their agenda (Zilla 2018). In Guatemala, these groups backed a law that threatens the rights of LGBT+ people, women, and non-traditional families in 'defence of the family' (IACHR 2022). Moreover, the Guatemalan Congress, highly influenced by evangelical groups, installed a commission to remove the Ombudsperson for Human Rights after he supported LGBT+ rights at a time when the country declared itself the 'pro-life' capital of the world (Government of Guatemala 2022). In Honduras, a recent constitutional amendment was approved to make it impossible for any kind of future constitutional reform to overturn the ban on same-sex marriage (Padgett 2021). And in El Salvador, the president recently publicly opposed same-sex marriage (Angelo and Bocci 2021).

Many factors explain the expansion of gender- and LGBT+-rights backlash in Latin America. The aversion to rights connected to sexual orientation, gender identity and/or expression and sexual characteristics, and women's rights is not an isolated argument; it draws on deeply rooted sociocultural dynamics in these societies, where histories of colonialism and imperialism have rooted rhetorical narratives that can securitise social identities deemed 'subversive'. These groups have promoted their ideas though a very well-articulated network that gathers economic support to promote populist politicians, discourse, and even violent action. Politicians have taken advantage of this productive capacity of political homophobia to expand their base of electoral support and consolidate power. This alliance between religious groups and populist politicians proves to be mutually beneficial, and has served repeatedly as a blueprint for the transnational spread of right-against-rights backlash as these mobilisations continue to garner success.

Conclusion

This chapter has explored the transnational backlash against LGBT+ and gender inclusion in Latin America through the effective framing techniques utilised by right-against-rights mobilisations. Using Payne's (2000; Chapter 2 of this volume) framework, we have illustrated how anti-rights groups 'name' gender-inclusive state practices as representative of a perceived national decline and social threat. We look at how these actors 'blame' political leaders and LGBT+ communities for this issue, thereby producing new social alliances between previously unaligned parts of society. From there, we then consider how they 'aim' to remove any political actor that might threaten the perceived social body of

THE TRANSNATIONAL FORCE OF ANTI-LGBT+ POLITICS   109

the nation, epitomised by the construction *childfamilynation*. We conclude by revealing how the 'claims' of these movements within a country facilitate their transnational spread in the region.

The backlash of anti-rights movements against LGBT+ and women's rights should be placed in a broader perspective of the growing discontentment with neoliberal orders in much of Latin America. While governments in Latin America strive to deliver on certain commitments to their own populations, minor political actors politicise gender inclusion as a populist scapegoat for discontentment with poverty and inequality, which facilitates a synergy for conservative religious groups and secondary politicians to present populistic solutions to these problems. As the rise of Bolsonaro showed in Brazil, populist rhetoric, already fuelled by socioeconomic frustrations, can reach a fever pitch when political homophobia is used to channel these frustrations toward a new 'enemy' or perceived source of discontent.

The arguments made produce a self and an 'other', which turns vulnerable populations into enemies as opposed to compatriots. The logic of politics then achieves a Schmittian logic where the goal is the total annihilation of the other, and the discourse of 'defeating' the enemy contributes to an extreme polarisation of societies. In extreme cases, such as in Brazil, where activists have raised concern about a potential 'homocaust' of anti-LGBT violence in the wake of Bolsonaro's election, countermovements can produce radical factions that use uncivil movement techniques such as extralegal violence to actualise these prejudices. Moreover, the influence of religious groups from outside the region – mainly from the United States – further worsens polarisation and makes societies more susceptible to the politics of extremism because foreign actors' involvement further isolates mobilising anti-rights groups from their targets. As countermovements rely more on foreign support, there are fewer incentives to build social networks within society, further reducing the mechanisms of restraint.

Despite this concerning pattern, Benjamin's interpretation of the concept of history finds that winds of progress can occur even in a storm. While religious groups increase their effort to dial back the gains of LGBT+ and feminist progress, as evidenced in Costa Rica, new coalitions can sometimes come together in the face of great challenges and serve as Benjamin's 'angel of history', reviving pluralistic politics supported by civil societies that can maintain stability in the human rights progress achieved in recent years.

References

Agamben, G., A. Badiou, D. Bensaid, *et al.* (2011), *Democracy in What State?* New Directions in Critical Theory, 11 (New York, Columbia University Press).

Angelo, P. and D. Bocci (2021), 'Are Latin American Nations Turning Their Backs on LGBTQ+ Rights?', *Council on Foreign Relations*, 9 February, https://www.cfr.org/blog/are-latin-american-nations-turning-their-backs-lgbtq-rights.

Arguedas-Ramírez, G. (2018), 'Gender Ideology, Religious Fundamentalism and the Electoral Campaign (2017–2018) in Costa Rica', *Religion and Global Society*, 6 December, https://blogs.lse.ac.uk/religionglobalsociety/2018/12/gender-ideology-religious-fundamentalism-and-the-electoral-campaign-2017-2018-in-costa-rica/.

Benjamin, W. (2020), 'Theses on the Philosophy of History', in *Critical Theory and Society: A Reader* (London, Routledge), pp. 255–63.

Biroli, F. (2019), 'The Crisis of Democracy and the Backlash against Gender', expert paper, UN Women Expert Group Meeting, 25–6 September, https://www.academia.edu/41142806/The_crisis_of_democracy_and_the_backlash_against_gender.

Bosia, M. J. and M. L. Weiss (2013), 'Political Homophobia in Comparative Perspective', in *Global Homophobia: States, Movements, and the Politics of Oppression* (Champaign-Urbana, University of Illinois Press), pp. 1–29.

Butler, J. (2002), 'Is Kinship Always Already Heterosexual?', *Differences*, 13:1, 14–44.

Calixtre, A. and F. Vaz (2015), 'Nota técnica: PNAD 2014 – breves análises', *IPEA*, 22, 49.

Castañeda, J. G. (2006), 'Latin America's Left Turn', *Foreign Affairs*, 85:3, 28–43.

Cordero, M., D. Cariboni, and L. Ferreira (2021), 'US "Dark Money" Groups behind Mississippi Abortion Case Spend Millions Overseas', *openDemocracy*, https://www.opendemocracy.net/en/5050/us-rightwing-mississippi-abortion/.

Corrales, J. (2015), 'The Politics of LGBT Rights in Latin America and the Caribbean: Research Agendas', *European Review of Latin American and Caribbean Studies/Revista Europea de estudios latinoamericanos y del Caribe*, 100, 53–62.

Corrales, J. (2017), 'Understanding the Uneven Spread of LGBT Rights in Latin America and the Caribbean, 1999–2013', *Journal of Research in Gender Studies*, 7:1, 52–82.

Corrales, J. (2020), 'The Expansion of LGBT Rights in Latin America and the Backlash', in *The Oxford Handbook of Global LGBT and Sexual Diversity Politics*, ed. M. J. Bosia, S. M. McEvoy, and M. Rahman (Oxford, Oxford University Press), pp. 184–200.

Curiel, O. (2013), 'La nación heterosexual: Análisis del discurso jurídico y el régimen heterosexual desde la antropología de la dominación', *Maguaré*, 27:1, 310–13.

De la Dehesa, R. (2010), *Queering the Public Sphere in Mexico and Brazil* (Hanover, NH, Duke University Press).

Enloe, C. (1991), 'Womenandchildren: Propaganda Tools of Patriarchy', in *Mobilizing Democracy: Changing the US Role in the Middle East* (Monroe, ME, Common Courage Press), 29–32.

Gómez-Suárez, A. (2016), *El triunfo del No: La paradoja emocional detrás del plebiscito* (Bogotá, Icono).

Government of Guatemala (2022), 'Guatemala es oficialmente reconocida como Capital Provida de Iberoamérica', https://www.maga.gob.gt/guatemala-es-oficialmente-reconocida-como-capital-provida-de-iberoamerica/.

IACHR [Inter-American Commission on Human Rights] (2017), 'IACHR Regrets Ban on Gender Education in Paraguay', 15 December, https://www.oas.org/en/iachr/media_center/PReleases/2017/208.asp.

IACHR [Inter-American Commission on Human Rights] (2018), 'Advances and Challenges towards the Recognition of the Rights of LGBT+ Persons in the Americas', OEA/Ser. L/V/II. 170 Doc. 184, December, https://www.oas.org/en/iachr/reports/pdfs/LGBT+-RecognitionRights2019.pdf.

IACHR [Inter-American Commission on Human Rights] (2022), 'CIDH Saluda anuncio de veto presidencial a proyecto de ley "Protección de la vida y la familia" en Guatemala', March, http://www.oas.org/es/CIDH/jsForm/?File=/es/cidh/prensa/comunicados/2022/052.asp.

THE TRANSNATIONAL FORCE OF ANTI-LGBT+ POLITICS   111

Lancaster, R. N. (2011), *Sex Panic and the Punitive State* (Berkeley, University of California Press).

Leão, D. (2012), 'Cotidiano – Ser especial', *Folha de São Paulo*, 25 December, https://www1.folha.uol.com.br/paywall/login.shtml?https://www1.folha.uol.com.br/fsp/cotidiano/80046-ser-especial.shtml.

Meneses, D. (2019), 'Con Mis Hijos No Te Metas: Un estudio de discurso y poder en un grupo de Facebook peruano opuesto a la "ideología de género"', *Anthropologica*, 37:42, 129–54.

Monte, M. E. and J. M. Vaggione (2018), 'Cortes irrumpidas: La judicialización conservadora del aborto en Argentina', *Revista rupturas*, 9:1, 107–25.

Mouffe, C. (2004), 'Le politique et la dynamique des passions', *Rue Descartes*, 3:3–4, 179–92.

Mujica, J. (2010), 'La tradición y la vida: Sobre los grupos conservadores y la democracia contemporánea', in *El activismo religioso conservador en Latinoamérica*, ed. J. M. Vaggione (Córdoba, Ferreyra/CIECS), pp. 171–91.

Padgett, D. (2021), 'Honduras Makes Overturning Same-Sex Marriage Ban Near Impossible', *Out Magazine*, https://www.out.com/news/2021/1/28/honduras-makes-overturning-same-sex-marriage-ban-near-impossible.

Payne, L. A. (2000), *Uncivil Movements: The Armed Right Wing and Democracy in Latin America* (Baltimore, Johns Hopkins University Press).

Quintero Garzón, C. J. (2019), *Discursos acerca de la infancia y el acuerdo de paz en Colombia: Un relato de los lugares de visibilidad e invisibilidad de los niños en la prensa (2012–2016)* (Bogotá, Universidad Pedagógica Nacional).

Rodríguez Rondón, M. (2016), 'La infancia como símbolo y moneda de cambio', Centro Latinoamericano de Sexualidad y Derechos Humanos, http://www.clam.org.br/busca/conteudo.asp?cod=12437.

Rodríguez Rondón, M. A. (2017), 'La ideología de género como exceso: Pánico moral y decisión ética en la política colombiana', *Sexualidad, salud y sociedad*, 27, 128–48.

Schmitt, C. (2008), *The Concept of the Political* (Chicago: University of Chicago Press).

Serrano-Amaya, J. F. (2017), 'La tormenta perfecta: Ideología de género y articulación de públicos', *Sexualidad, salud y sociedad*, 27, 149–71.

Tabosa, F. J. S., P. U. de Carvalho Castelar, and G. Irffi (2016), 'Brazil, 1981–2013: The Effects of Economic Growth and Income Inequality on Poverty', *CEPAL Review*, 120, 153–70.

Tilly, C. (2003), *The Politics of Collective Violence* (Cambridge, Cambridge University Press).

Vaggione, J. M. (2017), 'La Iglesia Católica frente a la política sexual: La configuración de una ciudadanía religiosa', *Cadernos Pagu*, https://www.academia.edu/41142806/The_crisis_of_democracy_and_the_backlash_against_gender.

Velasco, K. (forthcoming), 'Transnational Backlash and the Deinstitutionalization of Liberal Norms: LGBT+ Rights in a Contested World', *American Journal of Sociology*, preprint available at https://osf.io/preprints/socarxiv/3rtje/.

Zilla, C. (2018), Evangelicals and politics in Latin America: Religious switching and its growing political relevance (No. 46/2018). SWP Comment, Stiftung Wissenschaft und Politik (SWP), Berlin.

Žižek, S. (2008), *Violence: Six Sideways Reflections* (New York, Picador).

6

'In the Name of the Family': The Evangelical Caucus and Rights Rollbacks in Brazil

ANDREZA ARUSKA DE SOUZA SANTOS

EVANGELICALS HAVE BECOME highly influential in Brazilian politics and society, succeeding in gaining political power by electing candidates to public office (Oro 2005; Rodrigues-Silveira and Cervi 2019; Ferreira and Fuks 2021). This chapter explores how some religious organisations have created a powerful bloc – and countermovement – capable of rolling back rights championed by social movements. It thus contributes to Payne's conceptual framework (Chapter 2) by outlining some of the mechanisms underlying the right-against-rights success.

I argue that in the case of evangelical movements, success can be related to organisational structure. I focus on the impact of a church structure common among evangelical denominations in Brazil where the church is subdivided into smaller units (church-in-cells) that provide members with a sense of belonging to an intimate community (Andrade 2010). Leaders of cells are trained for their role through a similar small-group alliance. A hierarchical pyramid structure evolves: the main leader organises a dozen subleaders; each of those subleaders organises a dozen followers of their own (this is called G-12), and so on until the bottom of the pyramid is reached. The structure reinforces a system that promotes obedience through the notion that good leaders must also be good followers. This chapter uses the church structure as a framework for understanding how evangelical churches in Brazil can form a powerful mobilisation with profound impact on the Brazilian Congress.

Right-against-rights countermovements promote politicians both within and outside church structures to influence political outcomes in efforts to roll back abortion rights and LGBT+ rights. A key argument is that LGBT+ rights pose a key threat to Christian families. Evangelical structures such as the one presented here can use such arguments in the making of political leaders. However, the argument of the chapter is that there are competing views in Brazilian society and within the Church on what a family is and how to defend its structure. Because of that, when

Proceedings of the British Academy, **255**, 112–128, © The British Academy 2023.

THE EVANGELICAL CAUCUS AND RIGHTS ROLLBACKS: BRAZIL   113

centring political efforts on debates around the topic, church followers often tilt against windmills – fighting enemies that do not exist – sensing a 'moral panic'. *Gender ideology* and the 'gay kit', or the perceived indoctrination of school children in Brazil to become gay, as I will explain, are examples of this moral panic (Lehmann 2021).

I build this argument by looking at three main points for discussion. First, the prosperity theology is oriented around securing power (da Costa 2020), including in politics. Second, promoting a positive image of the Church enhances trust and the capacity to control narratives regarding the family. Churches are among the most trusted institutions in Brazil, while the Congress is historically associated with distrust and corruption (Machado 2012). This means that candidates supported by churches or coming from churches have a moral advantage. The Church has acquired interpretative authority over certain emotionally charged topics, such as the family. A narrative of persecution of the (heterosexual) majority by a (LGBT+ or feminist) minority can unite evangelical congregations against these perceived threats to the family. Third, the religious-right nexus has consolidated a cross-party consensus around values. The Brazilian Congress is famously splintered into a large number of parties (Zucco and Power 2020), which typically prevents consensus. The Evangelical Caucus, in contrast, has united across party lines on key right-against-rights topics, specifically the family, reproductive rights, LGBT+ rights, and education (Lehmann 2021; Smith 2019). The caucus fixes on these political and social issues with the aim of gaining influence over them.

After presenting this argument, the chapter concludes by discussing the future of church politics in Brazil. I close by saying that Church and politics have different structures. The missionary vision of church-in-cells conflicts with politics; the Church aims to reach the heart of all, while politics take sides and makes enemies. The Church, moreover, is organised around leadership and obedience values, and may feel threatened by the very structure of politics with its divisions and fragmentation. In addition, church candidates portray narrow electoral bases, frequently switch parties, and have a propensity for corruption (Reich and dos Santos 2013). Corruption scandals involving church candidates potentially undermine the Church's trustworthy image, a key power resource. Last, and most importantly for this chapter, the Church-in-politics is also vulnerable with regard to its assumed monopoly over family protection against threats. No coherent definition of the family or threat has emerged. Neither have evangelical temples created a space for discussion on the topic. Members may find the Church's position at odds with their own self-interest.

A Note on Methodology

The research for this chapter involved a multi-methods approach. I interviewed members of Congress in Brasília in 2019 under an umbrella-ethics guideline

114   *Andreza Aruska de Souza Santos*

for this book that supported semi-structured recorded interviews. I only identify interviewees when I discuss specific passages of our conversations and when I have received authorisation to do so. I also looked at draft policies that are closely followed by the Evangelical Caucus in Brazil. The list of draft policies followed by the Evangelical Caucus was obtained through verbal request to a member of Congress who is part of the caucus. The list is a collection of draft laws publicly available, but constantly changing owing to the frequent creation of new draft laws. The list used for this analysis is from early 2019. I offer a brief analysis of key interests represented on this list. Finally, I selected churches organised in cells from a review of secondary literature. From this review, two temporal moments emerge. In the first, during the early 2000s, the church-in-cells vision gains traction within some evangelical churches. I examine those connected to G-12, which was introduced by Pastor Rene Terra Nova (although some of my interviewees have mentioned that the movement started in the Catholic Church), who still offers guidance to dozens of churches using this methodology. The second, in the 2010s, captures the period when evangelicals consolidated their position in Brazilian politics and advanced a conservative agenda in the corridors of power and on social media. I do not focus on one specific church, as the structure is common to different denominations. Some of the Brazilian churches that follow a cell structure are: Sara Nossa Terra Evangelical Church, Bola de Neve, Metodista, Evangelho Quadrangular, Igreja Internacional da Restauraçao, and Igreja Batista da Lagoinha, amongst others. Churches most commonly studied in Brazil, such as the Universal Church of the Kingdom of God, do not follow the same structure.

The Church Enters Politics, Not the Other Way Around

Although evangelical churches are known for their institutional fragmentation – e.g. new churches appearing, others merging, and unstable congregations (Ribeiro and da Silva Cunha 2012) – the pyramid model of church organisation described above is common among some prosperous evangelical churches in Brazil. The church-in-cells model is based on a missionary strategy aimed at overcoming non-believers' hesitance to enter a church temple. Meetings take place in family homes, are small in size (having usually between five and 10 people), and present easy and quick messages that are successful in attracting new members. A sense of belonging and a social bond are formed in these intimate settings that provide the foundation for conversion and new church membership.

The cell structure facilitates evangelism, but also facilitates the sharing of political messages. Leaders of cells who may not feel comfortable backing a political candidate on large electoral platforms do so in small gatherings where they present the church candidate to the cell members. Dos Santos Sousa (2020) discusses how political campaigns enter the cell structure by looking at the Igreja do Evanvelho Quadrangular in Pará. In his study, cell members are encouraged to give their details (identification number, CPF (a Brazilian unique tax identification number), and voting number – *título de eleitor*) to the leader if they agree to vote for the church candidate. Such details are non-binding and voting is secret in Brazil. By giving personal details, however, a sense of commitment, a kind of oath, is established. In addition, the cell is a place for bonding and belonging to a community, a description that supports the findings of Saroglou (2011). The author looks at the psychological dimensions of religion – cognitive, emotional, moral, and social – and sees that some aspects are universally present in religious forms, such as belief, bonding, behaviour, and belonging. This means that despite individual electoral freedom and secrecy, members' declared support for church candidates is secured through bonds and belonging, and a desire to avoid alienation from the group. Any opposition or dissent is hidden to protect the values of friendship, obedience, and a family environment cultivated by the Church. By discouraging open disagreement, the Church's narrative, unsurprisingly, remains uncontested by its members, at least in public (Ribeiro and da Silva Cunha 2012).

The Church thus allows politics in, but in a highly controlled mechanism. It holds the door open to let some select politics in, but closes the door to open politics and open political debate. In house gatherings, there is little space to oppose or even discuss candidates or their political positions. In turn, the large size of the congregation as well as the model of one-way preaching preclude open debate in the temple. Whereas dissent exists at the individual or personal level, open disagreement, debate, or confrontation are strongly discouraged within church confines. The monocratic structure closes off opportunities for democratic practices of contestation, debate, and change. The leadership structure and family-centric organisation, allows for church authorities to select acceptable candidates, even if followers will vote for someone else. Below, I describe this leadership structure, followed by how the family constitutes the core of church–politics relations.

Church Structure and Human Empowerment

The importance of religion in Brazil goes beyond territories of faith, celebrations of life and death, and the rites of passage in between. Most religious groups in Brazil have a charity component (Machado 2012). Social projects range from distribution of clothes, toys, and food, to visits to hospitals and prisons. In Spiritism (influenced by Allen Kardec), charity is a means for redemption from offences in previous lives, and it is common that those belonging to a religious group will participate in social causes through volunteer work or financial donations. Orphanages, nurseries, and hospitals are often entirely run by *espirita* volunteers; these members also tend to adopt orphaned children.[1]

---

[1] Catholics and Protestants too, especially in the 1980s under the theology of liberation that some identified with, had a strong social and human rights agenda (Machado 2012, 80). Some sectors of the Catholic Church largely led social movements' emergence in Brazilian peripheries during and after the military dictatorship.

116 *Andreza Aruska de Souza Santos*

There is a strong association between religion and vulnerable populations. The church becomes a shelter for the vulnerable; it aids and supports those excluded from the state's socioeconomic welfare policies or who face personal crises unrelated to the state, such as the death of a loved one, an illness, or the end of a relationship. Offering emotional shelter in a country where unemployment or precarious employment, domestic violence, shortage in healthcare, and mental health problems, to name a few, have left many scarred, means that religion reaches far beyond faith boundaries. Members join cells and the church (usually in that order) because they might be new to a city and need to make friends, or because they are going through life crises and need emotional support. If a family loss, job-related problems, loneliness, or a friendly invitation may explain a first visit to a cell, long-term commitments to the church need further examination. The formation of friendships, belief, bonding, and belonging, as Saroglou (2011) would put it, as well as loyalty to those who were around when support was needed, and the positive benefits of faith as a transformative power are among the reasons for sustained adherence to the church.

Loiola (2020), when studying the Sara Nossa Terra Evangelical Church in Brasília, which is structured in cells and uses G-12, demonstrated that the church grows because its leadership model works. Moving beyond a theology of prosperity, which I explain in detail below, the author refers to the temple he examined as a 'coaching church', emphasising that the church's capillarity (cells and G-12) allows leaders to know their members well and offer practical advice to improve their human potential. From time-management to financial planning, leadership includes training and motivational strategies, making the congregation a management-theology church-type. While other churches may fail to offer the same coaching that, for Loiola, is what makes that church unique, neo-Pentecostal evangelical churches usually do emphasise financial prosperity. Adherents to the theology of prosperity see in material rewards the symbol of God's grace (da Costa 2020).

Financial well-being epitomises blessing. To receive that blessing, a healthy lifestyle and assuming leadership roles in diverse areas of life are encouraged. Ribeiro and da Silva Cunha (2012), studying Bola de Neve church, recognise in the church-in-cells structure a way in which the church appeals to young people by promoting a kind of lifestyle. Sports, parties, and opportunities to socialise are offered to youths as a 'positive confession'. Whereas Christianity has long been associated with enduring suffering, adherents to prosperity theology see faith working toward success in various aspects of life, such as relationships, health, education, and finance. Poor members of the church who have not experienced financial gains are not, however, excluded or judged to be individuals without blessing. On the contrary, the church offers workshops and role models, working with those individuals to enhance their confidence, aspirations, and strategies for success (Loiola 2020).

A charity focus (collective aims) is thus not incompatible with entrepreneurship (individual gain). To become a leader and to achieve in all areas, including politics, is a sign of faith (Yong 2012). Empowerment is a result of faith, 'individual material and spiritual success is a reward for the committed believer' (Reich and dos Santos 2013, 7). In this way, the church targets the most vulnerable. Theology of prosperity, political engagement, and the defence of the vulnerable converge. The protection of the (vulnerable) family, perceived as under threat, thus demands collective political engagement.

Historically, different walks of faith have long supported those in situations of emotional and social vulnerability. In Brazil, then, it is not surprising that, when it comes to trust, families are named as the most reliable institutions, followed by the Church, an institution that has historically worked at closing gaps between the wealthy and the poor (Pew Research Center, as discussed in Machado 2012, 76). Politicians are near to the very bottom of the trust list, well after neighbours, the armed forces, and the media (Machado 2012, 76). An underlying contradiction seems to emerge around religion and politics. On the one hand, the population trusts the Church and not politicians. On the other hand, prosperity theology promotes the Church as an institution to protect and empower the vulnerable through political engagement. The mission to defend the family from threat becomes the means by which this contradiction is overcome, and the Church enters politics in the name of the family, as I discuss below.

In the Name of the Family

> Brazil is a Christian and conservative country that has its foundation in the family. God bless all! (Former president Jair Bolsonaro 2020)[2]

In this section I explore the timing of the move to frame the struggle by minority groups to obtain rights as a threat against the majority. I agree with a body of literature that emerged in Brazil, which identifies 2013 as a key moment when different views on sexual rights became more contentious (Payne and de Souza Santos 2020; Smith 2019; do Nascimento Cunha 2013; Saad-Filho 2013).

In the field of psychology, high intensity in religion is explored in theological, social, ritualistic, and political spheres (Wibisono *et al.* 2019a, b). Any group at a particular time may become extreme in faith, discourse, or action (Wibisono *et al.* 2019a). The model of church-in-cells and leadership through small groups, in general, reflects tolerance in ritual practices. Clothes, hair style, music, and dancing, amongst other things, resemble non-believers' practices (Ribeiro and da Silva Cunha 2012). However, extreme political views held by church members are sometimes out of the mainstream, especially after 2013. Two critical political rights issues emerged that prompted the evangelical church to become engaged in efforts to defend, in their view, the vulnerable family: abortion and same-sex marriage rights.

Brazil has a long history of contestation over abortion. Internationally, the framing of abortion rights as a public health concern gained traction in the 1970s; in Brazil this was the period of the dictatorship (1960–84). Although the military dictatorship had the support of Catholic religious groups, the struggle against the

---

[2] Former president Jair Bolsonaro, speech in the United Nations General Assembly, 22 September 2020.

military dictatorship was also particularly connected with the Catholic Church, thus slowing down the abortion rights struggle, which regained strength only in the late 1980s (Sarti 2004). Since the 1940s, abortion rights in Brazil have had legal protection under law in specific cases, such as a pregnancy following rape. Decriminalising abortion in all cases became a key emphasis for feminist movements, but the strategy adopted in the 1990s sought first to secure safe abortions for those whose rights were already protected (rape). At the time, the law did not require doctors to perform abortions in these cases, and many refused to do so. Advancing a universal right to a safe abortion seemed too ambitious in this context. The right to abortion advanced in slow motion in Brazil after the 1990s but gained speed in the 2010s, as I discuss below.

Same-sex marriage rights followed a similar process. Brazil has moved slowly in terms of adopting legal protections for the LGBT+ community, and same-sex marriage in particular (dos Santos Gonzaga and Brasil 2020). Advances since the 2000s in the legislature have mainly focused on protection against discrimination. When the Supreme Court advanced rights related to inheritance, adoption, and recognition of civil union between same-sex couples, it established equality for the LGBT+ community to enjoy the same civil rights as heterosexual couples (dos Santos Gonzaga and Brasil 2020).

Each of these rights faced opposition from the evangelical community and others. Conservative movements had long opposed the extension of abortion to all women and that of marriage rights to encompass same-sex relationships. On the other side of the spectrum, the main voice advancing such agendas in Congress came from representatives of the Workers' Party (PT), with well-known leaders Luiza Erundina and Marta Suplicy at the helm in the 1990s. The right against rights vociferously opposed politicians who promoted abortion and same-sex union rights. They mobilised against the rape case exception to the abortion law, claiming that women would lie about rape to receive a legal abortion. They claimed that abortion would become not an exception, but standard practice. Correspondingly, right-against-rights movements resisted same-sex marriage because it would force church leaders into celebrating same-sex marriages in their temples. The right against rights is thus not new in Brazil, but 2013 marked a watershed moment for this mobilisation. The countermovement to rights began to frame abortion and same-sex marriage as threatening the rights of the majority heteronormative family structure in the country.

This 2013 turning point occurred when the evangelical pastor and deputy Marco Feliciano (São Paulo State) assumed the presidency of the Human Rights and Minorities Commission (Comissão de Direitos Humanos e Minorias, CDHM). From that moment onwards, turmoil reached a crescendo in Congress. Most laws drafted by the CDHM address topics related to minors (childcare, sex education, minimum age for alcohol consumption, minimum age for criminal sentence, among others); civil union (marriage and divorce); and issues around abortion, adoption, and legal guardianship. Such topics first reach that commission when discussed in Congress, where bills are assigned a rapporteur by the president.

THE EVANGELICAL CAUCUS AND RIGHTS ROLLBACKS: BRAZIL   119

Political party leaders select the president of each thematic commission. Feliciano's party – the Social Christian Party (Partido Social Cristão; PSC) nominated him. The decision to offer the PSC the presidency of such an important commission came from another evangelical political leader, the then president of the Lower House, deputy Eduardo Cunha. Cunha was a sworn enemy of Brazil's president at the time, Dilma Rousseff, and of the PT.[3] As a party on the left, the PT would have been expected to promote a feminist and LGBT+ agenda. The PT's national connection with evangelical churches, however, meant that it back-pedalled on these issues. Nevertheless, naming Marco Feliciano as president of the CDHM was not only a political rupture with the left stronghold over that body, but a provocative one.

Feliciano was already known for his racist and homophobic comments (do Nascimento Cunha 2013). His appointment led to a massive outcry on social media on 7 March 2013 (the day he was elected CDHM president) against his leadership of a commission aimed to protect the rights of the minorities he openly despised. Hashtags such as #MarcoFelicianoNaoMeRepresenta (Marco Feliciano does not represent me) or #ForaFeliciano (Out Feliciano) became popular (Paiva and Nicolau 2013). Street protests included *beijaços*, or 'kiss-ins', where gay couples would meet and kiss in public.

Within Congress, Jean Wyllys, an openly gay deputy, embraced the campaign against Feliciano. On the other side of the aisle, right-wing members of Congress, such as future president Jair Bolsonaro, unknown at that time to the majority of Brazilians, declared support for Feliciano. The presidency of CDHM thus created two opposing sides and leading figures: Bolsonaro and Wyllys (do Nascimento Cunha 2013). In this heated political moment, the right-against-rights mobilisation consolidated. What had been a fairly muted opposition to the LGBT+ and feminist movements became fierce. Those social movements on the left were framed by the right-against-rights counter-movements as Christianophobic, heterophobic, and threatening to the family. The escalation of conflict can be seen through an analysis of the law drafting process.

The Making, Unmaking, and Remaking of Families in the Brazilian Congress

I looked at bills under discussion in the Brazilian Congress between 2010 and 2019, and analysed their content, distribution (rapporteur), and processing (*tramite*). To filter family projects within the universe of proposed laws, I followed those targeted by the Bancada Evangélica leadership. The Evangelical Caucus is a multi-party group formed by evangelical members of Congress. In 2019, they consisted of 195 deputies and eight senators from 20 different political parties (Câmara

---

[3] Cunha would later lead the charge for Rouseff's impeachment in 2016.

dos Deputados 2019). They increased in number since 2016, when they had 87 deputies and held three senatorial seats. Some deputies are pastors and elected by members of a church; others represent other conservative sectors (police, teachers, and others) but declare their alliance to positions taken by the Evangelical Caucus. There are also those who have a declared faith and are part of the caucus, but they do not vote based on religious concerns alone. LGBT+ and feminist movements also follow the same draft laws as the Bancada – civil union, abortion, adoption, etc. – but for opposite reasons. Therefore, this list of proposed laws is an ideal place for this research, as it groups together projects where both, increasingly polarised, sides were interested. The list of projects that I analyse was obtained in March 2019. It was organised in the following columns: topic (two-word classification), commission (the thematic commission where the proposed law was distributed for analysis), project type, author, party, state, short abstract.

Looking at the topic and short abstract of each of the 1,277 proposed laws followed by the Evangelical Caucus in 2019, the breakdown of keywords is as follows: gender (302), family (289), and sex (221) were the most frequent words. While words already give a sense of the most important discussions, I created 10 broad categories to group the most frequent projects. They are: addiction, sexuality, society and culture, race, gender, LGBT+, religion, education, family, and human rights. I coded words according to frequency, where I excluded prepositions; I offer a translation below:

Bebida alcoólica = addiction
Bebida = addiction
Fumo = addiction
Jogatina = addiction
Drogas = addiction

Sexual = sexuality
Exploração sexual = sexuality
Sexual pornografia = sexuality
Sexual prostituição = sexuality
Preconceito = sexuality
Planejamento familiar = sexuality
Ensino sexual = sexuality
Vida aborto = sexuality
Vida = sexuality

Social = society and culture
Aplicativos e redes sociais = society and culture
Cultura = society and culture
Entretenimento = society and culture

Raça etnia = race
Raça e etnia = race

THE EVANGELICAL CAUCUS AND RIGHTS ROLLBACKS: BRAZIL   121

Sexo gênero = gender
Sexo ideologia de gênero = gender

Homossexualismolgbt = LGBT+
Homossexualismo = LGBT+
Discriminação = LGBT+
Homofobia = LGBT+

Outras religiões = religion
Ensino religioso = religion

Ensino = education
Ensino integral = education
Ensino domiciliar = education
Bullying = education

Família sexual = family
Família = family

Direitos humanos = human rights

Figure 6.1 aggregates projects according to the topics. Among these categories I investigate family and sexuality first and foremost, as they are the most recurrent topics. I offer below a few examples of projects that demonstrate how the family is a contentious topic. I also show that the distribution of rapporteurs epitomises polarisation. Furthermore, conservatives viewed the LGBT+ movements not as a group claiming rights, but as one threatening their rights.

Sexuality

The law proposed by the evangelical deputy Eduardo Cunha of Rio de Janeiro, PL 7382/2010, aimed to criminalise discrimination against heterosexuals. The deputy reporting on the rejection of the project was Erika Kokay, a famous LGBT+ militant from the PT in Brasília, Federal District. A number of projects advancing homosexual marriage were proposed by Marta Suplicy and Jean Wyllys, both left-wing politicians. On condemning gender ideology, Marco Feliciano, from São Paulo state, indicated that promoting gender ideology should be considered a crime under PL 3235/2015, and he also condemned *nome social*, name change by transgender people, proposing PDC 17/2015 (PL and PDC are acronyms that refer to the type of law proposed). Eduardo Bolsonaro, from Rio de Janeiro state, recommended against having an LGBT+ committee in the Ministry of Culture through PDC 235/ 2015. Cabo Daciolo, also from Rio de Janeiro state, contended that the law should bar gender ideology from schools, as per PL 10577/2018. Most such proposed laws had the opposing side as rapporteur, and the battle would often gain television attention (do Nascimento Cunha 2013, Paiva and Nicolau 2103).

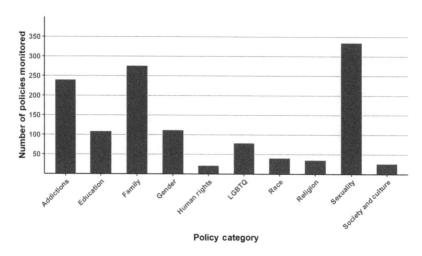

Figure 6.1 Draft laws on family in Brazil's Congress.

On abortion, Eduardo Cunha, from Rio de Janeiro, contended that compulsory support for victims of sexual violence encourages abortion in general, as discussed in PL 6033/2013. A similar proposal, PL 6061/2013, was offered by Congressman Hugo Leal, from the PSC, to replace the right to abortion with the right to information about the legal rights of victims of sexual violence. Several draft laws suggested punishment for women who seek abortion (e.g. PL 9104/2017, by Captain Augusto, from São Paulo). The evangelical Senator Magno Malta, in PSL 046/2017, suggested the criminalisation of abortion at any stage of pregnancy. In PL 4703/1998 it was proposed to make abortion a heinous crime, but rapporteur deputy Erika Kokay opposed it. Other proposals go in the opposite direction, expanding abortion services, such as PL 4403/2004, by Jandira Feghali from the Communist Party of Rio de Janeiro, who proposed decriminalising abortion when it is proven that the foetus is unable to live outside the mother's womb. The possibility of interrupting pregnancies in the Brazilian Health System (Sistema Único de Saúde; SUS) was detailed in INC 2627/2017, proposed by deputy Romulo Gouveia from a centrist party in Paraiba state, the Social Democratic Party. Marco Feliciano, on the other hand, defended the promotion of a 'National Day of Conscience against Abortion' in PL 5617/2016.

Issues related to sexuality exposed deep divisions within Congress. Proposed laws met fierce rejection from rapporteurs with little possibility of reaching agreement. On draft laws tagged as 'family' in the subject line, however, polarisation seemed less obvious.

Family

When looking at matters such as divorce, adoption, and domestic violence, sharp confrontations are not easily identified. For example, it is possible to say that among

THE EVANGELICAL CAUCUS AND RIGHTS ROLLBACKS: BRAZIL   123

44 draft laws clearly targeting domestic violence, centre and left-wing deputies were more dominant in initiating laws to prevent and define domestic violence, but clear opposition from conservative politicians did not emerge. On adoption, there seems to be a consensus on the need to speed up the process (e.g. PLS 031/2017, PLS 258/2014), guaranteeing a fair and fast process both to proposed adopters and to children.

Assisted reproduction techniques are also discussed under the broad 'family' umbrella. Most projects in this area are inclusive, e.g. supporting the expansion of the SUS to offer assisted reproduction as a basic health activity, as in PL 4725/2012, a proposed law by deputy Eleuses Paiva from the Social Democratic Party in the state of São Paulo. While PL 1184/2003 from Lucio Alcântara (from the Brazilian Social Democracy Party, Ceará state) seems to be restrictive, proposing the prohibition of surrogacy, that same draft proposes access to in-vitro fertilisation to those with genetic or infectious diseases.

What the examples above show is that there is a clear dispute over issues regarding sexuality, whereas those related to 'family' (adoption, domestic violence, assisted reproduction) usually reached a consensus. The fact that sexuality is disputed, but family is not, reveals a contradiction. I further analyse this aspect by looking at two specific cases: the highly disputed case of same-sex marriage, and the much less disputed field of assisted reproduction. What I found is that there is little resistance to in-vitro techniques of reproduction. This is in contrast to the right-against-rights mobilisation in the Inter-American human rights system as outlined by Kane and Moragas in this volume (Chapter 7).

Gamete donors are often members of same-sex couples. Lesbian couples frequently opt for in-vitro fertilisation where one partner offers the ovum that will form the embryo with donated sperm, and the other partner becomes pregnant. This process ensures that both are involved in the making of the baby (Thompson 2005). The use of fertility techniques by young and healthy homosexual couples is different from that of heterosexual couples using assisted techniques to conceive, often on account of perimenopausal or postmenopausal states, or other health issues. Such couples cannot always be donors to others, but young lesbian couples can. Heterosexual couples who hypothetically receive a gamete from a woman of same-sex orientation may follow a very different path from the same-sex donor couple outside a fertility clinic. Lesbian donors face legal obstacles in registering their civil union (Moreira 2012), in receiving a birth certificate (Campos Refosco and Guida Fernandes 2016), and in raising their child free from prejudice (Moreira 2012). Heterosexual recipients, however, face no legal barriers from the moment of conception. They may even denounce homosexual rights, not knowing who donated their ovum. Such an opinion that violates one's own interests can be the result of family platforms. In churches that suppress debate, broad understandings of bodily and emotional rights fail to emerge. In what follows, I discuss how some of those involved in disputes around sexuality and family were either fighting invisible enemies, or potentially producing arguments against their own interest.

124 *Andreza Aruska de Souza Santos*

Tilting at Windmills

> It penalises discrimination against heterosexuals and resolves that anti-discrimination public measures and policies pay attention to this possibility. (Eduardo Cunha, PL 7382/2010)

Projects to create the week of heterosexual consciousness or to criminalise perceived prejudice against heterosexuals reached a crescendo in Brazil in the 2010s. The logic behind such draft laws is that the struggle to overcome discrimination against homosexuals is equivalent to an attack on heterosexuals. Evidence does not back that view. 'At least 445 LGBT Brazilians died as victims of homophobia in 2017 – a 30% increase from 2016, according to LGBT watchdog group Grupo Gay de Bahia' (Cowie 2018). What these numbers represent is the violence against LGBT+ Brazilians and not documented claims of hate crimes aimed at heterosexuals. Heterophobia and Christianophobia are new terms in Brazilian politics used to mobilise the right against rights. The creation of an 'us'-versus-'them' situation led to the rise out of nowhere in the mid-2010s of political leaders, such as former president Jair Bolsonaro, achieving popularity for their defence of the family. What needs further investigation is who or what the enemy of the family is.

Family is an amorphous term in which everyone and everything represents harm or good. Draft laws opposing domestic violence are seen as promoting divorce. Anti-abortion projects may stimulate adoption. Draft laws that support in-vitro techniques of fertilisation stretch traditional boundaries of the body, science, and culture, but abortion is resisted using those same traditional notions of body, science, and culture. Contemporary kinship relations can include a pregnancy generated by more than two bodies. Parenthood can be denied to gamete donors; however, a heterosexual couple who make use of a sperm- or ovum-bank have legitimate parenting identities once the child is born (Thompson 2005). Assisted techniques for creating families show that heterosexual parenting has been biologically surpassed. The biological limits of parenthood have been technologically stretched. Reliance on intercourse for fertility and pregnancy is obsolete. Moreover, the Brazilian Congress agrees on the need to facilitate in-vitro techniques, an advance that supports heterosexual couples, though often it is often dependent on gamete donation by homosexuals. The support for assisted techniques for pregnancy, however, does not extend support for the interruption of pregnancy, even though in both cases the negotiation of the limits of the body is at stake. Cultural, physical, and technological prisms in the formation of a 'family' require dynamic negotiations. Debate over the notion of the family engaged the Evangelical Caucus in Congress, but such debate is stifled inside temples, as Deputy Israel (interview with the author, March 2019) explains:

> I cannot discuss with God, I cannot bring politics to God's house. I should not because that is not a space for discussion. That is a space for faith and belief. Faith is to believe. I do not need to think to have faith. This is the beauty of faith. But one cannot do politics without thinking. Those are different spaces. If a pastor defends a

candidate, he is authoritarian to the church, because if you disagree with the pastor, he will look at you and say: 'Are you praying enough, member?'.

Deputy Israel (Brasília) attracts votes within and beyond evangelicals. He is a member of a protestant church and a teacher. Education is his main platform. In a semi-structured in-depth interview in March 2019, Israel said that members of the church select candidates without debating complex family issues and, because of that, these church members are often tilting at windmills by fighting invisible enemies. He mentions current controversies about home-schooling, potentially to defend children against gay indoctrination, when the problem of education is actually the provision of schooling for the vast majority. Home-schooling is a privilege of an insignificant number of wealthy Brazilians who are able to afford it. To him, the creation of enemies to the 'family', and the bold tone used in the discussions, mobilise opinions and subvert priorities, as in the case of home-schooling against state school access. Another example is the defence of heterosexuality, when same-sex couples are the ones facing prejudice. When an important issue emerges, such as in the discussion of homosexual marriage, surrogacy, or in-family gamete donation, he explains, church politicians vote without any discussion in the temple: 'with god there is no discussion, but politics is the art of discussion'. Israel concludes that 'when we take politics to the church, we weaken both ... when religion embraces politics it gives up reaching the heart of all to have the heart of a few'.

Voting against one's own interest has already been the subject of analysis when looking at evangelical voting behaviour. In his Ph.D. dissertation, Victor Araújo (2019) discusses that evangelicals, although usually poor, may support an economic liberal right. This voting behaviour goes against their self-interest in public service provision and policies for poverty reduction – the platform of the left. Araújo explains that this is not an irrational voting behaviour, but that voters prioritise other moral agendas over economic gains. The argument presented in this chapter adds to Araújo's when it scrutinises the logic of a moral platform: although it is framed on the basis of an in-group–out-group narrative – us vs them, family vs family destruction, good vs evil (Smith 2019) – family rights are way more complex than that.

Conclusion

In Georg Simmel's essay on the bridge and the door, he highlights humans as a category that can only connect by means of separation. When we see a river that separates, we connect the two riverbanks with a bridge. Similarly, a door both closes us off and frees us (Simmel 1994). In this chapter I have discussed how evangelical churches-in-cells have simultaneously opened the door to politics but closed the door to political discussion and debate within the church. I show how politics and contention are on two separate banks. The bridge has not been built. Appealing to the vulnerable and providing protection for the fundamental values of family and the Church against perceived threat has involved closing the door on critical political debate and shoring up the Church's bank, rather than building bridges.

The success of the evangelical right-against-rights movement in Brazil has depended on this controlled engagement with politics. But the structure has not delivered unmitigated success. Electoral strength and control over congregants have influenced political decisions and legitimised divisive language and actions. Contradictions have emerged over the efforts to roll back rights for vulnerable people, especially the LGBT+ community. With evidence of corrupt practices by leaders in the evangelical church and its political bloc (Reich and dos Santos 2013; Hirabahasi and Cury 2022), the bond of trust that sustained an effective support of the Church in politics may become eroded. This is not to say that abortion and LGBT+ rights are safeguarded, but rather that opportunities exist to exploit the inherent weaknesses in right-against-rights mobilisations. In addition, for religion, a focus on political agendas may restrict rather than amplify its congregation, limit the reach of faith-messages, and create enemies.

References

Andrade, E. S. (2010), 'A visão celular no governo dos 12: Estratégias de crescimento, participação e conquista de espaços entre os batistas soteropolitanos de 1998 a 2008', M.Sc. dissertation, Universidade Federal da Bahia.

Araújo, V. (2019), 'A religião distrai os pobres? Pentecostalismo e voto redistributivo no Brasil', Ph.D. dissertation, São Paulo State University.

Câmara dos Deputados (2019), 'Frente Parlamentar Evangélica do Congresso Nacional', https://www.camara.leg.br/internet/deputado/frenteDetalhe.asp?id=54010.

Campos Refosco, H. and M. M. Guida Fernandes (2016), 'Same-Sex Parents and Their Children: Brazilian Case Law and Insights from Psychoanalysis', *William & Mary Journal of Women and the Law*, 23:2, 175–84.

Cowie, S. (2018), 'Violent Deaths of LGBT People in Brazil Hit All-Time High', *Guardian*, 22 January, https://www.theguardian.com/world/2018/jan/22/brazil-lgbt-violence-deaths-all-time-high-new-research.

da Costa, O. B. R. (2020), 'Mais que vencedores: As dinâmicas socioeconômicas nas/das igrejas neopentecostais', *Revista idere*, 12:3, 271–85.

do Nascimento Cunha, M. (2013), 'The Place of Media in the Process of Imaginary Constructions of the "Enemy" in Marco Feliciano Case', *Comunicação, midia e consumo*, 10:29, 51–76.

dos Santos Gonzaga, A. and D. R. Brasil (2020), 'Ativismo judicial: Meio necessário para criação e efetivação dos direitos fundamentais nas relações homoafetivas/Judicial Activism: The Necessary Way for Creating and Enforcing the Fundamental Rights in the Homoaffective Relations', *Brazilian Journal of Development*, 6:1, 1010–28.

dos Santos Sousa, D. D. (2020), 'Das casas ao congresso, igrejas nos lares: Um estudo sobre o modelo de células na igreja do evangelho quadrangular em santarém-pará', *Revista labirinto (unir)*, 32, 167–89.

Ferreira, M. G. M. and M. Fuks (2021), 'O hábito de frequentar cultos como mecanismo de mobilização eleitoral: O voto evangélico em Bolsonaro em 2018', *Revista brasileira de ciência política*, 34, 1–27.

THE EVANGELICAL CAUCUS AND RIGHTS ROLLBACKS: BRAZIL 127

Hirabahasi, G. and Cury, T. (2022), Justiça confirma prisão de pastores suspeitos de esquema de corrupção no MEC', CNN Brasil, 22 June, https://www.cnnbrasil.com.br/politica/justica-confirma-prisao-de-pastores-suspeitos-de-esquema-de-corrupcao-no-mec/.

Lehmann, D. (2021), 'Ritual, Text and Politics: The Evangelical Mindset and Political Polarisation', in *A Horizon of (Im)possibilities*, ed. K. Hatzikidi and E. Dullo (London, University of London Press), pp. 103–20.

Loiola, J. R. A. (2020), 'Neopentecostalismo e a "teologia de gestão": Uma leitura sociológica do "ethos" religioso da Igreja Sara Nossa Terra no Distrito Federal (1992–2018)', Ph.D. dissertation, Universidad Estadual Paulista, São Paulo.

Machado, M. D. D. C. (2012), 'Evangelicals and Politics in Brazil: The Case of Rio de Janeiro', *Religion, State and Society*, 40:1, 69–91.

Moreira, A. J. (2012), 'We Are Family! Legal Recognition of Same-Sex Unions in Brazil', *American Journal of Comparative Law*, 60:4, 1003–42.

Oro, A. P. (2005), 'The Politics of the Universal Church and Its Consequences on Religion and Politics in Brazil', trans. E. J. Romera, from *Revista brasileira de ciências sociais*, 18:53, 53–69, http://socialsciences.scielo.org/pdf/s_rbcsoc/v1nse/scs_a05.pdf.

Paiva, F. and M. Nicolau (2013), '"… e o Marco Feliciano não me Representa": As múltiplas formas de um meme no Instagram', in *XV Congresso de Ciências da Comunicação na Região Nordeste* (São Paulo, Sociedade Brasileira de Estudos Interdisciplinares da Comunicação), https://www.portalintercom.org.br/anais/nordeste2013/resumos/R37-0207-1.pdf.

Payne, L. A. and A. A. de Souza Santos (2020), 'The Right-Wing Backlash in Brazil and Beyond', *Politics & Gender*, 16:1 (*Special Symposium on Women's Parties*), 32–8.

Reich, G. and P. dos Santos (2013), 'The Rise (and Frequent Fall) of Evangelical Politicians: Organization, Theology, and Church Politics', *Latin American Politics and Society*, 55:4, 1–22.

Ribeiro, L. M. P. and D. da Silva Cunha (2012), '"Bola de Neve": Um fenômeno pentecostal contemporâneo', *Horizonte: Revista de estudos de teologia e ciências da religião*, 10:26, 500–21.

Rodrigues-Silveira, R. and E. U. Cervi (2019), 'Evangélicos e voto legislativo: Diversidade confessional e voto em deputados da bancada evangélica no Brasil', *Latin American Research Review*, 54:3, 560–73.

Saad-Filho, A. (2013). 'Mass Protests under "Left Neoliberalism": Brazil, June–July 2013', *Critical Sociology*, 39:5, 657–69.

Saroglou, V. (2011), 'Believing, Bonding, Behaving, and Belonging: The Big Four Religious Dimensions and Cultural Variation', *Journal of Cross-Cultural Psychology*, 42:8, 1320–40.

Sarti, C. A. (2004), 'O feminismo brasileiro desde os anos 1970: Revisitando uma trajetória', *Revista estudos feministas*, 12:2, 35–50.

Simmel, G. (1994), 'Bridge and Door', *Theory, Culture & Society*, 11:1, 5–10.

Smith, A. E. (2019), *Religion and Brazilian Democracy: Mobilizing the People of God* (Cambridge, Cambridge University Press).

Thompson, C. (2005), *Making Parents: The Ontological Choreography of Reproductive Technologies* (Cambridge, MA, MIT Press).

Wibisono, S., W. R. Louis, and J. Jetten (2019a), 'A Multi-Dimensional Analysis of Religious Extremism', *Frontiers in Psychology*, 10, article 2560.

Wibisono, S., W. Louis, and J. Jetten (2019b). 'The Role of Religious Fundamentalism in the Intersection of National and Religious Identities', *Journal of Pacific Rim Psychology*, 13.

Yong, A. (2012), 'A Typology of Prosperity Theology: A Religious Economy of Global Renewal or a Renewal Economics?', in *Pentecostalism and Prosperity: The Socio-Economics of the Global Charismatic Movement*, ed. K. Attanasi and A. Yong (New York, Palgrave Macmillan), pp. 15–33.

Zucco, C. and T. J. Power (2020), 'Fragmentation without Cleavages? Endogenous Fractionalization in the Brazilian Party System', *Comparative Politics*, 53:3, 477–500.

7

Framejacking Rights Discourse to Undermine Latin American Multilateral Human Rights Institutions

GILLIAN KANE, MIRTA MORAGAS, AND KIRAN STALLONE

THIS CHAPTER ANALYSES the ways in which the right against rights has impacted the world's oldest regional body – the Organization of American States (OAS) – and its Inter-American Human Rights System (IAS), comprising the Inter-American Commission on Human Rights (IACHR) and the Inter-American Court of Human Rights (IACtHR). The focus on right-wing movements has tended to be on their domestic politics. This is true in this volume on Latin America, as well as in the scholarship on Europe and the United States. Where an international dimension appears, it is largely around transnational advocacy networks (Keck and Sikkink 1998) that resist rights violations, with one exception in Clifford Bob's (2011) work on the 'global right wing'. There are very few academic studies on the impact of right-against-rights mobilisations on global multilateral institutions (see, however, Panotto (2020); Soley and Steininger (2018); Urueña (2019)). As demonstrated in this chapter, these institutions are increasingly vulnerable sites of contestation. Their efforts at promoting and protecting rights for marginalised groups are under attack by powerful and organised countermovements.

Conceptually, we draw on the notion of the right against rights to refer to *'collective extra-institutional and institutional mobilisation to check, roll back, or reverse specific rights promoted by previously marginalised groups and communities (i.e. gender and sexuality, ethnic, race, environment, accountability for crimes against humanity) and to restore, promote, or advance a status quo ante of traditional political, social, economic, and cultural rights'* (Escoffier, Payne, and Zulver (Chapter 1)). The right against rights that we examine moves beyond national borders to have a broader – regional – impact on the resistance to change. It falls into the category of a countermovement, in the sense that it 'aim[s] to roll back, reverse or block social movements' "undeserving" gains, and to promote an

Proceedings of the British Academy, **255**, 129–140, © The British Academy 2023.

130   *Gillian Kane, Mirta Moragas, and Kiran Stallone*

alternative set of rights … believe[d] to be fundamental and "worthy", such as the right to life, rights of the family, and religious rights' (Payne (Chapter 2)).

This chapter demonstrates that the right against rights is determined to expand and create an impact beyond national boundaries. Global anti-rights groups, and religious right-against-rights countermovements in particular, are on the rise worldwide (see Ritholtz and Mesquita (Chapter 5)). They have gained strength and traction. Multilateral Latin American human rights institutions, which were historically attentive to human rights issues in response to advocacy and demands for accountability from progressive civil society movements, are now being targeted by right-against-rights actors, who have developed the capacity to resist human rights gains. They do so by using the right-against-rights devices identified in this volume: forging alliances, mobilising, and appropriating social movements' rights language in an effort to undermine those rights. Put differently, these global mobilisations 'counter' social movements using those movements' own tactics (Payne (Chapter 2)). The appropriation of language is known as 'framejacking' (Bob 2011, 30), or the use of already existing social-movement language for an entirely different – even opposite – purpose. By specifically targeting the promotion of LGBT+ rights and sexual and reproductive rights, these countermovements reframe and accuse the OAS–IAS of violating fundamental rights, such as family rights, the rights of the unborn, the right to life, the right to religious freedom, and sovereignty rights.

To develop this analysis, the chapter first provides a brief background on the OAS–IAS and the emergence of religious anti-rights countermovements within them. It then analyses the use of right-against-rights discourse within the OAS General Assembly (GA) through the lens of framejacking, providing concrete examples of discourse appropriation in this space with textual evidence, as well as five anonymous interviews with high-ranking officials and activists who regularly participate in OAS spaces.[1] The subsequent section then takes an in-depth look at the potential impact of framejacking via an examination of coordinated anti-rights efforts and their use of sovereignty and anti-imperialistic discourse to successfully limit financial resources within the IAS. This anti-rights 'success' story reveals the vulnerability of the institution itself, as well as the possibility for more anti-rights action and more extensive rights reversals in the future. The chapter concludes with a discussion of recommendations on how to strengthen the OAS–IAS and safeguard them from future co-optation.

Background on the OAS–IAS and the Rise of Countermovements

The OAS was founded in 1889 and matured into its current iteration in 1948. This was the same year the United Nations adopted the Universal Declaration of Human

---

[1] All interviews for this chapter were carried out within the book project framework with individuals who are in leadership positions at non-governmental or intergovernmental organisations that regularly work in OAS spaces, including GAs.

Rights, and three years after the end of the Second World War. These events are meaningful; the OAS was designed to provide a conduit for strengthening continental security, peace, and democracy, while nurturing economic, social, and cultural development. It was also created to provide a space for civil society engagement across the Americas.

The OAS includes Latin American and Caribbean member states, as well as the United States and Canada. The OAS–IAS adjudicates issues and cases that impact and inform human rights at the national and regional level in Latin America through its two main bodies: the IACHR and the IACtHR. Civil society participation is encouraged through the GA, the OAS's main body for developing policy. The GA, IACtHR, and IACHR have all advanced human rights standards related to equality and non-discrimination.

The OAS has historically attended to global human rights issues and trends, including, in recent decades, sexual and reproductive health and rights. Until 2013, its regional human rights advocacy encountered little resistance. However, that year marked a dramatic shift. Since 2013, right-wing civil society organisations have engaged forcefully within the IAS and have begun challenging the OAS's mandate on rights promotion. While the OAS–IAS's human rights agenda and institutional structure are in large part responses to progressive social movements and government responses to the horrors of the Second World War, the recent right-against-rights mobilisation constitutes a direct challenge to this structure. This mobilisation has worked to block and roll back advances in women's rights, sexual and reproductive rights, and LGBT+ rights.

The right-against-rights countermovement in the OAS–IAS is primarily led by transnational alliances of Christian and secular organisations, including the Congreso Iberoamericano por la Vida y la Familia, Alianza Evangélica Latina, Alliance Defending Freedom, Con Mis Hijos No Te Metas, Human Life International, Frente Joven, Concerned Women for America, and CitizenGo. A unique feature of these alliances is their political partnerships outside Latin America, including the United States. They organise transnationally to challenge OAS–IAS advances on human rights, abortion rights, and LGBT+ rights. They have criticised the institutions' interpretations of human rights, parental rights, and national sovereignty. Using these arguments, they have tried to weaken OAS–IAS multilateral bodies and systems that advance and protect human rights issues.

The main site for the countermovement mobilisations analysed in this chapter is the OAS GA. The GA annually convenes all member states and is open to civil society groups to engage in dialogue over security, democracy, and human rights concerns such as gender equality, immigration, environment, Indigenous and Afro-descendant issues. These meetings also include a budget review, elections for new commissioners and judges, and the setting of policy for OAS agencies. Each of the 35 member states is entitled to send a delegation, and they have the mandate to participate in most OAS decisions, reached by consensus. Historically, member states participating in the GA have tended to approve resolutions on sexual and reproductive rights without major objections. Indeed, by 2008, the GA

132   *Gillian Kane, Mirta Moragas, and Kiran Stallone*

had become a progressive space for forwarding resolutions condemning discrimination on the basis of sexual orientation and gender identity. This was enabled by the vibrant participation of civil society representatives from the LGBT+, feminist, and women's movements.

The 2013 GA in Antigua, Guatemala, altered that course. Anti-rights groups arrived en masse to participate in the meetings. A right-against-rights alliance formed and attempted – without success – to block GA approval of the Inter-American Convention against All Forms of Discrimination and Intolerance (OAS 2013a) and the Inter-American Convention against Racism, Racial Discrimination and Related Forms of Intolerance (OAS 2013b).[2] They had objected to provisions within both conventions that included legal protection for people based on their sexual orientation, gender identity, and expression.

While the right-against-rights networks failed to block the two conventions, they nonetheless demonstrated their potential to impact this space; the 2013 GA set the groundwork to establish a foothold for their active and strengthened engagement in future assemblies. Since then, and in each subsequent GA, right-against-rights groups have increased their participation and coordination among themselves, while deepening their contacts with member states. They have also demonstrated their ability to adapt and modify strategies creatively. Initially they presented themselves as concerned secular organisations, even though many were backed by the Catholic Church. But by 2017 there was a shift, and blocks of evangelical groups emerged as the prominent anti-rights leaders at the GA, forming an identifiable 'Christian' alliance.

Beginning in the 1970s, the rise of evangelicals in the Americas, specifically US political advocacy and overseas outreach, is well-documented (Turek 2020, 181–8). A 2019 report by the Instituto de Estudios Sociales and Konrad Adenauer Stiftung on 'Evangelicals and Political Power in Latin America', for example, dates the growth of evangelical political participation to the 1980s, attributing that growth to outsized US evangelical influence. Considered 'religious sects', evangelicals operated on the political, geographic, social, and economic margins of Latin American society. Evangelical leaders over time began converting 'religious capital' into 'political capital'. This led to a burgeoning political movement, with a 'moral agenda (pro-life and pro-family)' at its core that successfully 'transcended denominational barriers' (Perez and Grundberger 2018, 12; de Souza Santos (Chapter 6)). Far-right evangelical leaders began mobilising politically and forging alliances around 'the only issue that could pull the great majority of Latin America's evangelicals together ... the moral proposal: pro-life and pro-family, and anti-abortion, anti-homosexual marriage and anti-"gender ideology" in general' (Perez and Grundberger 2018, 132). These moral issues also united previously competitive groups of evangelicals and Catholics. They worked together

---

[2] If there is no consensus, resolutions can be put to a vote. This almost never happens. In this case, the Conventions were approved in the GA without the right against rights succeeding in blocking them.

strategically during sessions at the GA, appropriating a rights discourse to reverse gains by women's and LGBT+ movements. This chapter looks at these far-right religious groups and their impact on the OAS–IAS.

Countermovements' Appropriation of Discourse in the GA

The strategic use of discourse involves the notion of 'framejacking' (Bob 2011, 30), through which the far-right Christian mobilisation within the OAS–IAS appropriated social movement rights language to fight against those very rights. Through distortions of prior social movement discourse, right-against-rights countermovements adapted previous rights language in new ways to attempt to overturn access to rights (Payne (Chapter 2)). The Christian anti-rights groups analysed in this chapter strategically used rights language (the right to life, children's rights, the right to family, freedom of religion, and national sovereignty rights (Panotto 2020)) to shift the debate and create an anti-rights environment within the OAS–IAS.

Policy leaders and activists who participate in OAS spaces commented that far-right-wing religious movements have been regularly using these linguistic tools to reverse rights gains. For example, a non-profit leader who has been to at least six OAS assemblies stated of far-right religious anti-rights groups: 'They started using the same terms. For example, the "criminalisation of something" or the "violation of the rights of some people"'. She then said that these far right-wing evangelicals are 'masters in storytelling'. Echoing this, a different OAS activist shared that such groups are highly coordinated and work together in articulated ways to strategise how to present their arguments; in particular, 'They talk about liberty, they talk about civil rights, they talk about freedom, and so on, but from a conservative perspective.' Another pointed out that such linguistic constructions are a way for anti-rights groups to manoeuvre within the OAS: specifically that a 'persuasive argument for that forum means it has to be based in rights [language]'.

At the 2019 GA, we see examples of such framing around the right to and protection of the family as a linguistic tool for right-against-rights appropriation. Fátima Oliva, an Evangelical Alliance member, spoke out against an LGBT+ rights resolution and asked member states not to sign in favour. At the OAS assembly, she framed her arguments around 'human rights', specifically the protection of children and prevention of 'the destruction of the family'. She stated: 'What we are seeing is very shameful … As women and men of faith we came here to defend our generation; to not allow children to be confused, or young people to be confused and taken to extremes. That is why as a church, as believers, we are here at the OAS Assembly' (*Evangelico Digital* 2019). During the 2018 GA the previous year, anti-rights coalitions similarly framejacked discourse to develop anti-abortion arguments. The Brazilian Coalition stated that it did 'not believe in development without the valorisation of the right to life and family', and implored the GA not to approve of directives supporting the legalisation of abortion or gay marriage (OAS 2018).

134   *Gillian Kane, Mirta Moragas, and Kiran Stallone*

Anti-rights groups have also strategically used a discourse on freedom of religion to attempt to roll back rights (Urueña 2019). A former OAS adviser to commissioners who witnessed many OAS gatherings noted that the Peru-based movement Con Mis Hijos No Te Metas (Don't Mess with My Kids) – one of multiple religious far-right-wing movements active in OAS spaces – focuses on freedom of religion in order to push back against rights gains.[3] She said that far-right movements such as Con Mis Hijos No Te Metas send representatives to OAS gatherings, including GAs, and receive cross-national funding and encouragement from right-wing religious conservatives from Argentina, the United States, Ecuador, Bolivia, Brazil, and Colombia. She noted that members of Con Mis Hijos No Te Metas, as well as other far-right religious groups, 'argue about freedom of religion and their right to educate their kids without the state interfering'. Another high-ranking organisational leader who regularly works in OAS spaces shared that religious faith is the driving force behind many demands to roll back rights, and that some (but not all) far-right religious groups consider themselves to be driven by a 'divine mandate' and base their actions on this.

These are just a few examples of how religious groups have framed religious views using rights language before the OAS. The use of this type of rights language is the kind of framejacking used by the right against rights to appropriate rights language used by those advancing rights to roll back those rights (Payne (Chapter 2)). In the aforementioned cases, while the groups did not successfully roll back rights as a result of their framing and presentations at the OAS, they shifted established discourse on human rights by introducing and legitimising regressive rights narratives into civil society and member states' debates. However, as illustrated by the anti-sovereignty framing analysis that follows, Christian groups have managed to weaken the OAS in other ways through discourse construction and coordination.

Framejacking to Reduce OAS Funding: Countermovements' Use of National Sovereignty and Cultural Imperialism Arguments

The OAS is funded by all member states, with the United States shouldering most of the financing – at over 40 per cent – as of 2017. Historically, the USA has benefited from playing this supportive role because the OAS typically aligned its position with US policy aims (Meyer 2018). However, this alignment has eroded in the last 15 years, because of disagreement on political crises such as Venezuela and Cuba, and in part because of the growing independence of member states. As a result, conservative forces within the US Congress have begun to question continued funding for an intergovernmental agency that no longer serves US

---

[3] For more on this religious group see Ritholtz and Mesquita (Chapter 5).

interests (see Lankford 2018). Congresspeople backed by far-right religious groups have begun to utilise discourse on threats to national sovereignty and cultural imperialism to question and call for reduced funding to the OAS–IAS. Activists and leaders interviewed for this chapter shared that sovereignty arguments are increasingly being used by the right against rights. This section narrates how politicians across nations backed by anti-rights groups used discourse on the right to sovereignty to secure reduced funding to the OAS.

In 2016, Senators Marco Rubio (Republican, Florida) and Mike Lee (Republican, Utah) drafted a letter to Secretary of State John Kerry. In it, they presented the OAS as a promoter of 'cultural imperialism' oriented against national self-determination, and questioned its integrity as a multilateral human rights institution. On 3 October of that year, the two senators held a press conference urging the 'State Department to re-examine the way US contributions to the Organization of American States (OAS) are utilised in light of ongoing concerns [that] the UN-backed entity is pushing an ideological agenda' (Rubio and Lee 2016). The senators were more concerned with their own ideological agenda than accuracy: the OAS is not, nor has it ever been a 'UN-backed entity'. The senators went on to claim that they 'have heard from Central and South American officials that their own national sovereignty is threatened by what they view as "cultural imperialism" imposed by an organisation that is seemingly more concerned with pushing an ideological agenda than respecting the local rule of law' (Rubio and Lee 2016).

The letter singled out the IACtHR, the IACHR, and the Inter-American Commission of Women (CIM), and focused on the landmark *Artavia Murillo* decision. That case ordered Costa Rica to end its ban against in-vitro fertilisation (IVF), rejecting Costa Rica's argument that embryos enjoy full human rights and personhood. Though broadly about IVF, the court's interpretation of the right to life transformed the case, and it became a hot-button reference point on the issue of abortion and reproductive rights in Latin America (CRR n.d.). Directly after mentioning the court's ruling on IVF in Costa Rica, Rubio and Lee said that the 'United States, through its sizable contribution to the general funds of the OAS is directly responsible for funding these attacks on national sovereignty and the rule of law' (Rubio and Lee 2016).

In subsequent paragraphs, the Rubio–Lee letter continued to focus on state sovereignty and the OAS: 'Whatever one's views about IVF, there is no justification for an international entity to impose its views on this issue on Costa Rica'. Ties between Rubio and Lee and conservative US anti-rights groups run deep. On his website, Rubio notes he sponsored a religious freedom resolution with the Alliance Defending Freedom (ADF) and the Family Research Council: two American conservative Christian legal groups that are anti-abortion; anti-LGBT+ rights; and, in the case of ADF, active at the OAS. Lee has also supported several ADF bills, including one to protect individuals who claim a religious objection to same-sex marriage. Most recently, Lee was linked to ex-president Donald Trump's illegal efforts to overturn the 2020 elections, which he lost to President Joe Biden (Rupar 2022).

The two senators concluded their letter by requesting a briefing and detailed information on the OAS budget. One year later, in 2017, Senator Lee joined forces with Texas Republican senator Ted Cruz to express alarm once again that US taxpayer dollars were going overseas to the OAS to advocate for abortion in an act of 'ideological colonialism' (Cruz and Lee 2017).

In December 2018, the demands to reduce US funding for the OAS continued. Nine staunchly anti-abortion US senators sent a letter to Secretary of State Mike Pompeo expressing concern over US funding for the IACHR and the CIM (Lankford 2018). This time, fears about abortion were centre stage, and the letter accused the two agencies of directly contravening US law through their support for the OAS: 'Time and again, IACHR and CIM have taken it upon themselves to be at the vanguard of those lobbying for the legalisation of abortion in a region where a great majority of the member states have chosen to protect the right to life in their constitutions' (Lankford 2018). The letter went on to state that it 'is the duty on the part of the OAS to respect the sovereignty of member states', and that 'sovereignty is the inherent right of nations to live according to their own values'. It ended with a plea to defund both organisations: 'we respectfully request the funding of those organs of the OAS, which are aggressively lobbying in favour of abortion, be stopped immediately through a proportional reduction in the United States contribution to the OAS general fund ... We also request a complete halt to all US voluntary fund contributions specially designated to those organs.'

But it was not only senators who were calling to defund the OAS–IAS during this period. Two months after the senatorial letter was published, on 14 February, Alfonso Aguilar, president of the International Human Rights Group, presented before the House Committee on Foreign Affairs, Subcommittee on the Western Hemisphere, at a hearing on 'Advancing US Interests through the Organization of American States'. While making a tacit nod to the importance of the OAS, his presentation became a rebuke of the IACHR and IACtHR, claiming that their 'intromissions' into 'the internal affairs of member states understandably cause great concern in the countries of the region and are perceived as an attempt against their sovereignty and constitutional order', while accusing the Court of 'judicial activism'. His speech ended with a call to ask that the USA 'demand that none of our funds are used to finance the Court' (GPO 2018).

The following month, on 13 March, the National Hispanic Christian Leadership Conference hosted a 'Justice Summit' at the Museum of the Bible in Washington, DC. Speaking at the gathering was Aguilar again, who is also a board member of ADF. Echoing Senator Cruz's earlier language around 'ideological colonialism', Aguilar lamented 'cultural colonialism' and said he was working closely with the Trump administration and its OAS ambassador, Carlos Trujillo, who personally told him that the administration was considering cutting funding to the IACHR. He added that it was important to build more partnerships with high-level politicians. Aguilar concluded his presentation saying 'We have, at the end, to reclaim human rights' (Montgomery 2019). Thirteen days later, on 26 March

2019, Pompeo reduced funding for the IACHR and the CIM (International Justice Resource Center 2019).[4]

There is a clear link between civil-society-led right-against-rights advocacy at the OAS and like-minded government stakeholders who move their agenda forward. Aguilar and others have cultivated these relationships for years. They telegraphed their intentions to defund the OAS as early as 2015 at a key networking conference for civil-society and government leaders in Washington, DC. The Political Network for Values Regional Summit for the Americas included over 120 conservative parliamentarians from Latin America, Spain, and the USA, including representatives Jeff Fortenberry (Republican, Nebraska) and Chris Smith (Republican, New Jersey). The event was sponsored by ADF; CitizenGo; and Aguilar's organisation, the International Human Rights Group. Speakers at the event expressed grave concern about the IACtHR and IACHR, worried that they were intervening in issues of national sovereignty. It was at this meeting that Aguilar proposed that activists begin working to stop the USA funding the OAS, insisting this needed to be a priority (Kane, private communication).[5] Ironically, the one-day meeting ended with cocktails at the OAS building, one of the most elegant buildings in Washington, DC.

These examples reveal the ways in which conservative anti-rights movements advanced their rights agendas through alliances and elite membership in the high ranks of United States and Latin American governments, and how the right wing's use of framejacked discourse ultimately led to reduced funding and support for IAS bodies. Put differently, elite leaders from member states are promoting the discourse of anti-rights groups and advancing the discourse of 'national sovereignty' to weaken the OAS–IAS mandate. Paradoxically, the sovereignty argument is not heard frequently when it comes to intervening in internal affairs of the states, or when the debate is transferred to the political setting, for example when dealing with Cuba and Venezuela. In other words, sovereignty seems to serve right-wing elites only to limit states' responsibility in upholding human rights.

Conclusion

This chapter has explored the ways in which conservative OAS member states, non-governmental organisations, right-wing Christian churches, and political parties have worked – often together – to reduce the power of the OAS and IAS. Through examining these examples of anti-rights activism at the OAS, three trends become evident: the growing influence of anti-rights religious groups, transnationally coordinated anti-rights mobilisation, and the manipulation of secular human

---

[4] For more information see Stull (2018).
[5] G. Kane, internal report to Ipas Partners for Reproductive Justice, 25 October 2015.

rights frameworks to advance religious agendas. By presenting a series of examples, the chapter has demonstrated right-against-rights countermovements' strategic deployment of rights discourse in order to limit rights advancements through the OAS–IAS.

At the GA, right-against-rights organisations have sought to limit advancements in sexual and reproductive rights. Although they have not yet made substantial gains against women's groups or LGBT+ organisations, they have contributed to an anti-rights environment, and they have shifted the dialogue in the OAS through framejacking. The subsequent and more in-depth study of anti-imperialism and sovereignty discourse reveals that these groups do have the potential to damage more than dialogue, however. They seek to hobble the IAS itself through defunding efforts, and by embedding within the system conservative leadership with regressive positions on gender and sexuality. We see a renewal and reinvigoration of their strategies, methods of organisation, and discourses to broaden their message and reach a wider audience. Also worrisome is the rapid growth of the evangelical movement in this space, which mirrors the political growth of the evangelical movement in Latin America and its influence in government settings.

Recent political wins for progressive movements and parties in several countries in Latin America will probably lead to continued backlash (Payne (Chapter 2)), as well as to more roadblocks to expanding human rights in the Americas. To this end, it is necessary to continue supporting and ensuring the sustainability of progressive sectors, feminists, and LGBT+ organisations in the OAS's political space. This is where decisions are made that directly impact the functioning of the IAS. In order to strengthen the presence of these progressive sectors, it is crucial to understand the strategies of anti-rights groups, as well as to strengthen progressive strategies and discourses. Several policy leaders and activists interviewed for this project also underscored that it is important to keep dialogue open. By keeping dialogue and debate open, and encouraging pluralism, the idea is to prevent even deeper hostilities from developing and truly to understand where motivations to roll back rights come from (Urueña 2019). Finally, activists and policy leaders interviewed underscored the need to engage with more progressive religious groups, many of which can help to broaden dialogue with the rigid, radical right-wing religious groups discussed in this chapter.

In 2019, the then US Secretary of State, Mike Pompeo, launched the Commission on Unalienable Rights to address discrepancies across human rights claims: 'As human rights claims have proliferated, some claims have come into tension with one another, provoking questions and clashes about which rights are entitled to gain respect' (Reuters 2019). This chapter has revealed the ways in which these clashes play out in OAS spaces, as well as the potentially huge impact of framejacked discourse. Moving forward, advocates for LGBT+ and sexual and reproductive rights must be aware of these tensions and the ways in which anti-rights movements are reframing rights discourse to their own advantage.

References

Bob, C. (2011), *The Global Right Wing and the Clash of World Politics* (Cambridge, Cambridge University Press).

CRR [Centro de Derechos Reproductivos] (n.d.), 'FIV en Costa Rica', https://reproductiverights.org/sites/default/files/documents/FIV-EN-COSTA-RICA_SPN.pdf.

Cruz, T. and M. Lee (2017), 'In Trump Era, It's Time to Reassess Western Hemisphere Alliances', *Houston Chronicle*, 22 June.

Evangélico Digital (2019), 'Fátima Oliva: 'En la OEA se promueve destruir la familia', 27 June, https://www.evangelicodigital.com/latinoamerica/8315/fatima-oliva-en-la-oea-promueven-la-confrontacion-hombre-mujer-y-la-destruccion-de-la-familia.

GPO [US Government Publishing Office] (2018), 'Advancing US Interests through the Organization of American States: Hearing before the Subcommittee on the Western Hemisphere of the Committee on Foreign Affairs House of Representatives. One Hundred Fifteenth Congress, Second Session', https://www.govinfo.gov/content/pkg/CHRG-115hhrg28645/html/CHRG-115hhrg28645.htm.

International Justice Resource Center (2019), 'US Resists International Oversight, Reduces IACHR Funding over Reproductive Rights', 8 April, https://ijrcenter.org/2019/04/08/u-s-resists-international-oversight-reduces-iachr-funding-over-reproductive-rights/.

Keck, M. E. and K. Sikkink (1998), *Activists beyond Borders: Advocacy Networks in International Politics* (Ithaca, Cornell University Press).

Lankford, J. (2018), 'Senator Lankford Leads Letter to Secretary Pompeo', 21 December, https://www.lankford.senate.gov/news/press-releases/senator-lankford-leads-letter-to-secretary-pompeo.

Meyer, P. J. (2018), 'Organization of American States: Background and Issues for Congress', 14 March, https://fas.org/sgp/crs/row/R42639.pdf.

Montgomery, P. (2019), 'Hispanic Evangelicals and Allies Hold "Justice Summit", Cheer Mike Pence', *Right Wing Watch*, 20 March, https://www.rightwingwatch.org/post/hispanic-evangelicals-allies-hold-justice-summit-cheer-mike-pence/.

OAS [Organization of American States] (2013a), Inter-American Convention against All Forms of Discrimination and Intolerance, https://www.oas.org/en/sla/dil/inter_american_treaties_A-69_discrimination_intolerance.asp.

OAS [Organization of American States] (2013b), Inter-American Convention against Racism, Racial Discrimination and Related Forms of Intolerance, https://www.oas.org/en/sla/dil/inter_american_treaties_A-68_racism.asp.

OAS [Organization of American States] (2018), 'Resumen de presentaciones de coaliciones de la sociedad civil y de actores sociales, 26 June, http://www.oas.org/es/49ag/docs/presentaciones-coaliciones/Insumos-de-Coalicion-49-Asamblea-General-OEA.pdf.

Panotto, N. (2020), 'Incidencia religiosa en clave multilateral: La presencia de redes políticas evangélicas en las asambleas de la OEA', *Revista cultura y religión*, 14:1, 100–20.

Pérez Guadalupe, J. L. and S. Grundberger (2018), 'Evangélicos y poder en América Latina', https://www.kas.de/c/document_library/get_file?uuid=35e0675a-5108-856c-c821-c5e1725a64b7&groupId=269552.

Reuters (2019), 'Pompeo Launches Commission to Study Human Rights Role', 8 July, https://www.reuters.com/article/us-usa-rights-pompeo-idUSKCN1U31SA.

Rubio, M. and M. Lee (2016), 'Rubio, Lee Call Out "Cultural Imperialism" of OAS', press release, 3 October, https://www.rubio.senate.gov/public/index.cfm/2016/10/rubio-lee-call-out-cultural-imperialism-of-oas.

Rupar, A. (2022), 'Mike Lee's Texts and the Coup in Search of a Legal Theory', 18 April, https://aaronrupar.substack.com/p/mike-lee-texts-mark-meadows-chip-roy?s=r.

Soley, X. and S. Steininger (2018), 'Parting Ways or Lashing Back? Withdrawals, Backlash and the Inter-American Court of Human Rights', *International Journal of Law in Context*, 14, 237–57.

Stull, M. (2018), 'State Department Emails between Mari Stull and White House,' 1 June, https://www.documentcloud.org/documents/6309201-State-Department-Emails-Between-Mari-Stull-and.html#document/p137/a569058.

Turek, L. F. (2020), *To Bring the Good News to All Nations: Evangelical Influence on Human Rights and US Foreign Policy* (Ithaca, Cornell University Press).

Urueña, R. (2019), 'Evangelicals at the Inter-American Court of Human Rights', *AJIL Unbound*, 113, 360–4.

8

Why Anti-Abortion Movements Fail:
The Case of Chile

SIMÓN ESCOFFIER AND LIETA VIVALDI

THE BILL TO decriminalise abortion was received by Chile's Chamber of Deputies in January 2015. After almost three years of discussions and modifications, this legislation began regulating women's ability to interrupt their pregnancies. Abortion became allowed in three cases: when women's lives are in danger, when the foetus will not survive after birth, and when the pregnancy is the result of rape.

This law may be understood as one of several progressive policy initiatives that sought to expand reproductive, sexual, and identity rights for sections of the population with a history of discrimination and marginalisation. In fact, while this abortion bill was being discussed in parliament, legislation on gender identity was slowly seeing its way through the Senate. Passed in 2018, the Gender Identity Law recognised transgender people's legal right to change their gender. Legislation securing women's free access to emergency contraception had been approved in 2010. In 2015, Congress also passed a law allowing civil unions between any people, regardless of their sexual orientation or gender identity. These policies were not only supported (and sometimes even drafted) by civil society organisations, but they also reflected the will of majorities within public opinion.

Far-right civil society organisers and think tanks, as well as conservative medical doctors, social scientists, and lawyers from some of the most prestigious institutions in the country, protested and lobbied against each one of these bills. They described this group of policies as a destabilising threat to the core moral norms underpinning Chilean culture and society.

In the years prior to the approval of the abortion law, several other, similar bills had also been discussed in parliament. Yet, in those cases these movements, together with other conservative political forces, had managed to prevent the approval of abortion policies. In this chapter we explore why anti-rights civil society organisations failed to block the abortion bill between 2015 and 2017.

Proceedings of the British Academy, **255**, 141–161, © The British Academy 2023.

142 *Simón Escoffier and Lieta Vivaldi*

Based on Leigh A. Payne's framework in this book (Chapter 2), we argue that a necessary condition for these movements' failure is a relatively unfavourable structure of political opportunity, in which their dominance is challenged. In that context, two combined mechanisms will work to prevent their success. On the one hand, our analysis shows how a powerful enough pro-choice opposition managed to counterbalance the influence of anti-abortion tactics in Congress and in other public environments. On the other hand, anti-abortion groups were unable to build a sense of crisis – moral panic – among key potential elite allies in Congress. Their framing tactics exceeded the confines of defence of the foetus, ridiculing, vilifying, and victimising women. They adapted for their own ends a distorted form of progressive and left-wing framing around human rights, disappearance, and sexism. These tactics came up against a consolidated pro-choice movement with advocates in grassroots and institutional organisations within and outside the state, most notably that of President Michelle Bachelet. This movement denounced anti-abortion tactics by highlighting their contradictions. Pro-choice groups also strategically based their argument on the three humanitarian grounds discussed in Congress, and emphasised an empathetic approach to women. Political actors perceived anti-abortion framing, in contrast, as dogmatic and radical, undermining their legitimacy among key potential elite political supporters in Congress.

The data we use for this chapter come from a comprehensive review of discussions in Congress on the abortion bill between 2015 and 2017. We analysed articles, opinion columns, and televised coverage on the abortion bill in Chilean mass media, which included four of the main newspapers and TV channels. Additionally, we conducted three interviews with government officials and consultants who assisted Bachelet's administration with the abortion bill in Congress. We also incorporated an analysis of interviews with seven activists and political consultants in Chile's most influential anti-abortion organisations.[1] Finally, we carried out triangulation by incorporating descriptive analyses of survey data from the 'Observatory of Conflicts' at the Centre for Social Conflict and Cohesion Studies (COES)[2] and the 'Encuesta Nacional Bicentenario' from the Pontificia Universidad Católica de Chile (PUC).

The chapter develops its argument in four steps. First, it provides a brief theoretical framework that follows Payne's Chapter 2 in this volume to explain how anti-abortion movements fail in blocking legislation in Latin America. Secondly, a historical context for the abortion bill is presented. Third, the chapter shows how anti-abortion organisations have experienced a shifting and narrower political opportunity structure. A part of this shift is the growing power of the feminist movement in the past couple of decades, as well as its institutional ramifications

---

[1] These organisations included the Jaime Guzmán Foundation, Community and Justice, Caring for Rights Chile, and the Society Studies Institute.

[2] The interviews we conducted for this chapter were part of a broader project reviewed and approved by Oxford University's Research Ethics Committee (CUREC) on 18 December 2018, ref. no. SIAS_LAC_C1A_18_101.

WHY ANTI-ABORTION MOVEMENTS FAIL: CHILE 143

within Bachelet's government. Fourth, the chapter ends by addressing the political dynamics within and outside Congress that undermined anti-abortion campaigners' support, thus leading to their defeat.

Why Latin American Anti-bortion Movements Fail

Debates over abortion spark discussions on women's right to determination over their own bodies, which is why its legalisation is a cornerstone struggle for feminist and pro-choice activists all over the world. Anti-abortion groups emerge in opposition. They partner up with elite allies, mobilise resources, and develop campaigns to counter pro-choice movements' progress. In particular, these anti-abortion groups mobilise to block pro-choice gains, such as progressive shifts in public opinion or new legislation put forth in Congress. They therefore oppose the expansion of women's reproductive rights and are what this book's framework calls countermovements.

Since the 1990s, a majority of the population in most Latin American countries have supported the decriminalisation of abortion if the mother's life is at risk, in the case of rape, and when the foetus is deformed (Htun 2003). Yet, until the mid-2000s, abortion legislation across the region remained highly restrictive. To a large degree the criminalisation of abortion endured in the region thanks to the concerted political influence of conservative civil society organisations and right-wing political parties, which effectively opposed pro-choice activism.

The Catholic Church and evangelical protestants are staunch supporters of anti-abortion activists and serve as permanent, influential links with those conservative factions that populate the state, regardless of the coalition in power (O'Brien and Walsh 2020; Kane 2008). Instrumental to this influence are what we call 'swing conservative allies', namely powerful political actors that may or may not provide their support to causes depending on contingent, pragmatic calculations regarding their political capital within their parties and constituencies. Anti-abortion movements have been successful in increasing the costs of publicly supporting progressive abortion legislation for politicians acting as swing allies within the government or Congress (Htun 2003; Heumann 2014). Simultaneously, the support of religious elites to anti-abortion campaigns has proved especially effective in the absence of electorally strong, secular left-wing party coalitions (Blofield 2006; Heumann 2014; Kampwirth 2008; Tabbush *et al.* 2016).

Anti-abortion tactics have been more effective in countries with weak feminist mobilisation and high levels of inequality. Comparing the cases of Chile and Uruguay with those of Portugal and Spain, Blofield (2008) argues that socio-economic inequality has undermined the power of feminist civil society organisers in the region. In highly unequal societies, women tend to have less cross-class solidarity. As middle- and upper-class Latin American women can illegally obtain abortions through private health services, decriminalising abortion is an urgent matter only for women in the lower class. In this context, women need an exceptional level of solidarity to coalesce into a powerful feminist movement. In more unequal societies, therefore, feminists tend to be weaker and more fragmented (Blofield 2008).

These factors explain the great effectiveness that Latin American anti-abortion movements have had when influencing legislative processes. Yet, despite their substantial power, these movements have endured failures in the past years. Progressive abortion reforms were passed in Colombia (2006 and 2022), Mexico City (2007), Uruguay (2012), Argentina (2012 and 2020), Brazil (2012 and 2016), the Dominican Republic (2014), and Chile (2017). Their failure in blocking pro-choice legislation can be theoretically explained as a mix of two broad factors.

First, as Payne's framework (Chapter 2) indicates, anti-rights activists are skilful at building or taking advantage of political opportunities. They promote a sense of moral crisis among allies and potential challengers that stimulates their support. This crisis-building is contingent on perception. In other words, the crisis may or may not exist in reality, and its traction among potential supporters depends on whether anti-abortion activists are able to develop the appropriate cultural cues capable of shaping people's interpretations of events. Therefore, their power to influence legislation is undermined when their framing tactics of naming, blaming, and aiming lose legitimacy among supporting actors. Key to this dynamic are swing conservative allies. As the validity of anti-abortion frames erodes, the costs of rejecting progressive legislation increase for swing allies.

Furthermore, anti-rights groups' framing tactics regularly play with contradictions and manipulations (Payne, Chapter 2), which necessarily hinders their empirical credibility (Benford and Snow 2000). In other words, anti-rights groups' naming and blaming tactics are more likely to promote cohesion among supporting elite allies when their movement entrepreneurs have enough cultural and social proximity to these influential actors. Otherwise, their messages can backfire by becoming 'radicalised', 'dogmatic' statements in the eyes of potential supporters (Davis 1999).

Second, anti-abortion movements are more likely to fail in blocking progressive legislation when they face a powerful opposition. A cohesive network of pro-choice and feminist organisations, able to exert influence within the political process, can hinder the impact of anti-rights framing tactics and their access to political allies (Maira and Carrera 2019; Blofield and Ewig 2017; Htun 2003; Lamas 2015; Reuterswärd *et al.* 2011). Htun (2003) speaks of 'elite issue networks' to describe coalitions of elite associations and individuals with different backgrounds that act on gender issues. They include lawyers, feminist activists, legislative consultants, doctors, state officials, grassroots organisers, and politicians. More diverse and collaborative issue networks make feminist actors more likely to acquire public visibility and challenge anti-rights framing tactics. Resonance and legitimacy are fundamental variables in this regard.

Resonance describes the reaction that movements' messages produce in the public realm (Koopmans and Olzak 2004). When a message becomes public it is

WHY ANTI-ABORTION MOVEMENTS FAIL: CHILE   145

more likely to be reproduced by others. The expansion of the message may enhance resonance in two ways. On the one hand, it can allow the movement's rhetoric to reach new groups. On the other hand, it makes the message's events and actors more prominent in the eyes of potential supporters. However, as Koopmans and Olzak note, the message may trigger different levels of support in people. The message's legitimacy is 'the degree to which, on average, reactions by third actors in the public sphere support an actor's claims more than they reject them' (Koopmans and Olzak 2004, 205). Strong pro-choice issue networks able to denounce tactically the contradictions and manipulations of anti-rights organisers (Payne, Chapter 2) can make their messages more controversial. This would decrease the legitimacy of anti-abortion messages while increasing their resonance among potential elite allies and their constituency, which in turn would hinder their ability to affect policy.

This factor also has an institutional layer. Institutionalised and movement-based left-wing parties in government make it more likely that anti-abortion movements will experience defeat (Blofield and Ewig 2017). Institutionalised parties enjoy a stable internal organisation with a relatively decentralised political authority. They have cohesive identities, strong networks, and leaders who are accountable to the party organisation and the rules of the political system. Left-wing governments in Uruguay, Brazil, and Chile would qualify for this category. Movement-based parties are strongly connected to social movements, which makes them more likely to give a voice to organised citizens (Levitsky and Roberts 2011). When in power, these types of parties have demonstrated a higher disposition toward incorporating feminist organisations in the political process, adopting international human rights standards, and limiting the influence of evangelical and Catholic churches on swing potential allies (Reuterswärd et al. 2011; Blofield and Ewig 2017).

The recent defeat experienced by anti-rights groups in the passing of Chile's abortion bill depicts how this framework works. Our analysis illustrates that process. Before examining the right-against-rights failure, we provide a brief historical context of Chile's abortion legislation.

The History of Chile's Abortion Legislation

In the first decades of the 20th century, child mortality in Chile was among the highest in the world. No healthcare programme dealt with reproductive rights, and women carried out abortions at great risk. In 1923, 7,000 illegal abortions were estimated for Santiago alone (Campo 2008, 138). To deal with this dramatic situation, so-called 'therapeutic' abortion was legalised in 1931, which allowed a pregnancy to be ended when the health of the foetus was in danger. The authorities' interpretation of what 'therapeutic purposes' meant was, however, ambiguous, and changed from one administration to the next (Matamala 2014, 8).

In 1964, a subsidised 'family planning programme' was implemented during Christian Democrat President Eduardo Frei's administration. Maternal deaths and hospitalisations decreased sharply (Faúndes and Barzelatto 2006). The law

146 *Simón Escoffier and Lieta Vivaldi*

regarding abortion remained unchanged until 1989, when General Augusto Pinochet's dictatorship (1973–90) prohibited abortion in every circumstance.

From 1990 to 2013, abortion was continually kept off governmental or ministries' agendas, and the feminist movement's demands regarding reproductive rights were systematically ignored, based on agreements between the different political factions (Richard 2001; Blofield and Haas 2005). However, several bills were presented, either to permit abortion in some circumstances, or to toughen its criminalisation (Casas and Vivaldi 2014). Simultaneously, other efforts to expand women's reproductive and sexual rights were pushed forward by political actors on the left. The Framework Law on Sexual and Reproductive Rights proposed in Congress in 2000 is one example. Between 2000 and 2010 the bill to provide women with emergency contraception sparked heated debates in Congress and revealed some of Chile's legal shortcomings when it came to regulating women's rights.

A bill to liberalise abortion was discussed in Chile's Senate for the first time in 2011. Although the three abortion bills introduced that year were rejected in April 2012, the discussions they generated contributed to an expanding national debate on reproductive rights. In 2013, President Bachelet explicitly included the legalisation of abortion on her administration's agenda. For the first time since Chile's return to democracy a president was pushing this legislation forward. Introduced in Congress in 2015, the bill was finally approved in September 2017. The new Abortion Act allowed the end of pregnancies only when the woman's life is at risk, in cases of rape, or if the foetus will not survive on its own after birth.

Each of the specific details of the bill – such as the gestational limits during which time a woman can terminate her pregnancy; the necessity, or not, of reporting to the police in the case of rape; and the procedure to corroborate the specific grounds for termination, among others – was extensively debated. The bill's legislative process can be subdivided into four steps.

Firstly, after being introduced by the government to Congress, the bill was discussed and approved in general terms by the Committee on Health Affairs (CS) of the Chamber of Deputies.[3] The CS discussed the bill in 20 sessions, from 31 March to 4 August 2015. Civil society activists and several experts, who were suggested by members of the CS and other politicians, gave their opinion about different aspects of the bill in front of the committee.[4] Additionally, the ministers who promoted the bill also presented to the CS at least once.[5]

---

[3] The CS is one of the 24 permanent committees within the Chamber of Deputies. The committees discuss the bills or special issues required by the Chamber. Each committee includes 13 members, who proportionally represent their political party or coalition. The CS was composed of five women and eight men. Of these, three were from the right-wing party Independent Democratic Union (UDI), two from the centre-right party National Renovation (RN), two from the centrist party Christian Democracy (DC), one from the centre-left Social Democrat Radical Party (PRSD), two from the centre-left Party for Democracy (PPD), two from the Socialist Party (PS), and one from the Communist Party (PC).
[4] In total, 76 people presented to the CS: 47 against the bill and 29 in favour.
[5] The Minister of the General Secretariat of the Presidency, Ximena Rincón; the Minister of the National Women's Service (SERNAM), Claudia Pascual; the Minister of Healthcare, Carmen Castillo; and the Minister of Justice, José Antonio Gómez.

Second, the government proposed amendments to the original bill. It introduced modification suggestions, which were discussed and finally approved by the CS on 4 August 2015. Consequently, the Commission on Constitutional, Legal, Justice, and Regulations Affairs (CCLJR) in the Chamber of Deputies also invited experts to discuss technical issues.[6] These sessions occurred between 7 October 2015 and 1 March 2016, when the regulatory details were finally approved.

Third, the Chamber of Deputies discussed and voted on the bill over two days, approving it on 17 March 2016. This last debate had a huge impact on Chilean media. Especially visible were the arguments by anti-abortion groups. When opposing abortion, one deputy, for example, claimed that Teletón, the national institution for the treatment of disabilities, would have to be closed if abortion was permitted. Presumably, this deputy argued, all disabled children would be aborted. Another deputy gave Chile's recent dictatorship a higher moral status in comparison with abortion. While most of those assassinated by the dictatorship were adults, the left-wing's abortion policy would kill defenceless children, he argued.[7]

Fourth, the bill was discussed and approved by the Senate. Additionally, conservative members of Congress took the bill to the Constitutional Tribunal to question its legitimacy. This tribunal can judicially review and veto a bill on constitutional grounds during the discussion in the legislature or once it is approved. Against most odds, on 21 August 2018, the Constitutional Tribunal ruled in favour of the bill. However, it extended the right of conscientious objection to entire institutions.

The Growth of a Powerful Pro-Choice Opposition

Explaining how anti-abortion tactics failed at obtaining the support they needed to block the abortion bill in 2015–17 requires, first, a discussion of the political opportunity structure that shifted and strengthened the power of the pro-choice movement.

Although most of the population supported abortion on the three grounds discussed in the bill since 2001 (FLACSO-Chile 2001, 68),[8] conservative groups managed to hold the status quo until 2015. When debates over abortion began in Congress, popular support for the bill had been increasing for over a decade and was overwhelming. Over 64 per cent of the population agreed on allowing abortion under the three circumstances included in the debate (ICSO-UDP 2015).[9]

---

[6] In total, 28 people presented to the CCLJR, including five ministers, one secretary of the presidency, one doctor, and one representative of the Church. The rest were mostly scholars.

[7] For more remarkable phrases uttered in the Chamber of Deputies see *La Tercera* (2016).

[8] According to FLACSO-Chile (2001), 56.3 per cent of Chileans supported abortion when the foetus suffers a severe malformation, 58.3 per cent supported it in cases of rape and incest, and 65.6 per cent supported it when the pregnancy endangers the mother's life.

[9] According to the poll results (ICSO-UDP 2015), 71.7 per cent of the population supported abortion when the mother's life is at risk, 68.7 per cent when the foetus will die after birth, and 64.2 per cent when the pregnancy results from rape.

148 *Simón Escoffier and Lieta Vivaldi*

This circumstance gave pro-choice advocates a mandate that they would not have had otherwise. Yet, this evolution in public opinion resulted, to a large degree, from the increasing visibility and power that Chile's feminist movement had consistently and steadfastly built for over two decades.

Right after the democratic transition, the strong feminist mobilisation that had resisted the dictatorship weakened together with the rest of Chile's civil society. Soon afterwards, in 1991, the Healthcare, Sexual and Reproductive Rights Forum emerged as the main non-institutional response to women's issues. The Forum demanded access to therapeutic abortion. It gathered feminists, academics, medical doctors, and other practitioners, and organised actions that included public meetings, seminars, debates, and research. It also became Chile's main international non-state actor in matters of women's rights. Its institutional reach, however, was very limited, and conservative political groups succeeded in keeping the dictatorship's criminalisation of abortion in place.

In the early 2000s abortion became an increasingly public issue, and in 2003 the Feminist Coalition for Abortion began organising demonstrations to make the impact of the criminalisation of abortion more visible. They organised performances and petitions, and published hundreds of testimonies by women who had had abortions in the press.

In 2008 the movement coalesced in the struggle over a bill that would regulate the supply of emergency contraception pills. Publicly known as *Pildorazo*, this event united feminists and pro-choice activists, doctors, and lawyers behind the same cause and showed them that change was possible. After the law was passed, the intensity of demands over abortion increased. Feminists created a new alliance of pro-choice civil society organisations called Feminist Articulation over the Freedom to Decide (AFLD). This group created a telephone information service for safe abortions and gave increasing prominence to the need to legalise the procedure (Vivaldi and Stutzin 2017).

When President Bachelet took power in 2013 and declared her determination to push an abortion bill forward, pro-choice organisers united further, and new adherents joined their cause. The movement then created the Action for Abortion Coalition, a strong and highly diverse issue network that incorporated a myriad of civil society organisations, human rights lawyers, academics, healthcare practitioners, researchers, and activists. The coalition collaborated with activists and experts in different parts of Latin America. Furthermore, and unlike most previous pro-choice networks, this coalition included feminists who had joined the government and were well embedded in state institutions. For instance, Gloria Maira, a fervent feminist, took the undersecretariat of the National Women's Service (SERNAM) – before it turned into the Ministry of Women and Gender Equality (MMEG) – and became an influential advocate for abortion from within the government. Claudia Pascual, the head of SERNAM, and then MMEG minister, was also a staunch pro-choice advocate. Although the moderate position that defended advocating access to abortion only under three circumstances often clashed with those feminists who demanded full access to abortion, the backing of the government apparatus created a sense of unprecedented opportunity. Indeed, as our interviews suggest, pro-choice advocates enjoyed access to resources and political networks hitherto unavailable to them. 'The MMEG minister told us, whatever we needed, we had it. If we needed the money for a breakfast with Congress members, we only needed to organise it', we were told by a lawyer who worked in the MMEG lobbying in Congress in favour of the bill. The government's determination to defend women's rights became transparent when Bachelet created the MMEG in March 2015. Never had anti-abortion advocates faced an opposition that moved simultaneously on so many fronts and benefited from such a high level of support and resources. In fact, while the bill was discussed in Congress, in 2016 and 2017, protests over women's rights increased sixfold. The spike in mobilisations largely resulted from increasingly salient demands to address gender violence, which amounted to 91 and 87 per cent of protest events on women's rights in 2016 and 2017 respectively (Garretón et al. 2018, 47).

As Figure 8.1 shows, protests opposing the abortion bill increased more sharply than those supporting it. During the time the bill was in Congress, between 2015 and 2017, anti-abortion mobilisations were four times more frequent than pro-choice demonstrations. In fact, anti-abortion organisers coordinated 46 protest events during 2015 alone. This sharp difference is partial evidence of how readily available resources are for anti-abortion groups when they need to activate elite support and public protests. It also shows that while pro-choice demonstrations increased together with all other events over women's rights, a substantial proportion of pro-choice activists' resources may have been tailored toward maximising their influence within the bill's legislative process, which presumably involved many other non-public actions. Overall, while anti-abortion groups had a good many resources at their disposal, the expansion and visibility of progressive gender-associated demands in Chilean society also indicate feminists' increased resources in those years.

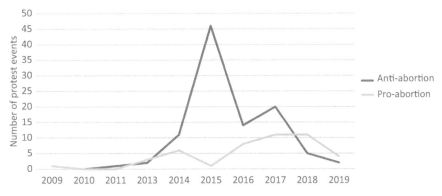

Figure 8.1 Protests over abortion by type of demand (2009–19). Authors' calculation using data from the Observatory of Conflicts Cumulative Dataset (COES 2020). Events were coded as pro- or anti-abortion depending on whether the organisation coordinating the protest supports abortion or not.

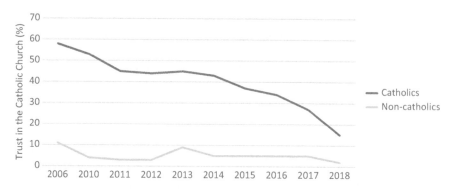

Figure 8.2 Catholics' trust in the Catholic Church (2006–18). Authors' calculation using data from the *Encuesta Nacional Bicentenario* (PUC 2021).

In addition to this favourable scenario for pro-choice groups, the power of the Catholic Church was diminished. Scandals over child abuses perpetrated by high-ranking Catholic priests in Chile had had increasing visibility since 2010, thus eroding trust in the Catholic Church (see Figure 8.2). Consequently, the religious elite within the Catholic Church enjoyed less and less public influence, especially among Catholic followers.

In addition, the structure of the political parties within which the bill was being discussed had suffered substantial changes in the previous years. As new actors with more progressive attitudes joined the political process, the dominance of the two main coalitions – Alianza por Chile (centre-right- and right-wing parties) and Concertación de Partidos por la Democracia (centre-left and left-wing parties) – eroded.

In 2013, a group of leftist former student movement leaders in their mid-twenties was elected to the Chamber of Deputies. For instance, Communist Party member and former head of the Universidad de Chile's student union Camila Vallejo would openly and proudly declare herself a feminist. At the time, that claim was bold and uncommon among politicians, even those on the left. Gabriel Boric (the current president of Chile) and Giorgio Jackson, also former student union leaders new to Congress, built their own parties and defended leftist policies. These new politicians gained increasing popularity by questioning the Concertación's strong commitment to market-oriented and conservative policies that sustained the dictatorship's legacy.[10]

The right wing experienced a similar situation. Representing a new branch of the right, the Political Evolution Party (Evopoli) combined the promotion of neoliberal policies with advocacy for diversity. Evopoli attracted politicians disappointed with the Alianza's radical right-wing views. It took centre stage within the new

---

[10] The Concertación de Partidos por la Democracia was a Chilean centre-left political coalition comprising the Christian Democratic Party (PDC); the Social Party (PS); the Party for Democracy (PPD); the Popular Socialist Union (USOPO); the Radical Party (PR); and other, smaller political parties.

WHY ANTI-ABORTION MOVEMENTS FAIL: CHILE   151

right-wing coalition created in 2014, Chile Vamos, which replaced Alianza por Chile with a very similar political configuration. Evopoli had no representation in Congress when the abortion bill was discussed, which marginalised those actors in the decision process. Yet, its more secular defence of gender rights and personal freedom became increasingly influential within the right wing in those years, thus contributing to the weakening of the position of anti-abortion hardliners within the Alianza. Furthermore, as public debate on the bill evolved in Congress, these new voices on the right fragmented the previous cohesiveness of anti-abortion arguments. The influential conservative lawyer and academic Magdalena Ossandón, for instance, declared in a statement at the CCLJR that the right to abortion should be rejected because on many occasions it means the assassination of the foetus (*feticidio*). However, in itself, she argued, interrupting pregnancy should not be considered a criminal act (Ossandón 2016). Although on highly technical grounds, her argument challenged the view of those on the right who defended criminal charges for women who abort, thereby fragmenting the right's position on abortion.

Defending the Unborn

Conservative groups implemented a diverse set of tactics in their attempt to build political opportunities in opposition to the abortion bill under discussion in Congress between 2015 and 2017. They used naming, blaming, aiming, and claiming (Payne, Chapter 2) to motivate action among their current and potential supporters. Their goal was to create a general sense of crisis within which the abortion bill was only one of the threats. As our interviews indicate, these groups' framing tactics focus on the dissolution of moral, social, and natural norms as damaging to the most intimate areas of human life. This attempt at creating a sense of moral panic tends to activate the support of religious, conservative, and radical right-wing groups.

Although many of the tactics implemented by anti-abortion groups aimed to influence public opinion, their goal was ultimately to tip the balance of votes in Congress to their side. Hence, while we pay attention to anti-abortion groups' actions both outside and within Congress, we focus on their ability to obtain support from key members of Congress, whom we call swing conservative allies. The following paragraphs show how anti-abortion groups failed to build a sense of menace and crisis among those potential supporters.

Unlike most other movements, anti-rights activism has enjoyed long-standing access to Congress. For example, one of the oldest and most powerful Chilean conservative think tanks, the Jaime Guzmán Foundation (FJG), keeps 10 permanent consultants exclusively dedicated to advising members of Congress. Our interviews reveal that the work of these consultants involves the staunch defence of Guzmán's principles of economic liberty and subsidiarity, as well as traditional Catholic values. Their work combines activism with technical and legal advice. They behave as tactical political whisperers on matters of legislation for politicians, especially for those of the UDI, one of the most conservative, right-wing parties along Chile's political spectrum. The FJG belongs to a network of think thanks, non-governmental organisations (NGOs), academics, and activists that oppose progressive legislation and use similar tactics to reach and influence members of Congress. As FJG, a set of organisations in this network devote most of their attention to political consultancy and research. They include Community and Justice, Republican Action, and Caring for Rights Chile. A group of conservative lawyers and academics from well-known local universities provide technical, legal support to these organisations. Simultaneously, a handful of passionate activists in this network, who head very small organisations with a more radical, conservative stance, conduct persistent advocacy work in Congress. In addition to their tactics of political influence in Congress, these organisations coordinate community development initiatives, workshops with school and university students, and internships. Most of these organisations present their political influence as collective and informal, rather than formal and institutional. A few with a more activist orientation coordinate rallies to support either politicians on the far right or public demonstrations. Activists across this network occasionally attend right-wing street mobilisations and protests.

Anti-abortion groups employed these tactics on different occasions within Congress during which they sought the support of politicians. Some of these occasions were more publicly visible than others. Most visible discussions were held in the CS and the CCLJR within the Chamber of Deputies and the Senate. This network of think tanks, NGOs, and activists both assisted conservative politicians' interventions in those commissions and gave speeches in opposition to the bill. In these cases, they deployed framing designed to oppose abortion. After sessions in these commissions were over, press releases were often held. Journalists then conducted multiple interviews with key actors in the meeting. These were also visible opportunities for anti-abortion advocates to seek the support of politicians and their constituencies. Less visible occasions included meetings arranged by anti-abortion advocates to persuade politicians, conversations in corridors, and other similar informal interactions. These less noticeable interactions with politicians also occurred outside Congress, in the party's branch, the presidential palace, or at a ministry.

In the past couple of decades, this conservative network had followed other campaigns in the rest of the world to oppose abortion. Like similar organisations abroad, their frames humanised the foetus, equating abortion with assassination (Braidotti 2011). They deployed this argument when attending meetings on the abortion bill in the CCLJR and CS commissions in the Chamber of Deputies. In meetings on the bill in commissions within the Chamber of Deputies and the Senate, they gave speeches supporting the right to life of the human embryo from its conception. In this view, ending its life is equivalent to murder (see InformAborto 2014, 2015, 2016). Those already born enjoy legal and social protections, these groups claimed. In contrast, the unborn is an 'innocent' and 'defenceless' being (BCN 2017). This logic brought them to assimilate the unborn with other 'vulnerable groups' in society. They therefore framed abortion as an act

WHY ANTI-ABORTION MOVEMENTS FAIL: CHILE   153

of 'discrimination' or even of 'war'. For example, with a speech in the Senate's CCLJR, legal scholar Fernando Londoño attacked the bill by highlighting its exclusionary quality:

> Those who defend the life of the unborn do not attack women (who are already weak and 'affected' in this unequal distribution of natural duties), but defend the voiceless, the weakest of the weak, the one 'hardly seen', the one that does not count. Those who defend the life of the unborn advocate for a more inclusive model of society, one in which – however painful the alternative may be – nobody is redundant. (Londoño 2016)

Their defence of the foetus also concealed these conservative advocates' religious, dogmatic notions of sexuality and the family. They developed secular arguments anchored in bioethics, medical language, and research. In his work on Argentina's anti-rights groups, Vaggione (2014) calls this tactic 'strategic secularism'. This secular framing was meant to increase their legitimacy both within and outside Congress.

In another example, the Women in White, a group of activists who carried out public performances against abortion, framed the anti-abortion cause in terms of justice and not religion. In 2015, one of their activists declared: 'We are not all Catholics. It is a matter of natural law and a right to truth. The government ... has lied to us women; it is a demon disguised as sensibility and as an angel of light to spare women suffering. Abortion is death, money, and a business. The right to be born is for everybody, it is not a religious matter' (Romero 2015).

Yet, their performances symbolised the purity of motherhood in a way that resembled the Christian bride and the Virgin (Bustamante 2015). Dressed in white, these women carried small white boxes representing coffins of aborted dead children. They increased their visibility by performing their act in public spaces and outside influential institutions, including Congress, the presidential palace, and Santiago's Constitutional Square (see Cooperativa 2015). On one occasion, they were joined by a few members of Congress who supported their cause. In addition, several of the Women in White's actions had religious connotations. Their 'white wall' performance, for example, filled a wall with white crosses symbolising a cemetery of dead foetuses, and they protested against abortion in Vatican City while President Bachelet was visiting Pope Francis in 2015.

With the goal of advancing their idea of crisis on all fronts, anti-abortion organisers conflated their cause with frames often used by progressive, pro-choice groups. Their discourse in congressional debates assimilated the threat to the foetus's life with the dictatorship's human rights violations. Campaigns by the InformAborto organisation in 2015 and 2016 displayed massive billboards on highways showing images of detention camps and explicitly equating political disappearances with aborted foetuses. One of these images showed political prisoners detained in Santiago's National Stadium in 1973. The caption at the bottom of the image read: 'Abortion is torture, death, and disappearance' (Elquintopoder 2016; Epicentro 2015).

As Payne indicates in this book's framework, these diverse tactics sought to build a cross-party, historically anchored myth of social threat. This focus on the

154   *Simón Escoffier and Lieta Vivaldi*

foetus, in fact, matched anti-abortion campaigners' broader framing devices, and received substantial support from moderate religious and right-wing sectors of the population. Campaigns organised by conservative university students, for example, in defence of the foetus, opposed the bill. Therefore, this was a potentially good platform to develop support against a larger social menace to the family and religious values. However, women's experience and decisions were largely absent from this line of argument, a key matter that pro-choice advocates would exploit.

Switching the Debate

The executive power built a team of pro-choice advocates and feminists located within different agencies of the state. A key element of this team comprised several lawyers in the MMEG who coordinated the work of other government officials and the General Secretariat of the Presidency, as well as the Health and Justice Ministries. This group created a strategy designed to push the bill all the way to the Constitutional Tribunal, which would be the last entity to assess its viability.

Their tactics were meant to achieve enough support for the bill to overcome each step of the legislative process. Two principles shaped these tactics. On the one hand, pro-choice advocates decided cautiously to narrow down the scope of their claims to the three conditions under which abortion enjoyed widespread support. This tactic meant resisting the tendency of many feminists to widen their goals and seek a bill that would allow abortion in all circumstances. On the other hand, they decided to locate women at the centre of the debate: a principle that involved approaching women empathetically, from a humane perspective.

Pro-choice advocates thus designed a cohesive and simple argument to back their actions: asking women to endure suffering and even death to uphold a moral principle is unfair. In congressional debates, progressive lawyers and advocates, for example, referred to the 'supererogatory act', or conditions in which a conduct might be good or desirable, but cannot be mandatory. As the legal scholar Alejandra Zúñiga argued in the CCLJR at the Senate, while the state can demand 'morally mandatory' acts from its citizens, it cannot demand 'morally good' actions from them. Acting heroically can only be acceptable if the person consents to it, as a matter of self-determination. It followed that nobody should be forced to accept conditions beyond duty, or that require personal sacrifice (Zúñiga 2016). Several other pro-choice activists and progressive politicians seconded this argument in Congress, and MMEG advocates used these ideas when meeting with politicians. In sum, pro-choice advocates focused the discussion on women and the difficult reproduction decisions they have to make in a range of contexts, a role that everyone could understand.

In this context, conservative advocates were forced to justify their position on women's role within the abortion equation in order to engage in the debate. They reacted to this challenge by creating a multifold, contradictory strategy that instrumentalised and stigmatised women. Their claims were plagued with generalisations that essentialised women as intrinsically mothers and wives. Marisol Turres, for example, justified the continuation of pregnancy in cases of rape by saying that 'we [women] have been blessed with the chance of motherhood ... [and] rape does not strip women of their dignity' (*La Tercera* 2015). According to her declaration, motherhood is a woman's core source of dignity, even when she has been raped. Additionally, in an interview in June 2015, the Women in White activist María Paz Vial attacked the pro-choice position as a 'Nazi ideology' that promotes women's 'pseudo-liberation', is ready to 'abandon children', and goes against 'women's three fundamental pillars: to be a virgin, mother, and wife' (Romero 2015).

Anti-abortion advocates represented women as victims. Abortion was, therefore, a way of reinforcing women's vulnerability and suffering. With this view, instead of providing access to abortions, the state should be protecting pregnant women. Therefore, women's rights are opposed to abortion. Former Christian Democrat Soledad Alvear reproduced this argument when she claimed that supporting abortion was *machista* (sexist) (Tele13 2016). As part of the congressional debate, the right-wing member of Congress Claudia Nogueira even conducted an interview with a woman who wanted to abort. The interview, again, showed women as vulnerable victims who need the state's support to make a morally correct decision. To the Healthcare Commission of the Deputy Chamber, Nogueira stated:

> Instead of the state informing you, as the bill suggests, how to get an abortion, how your baby will be taken away from you, where they will put the baby after the abortion, [it would be better] to change the discourse and have the state supporting and protecting you in order to guarantee a peaceful pregnancy ... it is because of the absence of the state that women conduct abortions in Chile. (Nogueira 2015)

In addition, women were portrayed as liars who are ready to instrumentalise the law with the goal of irresponsibly terminating their pregnancies. By claiming to have suffered rape, women would be able to access an abortion and avoid the consequences of their actions. The Cristian Democrat Pablo Lorenzini questioned women's integrity when he asked: 'How would we know if somebody was actually raped?' In his view, 'what a young girl declares [cannot be trusted] ... [With this bill] we would be allowing those girls to say "I was raped because I was a little forced to have it [sex]" whenever they have sex with their boyfriend' (SoyChile 2015).

Anti-abortion advocates even attacked women's wombs. In meetings at the Chamber of Deputies, they described wombs as threatening spaces, 'more dangerous than any country at war', and equated abortion with 'the largest genocide in the history of humanity' (Subercaseaux 2015).

These different notions portrayed women as villains who cannot be trusted. According to our interviews, the many generalisations and assumptions in these narratives often came across as hostility when conservative activists interacted with politicians in meetings and informal environments within Congress. Conservative groups implemented additional, violent tactics that further demonstrated hostility toward progressive politicians and government officials. At some point, for example, anti-abortion campaigners threw red paint at the MMEG minister and her

156 *Simón Escoffier and Lieta Vivaldi*

assistants. In another event, the minister received a bag of dead cats, symbolising what anti-abortion activists interpreted as her disrespect for life: 'The minister does not believe in life; that's why she is not a mother!', and 'they [pro-choice advocates] are assassins', anti-abortion advocates told the press and government officials on different occasions.

Getting the Votes

Anti- and pro-choice advocates' tactics involved identifying those key politicians who were more susceptible to changing their mind and support the bill in Congress. Bachelet's centre–left-wing coalition, the New Majority (and independent supporters), had over 50 per cent of the seats in Congress, in both chambers. Consequently, the challenge was seeking the required votes to pass the bill from conservative sections within the coalition, depending largely on Christian Democrats.

Belonging to the Communist Party, which had only recently joined the New Majority, the MMEG minister sought the assistance of skilful and well-connected female lawyers to promote the bill in Congress. Belonging to two of the most powerful parties within the coalition, the Cristian Democrat Elisa Walker and the Socialist Claudia Sarmiento led this effort. Well versed in human rights law, they both had additional attributes that made them a strategic choice and highly effective within Congress. They were very well connected within the political coalition and had a highly conciliatory approach to the bill. In fact, Walker's background would prove to be critical in passing the bill. She had personal relationships with several Christian Democrat swing conservative allies whose support was fundamental. In addition, she is Catholic. Her adamant support for abortion resulted from a personal experience in which she had to deal with a non-viable pregnancy (*La Tercera* 2017). She gave first-hand testimony on the injustices of criminalising abortion.

The government team of pro-choice advocates held countless meetings with swing conservative allies, within and outside Congress. On these occasions, these pro-choice advocates explored the concerns of members of Congress and sought gradually to influence their views. This tactic included treating those politicians with exceptional deference. For example, they arranged catering when meeting with them, and demonstrated care for their families and personal events. These government advocates also coordinated meetings with leading scientists and medical doctors who supported the bill and were ready to respond to politicians' concerns. As a result, the pro-choice team developed increasingly close interactions with swing conservative allies, which gave them the support they needed to pass the bill in Congress.

In parallel, anti-abortion advocates also approached swing conservative allies to promote their rejection of the bill. This task was more challenging because it involved reaching outside the right-wing coalition, within which they kept their closest political allies. To do so, they followed similar steps to those of the pro-choice advocates. They intervened in the Senate's commissions and held meetings with conservative politicians in the Christian Democratic Party. They also obtained substantial support from the Catholic Church. According to our interviewees several conservative politicians who were beginning to question their anti-abortion position received calls from high-level priests seeking their rejection of the bill.

Within commission sessions, meetings, and informal conversations, anti-abortion advocates conveyed their arguments to swing politicians. They maintained, however, the set of narratives interpreted as contradictory and offensive to women. Pro-choice advocates were poised to expose the problematic arguments made by the foes of abortion. In an informal conversation witnessed by one of our interviewees right after a commission session at the Senate, a conservative civil society advocate explained to a politician that 'Women will lie! This bill will open a door to any woman who wants to have an abortion! We cannot allow that!'. Quickly, however, a pro-choice government advocate intervened and told them: 'Rental contracts are very important, they are part of our economy. But people don't always comply with them, and we won't get rid of rental contracts because of this issue. Instead, we have mechanisms to respond to that problem. Let's not demand full compliance to [the] abortion [legislation] if we don't require it in other policy areas.'

Anti-abortion advocates' discourse appeared as fragmented, lacking cohesiveness and coherence, which made them less convincing. Additionally, their rhetoric and tactics in front of politicians seemed hostile. On several occasions, they even sought to use conspiracy theories as persuasive tools. In their interaction with potential allies, a few anti-abortion campaigners, for example, described the bill as a plot of the beauty industry, which would benefit from increasingly available (aborted) placentas in skin products and treatments. Rather than creating closeness and empathy among potential supporters in Congress, anti-abortion advocates consequently widened the distance. Had they faced a weaker pro-choice opposition, they might have had the chance to develop a sense of 'moral panic' to influence politicians' views. In that hypothetical context, their holistic diagnosis of a society in which conservative values are under attack might have triggered indignation among religious swing allies in Congress. Yet, their claims were systematically and persistently challenged with facts presented by pro-choice advocates.

Anti-abortion groups experienced a similar challenge in Argentina. There, pro-choice advocates turned to social media to mock a caption displayed in an anti-abortion protest under the image of a foetus, which read 'I want to be an engineer' (OhMyGeek! 2018). The caption was meant to equate the foetus with a human being and portray the abortion bill as a threat that precluded people's right to life. Pro-choice groups reacted by creating memes and jokes showing the absurdity of a foetus making life choices (Alma 2018). In other words, the tactic confronted anti-abortion narratives humanising the foetus. As in Chile, this action by Argentinean pro-choice groups undermined anti-abortion frames seeking to foster a sense of moral crisis. Conversely, similar anti-abortion frames that humanise the foetus have been successful in other Latin American countries. Only a few months ago, for instance, the right-wing-dominated Guatemalan Congress passed a draconian bill that criminalises abortion, further increasing punishments for women who induce their miscarriages and imposing prison sentences on anyone who 'promotes or

158 *Simón Escoffier and Lieta Vivaldi*

facilitates access to abortion' (Amnesty International 2022). Although President Alejandro Giammattei was forced to veto the bill on constitutional grounds, he supported conservative civil society organisations and Congress members behind the bill by publicly calling for the 'protection of life since its inception and until natural death' (Benotman 2022). Similar rhetoric has been successful in El Salvador, where abortion continues to be illegal in all cases. Presumably, the feminist movement in those countries has not yet created a platform powerful enough to publicly oppose conservative movements' frames.

Conclusion

This chapter addressed the question of when, why, and how anti-rights groups fail to block progressive legislation. It used the case of Chile's passing of a bill in 2017 that allowed abortion when birth is a threat to the mother's life, when the foetus will not survive after birth, and when the pregnancy is the result of rape.

The chapter showed how two combined mechanisms prevented the success of anti-rights civil society actors in contexts of a relatively disadvantageous political opportunity structure. First, a feminist and pro-choice opposition built up and became powerful enough to counteract conservatives' tactics in Congress and other public debates. We presented the growth of the feminist movement since the mobilisations that demanded access to emergency contraceptive pills in 2008. Eventually, Bachelet's government (2014–18) pushed to pass the abortion bill, having incorporated several pro-choice political actors into strategic government agencies. The most important one was the MMEG minister. Her team coordinated the tactics and efforts to obtain the support needed in Congress to pass the bill.

Second, anti-abortion groups were unable to build a sense of crisis among key potential elite allies in Congress. As pro-choice campaigners placed the focus of the debate on women's role, conservative groups were unable to produce a coherent and consensual set of arguments. In insisting on building a sense of crisis behind which supporters could unite, they stigmatised and vilified women. They also used aggressive tactics and conspiracy theories to seek support from Congress members that backfired. In contrast, pro-choice groups were able to represent women empathetically and as human beings. Consequently, anti-abortion advocates were unable to maintain a solid majority against the bill, even among conservative politicians in the governing coalition.

References

Alma, A. (2018), '#AbortoLegalYa: Reirse para sacar el aborto del melodrama'. *LATFEM*, 10 May, https://latfem.org/abortolegalya-reirse-para-sacar-el-aborto-del-melodrama/.
Amnesty International (2022), 'Guatemala: Discriminatory Law Foments Hate and Puts Lives, Rights and Families at Risk', 9 March, https://www.amnesty.org/en/latest/news/2022/03/guatemala-discriminatory-law-lives-rights-families-risk/.

WHY ANTI-ABORTION MOVEMENTS FAIL: CHILE 159

BCN [Biblioteca del Congreso Nacional de Chile] (2017), 'Historia de la Ley N° 21.030', https://www.bcn.cl/historia-de-la-ley/nc/historia-de-la-ley/6701/.

Benford, R. and D. Snow (2000), 'Framing Processes and Social Movements: An Overview and Assessment', *Annual Review of Sociology*, 26 (August), 611–39.

Benotman, A. (2022), 'Guatemala se declara "capital provida", aumenta penas por aborto y prohíbe el matrimonio igualitario', *France 24*, 10 March, https://www.france24.com/es/américa-latina/20220310-guatemala-aborto-derechos-homosexuales-giammattei.

Blofield, M. (2006), *The Politics of Moral Sin: Abortion and Divorce in Spain, Chile and Argentina* (London, Routledge).

Blofield, M. (2008), 'Women's Choices in Comparative Perspective: Abortion Policies in Late-Developing Catholic Countries', *Comparative Politics*, 40:4, 399–419.

Blofield, M. and C. Ewig (2017), 'The Left Turn and Abortion Politics in Latin America', *Social Politics*, 24:4, 481–510.

Blofield, M. and L. Haas (2005), 'Defining a Democracy: Reforming the Laws on Women's Rights in Chile, 1990–2002', *Latin American Politics and Society*, 47:3, 35–68.

Braidotti, R. (2011), *Nomadic Subjects: Embodiment and Sexual Difference in Contemporary Feminist Theory* (New York, Columbia University Press).

Bustamante, B. (2015), 'Mujeres de blanco denuncian contenido tendencioso en simposio sobre aborto en Chile', *ACI Prensa*, 22 November, https://www.aciprensa.com/noticias/mujeres-de-blanco-denuncian-contenido-tendencioso-en-simposio-sobre-aborto-en-chile-82975.

Campo, A. del (2008), 'El debate médico sobre el aborto en Chile en la década de 1930', in *Por la salud del cuerpo: Historia y políticas sanitarias en Chile*, ed. M. S. Zárate (Santiago de Chile, Universidad Alberto Hurtado), pp. 131–88.

Casas, L. and L. Vivaldi (2014), 'Abortion in Chile: The Practice under a Restrictive Regime', *Reproductive Health Matters*, 22:44, 70–81.

COES [Centre for Social Conflict and Cohesion Studies] (2020), 'Observatory of Conflicts – Cumulative Dataset', Harvard Dataverse, https://doi.org/10.7910/DVN/GKQXBR.

Cooperativa (2015), '"Mujeres de Blanco" marcharon este domingo en contra del aborto', 12 April, https://www.cooperativa.cl/noticias/pais/salud/aborto/mujeres-de-blanco-marcharon-este-domingo-en-contra-del-aborto/2015-04-12/191945_6.html#topgaleria.

Davis, D. (1999), 'The Power of Distance: Re-Theorizing Social Movements in Latin America', *Theory and Society*, 28:4, 585–638.

Elquintopoder (2016), 'Detenidos desaparecidos y no nacidos: Encuentre las diferencias', https://www.elquintopoder.cl/justicia/detenidos-desaparecidos-y-no-nacidos-encuentre-las-diferencias/.

Epicentro (2015), 'Gigantografías que comparan el aborto con torturados en dictadura causan polémica', 3 October, https://www.epicentrochile.com/2015/10/03/gigantografias-que-comparan-el-aborto-con-torturados-en-dictadura-causan-polemica/.

Faúndes, A. and J. Barzelatto (2006), *The Human Drama of Abortion: A Global Search for Consensus* (Nashville, Vanderbilt University Press).

FLACSO-Chile [Facultad Latinoamericana de Ciencias Sociales Chile] (2001), *Percepciones y actitudes de las y los chilenos a principios del siglo XXI: Encuesta nacional de opinión pública FLACSO 2001* (Santiago de Chile, FLACSO-Chile).

Garretón, M., A. Joignat, N. Somma, and T. Campos (2018), *Informe annual observatorio de conflictos 2018*, Notas COES de política pública, 17 (Santiago de Chile, Centro de Estudios de Conflicto y Cohesión Social).

Heumann, S. (2014), 'Gender, Sexuality, and Politics: Rethinking the Relationship between Feminism and Sandinismo in Nicaragua', *Social Politics: International Studies in Gender, State & Society*, 21:2, 290–314.

160 *Simón Escoffier and Lieta Vivaldi*

Htun, M. (2003), *Sex and the State: Abortion, Divorce, and the Family under Latin American Dictatorships and Democracies* (Cambridge, Cambridge University Press).

ICSO-UDP [Instituto de Investigación en Ciencias Sociales, Universidad Diego Portales] (2015), 'Encuesta Nacional UDP 2015', https://www.duna.cl/media/2015/11/Todos-los-Resultados-Encuesta-UDP-2015-1.pdf.

InformAborto (2014), 'Camión de InformAborto sigue mostrando la realidad del #Aborto en el centro de Santiago!', Facebook, https://www.facebook.com/informaborto/photos/835562923161176.

InformAborto (2015), 'Aborto es matar a un niño fruto de una violación', Facebook, https://www.facebook.com/informaborto/photos/1023363127714487.

InformAborto (2016), 'InformAborto en el Congreso mostrando la realidad de un aborto legal y seguro', Facebook, https://www.facebook.com/informaborto/photos/1112769368773862.

Kampwirth, K. (2008), 'Neither Left nor Right: Sandinismo in the Anti-Feminist Era', *NACLA Report on the Americas*, 41:1, 30–4.

Kane, G. (2008), 'Abortion Law Reform in Latin America: Lessons for Advocacy', *Gender and Development*, 16:2, 361–75.

Koopmans, R. and S. Olzak (2004), 'Discursive Opportunities and the Evolution of Right-Wing Violence in Germany', *American Journal of Sociology* 110:1, 198–230.

Lamas, M. (2015), *El largo camino hacia la ILE: Mi versión de los hechos* (Mexico City, Universidad Nacional Autónoma de México).

Levitsky, S. and K. M. Roberts (2011), *The Resurgence of the Latin American Left* (Baltimore, Johns Hopkins University Press).

Londoño, F. (2016), 'Intervención en Comisión de Constitución, Legislación, Justicia y Reglamento del Senado de la República de Chile', 6 January, https://www.bcn.cl/historiadelaley/nc/historia-de-la-ley/6701/.

Maira, G. and C. Carrera (2019), 'Estrategias feministas para la despenalización del aborto en Chile: La experiencia de la mesa acción por el aborto', in *Aborto en tres causales en Chile: Lecturas del proceso de despenalización*, ed. L. Casas and G. Maira Vargas (Santiago de Chile, Centro de Derechos Humanos UDP), pp. 181–202.

Matamala, M. I. (2014), 'Aborto en Chile: Cuerpos, derechos y libertades', in *Voces sobre el aborto: Ciudadanía de las mujeres, cuerpo y autonomía*, ed. Articulación Feminista por la Libertad de Decidir (AFLD) (Santiago de Chile, AFLD; Escuela de Salud Pública 'Dr. Salvador Allende G.', Facultad de Medicina, Universidad de Chile), pp. 7–20.

Nogueira, C. (2015), 'Intervención en Comisión de Salud de la Cámara de Diputados de la República de Chile', Boletín no. 9895-11: *Sesiones Comisión Salud, Cámara de Diputados* (March–July), 'Discusión de la Ley N° 21.030 que regula la despenalización voluntaria del embarazo en tres causales', transcribed by I. Palma, Programma de Investigación sobre el Aborto en Chile (Universidad de Chile), 13 July.

O'Brien, C. and S. D. Walsh (2020), 'Women's Rights and Opposition: Explaining the Stunted Rise and Sudden Reversals of Progressive Violence against Women Policies in Contentious Contexts', *Journal of Latin American Studies*, 52:1, 107–31.

OhMyGeek! (2018), '¿De dónde proviene el meme del "feto ingeniero"?', https://ohmygeek.net/2018/04/19/meme-feto-ingeniero/.

Ossandón, M. (2016), 'Intervención en Comisión de Constitución, Legislación, Justicia y Reglamento de la Cámara de Diputados de la República de Chile', 9 March, https://www.bcn.cl/historiadelaley/nc/historia-de-la-ley/6701/.

Pontificia Universidad Católica de Chile [PUC] (2021), Encuesta Nacional Bicentenario. Santiago de Chile. https://encuestabicentenario.uc.cl.

Reuterswärd, C., P. Zetterberg, S. Thapar-Björkert, and M. Molyneux (2011), 'Abortion Law Reforms in Colombia and Nicaragua: Issue Networks and Opportunity Contexts', *Development and Change*, 42:3, 805–31.

Richard, N. (2001), 'La problemática del feminismo en los años de la transición en Chile', in *Estudios latinoamericanos sobre cultura y transformaciones sociales en tiempos de globalización* (Buenos Aires, CLACSO), pp. 227–39.

Romero, J. (2015), '"Mujeres de Blanco" en Roma: El grito de las mujeres que busca defender la vida de los chilenos por nacer', InfoCatólica, https://www.infocatolica.com/blog/delapsis.php/1506040935-mujeres-de-blanco-en-roma-lel.

SoyChile (2015), 'Lorenzini: "Hay mujeres que tienen violaciones porque, a lo mejor, tomaron un traguito de más"', 6 February, https://www.soychile.cl/Santiago/Polit ica/2015/02/06/303544/Lorenzini-Hay-mujeres-que-tienen-violaciones-porque-a-lo-mejor-tomaron-un-traguito-de-mas.aspx.

Subercaseaux, F. (2015), 'Intervención en Comisión de Salud de la Cámara de Diputados de la República de Chile', Boletín no. 9895-11: *Sesiones Comisión Salud, Cámara de Diputados* (March–July), transcribed by I. Palma, Programma de Investigación sobre el Aborto en Chile (Universidad de Chile), 8 June.

Tabbush, C., M. C. Díaz, C. Trebisacce, and V. Keller (2016), 'Matrimonio igualitario, identidad de género y disputas por el derecho al aborto en Argentina: La política sexual durante el kirchnerismo (2003–2015)', *Sexualidad, salud y sociedad*, 22 (April): 22–55.

Tele13 (2016), 'Soledad Alvear: "El aborto es lo más machista que hay"', 26 October, https://www.t13.cl/noticia/politica/soledad-alvear-aborto-es-mas-machista-hay.

La Tercera (2015), 'Diputada UDI Marisol Turres: "Hay violaciones que no son violentas"', *La Tercera*, 16 September, https://www.latercera.com/noticia/diputada-udi-marisol-turres-hay-violaciones-que-no-son-violentas/.

La Tercera (2016), 'Las polémicas frases que marcaron el debate de la despenalización del aborto', *La Tercera*, 16 March, http://www.t13.cl/noticia/politica/las-frases-marcaron-discusion-despenalizacion-del-aborto.

La Tercera (2017), 'Elisa Walker: "Este proyecto es un gesto de humanidad y creo que el Catolicismo es parte de eso"', *La Tercera*, 27 August, https://www.latercera.com/noticia/elisa-walker-este-proyecto-gesto-humanidad-creo-catolicismo-parte/.

Vaggione, J. M. (2014), 'La politización de la sexualidad y los sentidos de lo religioso', *Sociedad y religión: Sociología, antropología e historia de la religión en el Cono Sur*, 24:42, 209–26.

Vivaldi, L. and V. Stutzin (2017), 'Mujeres víctimas, fetos públicos, uteros aislados: Tecnologías de género, tensiones y desplazamientos en las representaciones visuales sobre aborto en Chile', *Zona franca*, 25:25, 126–60.

Zúñiga, A. (2016), 'Intervención en Comisión de Constitución, Legislación, Justicia y Reglamento del Senado de la República de Chile', 2 November, https://www.bcn.cl/historiadelaley/nc/historia-de-la-ley/6701/.

9

The Violent Rollback of Indigenous and Environmental Rights: The Emblematic Case of Lenca Leader Berta Cáceres in Honduras

NANCY R. TAPIAS TORRADO

THIS CHAPTER EXAMINES a right-against-rights mobilisation that led to the murder of the Indigenous Lenca leader and prominent human rights defender Berta Cáceres. The explanation for this killing of the general coordinator and co-founder of the Council of Popular and Indigenous Organisations of Honduras (COPINH) is the reprisal for her leading role in defending the Lenca people from the abuses committed in connection to the Agua Zarca hydroelectric dam project in Honduras. I first situate the analysis in a dynamic of power and mobilisation – for rights and against them – briefly presenting the 'braided action' theoretical framework.[1] Then, after a succinct introduction to the mobilisation led by Berta Cáceres, I focus on the 'right-against-rights' analytical framework (Payne (Chapter 2)) in this case: the dynamics of an alliance of radical neoliberal, uncivil, and state actors that exercised a form of veto power to halt human rights change.[2] The chapter explores the who, when, why, how, and what behind this alliance and its impact.

---

[1] The analysis I offer in this chapter comes out of a much broader study, my doctoral investigation (Tapias Torrado 2020). The thesis provides a multilevel qualitative research study that involves three main comparisons of cases of 'success' and 'non-success' of Indigenous-women-led mobilisations: (1) within-country variation comparing Lenca-women-led organisations contesting abuses related to hydro-electric dam projects in Honduras; (2) within-case variation over time of a Binni'za-women-led mobil-isation against violations connected to wind farm projects in Mexico; and (3) a small-N cross-national comparison of mobilisations in Ecuador, Peru, and Colombia led by Sarayaku, Asháninka, and Wayuu women challenging the abuses related to oil extraction, hydroelectric dam projects, and coal mining respectively. Also, I develop a qualitative comparative analysis of all these cases, which includes a Boolean minimisation process. By success, I mean a favourable change in corporate practice.

[2] In my doctoral thesis (Tapias Torrado 2020), I adapt Payne *et al.*'s (2020) concept of 'veto players' to include an alliance of some state and corporate actors, and other groups – legal and illegal – supporting them. I explain that 'veto power' can be exerted, for example, through legal resources, media actions, social division, and undue pressures on or attacks against human rights defenders. Drawing on the frame-work presented in this book, in this chapter I refer to 'veto players' as the 'right-against-rights' alliance.

Proceedings of the British Academy, **255**, 162–180, © The British Academy 2023.

THE EMBLEMATIC CASE OF BERTA CÁCERES IN HONDURAS   163

The right-against-rights mobilisation that murdered Berta Cáceres unites a diverse range of actors with a range of interests. It includes private corporate and state actors backed by political and economic elites, and the hitmen who participated in the crime. These groups mobilise to advance their vested interests in the hydro-electric megaproject and protect the social and economic status quo behind it. This right-against-rights alliance used a series of tactics intending to reverse or roll back Indigenous rights, agency, leadership, and organisation that challenge abusive behaviour. In essence, this mobilisation used three broad tactics to achieve its goals. First, it rejected and devalued Indigenous people's collective identity, categorising them instead as impoverished people in need of aid. Second, it negatively framed and stigmatised the leadership and actions of Indigenous rights-defenders, in particular using gendered language to depict the Indigenous woman in the top leadership position as manipulative and deceitful. Aiming to undermine her legitimacy and credibility and that of her organisation further, the right-against-rights mobilisation used fabricated criminal charges against the Indigenous leaders. Third, it engaged in threats and extreme violence to intimidate, discourage, and eliminate Indigenous leaders mobilising against megaprojects. These actions occurred in a context, moreover, where the right against rights operates with impunity; domestic authorities have historically proved unwilling to hold elites accountable for even heinous acts of murder.

This right-against-rights alliance includes radical neoliberal or economic elite interests behind megaprojects. They, at times, even join forces with illegal actors to advance their objectives. In this case, as well as in other similar cases, the right against rights coordinated efforts to undermine Indigenous women human rights defenders, and their organisations and movements. Despite the violence used by these politically and economically powerful right-wing groups, they do not always succeed in their efforts. The 'braided action' framework presented below explores the factors that explain right-against-rights successes, that is, reversing human, Indigenous, and environmental rights gains. It also considers the explanation for failure, or when Indigenous rights and mobilisation power persist and deepen, reaffirming respect, protection, and advancement of human rights.

In the following sections, I first briefly introduce the 'braided action' theoretical framework, situating within it the role of the right-against-rights mobilisation that killed Berta Cáceres. I next briefly explore the struggle led by Berta Cáceres and COPINH, to then focus on the alliance on the right. I end with concluding remarks reflecting more generally on the patterns of the right-against-rights mobilisations against Indigenous and environmental movements.

The 'Braided Action' Theoretical Framework

The right against rights does not emerge in a vacuum. Indeed, as Chapter 1 suggests, the mobilisation by the contemporary right in Latin America reflects a shift away from the right's consolidated social, economic, political, and cultural power. Once that power and privilege was challenged by the 'rights revolution' in the region, a tense dynamic evolved, with traditional rights holders on the right opposed to 'new rights' seekers among previously marginalised groups. The 'braided action' model captures this dynamic, the underlying imbalance in power relations between a right-against-rights alliance and Indigenous women-led mobilisations. This model allows for variation in the outcome; the right against rights does not always win (Tapias Torrado 2020).

'Braided action', or *acción trenzada*, is a metaphor and framework that draws on the knowledge and experience of Indigenous-women-led mobilisations in the Americas, and legal, intersectional, and sociological studies (Tapias Torrado 2020). It builds on the Archimedes' Lever analogy proposed by Payne, Pereira, and Bernal-Bermúdez (2020), originally developed to study accountability efforts regarding economic actors' participation in human rights atrocities during past authoritarian and armed conflict periods. I adapt it to study contemporary cases of human rights violations committed in connection to megaprojects in the Americas. Corporate actors' involvement in grave crimes is not only a matter of past atrocities; it is a legacy of the past that remains a pressing issue.[3] It thus allows for the exploration of how traditional and powerful right-wing forces in the region confront the expansion of rights by previously marginalised groups.

Building on the Archimedes' Lever model, the 'braided action' framework acknowledges a dynamic of forces in the context of unbalanced power relationships. On either side of the lever are the forces aiming to suppress or lift up rights. Some of the most economically and politically powerful actors in the world, such as national and multinational corporations and state actors with vested interests in megaprojects, attempt to suppress those rights. This is where the right against rights is situated. On the other side, attempting to lift up rights, are the Indigenous communities affected by those projects, their leaders, and the national and international organisations supporting their rights claims. Indigenous-led mobilisations generally have far fewer material resources to defend their rights.

The 'weight' to be lifted in the specific context of Honduras is the rights of Indigenous peoples, including their free, prior, and informed consultation and consent, or FPIC. The alliance on the right attempts to 'veto' those rights, using its established power in the economy, in society, in the courts, and in government to attempt to suppress them. But in this case in Honduras, that radical neoliberal power was not enough. The right joined forces with illegal violent actors to block Indigenous rights.

By the time of the mobilisation by Berta Cáceres and COPINH, in Honduras and around the world Indigenous movements had articulated the rights to dignity and territory, and fundamental rights, and called for an end to abusive situations. There, the 'fulcrum', or the institutional and normative human rights framework, was in a minimally favourable position to lift up rights. In 1995, for example, Honduras ratified

---

[3] From 2015 to March 2022, the Business and Human Rights Resource Centre documented 3,881 attacks against human rights defenders. The most attacked are those who defend land and the environment, most often Indigenous leaders and groups (BHRRC 2022).

THE EMBLEMATIC CASE OF BERTA CÁCERES IN HONDURAS   165

the International Labour Organization Convention no. 169, concerning Indigenous and Tribal Peoples in Independent Countries (ILO 1989). Yet the approval of norms did not mean that Indigenous and tribal peoples in Honduras could achieve 'rights on the ground'. Even in this slightly favourable context, the struggle for rights remained highly unbalanced. The Indigenous peoples in Honduras would have to exert substantial pressure to lift up the weight of human rights from under the pressure of the right-against-rights alliance.

The 'braid of action' became an essential 'weapon of the weak' (Scott 1985) in this context. With a very strong 'braid of action', the Indigenous people could latch on to the lever, pulling it down, to lift up the heavy weight of rights from under the powerful pressure of the right-wing alliance.

Creating that powerful 'braid' involves weaving together four strands. Three emerge from the capacity of the movement: transforming the power in the territory into mobilisation power, effective leadership of Indigenous women, and human rights framing. The fourth is reacting to an external factor: a grave human rights violation –usually uncivil movement violence – overtly involving a corporation. These four strands woven together create a tough braid of action potentially capable of overcoming the counterweight of the right-against-rights alliance.[4] Indigenous women human rights defenders have continuously challenged dominant powers both inside and outside their communities to struggle for their rights and those of their peoples. In a minimally favourable context, and with appropriate tools, at times they have achieved success over these dominant forces (Tapias Torrado 2020).

However, if one or more strands are weak or frayed, the braid cannot achieve this impact. In some cases, Indigenous-women-led movements cannot build a strong braid because of challenges that are internal to their communities and organisations, or other types of obstacles in the broader context. Even with a minimally favourable context – 'fulcrum' – the conditions affecting Indigenous-women-led mobilisations continue to be adverse, and the right against rights overpowers them. Indigenous women, their organisations, and their communities continue to face many disadvantages, challenges, oppressions, and a history of discrimination and violence.[5] Indigenous-women-led efforts to build power and have an impact are challenged, targeted, and attacked by the right against rights. The alliance uses a wide range of tactics and even extreme violence to create fear, silence human rights defenders, and deter others from joining their mobilisation, seeking to unravel the 'braid of action'.

---

[4] The four strands overlap each other and, operating with their own mechanisms, they gather strength. To explain the strands' dynamics and mechanisms, I build upon the learnings of the cases studied in-depth in my doctoral investigation and analytical sociology (Hedström and Swedberg 1998; Hedström and Bearman 2017). See Tapias Torrado (2020) for a detailed explanation of the braid and its strands and mechanisms.

[5] The Lenca people, as well as all other ethnic groups in the country, are among the groups most affected by inequality and injustice. The average life expectancy in the country is 72.6 years, but for Indigenous people it is 36 for men and 42 for women (IACHR 2013, 293–6). Access to education, health, and other fundamental rights for Indigenous people is minimal (CIDH 2015, para. 418).

166   *Nancy R. Tapias Torrado*

The motivation behind the right's mobilisation is largely economic and a protection of certain privileges over how to do business. In this sense it is a radical neoliberal mobilisation (Payne (Chapter 2)). But their use of violence goes beyond those economic interests; the right-wing alliance also involves violent 'uncivil movements' (Payne 2000; Payne (Chapter 2)) that aim not only to roll back rights, but also to eliminate rights seekers: in this case Berta Cáceres and the COPINH. Indeed, it is because Berta Cáceres and the COPINH had begun to use effective tools – braided action – to lift up their rights that the right could no longer work behind the scenes to influence outcomes. It mobilised an alliance to halt and eliminate the Indigenous movement and its advances.

Berta Cáceres, the COPINH, and Braided Action

Through the 'braid of action', Berta Cáceres and the COPINH began to challenge power relations. Leadership proved key to the movement's impact. In the early 1990s, Berta Cáceres co-founded the COPINH. Thus, mobilisation for Indigenous rights had already begun when the Agua Zarca hydroelectric dam project arrived in Lenca territory. Most of the affected local communities were already part of the COPINH organisation, and they had begun to have an impact on local and national issues (Tapias Torrado 2020).

Berta Cáceres was a leading member of the organisation from its outset and led it for more than two decades. In 1994, COPINH, together with other Indigenous and tribal peoples and organisations in Honduras, mobilised in the first pilgrimage for 'life, liberty, and justice'. About 4,000 Indigenous people walked to Tegucigalpa to make rights demands. They successfully pressed for the ratification of ILO Convention 169, the creation of two Indigenous municipalities,[6] legal titles over some communal lands, the suspension of lumber mills' activities,[7] and the creation of the Prosecutor's Office on Ethnic Groups and the Cultural Patrimony of the Nation, among other achievements. Indigenous peoples became visible and crucial political and social actors in Honduras. They began to effect a slight shift in the power imbalance in the country.

Building on these and other achievements and the force of their social mobilisation, COPINH continued to grow and expand their human rights impact through educative workshops, judicial activism, solidarity actions, and spiritual gatherings, among others. Together, all these actions formed thick strands and, as a braid, harnessed their power to lift up their rights.

Drawing on Lenca spiritual ceremonies and ancestral social and cultural practices, and taking actions of 'territorial control', the COPINH was able to transform power in the territory into power to lift up rights. The leadership of Berta

---

[6] San Francisco de Opalaca and San Marcos de Caiquín.
[7] Previously, in 1993, after a protest of more than 1,500 people against a lumber mill in Yamaranguila, Intibucá, they managed to get some forest areas protected from logging.

Cáceres played a central role in this. She was a charismatic leader, and someone who also led by example and through concrete actions that addressed fundamental issues within and beyond the COPINH and the Lenca communities, such as women's participation and the eradication of violence against them. Furthermore, Berta's effective leadership strategically and frequently used human rights framing. The COPINH used that framing as a language useful in asserting the Lencas' legitimacy and rights and advancing their struggles in non-institutional and institutional channels, such as the many judicial and non-judicial complaints filed before diverse institutions. Over time, therefore, the COPINH mobilised its power in this slightly favourable context; it began to use that power to lift up rights.

Such power, however, did not mean the end to abuses. The 200 Lenca communities that are part of COPINH have faced many human rights violations, including abuses connected to several megaprojects, one of them the Agua Zarca hydroelectric dam project. In April 2015, Berta Cáceres received the Goldman Prize (also known as the 'green Nobel') in recognition of her achievements defending the Lenca people from the abuses committed in connection to megaprojects in their territory. A year later, after many other attacks against her and other members of COPINH, she was killed in reprisal for her human rights actions. The murder of Berta Cáceres was the consolidation of numerous previous attacks against her and many other leading members of the COPINH. This right-against-rights alliance behind her murder is the focus of the next section.

The Right-against-Rights Mobilisation to Reverse Indigenous Rights

Having lost influence over the rights achievements of Indigenous peoples in Honduras, the right against rights mobilised in more overt – violent – ways against those rights-seekers. This section analyses who formed part of this right-wing mobilisation; why they mobilised; and when, how, and with what impact.

The alliance of the right against rights involved a diverse range of actors with vested interests in the megaproject. In this case, the Agua Zarca project is owned by Desarrollo Energético S.A. (DESA), whose board of directors includes members of the Honduras economic and political elite (Global Witness 2017, 14). The Agua Zarca hydroelectric dam project originated soon after the 2009 coup d'état, with the national law on waters approved the same year. Under this law, the concession to build a dam in the Gualcarque River – to generate 21.3 MW – was approved. In 2011, the National Congress approved the contract of operation between DESA and the Ministry of Natural Resources and the Environment. All of these approvals were granted without the FPIC of affected Indigenous Lenca communities.[8] The COPINH thus mobilised to protect their communities from these procedurally flawed concessions.

---

[8] For an explanation of the content and centrality of the right to FPIC for Indigenous peoples, see UN (2018).

168   *Nancy R. Tapias Torrado*

That, then, explains the 'why' behind the right-wing alliance against COPINH. The economic actors involved in the project aimed to protect and advance their political and economic interests. They sought to consolidate and profit from the megaprojects that had been approved. They also aimed to protect their investments in time, money, and resources to plan, develop, and implement the megaprojects (Tapias Torrado 2020; 2022b). They had perhaps not anticipated confrontations with the Indigenous communities, or assumed that they could use traditional strategies – government intervention, divide-and-conquer, intimidation – to block Indigenous protests.

In this case, however, those strategies did not work. Rather than addressing the Indigenous communities and their leaders as rightful human rights defenders,[9] the strategy used by the alliance involved demonising them (Payne (Chapter 2)). The Indigenous movement were identified as 'trouble-makers', 'obstacles', and 'threats' to national development and progress. In a slightly favourable global and local context for Indigenous and environmental rights, the appeal to corporate privilege and the use of thinly veiled racism did not have the same effect. This, then, led to more overt forms of mobilisation by the right against rights.

The alliance formed well before Agua Zarca arrived in Lenca territory, and it persisted after the killing of Berta Cáceres. The alliance had begun within the institutional sphere to promote legal and political conditions favouring their economic interests. On 28 June 2009, a de facto government led by the then president of the National Congress, Roberto Micheletti, was established. He was a member of President Manuel Zelaya's Liberal Party, but he formed an alliance with the armed forces and the business elite to overthrow Zelaya (Cunha Filho *et al.* 2013). It was a violent and abrupt way to shift crucial political debates and to prioritise the interests of economic and political elites. The context created by the coup was used to advance economic projects: for example, the previously mentioned 2009 national law on waters, which allowed for the privatisation of once protected waterways. In September 2010, 40 out of 47 renewal energy contracts adjudged by the National Electric Power Company were approved by the National Congress without the FPIC of affected Indigenous communities, and most of the contracts were concessions for hydroelectric dam projects. Also, in 2013, the National Congress reformed some articles of the 2007 Law on the Promotion to the Generation of Electric Power with Renewable Resources to provide additional incentives to those already included in the 2011 Law on the Promotion and Protection of Investments. Consequently, in 2018, more than 80 per cent of Honduras's energy production was in the hands of private corporations, and the electricity supply in the country depended on 94 contracts with private companies, 40 of them for hydroelectric projects (CEHPRODEC 2018).

---

[9] States must regulate and monitor corporations, and provide effective mechanisms of accountability and redress when corporations violate human rights at home or abroad (ISHR 2015, 15–16; UNGA 2017, para. 33). Corporate actors also have human rights responsibilities, including some explicitly addressing the situation of human rights defenders. In 2011, the UN Guiding Principles set essential standards on corporate responsibility (Ruggie 2011).

Consequently, hydroelectric dam projects became a priority for the Honduran government.[10] In this context, Indigenous rights were not respected, protected, or guaranteed. In August 2011, for example, President Porfirio Lobo agreed with COPINH that hydroelectric dam projects in the Lenca territory had to be validated in *cabildos abiertos* (town meetings), according to ILO Convention 169 and with the participation of COPINH (Korol 2018). This intention, however, was never implemented, as the agreed standards were never respected.

With legal and political conditions in their favour, the right-wing alliance approached local government authorities and landowners.[11] At the end of 2011, the mayor granted a construction permit to DESA without the authorisation of the affected communities. At that moment, DESA had already bought some lands in the area. In 2012, the project started with no warning to the local communities. Local community members only became aware of the project's implementation as they saw DESA machinery driving over their lands and destroying their crops. The right-against-rights mobilisation then continued a strategy to push the affected Lenca communities off their lands. Later that year, the company built a fence that prevented the Lenca people of La Tejera from accessing their source of potable water (Bird 2013, 4). This tense situation escalated further in March 2013, when security guards and new signs in the area prevented the Lenca communities from accessing the Gualcarque River, a key site for the spirituality and livelihoods of the Lenca communities.

On 1 April 2013, COPINH and the Lenca communities affected by Agua Zarca created the blockade known as 'El Roblón', a roadblock preventing access to the construction project. They demanded the immediate stop to the Agua Zarca project, which Lenca organisers considered a *proyecto de muerte* – a 'project of death'. Lenca leaders called on all corporate actors involved to withdraw from the project and their lands because they had not authorised its development, as was their right. Corporate representatives of DESA and Sinohydro (the largest hydroelectric dam builder in the world, hired by DESA for the Agua Zarca project) visited El Roblón but used the encounter to insist on the importance of continuing the project. Corporate representatives were accompanied by local authorities, the police, and some members of a community in favour of the project. The encounters also often involved verbal harassment of Berta Cáceres and other COPINH leaders (COPINH 2013a). When these tactics did not work, and COPINH and the local communities continued to make their human rights claims, right-wing mobilisation intensified,

---

[10] This was indeed the approach of President Juan Orlando Hernández, fraudulently re-elected in 2017 (IACHR & OHCHR 2017; OAS 2017). President Hernández was a congressman and the National Congress president in 2010, when the 40 renewable energy contracts were approved. In January 2022, Xiomara Castro, wife of former president Manuel Zelaya, took office as the first female president in Honduras. Her arrival brings high hopes for better protection of women's and Indigenous rights in the country.

[11] Collective legal titles over lands are a way to protect communities' territories. Buying individual property land titles is a way to bypass collective protections over the territory.

170   *Nancy R. Tapias Torrado*

with intimidation, threats, persecution, and attacks against COPINH and La Tejera's local leaders (COPINH 2013b, c).

Additional actors joined the alliance and the right-against-rights mobilisation. At the end of April 2013, the military was active in the area. In May 2013, a permanent military and police presence was installed on the premises of DESA.[12] Aggressive tactics escalated. On 24 May 2013, Berta Cáceres was detained and accused of carrying an unlicensed gun in the back of the pickup truck she was driving. She insisted that the gun had been planted by the military officers when they searched the car. Three months later, Berta Cáceres and two other COPINH leaders faced new criminal charges of usurpation, coercion, and damages to the DESA company. Although unfounded, this criminal investigation could have led to Berta Caceres's detention and imprisonment; she was forced into hiding to avoid that outcome (Amnesty International 2013a, c). During the proceedings, 'DESA's lawyers went as far as to call on the Honduran state to "act with all resources at its disposal to persecute, punish and neutralise" COPINH's actions' (Global Witness 2017, 16).[13]

As COPINH continued mobilising over the Lenca people's rights, the right-against-rights alliance intensified its actions. On 15 July 2013, Tomás García, one of COPINH's local leaders, was shot together with his 17-year-old son, Allan, by a soldier guarding the company's premises. They were participating in a march protest against DESA. Tomás was killed, and his son was severely injured in the incident. Although the soldier who attacked them was later detained, DESA supported him and paid for his legal defence (GAIPE 2017).[14] After Tomás was killed, the staff of Sinohydro left Agua Zarca (Korol 2018, 173). Four months later, Sinohydro publicly explained:

> Right from the very beginning of our mobilisation, it was noticed that there were serious interest conflicts between the Employer of the Project, i.e. DESA, and the local communities, which were treated as unpredictable and uncontrollable to the Contractor. Therefore, Sinohydro Corporation Limited instructed to suspend all the site performance and ongoing preparations, and demobilised all its manpower from the project site on July 15th, 2013. On August 24th, 2013, the Contract Agreement ... was officially terminated.[15] (Sinohydro Group 2013)

Despite these public declarations and Sinohydro's withdrawal from the initial site, the Agua Zarca project continued to be developed in the area. The project only moved a few kilometres away, near to the San Francisco de Ojuera community, still on the Gualcarque River. The company again violated local communities' right to

---

[12] It was established after the death of COPINH leader Paula González in a car accident, which her family and COPINH consider a direct consequence of the imposition of Agua Zarca.

[13] A few months later, all these baseless charges were dropped.

[14] On 10 December 2015, the soldier was found guilty of the killing of Tomás, but the attempted murder of his son remains unpunished.

[15] This communication responds to the 2013 report by the Non-governmental organisation Rights Action on the situation (Bird 2013).

THE EMBLEMATIC CASE OF BERTA CÁCERES IN HONDURAS   171

FPIC. In this scenario, COPINH insisted on its demands for Lenca people's rights. The right-wing alliance responded with even more violence than before. On the night of 2 March 2016 two men broke into Berta Cáceres's house in La Esperanza and shot her dead.[16] Initially, and during the criminal proceedings, the company denied any involvement in the crime and tried to blame it on COPINH. Only a year after her killing did the Netherlands Development Finance Institution (FMO) and the Finnish Fund for Industrial Cooperation (FinnFund) pull out of their participation in the Agua Zarca project.

The murder of Berta Cáceres was the culmination of a myriad of previous attacks, which aimed to intimidate, silence, and demobilise COPINH. The right-wing alliance's persistent and violent tactics ultimately sought to reverse Indigenous rights in order to tip the balance of power to their advantage and profit from economically exploiting the area's resources.

The alliance of the right against rights used a series of tactics to reverse or roll back Indigenous rights, agency, leadership, and mobilisation. The alliance moved from traditional forms of mobilisation to 'uncivil' actions (Payne 2000; Payne (Chapter 2)). Initially those traditional forms of mobilisation involved promoting laws favourable to private economic interests and buying up private lands to achieve economic goals. Although these actions were legally permitted under Honduran norms, they regularly violated the rights of Indigenous communities (e.g. FPIC and collective ancestral legal titles over lands).

In a second stage, the alliance adopted more direct forms of mobilisation that attempted to impose the megaproject development on Indigenous territory, even if those actions went against local communities and their rights. The project was, for example, approved by the local mayor, disregarding the affected Indigenous communities' lack of consent. In these cases, the consultations and consent of local Indigenous communities is mandated by human rights law (e.g. ILO Convention 169).

The right against rights mobilised more aggressively in a third stage to the conflict. In this case, it perceived the local community's mobilisation as a 'threat' or 'obstacle' to the project. Consequently, it used three 'uncivil' mobilisation tactics against rights-seekers: the rejection of their Indigenous identity, the negative framing of Indigenous women leaders and their organisations, and the use of extreme violence.

The affected Indigenous communities that COPINH comprised based their claims on their Indigenous identity and rights, on their cultural and social practices, and on the concerns over their ancestral territory and their long history defending it. The right-against-rights alliance, however, refused to acknowledge their rights as Indigenous communities, or to respect them as collective actors. This tactic was

---

[16] For a detailed account of the crime and investigation that followed, see Lakhani (2020). After the murder social divisions deepened, with the local community favouring Agua Zarca (Dada 2016; COPINH 2018; Vinal 2021).

172   *Nancy R. Tapias Torrado*

demonstrated by DESA, for example, in a letter I received from them on 23 June 2017. In response to several of my questions, they revealed their views on the Lenca people's Indigenous identity. The letter said:

> There is an important level of misinformation regarding the ethnic groups in the area. The majority of people in the area are non-Indigenous. Some sectors of the population self-denominate as Indigenous, but they do not speak the language or follow Lenca traditions ... Furthermore, an Independent Commission hired by FMO and FinnFund established that, based on anthropological studies in the area, there is no Indigenous presence in the area influenced by the Agua Zarca project.[17]

According to the letter, DESA has consistently followed Municipal Law and organised town meetings to consult the affected population. The company erroneously ignored the fact that self-identification is the decisive criterion in defining who are Indigenous peoples, and understood professional experts as those certified to decide on people's ethnicity and identity.[18]

The rejection of Indigenous identity and rights by the right-against-rights alliance draws on a colonial legacy that persists in Honduras and across the region. The Lenca people lost important parts of their culture during the colonisation period and the subsequent long process of assimilation (Tapias Torrado 2020). The Lenca people have always been aware of their Indigenous identity but, as my fieldwork shows, until relatively recently they hid their ethnicity to avoid further discrimination and violence. The processes of colonisation, assimilation, and other forms of violence and discrimination affecting many Indigenous peoples in the Americas – including the Lenca people – have weakened their social fabric and culture. Those destructive processes have made some Indigenous peoples less connected to their ancestral traditions and livelihoods and more dependent on the dominant capitalist system. Additionally, many Indigenous communities rely on external state and private sector services and assistance to survive. Therefore, they are not always likely to protest investment projects that offer jobs and other resources, even when those projects threaten their ancestral territories.

The right-against-rights tactic of rejecting Indigenous identity allows for the diminishment of legitimacy claims, contending instead that they are 'poor people', living on 'barren lands' and needing 'development' (Hale 2011). In its letter, DESA, in fact, used the local community's impoverishment as a justification for its actions associated with the project. In DESA's words, the project meant the 'opportunity to overcome poverty' in the area. This is a commonly used argument to justify the development of megaprojects, and goes against the lived experience of those in the community who have suffered from its impact. In essence, denying Indigenous communities' identity is a disempowering tactic. It affects Indigenous

---

[17] My translation from the original Spanish.
[18] Given the broad diversity and heterogeneity of Indigenous people and peoples, a precise definition risks excluding some of them. Therefore, per Article 1(2) of the American Declaration on Indigenous Peoples, the decisive criterion is self-identification (OAS 2016). Other additional considerations – both objective and subjective – are in Article 1.1 of ILO Convention 169 (ILO 1989).

THE EMBLEMATIC CASE OF BERTA CÁCERES IN HONDURAS   173

subjectivity, agency, and mobilisation. It is part of a series of processes that precede the development of megaprojects, and extends to a continuum of accumulation of power and capital by subordinating and dispossessing others, including modernisation, industrialisation, colonialism, and development (Petras and Veltmeyer 2001; Harvey 2003; Veltmeyer and Petras 2015). While reaffirming their identity as Indigenous people was crucial for the COPINH's mobilisation, it was essential for the right against rights to counter that 'there is no Indigenous presence' in the area. It resembles the *terra nullius* doctrine used in the region in colonial times.[19]

Another 'uncivil' mobilisation tactic was the negative framing of COPINH and the local communities. For example, DESA ended its letter to me of 23 June 2017 with this paragraph: 'the strength of opposition groups responds in many cases to a particular national and international strategy, but it is possible to ... avoid misunderstandings and misinterpretations when the correct story is told correctly. Everything that has happened in recent years has been marked by different deceptions and manipulations from organisations such as COPINH, which creates confusions that need to be later corrected.'[20]

Portraying COPINH as manipulative and deceitful belongs to a negative framing tactic consistently used by the right against rights. The company, in alliance with others, attempted to undermine COPINH's public credibility and legitimacy. It attempts to weaken rights-seekers' mobilisation potential and unravel their 'braid of action' by using discrediting tactics in the legal, social, and political fields. It directly mobilises to counter ideas and meanings generated by COPINH in defence of human rights (Benford and Snow 2000).

The denigrating framing of COPINH is identified by Payne (Chapter 2) as a tactic used by right-against-rights mobilisations, and uncivil movements in particular, to weaken social movements' appeal and legitimacy. In the COPINH case, this involved fabricating criminal accusations; digital harassment; and stigmatisation, such as creating fake Facebook and Twitter profiles to defame COPINH leaders. The right against rights mobilised behind a campaign 'claiming to reveal "the truth about COPINH" [to show that its] members have committed serious crimes while advocating [for rights]' (Amnesty International 2013b).

The negative framing continued before and after Berta Cáceres's murder, and throughout the criminal procedures related to it. The criminal investigation began with the hypothesis of 'a crime of passion'. Then, it changed to a 'crime that resulted from conflicts within COPINH'. Both claims ignored DESA's possible role. In the face of this situation, and fearing that the state authorities would not investigate the intellectual actors of the crime, COPINH and Berta Cáceres's family demanded an effective and independent investigation before the United Nations (UN), the Inter-American Commission on Human Rights (IACHR), and many other international

---

[19] *Terra nullius* generally means the disposition of Indigenous lands justified on their alleged inferiority, and the occupation of the so-called 'empty lands.'

[20] My translation.

174   *Nancy R. Tapias Torrado*

and national organisations, but the Honduran state denied their request. They thus worked with the Honduran Broad Movement for Dignity and Justice, the Centre for Justice and International Law, and other national and international organisations to form the International Advisory Group of Experts (GAIPE) to advance their demand. An investigation was conducted by GAIPE, and a report issued presenting evidence of the company's involvement in the murder.

In turn, DESA hired the international law firm Amsterdam & Partners LLP (AP LLP) and a public relations company to handle its side of the case. In 2018, AP LLP issued the report 'War on Development: Exposing the COPINH Disinformation Campaign Surrounding the Berta Cáceres Case in Honduras'. It claims DESA employees' innocence by arguing, among other things, that the report issued by GAIPE is 'blatantly non-objective, and has served as COPINH's most important foundational propaganda instrument to recruit allies among the NGO community who have neglected to independently analyse the facts of the case', while COPINH 'has carried out a fraud by misinforming the public and twisting the facts to fit their story' (AP LLP 2018, 4, 26). The view of AP LLP is based on a report that it commissioned from a Canadian criminal lawyer (Greenspan 2018). The document frames COPINH as a violent and radical organisation, which misled and misinformed others (for example 'deceiving' international media and organisations, and 'fooling' the UN Special Rapporteur on the Rights of Indigenous Peoples) (AP LLP 2018, 16).

As an Indigenous female leader, in a predominantly patriarchal society, Berta Cáceres had her image viciously attacked. She was frequently and publicly accused of being 'a bitch', 'a witch', a 'mad woman', and the mother of a 'dysfunctional family' (Korol 2018, 178).

Violence was also used by the right-against-rights alliance. Even before the taking of her life, Cáceres and COPINH suffered numerous violent incidents, including death threats against COPINH members and the killing of Tomás García. In the last few weeks before her murder, Berta Cáceres filed more than 30 complaints about the most recent death threats against her. These threats were not investigated. In fact, according to the GAIPE report:

> The company appears to have used funds originating from the financial system to increase the levels of violence in the company's zone of influence and to systematically attack members of COPINH and Berta ... GAIPE has been able to establish the participation of executives, managers, and employees of DESA; of private security personnel hired by the company; and of state agents and parallel structures to state security forces in crimes committed before, during, and after March 2, 2016. (GAIPE 2017, 2–3)

The evidence was so strong that even the Honduran courts had to recognise the company's involvement. In December 2019, seven men were sentenced to between 30 and 50 years' imprisonment for the murder of Berta Cáceres. They were DESA's Manager of Social, Environment, and Communications Affairs; DESA's Head of Security; a major on active duty in the armed forces; and four paid hitmen. On 5 July 2021, David Castillo, DESA's Executive Director at the time of Berta's killing, was found guilty of participating in her murder.

THE EMBLEMATIC CASE OF BERTA CÁCERES IN HONDURAS 175

In the end, and despite the power imbalance between the company and its allies and the Indigenous movement, justice prevailed. Justice in this one case, however, does not necessarily signify the capacity of Indigenous and environmental social movements to prevent the rollback of rights. This topic is explored in the next section.

The Impact of the Right against Rights and Violent Mobilisation

Human rights defenders in Honduras have faced a critical situation of risk for many years. Between 2009 and 2017, over 120 defenders of land, territory, and Indigenous rights were killed (Global Witness 2017). Between 2016 and 2017, 1,232 attacks against women human rights defenders were registered, and 444 of these attacks were against those defending Indigenous people's land and environmental rights (Red Nacional de Defensoras de Honduras 2018, 40).[21] In 2021, Honduras continued to be among the countries with the highest number of land, environmental, and Indigenous rights-defenders killed (Front Line Defenders 2021). The many attacks against COPINH members and the killing of Berta Cáceres belong to a larger pattern of attacks against human rights defenders in Honduras. These 'uncivil' actions, their impunity,[22] and the lack of effective protection measures for those at risk have perpetuated a spiral of violence that emboldens aggressors and increases the vulnerability of activists. The fragility of their situation was even more evident with the murder of Berta Cáceres. She was killed despite being one of the most prominent, recognised, and supported human rights defenders in the country, who had valid Precautionary Measures ordered by the IACHR.[23] These 'uncivil tactics' have indeed created fear and made human rights defenders increasingly vulnerable to attacks, especially because the Honduran state has failed in its human rights obligations to protect them and investigate the attacks (UN 1998).

A closer look at Berta Cáceres's case shows two additional impacts of the right-against-rights mobilisation. First, the tactics of denying COPINH's Indigenous identity and denigrating its members had the reverse of the intended effect, in strengthening their need to reaffirm their identity, legitimacy, and claims. For example, when Berta was facing fabricated criminal charges and was forced into hiding, she said: 'We decided to sustain the struggle and to intensify the national

---

[21] They comprised six killings and numerous cases of intimidation, death threats, domestic violence, and sexual violence, among other things. In most of these cases, the aggressors are unknown. Where known, they were mostly from the police, the community, the corporations, the social movement, or the military, or were a family member or the partner of the victim.

[22] In a report dedicated to impunity, the UN Special Rapporteur on Human Rights Defenders (HRDs) corroborated that the overwhelming majority of attacks against HRDs remain unpunished. Worryingly, 'it has not been possible to produce statistics that reflect the magnitude of this issue owing to the lack of any official record' (UNGA 2019, paras 23–4).

[23] Between 2012 and 2017, 14 HRDs with measures issued by the IACHR were killed. Ten of them were defending rights in relation to land and territory, and five were Indigenous leaders, including COPINH members Berta Cáceres and Nelson García.

176   *Nancy R. Tapias Torrado*

and international activities in our protest. I feel very supported; I do not feel alone. They have been unable to impose fear or terror. We remain firm. I feel safe, dignified and strong' (Korol 2018, 176–7). When rights-defenders have already created a strong 'braid of action', targeted attacks can trigger reinforcing reactions.

Furthermore, building on that idea and the fourth strand of the 'braid of action', I argue that COPINH harnessed even more power, reacting with further cohesion and mobilisation for rights, and against these acts of severe repression. This mobilisation was strong at many levels, and when the right against rights committed grave crimes against COPINH's mobilisation, there was a backlash against them; the mobilisation for rights was reaffirmed and strengthened. All these strands together in one braid managed to harness a strong force to lift up rights. Thus, the most extreme violence used by the right-against-rights alliance ended up negatively affecting the alliance, an outcome anticipated in some of the social movement literature (Hess and Martin 2006) and reinforced in this volume (Chapter 2). After Tomás García was murdered and mobilisations intensified, Sinohydro left the project and ceased its participation in Agua Zarca. After Cáceres's murder, FMO and FinnFund suspended their support for the project (FMO 2016), and ended their contracts with DESA a year later (FMO 2017). Even state actors in the courts distanced themselves from the company, by holding its staff legally accountable for murder (Tapias Torrado 2022a). This seems to confirm that extreme positions, especially supporting violence, can fragment unity within the right against rights, weakening its power (Payne (Chapter 2)).

In sum, the case of DESA and COPINH in Honduras shows how the right against rights is willing to use all of the resources at its disposal to defend its own traditional rights and prerogatives over investment, production, and profits. In this case, radical neoliberalism confronted a powerful Indigenous and environmental social movement in a context of international and national rights victories, at least in normative and institutional terms. To roll back those rights, the right against rights expanded its mobilisation from within the state to outside, using 'uncivil' tactics. Ultimately, however, the 'uncivil' mobilisation could not overcome the power of COPINH, garnered through the 'braid of action'.

Conclusion

This chapter explored the right-against-rights alliance in the mobilisation that consolidated the murder of the Lenca leader Berta Cáceres, and how this alliance pursued a violent agenda in the conflict over Indigenous and environmental rights between DESA and COPINH. In this conflict, the right against rights attempted to reverse Indigenous rights and the mobilisation defending it with the use of 'uncivil' tactics, including extreme violence. They failed, however, to consolidate their hydroelectric dam project by violating and rolling back Indigenous rights. The power harnessed by the 'braid of action' did not fray, it became stronger, and COPINH was able to advance its struggle for rights and justice. After her murder, Berta Cáceres became an iconic figure and an inspiration for Indigenous, environmental, and women's rights defenders. Instead of being silenced and forgotten, she continues to be widely remembered. Her words continue to resonate around Latin America and the world, where the situation of Indigenous and environmental defenders challenging the abuses committed in connection to megaprojects continues to be a pressing issue.

The emblematic case of Berta Cáceres has revealed the several tactics – legal and illegal – by which economic actors pursue their economic interests, even rolling back Indigenous, environmental, and other human rights. However, economic actors and their alliances may not be grouped as a unified, single right-wing movement or conservative force. The right against Indigenous and environmental rights includes countermovements, uncivil movements, and radical neoliberal mobilisations. It aims not only to reverse, roll back, or block rights, but also, at times, to eliminate rights-seekers, such as Berta Cáceres. Strong alliances within state and society have tended to allow them to expand rights and prerogatives for investment, production, and profits at the expense of communities. When that has failed, recourse to violence may occur.

The case of Berta Cáceres and COPINH is particularly important to highlight that while the tactics of the right against rights usually win the battles they engage in, this is not always the case. As Payne shows in Chapter 2, where the right against rights comes up against powerful social movement mobilisation with strong domestic and international linkages, it may itself be rolled back. Berta Cáceres and COPINH had already created an enduring, transformative mobilisation, which was able powerfully to oppose the right-wing alliance that was defending the Agua Zarca project in Honduras. In other words, Berta Cáceres and COPINH managed to overcome both legal and legitimate and 'uncivil' tactics implemented by the right against rights. The COPINH continues to seek justice and to defend the Lenca communities, and the voice of Berta Cáceres still resonates throughout Honduras and the world.

References

Amnesty International (2013a), 'Defending Human Rights in Honduras Is a Crime', https://www.amnesty.org/en/latest/news/2013/11/honduras-human-rights-defenders-under-threat/.

Amnesty International (2013b), 'Further Information on UA: 244/13', https://www.amnesty.org/es/wp-content/uploads/2021/06/amr370132013en.pdf.

Amnesty International (2013c), 'UA: 244/13. Indigenous Leaders Face Unjust Charges', https://www.amnestyusa.org/files/uaa24413.pdf.

AP LLP [Amsterdam & Partners LLP] (2018), 'War on Development: Exposing the COPINH Disinformation Campaign Surrounding the Berta Cáceres Case in Honduras', https://amsterdamandpartners.com/wp-content/uploads/2019/03/War-on-Development-Ver-4.pdf.

178   *Nancy R. Tapias Torrado*

Benford, R. D. and D. Snow (2000), 'Framing Processes and Social Movements: An Overview and Assessment', *Annual Review of Sociology*, 26 (August), 611–39.

BHRRC [Business & Human Rights Resource Centre] (2022), 'Human Rights Defenders & Civic Freedoms', https://www.business-humanrights.org/en/big-issues/human-rights-defenders-civic-freedoms/.

Bird, A. (2013), 'The Agua Zarca Dam and Lenca Communities in Honduras: Transnational Investment Leads to Violence against and Criminalization of Indigenous Communities', http://rightsaction.org/sites/default/files/Rpt_131001_RioBlanco_Final.pdf.

CEHPRODEC [Honduran Centre for the Promotion of Community Development] (2018), *La producción de energía eléctrica en honduras* (Tegucigalpa, CEHPRODEC).

COPINH [Council of Popular and Indigenous Organisations of Honduras] (2013a), 'COMUNICADO URGENTE: A cuatro días de lucha continuamos firmes en defensa de nuestros ríos exigiendo la salida del proyecto hidroeléctrico Agua Zarca', https://cop inh.org/2013/04/comunicado-urgente-a-cuatro-dias-de-lucha-continuamos-firmes-en-defensa-de-nuestros-rios-exigiendo-la-salida-del-proyecto-hidroelectrico-agua-zarca/.

COPINH [Council of Popular and Indigenous Organisations of Honduras] (2013b), 'COPINH – COMUNICADOS URGENTES: ¡A SIETE DÍAS LA LUCHA SIGUE!', https://copinh.org/2013/04/copinh-comunicados-urgentes-a-siete-dias-la-lucha-sigue/.

COPINH [Council of Popular and Indigenous Organisations of Honduras] (2013c), 'COPINH toma de carreteras en Rio Blanco', YouTube, https://www.youtube.com/watch?v=Bf9vJyrF894.

COPINH [Council of Popular and Indigenous Organisations of Honduras] (2018), 'Alerta! Familia Madrid empleados de la empresa DESA ataca a comunidad de Río Blanco', https://copinh.org/2018/09/alerta-familia-madrid-empleados-de-la-empresa-desa-ataca-a-comunidad-de-rio-blanco/.

Cunha Filho, C. M., A. L. Coelho, and F. I. Perez Flores (2013), 'A Right-to-Left Policy Switch? An Analysis of the Honduran Case under Manuel Zelaya', *International Political Science Review*, 34:5, 519–42.

Dada, C. (2016), 'Por aquí pasó Berta Cáceres', *El Faro*, https://elfaro.net/es/201609/centro america/19291/Por-aqui-paso-berta-caceres.htm.

FMO [Netherlands Development Finance Institution] (2016), 'FMO Suspends All Activities in Honduras Effective Immediately', https://www.fmo.nl/news-detail/9483b943-4b56-487e-b392-a1464c781a2b/fmo-suspends-all-activities-in-honduras-effective-imme diately.

FMO [Netherlands Development Finance Institution] (2017), 'FMO and Finnfund Finalize Exit Agua Zarca', https://www.fmo.nl/news-detail/21a7c615-a32b-471c-9378-60317 196daf6/fmo-and-finnfund-finalize-exit-agua-zarca.

Front Line Defenders (2021), 'Global Analysis', https://www.frontlinedefenders.org/sites/default/files/2021_global_analysis_-_final.pdf.

GAIPE [Grupo Asesor Internacional de Personas Expertas] (2017), 'Dam Violence: The Plan that Killed Berta Cáceres', November, https://www.gaipe.net/wp-content/uploads/2017/10/GAIPE-Report-English.pdf.

Global Witness (2017), 'Honduras: The Deadliest Country in the World for Environmental Activism', https://www.globalwitness.org/en/campaigns/environmental-activists/honduras-el-país-más-peligroso-del-mundo-para-el-activismo-ambiental/.

Greenspan, B. (2018), *The Greenspan Report*, https://casocaceres.com/en/el-informe-greenspan/.

Hale, C. R. (2011), 'Resistencia para que? Territory, Autonomy and Neoliberal Entanglements in the "Empty Spaces" of Central America', *Economy and Society*, 40:2, 184–210.

THE EMBLEMATIC CASE OF BERTA CÁCERES IN HONDURAS   179

Harvey, D. (2003), *The New Imperialism* (Oxford, Oxford University Press).

Hedström, P. and P. Bearman (2017), *The Oxford Handbook of Analytical Sociology* (Oxford, Oxford University Press).

Hedström, P. and R. Swedberg (1998), *Social Mechanisms: An Analytical Approach to Social Theory* (Cambridge, Cambridge University Press).

Hess, D. and B. Martin (2006), 'Repression, Backfire, and the Theory of Transformative Events', *Mobilization*, 11:2, 249–67.

IACHR [Inter-American Commission on Human Rights] (2013), 'Annual Report, Chapter IV, Honduras', http://www.oas.org/en/iachr/docs/annual/2013/TOC.asp.

IACHR [Inter-American Commission on Human Rights] and OHCHR [Office of the High Commissioner for Human Rights] (2017), 'IACHR and OHCHR Express Concern over Post-Election Violence in Honduras', http://www.oas.org/en/iachr/media_center/PReleases/2017/197.asp.

ILO [International Labour Organization] (1989), 'Indigenous and Tribal Peoples Convention (no.169),https://www.ilo.org/dyn/normlex/en/f?p=NORMLEXPUB:12100:0::NO:12100:P12100_INSTRUMENT_ID:312314:NO.

ISHR [International Service for Human Rights] (2015), 'Human Rights Defenders and Corporate Accountability', http://www.ishr.ch/sites/default/files/documents/business_and_human_rights_monitor_-_english_november_2015-final_last_version-2.pdf.

Korol, C. (2018), *Las revoluciones de Berta* (Buenos Aires, América Libre).

Lakhani, N. (2020), *Who Killed Berta Cáceres? Dams, Death Squads, and an Indigenous Defender's Battle for the Planet* (London, Verso).

OAS [Organization of American States] (2016), 'American Declaration on the Rights of Indigenous Peoples', AG/RES. 2888 (XLVI-O/16)), https://www.oas.org/en/sare/documents/DecAmIND.pdf.

OAS [Organization of American States] (2017), 'Declaration of the OAS General Secretariat Regarding the Presidential Elections in Honduras', http://www.oas.org/en/media_center/press_release.asp?sCodigo=E-090/17.

Payne, L. A. (2000), *Uncivil Movements: The Armed Right Wing and Democracy in Latin America* (Baltimore, Johns Hopkins University Press).

Payne, L. A., G. Pereira, and L. Bernal-Bermúdez (2020), *Transitional Justice and Corporate Accountability from Below: Deploying Archimedes' Lever* (Cambridge, Cambridge University Press).

Petras, J. and H. Veltmeyer (2001), *Globalization Unmasked: Imperialisms in the 21st Century* (Halifax, NS, Fernwood).

Red Nacional de Defensoras de Honduras (2018), *Informe sobre la situación de defensoras*, http://im-defensoras.org/wp-content/uploads/2018/05/Informe-de-Agresiones-a-defensoras-2016-2017.pdf.

Scott, J. C. (1985), *Weapons of the Weak: Everyday Forms of Peasant Resistance* (New Haven, Yale University Press).

Sinohydro Group (2013), 'Response to Report by Rights Action about Alleged Violence & Intimidation against Lenca Indigenous Communities Related to the Constructions of Agua Zarca Dam, Honduras', Business & Human Rights Resource Centre, https://www.business-humanrights.org/en/latest-news/sinohydro-group-response-to-report-by-rights-action-about-alleged-violence-intimidation-against-lenca-Indigenous-communities-related-to-the-constructions-of-agua-zarca-dam-honduras/.

Tapias Torrado, N. R. (2020), 'Indigenous Women Leading the Defence of Human Rights from the Abuses by Mega-Projects in Latin America, in the Face of Extreme Violence', D.Phil. dissertation, University of Oxford, https://ora.ox.ac.uk/objects/uuid:3a1393b3-1a8b-4341-bb6e-7a33897db5c7.

Tapias Torrado, N. R. (2022a), 'Honduras: ¡Berta vive, la lucha sigue! Corporate Accountability for Attacks against Human Rights Defenders', in *Economic Actors and the Limits of Transitional Justice: Truth and Justice for Past Business Complicity in Human Rights*, ed. L. A. Payne, G. Pereira, and L. Bernal-Bermúdez (Oxford, Oxford University Press), pp. 214–35.

Tapias Torrado, N. R. (2022b), 'Overcoming Silencing Practices: Indigenous Women Defending Human Rights from Abuses Committed in Connection to Mega-Projects: A Case in Colombia', *Business and Human Rights Journal*, 7:1, 9–44.

UN [United Nations] (1998), 'Declaración sobre las defensoras y los defensores de los derechos humanos, Asamblea General', http://www.ohchr.org/Documents/Issues/Defenders/Declaration/declaration_sp.pdf.

UN [United Nations] (2011), 'Guiding Principles on Business and Human Rights: Implementing the United Nations "Protect, Respect and Remedy" Framework' (New York, United Nations Office of the High Commissioner for Human Rights), https://www.ohchr.org/sites/default/files/documents/publications/guidingprinciplesbusinesshr_en.pdf.

UN [United Nations] (2018), 'Free, Prior and Informed Consent: A Human Rights-Based Approach – Study of the Expert Mechanism on the Rights of Indigenous Peoples', 10 August, A/HRC/39/62, https://www.ohchr.org/en/documents/thematic-reports/free-prior-and-informed-consent-human-rights-based-approach-study-expert.

UNGA [United Nations General Assembly] (2017), 'Report of the Special Rapporteur on the Situation of Human Rights Defenders', A/72/170, https://undocs.org/en/A/72/170.

Veltmeyer, H. and J. Petras (2015), *El neoextractivismo: ¿Un modelo posneoliberal de desarrollo o el imperialismo del siglo XXI?* (Mexico, Crítica).

Vinal, S. (dir.) (2021), *La lucha sigue (The Struggle Continues)*, documentary film (Mutual Aid Media).

10

Opposing Affirmative Action: Covert and Coded Challenges to Racial Equality in Uruguay*

DEBBIE SHARNAK

IN LATE 2013, Bertha Sanseverino, an elected representative to the Uruguayan Chamber of Deputies from the governing leftist party Frente Amplio, wrote a message on Facebook to her supporters about the previous year's legislative achievements. She commended the party's accomplishments, asserting that parliament had 'passed good laws that consolidated rights … and promoted more equality' (Sanseverino 2013). First among her list of achievements was Law 19.122, the Affirmative Action Law for People of African Descent: a significant piece of legislation that sought to address the country's history of racism and discrimination. It was a noteworthy accomplishment for the rights it sought to further for Afro-Uruguayans. Yet, it was also significant because the law had overcome opposition during its path toward passage in parliament – and it would continue to face challenges in its implementation from the country's right-wing mobilisations. This chapter explores this opposition, analysing the nature and means of the right's pushback against legislative attempts to further racial equality in Uruguay.

The 2013 affirmative action law ultimately centred on three main provisions. First, it mandated teaching about Afro-Uruguayan history, which until 2013 had been completely omitted from state schools' curricula. Second, it granted Afro-descendants access to more scholarships and vocational training to increase and improve employment opportunities. Last, the law established a quota in government employment, setting aside 8 per cent of vacancies for Afro-Uruguayans

---

* I wish to thank Ariette Escobar for her help with research; my colleagues at Rowan University for feedback on a talk I gave on this chapter at the Rowan Center for the Study of the Holocaust, Genocide, and Human Rights; and Rachel Gross, Christine Lamberson, Britt Tevis, Leigh A. Payne, Julia Zulver, Simón Escoffier, Cristóbal Rovira Kaltwasser, and Lindsay Mayka for their comments on earlier versions of the chapter.

Proceedings of the British Academy, **255**, 181–204, © The British Academy 2023.

(ROU 2013c). The law marked the culmination of decades of Afro-Uruguayan organisation for rights that largely began when the country transitioned back to democratic rule in 1985.[1] After exclusion and discrimination from the nation's founding was exacerbated during the Cold War dictatorship, Afro-Uruguayans utilised the transitional context and joined a global movement of growing racially based activism to push for official inclusion in the Uruguayan state. They formed organisations, founded newspapers, and protested against racism and discrimination, injecting a discourse about race into the national conversation that had previously been largely absent. In this way, the restoration of democracy after the depths of despair during the dictatorships led to the creation of a vibrant civil rights movement that empowered Afro-Uruguayan citizens to mobilise for inclusion and racial equality. One of the most tangible results of these efforts was the 2013 affirmative action law.

To date, very few scholars have studied the law, its passage, or attempts at its implementation.[2] Moreover, no scholarship exists on those who opposed it. Part of this absence is explained by the fact that forces against Afro-Uruguayan rights are not part of traditional approaches to right-wing mobilisation (Payne (Chapter 2)). There is no formal movement or concerted organisation, voice, or vision against Afro-Uruguayan rights or equality of opportunities. There are no protests in the streets against them, or anyone arguing in newspapers that the idea of racial equality is not a worthwhile goal. Uruguay sees itself as a historically tolerant and progressive country; consequently, very few overt instances of race-based hostility have occurred in response to the law, making opposition to it difficult to identify. Instead, a coded discourse (Payne (Chapter 2)) emerged in opposition to the law and its implementation from a disparate group of right-wing actors operating both within and outside government. By coding its racist elements, the mobilisation against the law appealed to diverse constituencies that may reject overt forms of racism, such as the business community, but also political figures and political party members. This strategy served to avoid losing adherence among those who would not like to be identified as racists. Yet, this pushback also functions as a continued form of structural racism, whereby people are in favour of symbolic and limited gestures toward acknowledging Afro-Uruguayan equality, but want to constrain

---

[1] During the dictatorship, the military sought to eliminate perceived leftist subversives, often exerting its control through political imprisonment, torture, and disappearances. Afro-Uruguayans were victims of these systematic human rights violations, which affected the entire nation, but they also suffered high rates of internal displacement as the military targeted historic Afro-descendant communities as part of the capital city's gentrification process. In these cases, the military forced Afro-Uruguayans out of their communities, often with no compensation, dispersing them to the literal and figurative margins of the country. With the fall of the regime in the mid-1980s, however, Black civic mobilisation surged as part of the 'rights revolution' identified in Chapters 1 and 2 of this volume (Olaza 2017a). See also D. Sharnak, 2022 and 2023.

[2] Two notable exceptions are Olaza (2017b) and Townsend-Bell (2021).

more radical measures for addressing the root causes of this inequality, such as poverty, access to education, and jobs. They utilise a remarkably consistent language and set of actions that seek to preserve the status quo and limit gains by the left.

Thus, this chapter takes the case of Uruguay to analyse and uncover the backlash against rights that does not fit easily within the existing literature and categorisation of right-wing mobilisations. By exploring the racially coded debate in parliament that sought to limit the law's effects, as well as the struggles to realise its implementation, the chapter seeks to recognise how, even in progressive Uruguay, informal 'mobilisations' against rights can emerge in coded and covert terms where political actors oppose and obstruct legislation. This pushback is perhaps not as easy to identify or call out as anti-abortion activists in El Salvador or the anti-LGBT+ movement in Brazil that Leigh Payne writes about in Chapter 2. In those cases, it is socially and politically acceptable to invoke religion against these rights initiatives; it is much more out of fashion politically to invoke explicit racial difference and organise around it. However, political actors utilised the legislative debate process and somewhat lax implementation efforts to limit the advancement of rights, in spite of the progressive political agenda of the governing party. Indeed, because there was no formal right-wing movement with a title, official organisation, or charismatic leader, those who opposed the law were able to act more stealthily within parliament and state agencies. Uruguay's case compels scholars to expand the typologies of right-wing mobilisation to consider less overt countermovements from the right-against-rights gains, and deserves further exploration as another form of effective pushback that operates against equality in Latin America.

To show as much, this chapter is organised as follows. First, it briefly explores the history of Afro-descendants in Uruguay, uncovering a larger pattern of invisibility and struggle for official recognition to understand the particularities of Uruguay's racial past. Next, it examines the parliamentary debates around the affirmative action law in 2013, focusing on arguments against the law and reading against the grain to uncover coded forms of discrimination and attempts at limiting its scope. Third, it uses government reports and public discourse about the law after its passage to analyse its slow implementation. While legislators failed to prevent the law's passage in parliament, anti-rights activists have succeeded much more in slowing its implementation, particularly in the case of filling the quotas of state agencies. Finally, it concludes by contextualising opposition to Afro-Uruguayan rights within recent, more formal right-wing mobilisation against the Frente Amplio agenda after the law's passage, revealing how the same right-wing activists who opposed the affirmative action law gained ground in other anti-democratic efforts, such as anti-LGBT+ rights. This section connects traditional anti-rights mobilisation to more covert forms against racial equality. Ultimately, this chapter uses the case of Uruguay to show how, even in the absence of mobilisation in the streets, the right against rights has adapted racially coded language to undermine the implementation of legislation that would advance rights for previously marginalised groups. This tactic expands our understanding of how the right blocks rights in Latin America.

A History of Invisibility

Uruguay has long denied the presence and impact of its Afro-Uruguayan population in the country's history and social life. Montevideo was the official port of entry for African slaves for the entire Río de la Plata region starting in the colonial period, and historian Alex Borucki (2015) notes that Afro-descendant invisibility began simultaneously. In his vignette-laden historical overview of Latin America, *Faces and Masks*, famous Uruguayan writer Eduardo Galeano (1987, 21) writes: 'From Buenos Aires come the first settlers, fifteen young people, nineteen children, and a few slaves who do not figure on the list – black hands for the axe, the hoe, and the gallows, breasts to give milk, a voice to cry wares.' Yet, as he points out, many slaves came to the territory. They played a critical part in the functioning of colonial society, which ranged from producing cattle hide, the country's most valued export; to harvesting and cooking food; to working in industries such as carpentry, shoe-making, and tailoring (Borucki 2015, 3, 8). Afro-descendants were important to the social and cultural fabric of the colony in the earliest days of outsiders' arrival. Yet, they were still overwhelmingly ignored in both official registers and in the historical memory of this period.

Afro-Uruguayans' invisibility continued during the post-independence period as well. On the eve of independence in 1825, Africans or Afro-Uruguayans constituted as much as 25 per cent of the population. In the subsequent years, many fought in the wars for independence in exchange for their freedom, and slavery was officially abolished in 1842 (Andrews 2011; Borucki 2015, 17).[3] The Dirección General de Estadística y Censos carried out the country's first census in 1852 and included a question about race, but it did not appear again until 2011 (Loveman 2014, Chapter 2; Andrews 2004, 7, 117–24).[4] Further, by the late 19th century, Uruguay began a process of *blanqueamiento*, or whitening, which, by the turn of the century, meant promoting an image of its population as made up of immigrants from western and southern Europe as proof of its modernity and racial progress (Hernández 2013, 20; Loveman 2014, 208–9; Arocena Armas 2013, 140; Quijano 2000, 562–3; Cottrol 2013, 16–17, 113–142; Andrews 2010b, 117–51; Wade 1993, 12). As a result, most official histories of the country largely ignored the tens of thousands of slaves brought to its shores from Africa, their descendants, and their subsequent collective impact on the nation (Bucheli and Porzecanski 2011, 113; Sans 2011, 197–8). Textbooks used in primary schools in Uruguay as late as the 1980s reinforced a strong European lineage and the whiteness of Uruguay's population, relegating Afro-descendants to the literal and figurative margins of national

---

[3] Slavery was officially abolished in 1842 by the Uruguayan Senate during the Guerra Grande, when most able-bodied Black men were conscripted to fight for either the Blancos or the Colorados (Goyena and Canstatt 1874).

[4] In the 1852 census, 'Black and Brown' categories represented a total of 8.8 per cent of the population. Race was also included in the 1884 municipal census in Montevideo, but not at the national level.

OPPOSING AFFIRMATIVE ACTION: URUGUAY 185

consciousness (*Brecha* 1985b).[5] This characterisation of a 'white' Uruguay has proven remarkably persistent. Indeed, Bucheli and Porzecanski (2011, 116) conclude that Uruguayans tend to accept the myths of 'racial democracy, homogeneity, and equality of opportunity'.

This myth of whiteness, however, belies a much deeper history of Afro-Uruguayan presence in Uruguay's cultural and political history, including that of those who organised in reaction to the *blanqueamiento* process. While Afro-Uruguayans often suffered from discrimination and higher rates of poverty, there was an active Black press, and *candombe* – a Uruguayan dance with rhythmic music adopted from slave traditions – proved incredibly popular across the entire country. Likewise, Uruguay was the first country in the world to have Black players on its national football team, many of whom indeed made an impact on their World Cup winning teams (Andrews 2010a, 83–4; Persico 2015; Galeano 2013, 53; Nadel 2014, 152). Afro-Uruguayans also organised social clubs and founded a short-lived political party (Andrews 2010b, 88, 92–3, 96–111). In 1941, the white poet and anthropologist Ildefonso Pereda Valdés led the charge to establish Afro-Uruguayan studies as a reaction to the *blanqueamiento* process, helping to elevate the presence and work of Afro-Uruguayans (Pereda Valdés 1941). This helped puncture the nation's homogeneous self-image and brought Afro-Uruguayan contributions to mainstream consciousness (Andrews 2010b, 99–100; Carvalho Neto 1954; Holmes 1944; Pereda Valdés 1965). Still, despite the considerable and varied impacts of Afro-Uruguayans on the country's political and cultural landscape, through the mid-20th century, Uruguay promoted an image of its white citizenry and largely excluded its African-origin population.

During the country's dictatorship from 1973 to 1985, the nature of discrimination and exclusion of Afro-Uruguayans changed. They not only suffered under the repressive conditions that the military government imposed on the entire population, but also experienced higher rates of forced removal from historic Afro-Uruguayan centres of community life in *conventillos*, a type of planned housing tenement building, as part of the dictatorship's neoliberal project to modernise the capital (Sztainbok 2009; *Diario* 1978; Ruetalo 2008, 39–40). The effects of this forced displacement were profound for Afro-Uruguayan populations. While they had been ignored and discriminated against throughout Uruguayan history, the population's forced displacement by the military in Montevideo brought into focus the physical, social, and psychological ways that Afro-Uruguayans could be displaced from the centres of Uruguayan life, especially without a formal recognition of their population from the state.

Thus, in the aftermath of the dictatorship, forceful efforts to challenge this marginalisation and discrimination emerged. Societal discussions about democratisation provided an opening for a renegotiation of the relationship between states

---

[5] People often refer to the enduring idea that Uruguay, until very recently, was characterised as 'a white, European country that did not have a black population'. See Luz (2013, 113) and Cottrol (2013, 124).

186   *Debbie Sharnak*

and citizens in the newly reconstituted democratic state (Loveman 2014, 266–7; Kenny 2018, 64–5; Andrews 2004, 82–3). In the post-dictatorship period, a group of younger and more politically left-leaning Afro-Uruguayans utilised the transitional environment to vocalise collective dissent and to advocate for a broad range of social, political, and economic rights. They organised a racially defined Black mobilisation effort in direct response to the plight of those who had been displaced during the dictatorship, and to the racism that their communities had faced historically, which continued unabated (*Brecha* 1985a).[6] These activists formed numerous non-governmental organisations, such as Organización Mundo Afro, Casa de la Cultura Afro, Mizangas, and Grupo Cultural Afrogama (Rodríguez 1988; CPDI 2013b). Together, these groups worked to increase Afro-Uruguayan presence and visibility within the state to promote recognition of the profound cultural presence that Afro-Uruguayans had in the country, and to counter discrimination in schools, the workplace, and larger society. Their efforts found success by providing an organising force to push forward measures in both municipal and national spheres, such as passing a law to declare a National Day of *Candombe*, Afro-Uruguayan Culture, and Racial Equity in 2006 (ROU 2006).[7] They also began to advocate for race to be accounted for in the next census, a move for recognition that was part of a larger effort occurring around Latin America during this period.

Across the region, Afro-descendants had begun mobilising for racially aware censuses in the late 20th century to address the absence of an official Afro-Latin presence in these nations. Without censuses that included racial demography in any country except Brazil and Cuba at the time, however, there was no way to document the presence of Afro populations. Nor could they document their conditions, a key process needed to generate proposals to address gaps in social equality. As historian George Reid Andrews (2018, 38–40) explains, movements to secure official recognition and inclusion in the census pressured national governments 'to acknowledge the disparities between racial democracy in theory and racial democracy in practice, and to take action to close those gaps'.

In Uruguay, the census movement became particularly prominent in 2005 when Tabaré Vázquez was inaugurated as president. The occasion marked the first time that the leftist Frente Amplio Party had won the presidency in Uruguayan history. In addition, during the same election cycle, Edgardo Ortuño became the

---

[6] Many Afro-Uruguayans were influenced by broader international movements, and brought their ideas on how to improve the lives of Afro-Uruguayans back with them from their time abroad during the dictatorship. Romero Jorge Rodríguez spent time in exile in Brazil in the mid-1970s, where he joined with those organising around racial consciousness. Rodríguez drew on this experience upon his return to Uruguay from exile as he began to advocate for a Uruguayan racial consciousness. His experience was replicated by many Afro-Uruguayans who became involved in the organisation mobilisations and leftist politics of the post-dictatorship period (Rodríguez 2003; Rodríguez 2014).

[7] An earlier law acknowledging a vague commitment to studying and fighting discrimination also came in 2004 in the form of Ley no. 17.817 (ROU 2004).

first Afro-Uruguayan elected to parliament since 1932.[8] As a result, when Afro-Uruguayan civil society groups continued to lobby to have the next census explicitly ask citizens whether they self-identified as 'Afro o Negra' for the first time in over 150 years, they now had powerful allies both in parliament and from the presidency.[9] When this movement succeeded, the results were stunning. Previous estimates cited Uruguay's Afro-descendant population as a mere 4 per cent of the country, but the results of the explicit question on race revealed that the actual numbers were more than double previous projections, at 8.1 per cent (Cabella *et al.* 2013; INE 2011). The data also revealed striking socioeconomic differences between what was revealed to be a sizable minority population of Afro-Uruguayans and the rest of the population. For example, Afro-Uruguayans had less than half the number of people going to university as the rest of the population, a substantially higher rate of unemployment (which was even higher for Afro-Uruguayan women), and a much higher number of people whose basic needs were not being met.[10]

As a movement for a racially aware census arose, ideas started to circulate about an affirmative action law. Momentum for the legislation first gained real traction in the early 21st century at a regional workshop for the Adoption and Implementation of Affirmative Action Policies for *Afrodescendientes* in Latin America and the Caribbean (Torres-Parodi 2003; Olaza 2017b, 95). Uruguay actually hosted this workshop in Montevideo in 2003 and was an active participant in debating the possibilities and benefits. Romero Jorge Rodríguez, the founder of the Afro-Uruguayan group Mundo Afro, also published a book the same year, describing the need for an affirmative action programme that would help combat modern forms of racism and discrimination, as well as help remedy the persistent inequality that had existed since slavery (Rodríguez 2003, 119–20). These efforts built on powerful models gaining traction in other Latin American countries.

Indeed, Uruguay benefited from and drew on other countries in the region that were working to implement affirmative action laws. Colombia and Brazil possess

---

[8] According to Andrews (2010b, 164–5), there is some evidence suggesting that Alba Roballo, who served as a senator from 1958 to 1968 and from 1971 to 1973, was also Black. Ortuño was in office for one term from 2005 to 2010. Afro-Uruguayans remain underrepresented in parliament (Riguetti 2019).
[9] The exact question on the census was '¿Cree tener acendencia ... afro o negra; asiática o amarilla; blanca; indígena; otra?' (What do you consider to be your principal racial-ethnic identity: African or Black; Asian or yellow; Indigenous; white; or other?). Earlier household surveys in Uruguay in 1996 and 2006 had also pointed to a larger percentage of Afro-Uruguayans, but without a country-wide census these numbers were not comprehensive.
[10] According to Cabella *et al.* (2013), only 10.6 per cent of Afro-Uruguayans go to university, as compared to 23.1 per cent of the rest of the population. Unemployment among Afro-Uruguayan women is 12 per cent, compared to only 8.4 per cent of non-Afro-Uruguayan women. Basic needs include factors such as habitable living space, and access to potable water, electricity, and education from the age of four on. Only 48.7 per cent of Afro-Uruguayans have all their basic needs met, compared to 67.9 per cent of non-Afro-Uruguayans. Among Afro-Uruguayans, 11.8 per cent have three or more basic needs unmet, compared to only 5.3 per cent of the population as a whole.

188   *Debbie Sharnak*

larger Afro-Latin populations than Uruguay and offered models for this type of legislation.[11] For example, Colombia passed a series of measures starting in the 1990s that sought to recognise discriminatory practices against Afro-Colombians and attempted to promote equality. The government passed Law 70 (MADR 1993), which recognised Afro-Colombians' right to territorial lands along the pacific coast. Further laws included the *Programa de Créditos Educativos para Comunidades Afro-Colombianas* (Programme of Education Credits for Afro-Colombians) in 1996, which sought to give university credit to Afro-Colombians for community service. This measure was complemented by several public and private universities creating special admissions programmes for ethnic minorities (both Afro-Colombians and Indigenous students) (Olaza 2017b, 56–7; Hernández 2012). In Brazil, progress has often occurred at a state level first. For example, in 1999, in Porto Alegre, the municipal government passed a regulation stipulating that 5 per cent of the public workforce had to be Afro-Brazilian. At a national level, the Minister of Agrarian Development, Raul Jungman, issued an executive order reserving administrative positions in the ministry for Afro-Brazilians, which was then followed by various other government ministries. A 2002 presidential decree promulgated the *Programa Nacional de Acción Afirmativa* (National Affirmative Action Programme) promoting the implementation of goals for Afro-Brazilian participation in federal agencies and contract firms as well (Olaza 2017b, 49–50; Hernández 2012).[12] This effort was expanded in 2012 when then president Dilma Rouseff passed the Law of Social Quotas, which strengthened the previous affirmative action policies by requiring that university admissions be in accordance with the racial makeup of each state and implementing quotas on the basis of attendance at state high school; family income; or being Indigenous, Black, or brown (Romero 2012). In summary, as state-sponsored multiculturalism grew as a *cause célèbre* in the late 20th and early 21st century, it eventually extended to Afro-Latin populations. Many Latin American countries began to grapple with their own racial inequity and attempted to address these issues through the law.[13] In Uruguay, this growing regional movement, combined with the coming into power of the leftist governing party – the Frente Amplio – and stark evidence from Uruguay's first racially aware census in over 150 years, led to Uruguay's own affirmative action law finally gaining momentum. There were, however, detractors.

---

[11] Colombia is estimated to have a 10.3 per cent Afro-Colombian population. Brazil has a 7.6 per cent Black population, but 43.1 per cent mulatto, or mixed race (CIA n.d.; DANE 2005; IBGE 2010a, b).

[12] For more on the move toward affirmative action programmes see Alberto (2011, 298–9).

[13] In discussions about the law, figures such as Beatriz Santos referenced other countries in the region, including comparative cases of Brazil, Argentina, and even the United States to some extent. One should also note the differences across the region in gains made by Indigenous groups, and the way that Afro-Latin populations struggled to achieve protections by governments, in large part as a result of the way states have been more receptive to claims on the basis of protecting cultural difference. While Indigenous populations gained these protections earlier, it took Afro-Latin groups much longer to begin to see measures where states addressed discrimination on the basis of race (Hooker 2005).

OPPOSING AFFIRMATIVE ACTION: URUGUAY

The Struggles to Pass Law 19.122

Uruguay's Law 19.122, *Afrodescendientes: Normas para favor su participación en las áreas educative y laboral* (Afrodescendants: Norms to Increase Participation in the Areas of Education and Employment), was signed into law on 21 August 2013. Its ultimate passage took years of negotiations. Parliamentary discussions began in earnest in 2011 with a newly elected parliament. For the second election in a row, the Frente Amplio held majorities in both chambers of parliament and controlled the presidency.[14] They used their electoral mandate to pass a range of progressive legislation, including legalising abortion and gay marriage, and eventually the passage of an affirmation action law. The law addressing racial discrimination had the additional support of Afro-Uruguayan activists and a growing international movement, which added a new level of urgency to the process, especially after the census results had painted such a stark picture of racial disparity.[15] Thus, at the second session of the new parliament, the Chamber of Deputies made reference to the way it was responding to international momentum. Representatives officially recognised 2011 as the UN's 'International Year for Afro-Descendants' and recommended that parliament address the UN's mandate (ROU 2011a). By the end of the year, eight representatives introduced the first version of an affirmative action law, in part recognising the initiative as tied to the UN's project (ROU 2011b). Pointing out the disparity in education and poverty levels, the representatives who introduced the bill stressed that the 'system alone would not correct these inequities, and therefore required state intervention to help the most vulnerable sectors of the population that could not escape these structural barriers without direct assistance' (ROU 2011b). The call recognised both the current inequality and historic discrimination. As political scientist Erica Townsend-Bell (2021, 245) points out, 'the legislation's proponents, especially Black civil society and institutional actors, spent a significant portion of their time focused on the case for symbolic remedy'.

In early 2012, the process moved toward broad consultation with both civil society and government agencies to respond to the initial proposed law (CEPDS 2012b, d). Parliament eventually called in over 40 people representing a variety of Afro-Uruguayan voices from institutions and organisations around the state, almost all of whom were strong supporters of the law. Collectively, they laid out varied reasons for the law's necessity, debated whether to include a gendered component that specifically targeted divergence between Afro-Uruguayan men and women, and made regional comparisons with Brazil and the United States (CEPDS 2012c, d). Over the course of 2012 and 2013, these experts and representatives regularly briefed and responded to legislators who were tasked with amending the law.

---

[14] The Frente Amplio was created in 1971 but had never held power at a national level before 2005.
[15] Some of the Afro-Uruguayan groups who were essential to getting the law passed include: Acsum, Mundo Afro, Cecau, Ubuntu, Movimiento de Afrodescendientes, Organización Salvador, and Movimiento Afro Nacionalista. See their explicit mention in parliament (ROU 2012).

190 *Debbie Sharnak*

The law itself revolved around three main provisions: teaching Afro-Uruguayan history in schools, scholarships for Afro-Uruguayan students, and employment quotas. The final version passed unanimously – an incredible feat considering how difficult it was to pass other progressive legislation during the parliamentary session, such as the law decriminalising abortion, which passed by only one vote (Townsend-Bell 2021, 243). Yet, the final version was ultimately scaled down, largely as the result of negotiation with conservative legislators who sought to limit the reach of the affirmative action law. While there were proponents of the law from opposition parties who earnestly sought to improve the legislation, those opposed to the law's broad mandate came primarily from the representatives in the Colorado Party, but with some Blanco Party representatives as well.[16] Throughout most of Uruguayan history, these two groups had fought vociferously and traded governing power back and forth. However, the emergence of the Frente Amplio as a legitimate political contender in the 1990s drove these once-sparring parties to, at times, work in concert against the Frente Amplio governing agenda in a bipolar competition between the traditional parties and the Frente.[17] This divide became even more acute when the Frente Amplio won the presidency and controlled both houses in parliament. In large part, the representatives who were loudest in their opposition were part of the traditionally political conservative *sublemas* (faction within the party), particularly the Vamos Uruguay group, which was one of the most conservative factions within the Colorado Party. For instance, in the 2009 election, Vamos Uruguay championed the candidacy of Pedro Bordaberry, son of Juan María Bordaberry, the first civilian head of the Uruguayan dictatorship. Further, this group of legislators led the ultimately failed referendum campaign to lower the age of criminal responsibility from 18 to 16, arguing that trying younger citizens as adults would prove a more effective deterrent to rising crime in the region, demonstrating its broader right-wing agenda. While the Colorados were the most outspoken critics of the affirmative action law, certain members of the Blanco Party, which boasted a strong, rural base, also pushed for certain limits to be built into the legislation (Rosenblatt 2018, 170–6). In sum, representatives from these parties were most vocal against aspects of the affirmative action law, but also presented a broader right-wing mobilisation against the governing leftist party's agenda in other areas that will be discussed later.

In response to the affirmative action law, these elected representatives in both the parliamentary bodies did not overtly oppose the law for racial equality but began questioning the logic of creating special conditions for Afro-Uruguayans.

---

[16] In the parliamentary debates, those who gave voice to their party's position in opposition to the law were the representatives to the special commission that drafted and debated its provisions in depth before the law reached the floor of parliament for broader debate.

[17] Rosenblatt (2018, 170) demonstrates how the two parties even presented a unified party in 2015 in departmental and municipal elections in Montevideo.

OPPOSING AFFIRMATIVE ACTION: URUGUAY 191

They based their argument, in part, on fear of the idea of 'reverse discrimination'.[18] Representatives argued that creating special quotas would undermine the concept that all Uruguayans were equal before the law (ROU 2012).[19] For example, Gustavo Cersósimo of the Colorado Party contended that white Uruguayans also suffered from poverty and should not be disadvantaged because of this law. Instead of recognising that the ideas and importance of the law came from historic exclusion and continued discrimination, Cersósimo and others focused on poverty and worried about poor, white Uruguayans who might lose out on jobs or scholarships if they were reserved for Afro-Uruguayans (CEPDS 2012f; ROU 2012).[20]

Other representatives focused on limiting the reach of the affirmative action provisions. For example, some representatives sought to reduce the percentage of public sector jobs that would be reserved for Afro-Uruguayans – to 4 per cent instead of 8 per cent – in the quotas for filling state vacancies. These numbers relied on the already debunked assumption that Afro-Uruguayans only represented 4 per cent of the population, and ignored the results of the new census. Another representative of the Blanco Party, Senator Alfredo Solari, suggested limiting affirmative-action hiring to when it could be proven that Afro-Uruguayans had exactly equal qualifications to white Uruguayans, lest the bill 'jeopardise the functioning of the state' by employing unqualified candidates (CEPDS 2013b).[21] Representative Pablo Abdala of the Blanco Party also pushed for a sunset provision that limited the affirmative action programme to a 10-year period (CEPDS 2013b; ROU 2012; CEPDS 2013a).

The other area of the affirmative action law that conservative legislators targeted was the provision regarding private employers. In fact, in the initial draft of the law (ROU 2011b), legislators proposed both a required quota for government jobs and an article to encourage the increased hiring of Afro-descendants in private employment by as much as 'one and a half times' the current rate.[22] The acting Minister

---

[18] Representatives even referred to the Supreme Court case of *University of California v. Bakke* in the USA, which made this same argument and ended up rejecting specific quotas but allowing race to be a factor in admission decisions (CEPDS 2012f).

[19] Diputado Juan C. Souza was unique in acknowledging that most of the representatives in the room had heard these comments, even if they were 'whispers' because people recognised that they were not politically correct.

[20] Even the proposed October 2012 law that went forward to further discussion from the subcommittee was approved only 'with conditions' by Cersósimo (CEPDS 2012a). He reiterated this line of argument, vociferously arguing the idea of affirmative action as a form of reverse discrimination, even while voting to approve the law in 2013 (ROU 2013b). The leader of the Vamos Uruguay faction, Pedro Bordaberry, remained a member of the Senate even after the failed presidential bid. He was also an outspoken opponent of the law on many of these grounds (ROU 2013a).

[21] CPDI (2013a). This argument was quickly rejected by the other members of the commission.

[22] The initial law also had a target of 10 per cent of state jobs going to Afro-Uruguayans, but was amended to 8 per cent by the October 2012 version of the law to align with the exact number of the census rather than rounding up from an earlier household survey.

192 *Debbie Sharnak*

of Labour and Social Security at the time, Nelson Loustaunau, even stressed the importance of targeting private industry, where more pervasive and 'veiled' discrimination toward Afro-Uruguayans often took place (CEPDS 2012e).[23] Yet, despite the initial proposals, and calls from experts that it would be essential to target private industry to have a broader societal impact, the Senate weakened the provision for private industry by eliminating any specific numbers from later versions of the law. They replaced the initial provision with an article noting simply that private industry should 'incorporate' Afro-Uruguayans. In all these ways, the conservative legislators pushed back against the affirmative action law by seeking to limit its coverage in terms of the language, targets, and population included in its provisions, rather than argue against the idea of the law directly.

Mobilisation within the legislature partly succeeded. While reducing the percentage of the quota failed, opposition forces amended the proposed legislation to include a time horizon on the law at 15 years, although senators increased the sunset to 15 years from the proposed 10-year limit, and even one proposal by Cersósimo for a five-year limit (CEPDS 2012f; ROU 2013a). Blanco and Colorado legislators also struck the provision that gave any teeth to a quota for private employers. These pushbacks did not come in the form of overt opposition to the law or justification that rested on explicit racist language; in fact, each person arguing for a limit mentioned in their statements that they believed in the idea of equality. Yet, the changes pushed against the law's broad mandate and limited the redress for stark inequality by seeking to constrain the scope of the proposed legislation. In this way, the movement against affirmative action included an element of radical neoliberalism, succeeding in arguing that the law constrained business choice in employment practices in order to remove any targeting of the law's potential effects beyond state agencies.

At a time of increasing global and regional investment in multiculturalism, scholars such as Charles Hale (2002, 2005, 2006) have demonstrated how governments sometimes embraced limited forms of multiculturalism to control broader or more radical forms of empowerment. Hale's research focused on Indigenous rights in Guatemala, where neoliberal governments proactively recognised minimal rights in order to stave off broader measures. One could see how members of the Colorado Party embraced this form of pushback in respect to racial rights in Uruguay. (For another example, see Krausova's Chapter 11.) Instead of fighting a losing battle against the law that had support from the majority party in parliament, representatives intended to vote for the law, but to do so in as limited terms as possible. In this way, challenges to the affirmative action came primarily in the form of limiting its potential reach and scope. It did so not in explicitly racist terms, but in neoliberal arguments and coded ways that seemingly embraced the global movement toward multiculturalism in theory, but ultimately sought to limit

---

[23] The discussion about cutting the incentive language occurred in the Senate, largely at the urging of Alfredo Solari (CPDI 2013d).

OPPOSING AFFIRMATIVE ACTION: URUGUAY   193

its impact in practice. To have used a more overly racist discourse would probably have undermined the alliance against the legislation. (See Escoffier and Vivaldi (Chapter 8), for an example.)

Despite some successes in limiting the scope and reach of the law, a fairly robust version successfully passed the Chamber of Deputies in December 2012, and the Senate in August 2013 – both unanimously (Parlamento del Uruguay 2013). It had taken almost two years from initially being introduced, but groups that had been mobilising for official recognition and inclusion in the state since the transition back to democratic rule almost 30 years prior viewed its passage as a major victory.[24] The road to implementation, however, proved rockier. While the law's detractors had failed to prevent the its mandate, it was ultimately easier to push back against the legislation by not implementing the law – particularly with respect to fulfilling the hiring quotas across state agencies.

Uneven Implementation

Even at the time of the bill's passage, Frente Amplio legislators worried about the ability to enforce and implement the law across all levels of the government (ROU 2012). Their fears proved well founded. As of 2022, some provisions have achieved great success. Particularly in the realm of curricular changes and the distribution of scholarships, the mandate of the law has been implemented. For example, the Administración Nacional de Educación Pública (National Public Education Administration (ANEP)) (2016) published a teaching guide for *Afrodescendencia* and sent it out to the entire country. The guide provides background on teaching about Afro-descendants in Uruguay's history, as well as concrete lesson plans for teachers in initial, primary, and secondary education. There were also workshops around the country to meet with teachers preparing its inclusion in the curriculum (Recagno 2016). Similarly successful, scholarships for Afro-Uruguayans increased substantially after Law 19.122 was passed. In 2011, before the law, only 20 scholarships went to Afro-Uruguayans, well below 1 per cent of all the scholarships available. However, in 2016, a few years after implementation, awards for Afro-Uruguayans reached 817 students (*Diaria* 2017). By 2019, ANEP and the Ministries of Social Development and Education and Culture reported that 20 per cent of state scholarships had gone to Afro-Uruguayans (Uruguay Presidencia 2019). In this way, the less controversial aspects of the law saw a relatively easy path to implementation.

Progress toward 8 per cent of state vacancies going to Afro-Uruguayans has been much slower, revealing persistent and subtle forms of racism, as well as the

---

[24] Future research on this topic could examine closely the newspaper reporting at the time of the law's passage. Online archives show an absence of coverage of its passage in mainstream papers in August 2013. This suggests some foreboding for the law's implementation, as well as an intransigence within the press and society with regard to ending the marginalisation of Afro-Uruguayans.

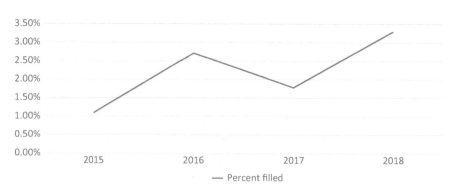

Figure 10.1 Implementation of Ley 19.122: percentage of state vacancies that went to Afro-Uruguayans. Author's calculation based on secondary data.

relative success of the pushback against the law. As shown in Figure 10.1, while jobs increased in the first two years, the law did not reach even 3 per cent of state vacancies. (Even that increase, however, was amazingly still a 144 per cent improvement from 2014 (Castineiras and Urwicz 2016)). In 2017, the numbers dropped again below 2 per cent of public positions – less than a quarter of the 8 per cent stipulated by law. As Townsend-Bell (2021, 255) notes, between 50 and 89 per cent of the positions filled fell in the categories of military and peon labour, areas that Afro-Uruguayans did not require affirmative action to access.

The state's five-year report indicated that through 2018, state agencies finally reached 3.29 per cent, which, when broken down by state agency, equalled 14 out of 38 organisations managing to reach the quota (Isgleas 2019; *Diaria* 2017). Some of the improvement was due to extensive education campaigns for hiring within the ministries that sought to address the gaps in implementation of the law, which included targeting people who claimed not to know about the law as an excuse for their agency not reaching the quota (Olaza 2017b, 145). Only a year later, though, there was another dip, with numbers falling to 2.24 per cent of state bodies and only seven organisations reaching the quota, demonstrating at best uneven progress (Oficina Nacional del Servicio Civil 2019). It is impossible to prove definitively that overt racism is directly tied to the failure to reach or enforce the quota. However, the persistent forms of covert discrimination, implicit bias, and the excuses tied to cultural racism used to justify the state's failure to fully implement the law demonstrate persistent and concerted forms of racist pushback.

As such, there were several categorical problems related to the gaps in reaching the mandated quota numbers. First, there are no penalties for lack of enforcement. While legislators discussed enforcement during the parliamentary debates, it was not fully addressed in the writing of the law (CEPDS 2012e; ROU 2013b). Thus, agencies have largely complied on a case-by-case basis depending on who was in a position to hire, stated awareness of the law, and willingness to comply. Those who did not comply have faced few consequences. Given the pushback from various individuals and political parties against the law's initial passage in parliament, it is unsurprising that, without any penalties, certain agencies might resist implementation for a range of discriminatory reasons that will be explained below. Further, certain government agencies have indicated more resistance than others. The Judicial Branch and the Retirement and Pension Fund, for example, have particularly low rates of Afro-Uruguayan hiring in the first five years of the law, signalling intransigent discriminatory attitudes in the absence of penalties (Isgleas 2019).

Without specific penalties, persistent, implicit racist attitudes justify noncompliance. Interviews and statements from Afro-Uruguayans attest to this phenomenon. For example, Néstor Silva, the national director of Mundo Afro, believes that both a lack of interest and an undertone of racism produced the gap between the law's mandate and state compliance. He argues that it is hard to overcome structural racism premised on the belief that Black people do not belong in certain spaces (*ECOS Latinoamérica* 2018). Indeed, scholars have posited that instead of overt racial discrimination, language about exclusion tends to rely more on pointing to 'cultural deficiencies', arguing that a lack of training or education about the viability of Afro-Uruguayan candidates has replaced overt forms of hiring discrimination (Buffington and Fraley 2011, 335). In this way, people invoke powerful explanations, or, as some scholars argue, justifications, for continued inequalities, that rely on outside factors and not their own discrimination or racism (Bonilla-Silva 2003, 3). While most scholars have studied this phenomenon in other countries, particularly the USA, the parallels with Uruguay are striking for the ways that coded language about qualifications masks racist attitudes toward a population.

Two other factors regarding the law's uneven implementation are important to mention in identifying structural and covert racism as well. First, private industry remains even more woefully behind in employment of Afro-Uruguayans, particularly in leadership positions. Only 0.2 per cent of leadership positions in medium and large companies in Uruguay are occupied by Afro-descendants as of 2019. While some analysts have attributed this disparity to lower levels of education among Afro-Uruguayans, under close examination, the justification reveals unjust biases and displays the ways that employers invoked claims about the cultural deficiencies of Afro-Uruguayans to explain discriminatory hiring practices. Even Afro-Uruguayans who earn advanced degrees, develop impressive careers abroad, and then return home with both the requisite education and experience, have noted the difficulty of securing employment in Uruguay. Perversely, hiring committees or bosses often claim that they are overqualified. Indeed, these lows numbers can be traced to what former Afro-Uruguayan representative Egardo Ortuño has called 'undercover' discrimination, or covert discrimination. Employers are not outwardly saying they do not want to hire Afro-Uruguayans but instead make excuses from the perspective of racially coded language that finds Afro-Uruguayans either 'underqualified' because of a perceived lack of education, or not right for the position for another reason, such as being overqualified. This exclusion is an example

196 *Debbie Sharnak*

of a type of coded discrimination that keeps Uruguayans out of powerful positions within private industry and mirrors many of the challenges one sees in compliance with state vacancies as well (Mujica 2018).[25]

There is also the case of overt discrimination against Afro-Uruguayans, which belies claims of tolerance in Uruguay. One particular case broke through a general silence on this topic because it affected a US diplomat. In December 2014, a year after the affirmative action law was passed, the diplomat was turned away from the door of a restaurant called Circus, a gastropub in the Pocitos neighbourhood of Montevideo. While the host said it was due to the diplomat's casual dress – since she was at a fancy restaurant wearing a tank top and flip-flops – the embassy staff pushed back against this justification, arguing that their outfits were similar to those of many people already seated in the restaurant. Eventually, the host insinuated that they could not enter because a member of their party was Black. Since the person turned away was a visiting US diplomat and not Uruguayan, they reported the incident to the US ambassador to the country, Julissa Reynoso (Rainey 2014).[26] The US embassy under Ambassador Reynoso had signed a joint memorandum earlier in her tenure to work on issues of social inclusion, particularly toward Afro-descendants, and thus the embassy made the restaurant's refusal to serve an Afro-descendent a public issue. Newspapers and social media covered the case in the weeks that followed. As Ambassador Reynoso explained (2019), the embassy believed that these issues probably happened more frequently but never become part of the public conversation. In this way, the incident is one where discrimination against Afro-Uruguayans occurred in a covert and coded way, centred on inappropriate dress, and brought continued discrimination out into view. While not related specifically to the affirmative action law, the incident is important for bringing to light the various ways that discrimination exists and persists in Uruguay, despite claims of tolerance. While most of these incidents are not brought into public view, this specific case shone a light on the ways that denials of racism obscure the various ways that it does in fact operate in the country, and extends from entering public places to exclusion in hiring.

Conclusion

Uruguay has been regarded as one of, if not the most, progressive country in the region. It surpasses many of its regional counterparts on abortion, gay marriage, and trans rights. Yet, there is an emerging pushback against some of this rights agenda by an increasingly organised, but largely invisible, right-wing mobilisation.

---

[25] This type of exclusion is also an example of the type of neoliberal mobilisation oriented toward defending the rights of businesses against rights advancements for minority groups that Escoffier, Payne, and Zulver outline in Chapter 1 of this volume.

[26] Another case was alleged the following year at another establishment (*Observador* 2015).

This opposition has occurred in multiple venues. First, at the ballot box, the Frente Amplio lost the presidency to Luis Lacalle Pou from the centre-right Blancos Party in the November 2019 election after 15 years in power. While neither José Mujica nor Tabaré Vázquez was particularly fervent in moving the implementation of the affirmative action law forward (Townsend-Bell 2021, 255), the parliamentary debates demonstrate even less willingness to do so among Blanco politicians. Perhaps the most worrisome aspect of the election was the emergence of the Cabildo Abierto, a far-right group that embraced militarism and earned 11 per cent of the vote.[27]

In addition to these electoral trends, pushback has occurred in the streets, where groups have mobilised against some of the laws passed by the Frente Amplio, employing more traditional modes of social mobilisation against rights. For example, members of the Blanco Party launched an ultimately unsuccessful referendum against the trans rights law in early 2019. The law (ROU 2018), which had passed through parliament and been signed by Vázquez in late 2018, allowed trans people aged 16 and older to self-identify and change their gender. It also included financial compensation for trans people persecuted under the Uruguayan dictatorship, and access to education scholarships and the national healthcare system if they choose to get hormone treatment. Early in 2019, an election year, representatives of Blanco Party, Carlos Iafigliola and Álvaro Dastugue, mobilised a coalition of conservative groups against the law, claiming that it denied 'biology' and was intruding on parental authority, since it allowed people as young as 16 to declare their own gender (*Catholic News Agency* 2019). However, reminiscent of the arguments that their compatriots made in parliament against the affirmative action law, they also claimed reverse discrimination, saying that the law violated constitutional guarantees of equality by granting preferential treatment to transgender people. The referendum attempt was ultimately defeated, as less than 10 per cent of the necessary 25 per cent needed came out in support of overturning the law (*Pais* 2019). Yet, it foretold an emboldened and strengthened national movement against the Frente Amplio's progressive legislation in more traditional forms of activism and mobilisation.[28] In 2022, one Cabildo Abierto legislator, Inés Monzillo, who was elected in 2019 to the House of Deputies, demonstrated this impulse when she defied the strategy of covert opposition to the affirmative action law and openly stated that she was bothered by the quotas, questioning why the state should offer such benefits. Further, despite the lack of success in actually achieving measurable improvement over the previous nine years, she believed people 'abused' those rights (*Búsqueda* 2022).

---

[27] Cabildo Abierto, particularly its leader Manini Ríos, positively assessed the Cold War dictatorship that had caused Uruguay to be referred to as the 'torture chamber of Latin America', and argued for the resurrection of the *Ley de Caducidad*, or amnesty law, for members of the military.

[28] Leaders of the movement against the trans rights law also sought to overturn the country's abortion law. For more on regional conservative backlash against gender equality see Biroli (2020).

Monzillo, however, is still largely an exception. What one typically sees in terms of resistance against the advancement of Afro-Uruguayans rights is actually trickier to denounce. Anti-rights activism does not always occur through overt organisational efforts. By attempting to highlight arguments about reverse discrimination, using coded language to point to cultural deficiencies that justify not fulfilling the quota mandate, and invoking claims of radical neoliberal business rights, this chapter has underlined the multiple forms of opposition from around the country. Examining this pushback expands our typology of right-wing backlash and how it can occur in stealthier and more covert ways, even as we can trace links between covert discrimination and more traditional forms of pushback against the Frente Amplio's progressive agenda. This opposition is more difficult to address, since it invokes stereotypes or focuses on the freedom of companies' employment practices, which is not always overtly discriminatory. In fact, it often works by avoiding any language that could be perceived as racist. Its proponents espouse equality but focus on their existing political power and hide racist views in order to roll back rights. This pushback manifested in Uruguay in the limiting of the initial reach of the law, and then successfully delaying the law's full implementation. In this way, however, the Uruguayan case of Afro-descendant rights outlines another form of mobilisation that emerged in the form of coded language in the discussions in parliament, as well as attempts to delay the law's enforcement. Covert activity allows room for members of the business community and others who are uncomfortable with street mobilisations nonetheless to influence political and policy outcomes that protect their interests behind the scenes.

Thus, this study offers a view into a resurgent force – in fact, a countermovement with an element of radical neoliberalism – against *Afrodescendiente* rights, whereby many Uruguayans are seeking to maintain the status quo, to ignore discrimination, and to reinforce the invisibility of a minority population. This non-traditional mobilisation against rights demonstrates how even under leftist and progressive governments, pushback flourishes in various forms and offers a broader conceptual frame of the threat found in right-wing attempts to preserve the status quo.

At the beginning of the chapter I mentioned Representative Bertha Sanseverino, who, after the law's passage, so proudly proclaimed it as part of Uruguay's march toward greater equality. Yet, her concerns during the debate in Chamber of Deputies in 2012 revealed a healthy degree of scepticism about how difficult the law would be to achieve. She noted that, if passed, an affirmative action law needed to be accompanied by campaigns where there were 'debates about ideas and values ... otherwise the results will be much poorer ... it would leave us with a functional instrument without substance' (CEPDS 2012d). With this statement, Sanseverino explained that cultural norms and racist discrimination would persist if there were not a broader grappling with the circumstances and prejudices that undergirded discrimination. Unfortunately, the struggles with implementation realise this well-founded fear. In conversations about the law that I had with Uruguayans while living there and on other shorter research trips, I found that many Uruguayans either did not know about the law or said that they remembered it had been passed but did not know its outcome, especially because 'there is such a small Afro-Uruguayan population' to begin with. In this way, despite the census results and attempts to recognise Afro-Uruguayan contributions in the country through legislation, the challenges of recognition and discrimination still remain. Anti-rights mobilisation against racial equality in Uruguay has largely occurred in the form of the retrenchment of neoliberalism with coded and covert discrimination as justification for non-compliance with quotas. Without a broader grappling with the underlying racism and stigma that undergirded these inequalities in the first place, many of the same challenges in Uruguay persist. Indeed, the forces that have led the fight against the law's initial passage and implementation reveal the many forms of pushback against the advancement of rights, which, as the case of Uruguay shows, occurred in coded ways as a fight against the country's progressive legislation.

References

Alberto, P. L. (2011), *Terms of Inclusion: Black Intellectuals in Twentieth-Century Brazil* (Chapel Hill, University of North Carolina Press).

Andrews, G. R. (2004), *Afro-Latin America 1800–2000* (New York, Oxford University Press).

Andrews, G. R. (2010a), 'Afro-World: African-Diaspora Thought and Practice in Montevideo, Uruguay, 1830–2000', *The Americas*, 67:1, 83–107.

Andrews, G. R. (2010b), *Blackness in a White Nation: A History of Afro-Uruguay* (Chapel Hill, University of North Carolina Press).

Andrews, G. R. (2011), 'Afro-Uruguay', *Black Past*, http://www.blackpast.org/perspectives/afro-uruguay-brief-history.

Andrews, G. R. (2018), 'Afro-Latin America by the Numbers: The Politics of Census', *ReVista*, 17:2, https://revista.drclas.harvard.edu/afro-latin-america-by-the-numbers/.

ANEP [Administración Nacional de Educación Pública] (2016), 'Guía didáctica: Educación y afrodescendencia', https://www.anep.edu.uy/sites/default/files/images/Archivos/publicaciones-direcciones/DDHH/educacion-afrodescendencia/GuiaDidacticaEducacionyAfrodescendencia.pdf.

Arocena Armas (2013), 'Uruguay: Un país más diverso que su imaginación. Una interpretación a partir del censo de 2011', *Revista de ciencias sociales*, 26:33, 137–58.

Biroli, F. (2020), 'The Backlash against Gender Equality in Latin America: Temporarility, Religious Patterns, and the Erosion of Democracy', *LASA Forum: The Quarterly Newsletter for the Latin American Studies Association*, 51:2, 22–6.

Bonilla-Silva, E. (2003), *Racism without Racists: Color-Blind Racism and the Persistence of Inequality in the United States* (New York: Rowman & Littlefield).

Borucki, A. (2015), *From Shipmates to Soldiers: Emerging Black Identities in the Río de la Plata* (Albuquerque, University of New Mexico Press).

Brecha (1985a), 'Las dificultades para insertarse en una sociedad blanca', 23 December, 2.

Brecha (1985b), '¿Libros que enseñan a ser racistas?', 20 December, 9.

Bucheli, M. and R. Porzecanski (2011), 'Racial Inequality in the Uruguayan Labor Market: An Analysis of Wage Differentials between Afro-Descendants and Whites', *Latin American Politics & Society*, 53:2, 113–50.

Buffington, D. and T. Fraley (2011), 'Racetalk and Sport: The Color Consciousness of Contemporary Discourse on Basketball', *Sociological Inquiry*, 81:3, 333–52.

Búsqueda (2022), 'Uruguay está pasando de un "patriarcado a un matriarcado", dice diputado de Cabildo Abierto que critica al "feminismo del 8m"', 9 March, https://www.busqueda.com.uy/Secciones/Uruguay-esta-pasando-de-un-patriarcado-a-un-matriarcado--dice-diputada-de-Cabildo-Abierto-que-critica-al-feminismo-del-8M--uc51446.

Cabella, W., M. Nathan, and M. Tenenbaum (2013), 'La población afro-uruguaya en el Censo 2011', *Atlas sociodemográfico y de la desigualdad del Uruguay*, http://www.ine.gub.uy/c/document_library/get_file?uuid=1726c03f-aecd-4c78-b9be-f2c27dafba1d&groupId=10181.

Carvalho Neto, P. de (1954), 'Temas de la obra afro-uruguaya de Ildefonso Pereda Valdés', *Boletín bibliográfico de antropología americana*, 17:1, 235–8.

Castineiras, M. and T. Urwicz (2016), 'Ser negro en el país de racismo invisible', *Brecha*, 6 July.

Catholic News Agency (2019), 'Efforts Build to Repeal Uruguay's Controversial Transgender Law', 28 March, https://www.catholicnewsagency.com/news/efforts-build-to-repeal-uruguays-controversial-transgender-law-87180.

CEPDS [Comisión Especial de Población y Desarrollo Social] (2012a), 'Afrodescendientes: Normas para favorecer su participación en las áreas educativa y laboral', Carpetas no. 1288, Anexo I, Repartido no. 761, https://legislativo.parlamento.gub.uy/temporales/D2012100761-01366631.pdf.

CEPDS [Comisión Especial de Población y Desarrollo Social] (2012b), 'Versión taquigráfica no. 1030 de 2012', 4 May, https://legislativo.parlamento.gub.uy/temporales/D20120503-1008-10303160990.HTML.

CEPDS [Comisión Especial de Población y Desarrollo Social] (2012c), 'Versión taquigráfica no. 1039 de 2012', 10 May, https://legislativo.parlamento.gub.uy/temporales/D20120510-1008-10392401713.HTML.

CEPDS [Comisión Especial de Población y Desarrollo Social] (2012d), 'Versión taquigráfica no. 1090 de 2012', 7 June, https://legislativo.parlamento.gub.uy/temporales/D20120607-1008-10909762930.HTML#.

CEPDS [Comisión Especial de Población y Desarrollo Social] (2012e), 'Versión taquigráfica no. 1104 de 2012', 14 June, https://legislativo.parlamento.gub.uy/temporales/D20120614-1008-11044382054.HTML#.

CEPDS [Comisión Especial de Población y Desarrollo Social] (2012f), 'Versión taquigráfica no. 1251 de 2012', 13 September, https://legislativo.parlamento.gub.uy/temporales/D20120913-1008-12512493283.HTML#.

CEPDS [Comisión Especial de Población y Desarrollo Social] (2013a), 'Versión taquigráfica no. 2172', 16 June, https://legislativo.parlamento.gub.uy/temporales/S201321723622273.HTML#.

CEPDS [Comisión Especial de Población y Desarrollo Social] (2013b), 'Versión taquigráfica 2126', Carpetas no. 1042/2012, 3 June 2013, https://legislativo.parlamento.gub.uy/temporales/S20132126939234.HTML#.

CIA [Central Intelligence Agency] (n.d.), 'Ethnic Groups,' *The World Factbook*, https://www.cia.gov/library/publications/the-world-factbook/fields/400.html#BR.

Cottrol, R. (2013), *The Long, Lingering Shadow: Slavery, Race, and Law in the American Hemisphere* (Athens, University of Georgia Press).

CPDI [Comisión de Población, Desarrollo e Inclusión] (2013a), 'Carpeta no. 1042/2012, Versión taquigráfica 2126', 3 June, https://legislativo.parlamento.gub.uy/temporales/S20132126939234.HTML#.

OPPOSING AFFIRMATIVE ACTION: URUGUAY 201

CPDI [Comisión de Población, Desarrollo e Inclusión] (2013b), 'Distribuido no. 1977', 18 March, https://legislativo.parlamento.gub.uy/temporales/S201319779113111.HTML.

CPDI [Comisión de Población, Desarrollo e Inclusión] (2013c), 'Versión taquigráfica no. 2172', 16 June, https://legislativo.parlamento.gub.uy/temporales/S201321723622 273.HTML#.

CPDI [Comisión de Población, Desarrollo e Inclusión] (2013d), 'Versión taquigráfica 2199', 1 July, https://parlamento.gub.uy/documentosyleyes/ficha-asunto/110651/tramite.

DANE [Departamento Administrativo Nacional de Estadística, Colombia] (2005), 'La visibilización estadística de los grupos étnicos colombianos', https://www.dane.gov.co/files/censo2005/etnia/sys/visibilidad_estadistica_etnicos.pdf.

Diaria (2017), 'Qué pasa con la ley de cuotas para personas afro', *La Diaria*, 27 January, https://ladiaria.com.uy/articulo/2017/1/que-pasa-con-la-ley-de-cuotas-para-personas-afro/.

Diario (1978), "Remodelación del Puerto de Montevideo," *El Diario*, 7 December, 4.

ECOS Latinamérica (2018), 'La Ley de Afrodescendientes está "en falta" desde su creación', 2 July, http://ecos.la/LA/13/Sociedad/2018/07/02/24734/la-ley-de-afrodescendientes-esta-en-falta-desde-su-creacion/.

Galeano, E. (1987), *Memory of Fire*, Vol. II, *Faces and Masks* (New York, Pantheon Books).

Galeano, E. (2013), *Soccer in Sun and Shadows* (New York, Nation Books).

Goyena, P. V. and E. Canstatt (1874), 'Ley declarando que no hay esclavos en todo el territorio de la Republica', Law no. 242, 12 December, in P. V. Goyena and E. Canstatt, *La legislación vigente de la República Oriental del Uruguay*, Vol. I (Montevideo, Imprenta de el Uruguay).

Hale, C. (2002), 'Does Multiculturalism Menace? Governance, Cultural Rights, and the Politics of Identity in Guatemala', *Journal of Latin American Studies*, 34:3, 485–524.

Hale, C. (2005), 'Neoliberal Multiculturalism: The Remaking of Cultural Rights and Racial Dominance in Central America', *PoLAR: Political and Legal Anthropology Review*, 28:1, 10–28.

Hale, C. (2006), *Más que un Indio: Racial Ambivalence and Neoliberal Multiculturalism in Guatemala* (New Mexico, School of American Research Press).

Hernández, T. K. (2012), 'Affirmative Action in the Americas', *Americas Quarterly*, July 24, https://www.americasquarterly.org/fulltextarticle/affirmative-action-in-the-americas/.

Hernández, T. K. (2013), *Racial Subordination in Latin America: The Role of the State, Customary Law, and the New Civil Rights Response* (New York, Cambridge University Press).

Holmes, H. A. (1944), 'Ildefonso Pereda Valdés y su libro "Negro esclavos y negros libres"', *Revista Iberoamericana*, 8:15, 21–30.

Hooker, J. (2005), 'Indigenous Inclusion/Black Exclusion: Race, Ethnicity and Multicultural Citizenship in Latin America', *Journal of Latin American Studies*, 37, 285–310.

IBGE [Institute Brasileiro de Geografia e Estatistica] (2010a), 'Censo demográfico. Principais resultados: Caracteristicas da populaçao e dos domicilios', https://www.ibge.gov.br/estatisticas/sociais/populacao/9662-censo-demografico-2010.html?edicao=10503&t=destaques.

IBGE [Institute Brasileiro de Geografia e Estatistica] (2010b), 'Censo demográfico. Principais resultados: Sinopse', https://www.ibge.gov.br/estatisticas/sociais/populacao/9662-censo-demografico-2010.html?edicao=9673&t=destaques.

INE [Insituto Nacional de Estadística Uruguay] (2011), 'Census 2011: Manual del Censista', http://www3.ine.gub.uy/c/document_library/get_file?uuid=0025b663-abc5-4ab4-8517-e3302eb1f090&groupId=10181.

202   *Debbie Sharnak*

Isgleas, D. (2019), 'El Estado sigue lejos de cumplir la cuota de empleados "afro"', *El País*, July, https://www.elpfdiariaais.com.uy/informacion/politica/sigue-lejos-cumplir-cuota-empleados-afro.html.

Kenny, M. L. (2018), *Deeply Rooted in the Present: Heritage, Memory, and Identity in Brazilian Quilombos* (Toronto, University of Toronto Press).

Loveman, M. (2014), *National Colors: Racial Classification and the State in Latin America* (New York, Oxford University Press).

Luz, J. de la (2013), interview in *Triunfadores: Negros Profesionales en el Uruguay*, ed. Pamela Laviña (Montevideo, Editorial Psicolibros Universitario, 2013), 109–15.

MADR [Ministero de Agricultura y Desarrollo Rural] (1993), 'Ley 70 de 1993', 27 August, minagricultura.gov.co/Normatividad/Leyes/Ley%2070%20de%201993.pdf

Mujica, V. (2018), 'Gerentes afrodescendientes son casos atípicos en las empresas uruguayas', *El Observador*, 14 February, https://www.elobservador.com.uy/nota/geren tes-afrodescendientes-son-casos-atipicos-en-las-empresas-uruguayas-2018214500.

Nadel, J. H. (2014), *Fútbol: Why Soccer Matters in Latin America* (Gainesville, University of Florida Press).

Observador (2015), 'Institución de Derechos Humanos investigará denuncia de racismo en boliche del Cordón', *El Observador*, 22 September, https://www.elobservador.com.uy/nota/institucion-de-derechos-humanos-investigara-denuncia-de-racismo-en-boliche-del-cordon-201592212490.

Oficina Nacional del Servicio Civil (2019), *Ingresos de personas afrodescendientes en el Estado*, Ley no. 19.122, https://www.gub.uy/oficina-nacional-servicio-civil/sites/ofic ina-nacional-servicio-civil/files/documentos/publicaciones/Informe%20Afro%202 019.pdf.

Olaza, M. (2017a), 'Afrodescendencia y restauración democrática en Uruguay: ¿Una nueva visión de ciudadanía?', *Revista de ciencias sociales*, 30:40 (January–June), 63–82.

Olaza, M. (2017b), *Afrodescendientes en Uruguay: Debates sobre políticas de acción afirmativas* (Montevideo, Doble Clic Editoras).

Pais (2019), 'Fracasó el prereferéndum para habilitar consulta por la ley trans', *El País*, 5 August, https://www.elpais.com.uy/informacion/politica/fracaso-prerreferendum-habilitar-consulta-ley-trans.html.

Parlamento del Uruguay (2013), 'Ficha asunto Afrodescendencia', https://parlamento.gub. uy/documentosyleyes/ficha-asunto/110651/ficha_completa.

Pereda Valdés, I. (1941), *Negros esclavos y negros libres: Esquema de una sociedad esclavista y aporte del negro en nuestra formación nacional* (Montevideo, Imprenta Gaceta Comercial).

Pereda Valdés, I. (1965), *El negro en el Uruguay: Pasado y presente* (Montevideo, Instituto Histórico y Geográfico del Uruguay).

Persico, M. M. (2015), 'Afro-Uruguayan Culture and Legitimation: Candombe and Poetry', in *Black Writing, Culture, and the State in Latin America*, ed. J. C. Branche (Nashville, Vanderbilt University Press).

Quijano, A. (2000), 'Coloniality of Power, Eurocentrism, and Latin America', *Nepantla: Views from the South*, 1:3, 533–80.

Rainey, C. (2014), 'A US Diplomat in Uruguay Alleges She Was Denied Entry to a Restaurant because of Her Race', *New York*, 9 December, http://www.grubstreet.com/2014/12/cir cus-restauant-uruguay-allegedly-turned-away-black-diplomat.html.

Recagno, V. (2016), 'Ubunto', *La Diaria*, 18 August, https://ladiaria.com.uy/articulo/2016/ 8/ubuntu/.

Reynoso, J. (2019), Author Interview. Interviewed by Debbie Sharnak [by phone], October 30.

Riguetti, B. (2019), 'Gloria Rodríguez: La población negra no está representada en Parlamento', *La Diaria*, 2 January.

Rodríguez, R. J. (1988), 'Carta de Director', *Mundo Afro*, 1:1 (August), 3.

Rodríguez, R. J. (2003), *Racismo y derechos humanos en Uruguay* (Montevideo, Ediciones Étnicas).

Rodríguez, R. J. (2014), Author Interview. Interviewed by Debbie Sharnak [Montevideo, Uruguay], October 9.

Romero, S. (2012), 'Brazil Enacts Affirmative Action Law for Universities', *New York Times*, 30 August, https://www.nytimes.com/2012/08/31/world/americas/brazil-enacts-affirmative-action-law-for-universities.html.

Rosenblatt, F. (2018), *Party Vibrancy and Democracy in Latin America* (New York, Oxford University Press).

ROU [República Oriental del Uruguay] (2004), 'Ley no. 17.817: Lucha contra el racismo, la xenofobia y la discriminación', 6 September, https://www.gub.uy/ministerio-desarro llo-social/sites/ministerio-desarrollo-social/files/documentos/publicaciones/1774.pdf.

ROU (2006), 'Ley no. 18.059: Día nacional del candombe, la cultura afrouruguaya y la equidad racial', 20 November, https://www.gub.uy/ministerio-desarrollo-social/sites/ ministerio-desarrollo-social/files/documentos/publicaciones/1775.pdf.

ROU [República Oriental del Uruguay] (2011a), 'Diario de sesiones de la Cámara de representantes," 2nd session, 2 March, https://legislativo.parlamento.gub.uy/tempora les/20110302D0002_SSN6162605.html.

ROU [República Oriental del Uruguay] (2011b), 'Diario de Sesiones de la Cámara de representantes', 60th session, 6 December, https://parlamento.gub.uy/documentosyle yes/ficha-asunto/110651/tramite.

ROU [República Oriental del Uruguay] (2012), 'Diario de Sesiones de la Cámara de representantes', 59th session, 17 October, https://legislativo.parlamento.gub.uy/ temporales/70784335268641.PDF#pagina18.

ROU [República Oriental del Uruguay] (2013a), "Diario de Sesiones de la Cámara de senadores', 31st ordinary session, no. 229, Vol. 509, 16 July, https://parlamento.gub.uy/ documentosyleyes/ficha-asunto/110651/tramite.

ROU [República Oriental del Uruguay] (2013b), "Diario de Sesiones de la Cámara de representantes', 36th extraordinary session, 8 August, https://legislativo.parlamento. gub.uy/temporales/98357126751753.PDF#pagina126.

ROU [República Oriental del Uruguay] (2013c), 'Ley no. 19.122: Afrodescendientes. Normas para favorecer su participación en las áreas educativa y laboral' (2013), https:// www.gub.uy/ministerio-desarrollo-social/sites/ministerio-desarrollo-social/files/ documentos/publicaciones/1781.pdf.

ROU [República Oriental del Uruguay] (2018), 'Ley no. 19.684: Ley integral para personas trans', 7 November, https://www.gub.uy/ministerio-desarrollo-social/sites/ministerio-desarrollo-social/files/documentos/publicaciones/1922.pdf.

Ruetalo, V. (2008), 'From Penal Institution to Shopping Mecca: The Economics of Memory and the Case of Punta Carretas', *Cultural Critique*, 68 (Winter), 38–65.

Sans, M. (2011), 'National Identity, Census Data, and Genetics in Uruguay', in *Racial Identities, Genetic Ancestry, and Health in South America*, ed. S. Gibbon, R. Ventura Santos, and M. Sans (New York, Palgrave Macmillan).

Sanserevino, B. (2013), '2013: Aprobamos Leyes', https://www.facebook.com/notes/bertha-sanseverino/2013-aprobamos-leyes-que-consolidan-derechos/10151988482259351/.

Sharnak, D. (2022), 'The Road to Recognition: Afro-Uruguayan Activism and the Struggle for Visibility', in *Narratives of Mass Atrocity: Victims and Perpetrators in the Aftermath*, ed. S. Federman and R. Niezen (New York: Cambridge).

Sharnak, D. (2023), *Of Light and Struggle: Social Justice, Human Rights, and Accountability in Uruguay* (Philadelphia, University of Pennsylvania Press).

Sztainbok, V. (2009), 'Imagining the Afro-Uruguayan Conventillo: Belonging and the Fetish of Place and Blackness', Ph.D. dissertation, University of Toronto.

Torres-Parodi, C. (2003), *Acciones afirmativas para lograr la equidad de salud para los grupos étnicos/raciales* (Washington, DC, Organización Panamericana de la Salud).

Townsend-Bell, E. (2021), '"We entered as blacks and we left as Afro-descendants": Tracing the Path to Affirmative Action in Uruguay', *Latin American and Caribbean Ethnic Studies*, 16:3, 237–58.

Uruguay Presidencia (2019), 'Becas estatales son recibidas por 20% de adolescentes y jóvenes afrodescendientes de Uruguay', 1 July, https://www.presidencia.gub.uy/comunicacion/comunicacionnoticias/lanzamiento-mes-afrodescendencia-aumento-numero-de-becas.

Wade, P. (1993), *Blackness and Race Mixture: The Dynamics of Racial Identity in Colombia* (Baltimore, Johns Hopkins University Press).

11

Resisting Redistribution with Recognition: A Radical Neoliberal Countermovement in Santa Cruz, Bolivia

ANNA KRAUSOVA

INDIGENOUS PEOPLES IN Latin America are unrelenting in their political activism; often, so are those wishing to roll back the advances made. In October 2019, Bolivia suffered painful political polarisation as protests against the controversial re-election of Evo Morales forced the long-standing Indigenous president to flee the country. The electoral controversy gave the opposition the opportunity to capitalise on the growing disenchantment with Morales's 14-year rule, with further – often violent – protests snowballing across the country, nearly bringing it to a standstill (Lehoucq 2020). The anti-Indigenous racism that had been (at least partially) silenced since 2005 reared its ugly head again, including public burnings of the *Wiphala*, a highland Indigenous flag (Farthing and Arigho-Stiles 2019).

We know a lot about the trajectories of Indigenous movements, and about how different Latin American governments have reacted to Indigenous mobilisations (Albó 2008; Crabtree and Crabtree-Condor 2012; Postero 2017; Stahler-Sholk and Vanden 2011; Svampa 2017; Van Cott 2010; Yashar 2005). However, we still lack the tools to predict whether and *which* demands of Indigenous movements are likely to be met. While Bolivia had an Indigenous president for 14 years and now constitutionally recognises plurinationality, Indigenous rights, and even the rights of the Mother Earth, Indigenous groups, especially from the lowlands, have, since 2011, been protesting the government (Crabtree and Chaplin 2013; McNeish 2013; Postero 2017; *Razón* 2017). Apart from paying more attention to the varied strategies that different Indigenous collective actors use (Krausova 2020), we also need to study the non-state, non-Indigenous actors that aid or resist the changes Indigenous people(s) demand (Alvarez *et al.* 1998; Andolina *et al.* 2009; Lucero 2008).

This chapter focuses on how the regional right against rights in Bolivia's Santa Cruz region responded to the left-wing multicultural reforms of the Morales

Proceedings of the British Academy, **255**, 205–228, © The British Academy 2023.

administration. Viewed within the analytical framework developed by Payne in Chapter 2 of this volume, the actors studied here represent a coalescence of radical neoliberals *and* a right-wing countermovement. To date, this opposition movement has been studied as an elite backlash, a bourgeois retreat, or an ethnoterritorial project (Eaton 2007; Gustafson 2006; Peña Claros 2010; Perreault and Green 2013; Soruco 2008; Webber 2008c). Labelling it as a conservative autonomy movement, Kent Eaton points out that while 'private sector entrepreneurs, business associations, and local politicians are the most powerful advocates' of this movement – suggesting it fits within the *radical neoliberal* category – its agenda has 'resonated substantially beyond elite circles' (Eaton 2011, 291–2). This broader popular appeal extends beyond autonomy and is also explained by applying the countermovement category.

To elucidate the strategies and relative successes of this radical neoliberal countermovement, this chapter presents a mixed-method analysis, combining an analysis of qualitative data collected in Bolivia during field trips in 2011 and 2016, supplemented with online sources collected in 2020 and 2021 with a quantitative text analysis conducted in 2021, and builds on and extends the findings of the author's master's and doctoral theses (Krausova 2012, 2018). Overall, the chapter finds that neoliberal regional politicians, civil society organisations[1] involved in an autonomy struggle, and right-wing intellectuals – representing a radical neoliberal countermovement – do not uniformly oppose the reforms of the Morales administration.

As these have undermined both the economic and racial social order of Bolivia's most unequal region – Santa Cruz – the often violent resistance of Cruceño elites is well documented (Fabricant 2009; FIDH 2008; Gustafson 2006; Postero 2017). Yet while land redistribution and other left-wing economic policies were wholeheartedly rejected, Indigenous rights per se were not. As Escoffier, Payne, and Zulver elucidate in the introduction to this volume, the right tends to bestow rights only upon the 'worthy'. For the Santa Cruz countermovement, the contestation became both about what was considered legitimate for Indigenous people to claim, and who were the authentic Indigenous people in the first place. While recognition of cultural diversity was argued to be legitimate, claims for material redistribution were not, amounting to the resistance of redistribution with recognition.

We already know that in Latin America, those opposing Indigenous rights might try to separate Indigenous people's demands into categories of 'permitted' versus 'non-permitted' (Hale 2002, 2007; Lucero 2008; Rivera Cusicanqui 1987).[2] Yet, just because neoliberal elites or right-wing movements strategise to separate culture

---

[1] Calling them 'civil' might not be exactly appropriate (Payne 2000).

[2] Who is Indigenous? There are debates about this within Indigenous movements themselves. In October 2016, the Aymara sociologist Silvia Rivera Cusicanqui told me: 'putting on a poncho does not make you an Indian', in reference to Evo Morales (interview, 9 October 2016). For some, then, indigeneity is about a particular way of life. However, as social scientists, we are not in a position to adjudicate these debates. Arguably, we can use the word 'Indigenous' for someone who describes themselves as Indigenous, was born to an Indigenous family, and speaks an Indigenous language; this applies as much to the Guaraníes in Santa Cruz (including those living in the city) as it does to Evo Morales, who spoke to the UN in Aymara (Postero 2007, 2017).

from class does not mean that they will be successful. This is fought out in the political arena (Van Cott 2006, 276). Moreover, even a partial legitimation of Indigenous rights may open opportunities for further Indigenous activism toward more transformative goals (McNeish 2008; Van Cott 2006). However, this does not take place in all cases, nor do we have a good sense as to what explains the relative strength of neoliberal elites. One way to try and elucidate this is to study in more detail the movements that organise to support existing economic relations of production while adopting a language of multiculturalism, and *how* they frame their multiculturalism.

As the leading organisation of this movement, the Comité Pro Santa Cruz (Santa Cruz Civic Committee; CPSC) has made public speeches; organised citizen assemblies; led large demonstrations; and, through its youth wing, kicked off riots and violent racialised clashes. This is the stuff of social movements. To understand the emergence and continued strength of the right-wing pro-autonomy countermovement, then, we need to study it as a social movement. What strategies does it use specifically? What helps the movement's framing of Indigenous rights become accepted as legitimate beyond the countermovement's own ranks? It is social movement scholarship, and specifically framing theory, that will help us make sense of the strategies and successes of the Cruceño countermovement. Right-against-rights movements do not often fit well into the category of *social* movements empirically and politically, as Escoffier, Payne, and Zulver argue in the introduction to this volume. However, this chapter argues that applying the insights of social movement theories is essential in order to deepen our understanding of movements and mobilisation beyond the progressive cases.

Radical Neoliberals and Indigeneity in Santa Cruz

The iconic 1990 Indigenous March for Territory and Dignity originated in the Santa Cruz province, kick-starting a period of economically orthodox and multicultural reforms in 1994, including the establishment of *Tierras Comunitarias de Origen* (Indigenous Territories; TCOs) (Dunkerley 2007; Kohl 2010). Yet the 1996 agrarian reform, while recognising TCOs, also resulted in 'stabilising the property rights of Santa Cruz agro-businessmen' (Lucero 2008, 134). Indigenous people continued to experience systematic racism (Postero 2007, 225) and the citizenship regime that developed privileged ('permitted') Indigenous identities over others. Conversely, the 'process of change' of the Morales administration (Crabtree amd Chaplin 2013) made prominent the element of redistribution in its conception and implementation of Indigenous rights. In 2009, the new Constitution codified the term *indígena-originario-campesino* (Indigenous-originary-peasant[3]), seeking

---

[3] A unifying symbol like this was required in a country such as Bolivia, divided across class, ethnic, and rural–urban lines, in order to construct the Grasmcian 'people' for the MAS movement to represent. The term *originario* can be seen as analogous to the concept of 'first nations' in Canada or 'aboriginal' in Australia, and is translated here as 'original' for the lack of a better word. There seems to be little

208 *Anna Krausova*

to unify both politically and discursively Indigenous and popular (rural) sectors, something that became fiercely resisted by the Cruceño countermovement.

Indeed, Santa Cruz was at the epicentre of resistance to Morales's reforms, to the point that civil war and secession were considered a possibility in 2009 (Bebbington and Bebbington 2010; Dunkerley 2007; Gustafson 2006; Plata 2008; Postero 2017; Webber 2008c). Santa Cruz is the economic heartland of the country, with extensive agro-industrial as well as oil and gas production. Consequently, the land reforms of the Morales administration presented a direct challenge to the Santa Cruz landed elites (Plata 2008; Soruco 2008). The Santa Cruz region was hardly touched by the 1953 agrarian reform, which was intended to do away with colonial systems of land distribution and agricultural labour relations (Klein 1992; Kay and Urioste 2005; Webber 2008a). Soruco (2008) argues that local political and economic elites have largely reproduced without significant ruptures or pressure from below since colonial times. A temporary truce was only reached when the Morales administration realised it relied on Santa Cruz's agro-industry to feed the country, and Cruceño neoliberals realised they could not win against the president electorally at the national level (Crabtree and Chaplin 2013; Postero 2017; Webber 2008a, b, c).

As a product of the export-led economy with closer international than national ties, Santa Cruz elites had less need for a horizontal political dialogue with the local Indigenous population or the middle classes. This helps explain their economically neoliberal outlook. The lowland Cruceños were never able to challenge the claim to national hegemony of the highland Altiplano elites (Crabtree and Chaplin 2013; Klein 1992; Plata 2008; Yashar 2005). This elucidates the discursive construction of the *Nación Camba* (Camba Nation) of the Bolivian lowlands, portrayed as racially and culturally distinct from the highland *Nación Colla* (Colla Nation).[4] This claim to Camba nationhood and Cruceño exceptionalism is a crucial part of the framing of the countermovement, led by the CPSC.

---

difference in Bolivia in the usage of the terms 'Indigenous' and 'originary', except that the lowland identity-based organisations tend to use the word 'Indigenous' while the highland ones seem to prefer the term 'originary'.

[4] Still, it is important not to overstate the differences between the 'lowlands' and the 'highlands' (the Cambas and the Collas). The highland movements built on a historical experience of class-based, corporatist, union organisation, and were discursively constructed as *campesinos* (peasants) (Albó, 2008). Their lowland counterparts, having experienced much less integration into the state historically, only came to play an important political role at the national level during the 1980s and 1990s, partly as the result of a process of structuring through non-governmental organisations (NGOs), and building on the organisational frameworks left in place by the Jesuit missions. This shaped the ways in which indigeneity was constructed (Yashar 2005), favouring a more ethnic-based focus and emphasising an Indigenous 'mode' of life as protecting the environment. Moreover, while the Andes and the valleys tend to be populated mainly by the Quechua and Aymara peoples (the two largest Indigenous groups in Bolivia), there is great diversity of linguistic and cultural groups among Santa Cruz Indigenous peoples, including the Guaraníes, the Chiquitanos, the Ayoreos, the Yuracarés, the Moxeños, and the Quarayos. However, there has also been a long historical migration of Aymara and Quechua populations into the lowlands, thus making the distinction between the lowlands and the highlands less clear (Postero 2007).

The CPSC, established in 1950, presents itself as the 'moral government of the Cruceños'.[5] While historically it has provided a space for local political, business, and civic elites to come together (Soruco 2008), since the 2005 election of Evo Morales, its 'leaders built an urban base of support and ultimately created a powerful social movement' in opposition to that government (Fabricant 2009, 769). At the height of the regional resistance to Morales's reforms, the committee was able to mobilise hundreds of thousands of supporters (Rochlin 2007, 1334); in 2007, the CPSC 'held a public meeting attended by a million flag-waving protestors' (Postero 2017, 132).

During 2007 and 2008, the movement was also at its boldest. Its youth wing, the Unión Juvenil Cruceñista (Santa Cruz Youth Union; UJC), 'carried out numerous attacks against Andean migrants to the city' (Postero 2017, 121). Weakened by the 2009 constitutional reform that granted some regional autonomy on the one hand and accusations of racism, separatism, and even terrorism on the other, the movement then began to use the language of human rights and victimhood to advance its agenda (Fabricant and Postero 2013; Postero 2017). This fits the conceptualisation developed by Escoffier, Payne, and Zulver in the introduction to this volume, whereby the right against rights uses a language of rights-protection, but only for those deemed 'worthy'.

Latin American Multiculturalism(s) and the Framing of Indigeneity

The classificatory power of Latin American multiculturalism has been studied extensively. For many scholars, the period of neoliberal multiculturalism positioned only some Indigenous groups as the 'permitted Indian', a term coined by Bolivian Aymara scholar Silvia Rivera Cusicanqui and developed and popularised by Charles Hale (Hale 2002; Rivera Cusicanqui 1987). The dichotomy of the 'permitted' and 'non-permitted' Indigenous political subjects draws on long-standing debates in political theory about class versus identity, and recognition versus redistribution (Fraser 2003; Honneth 2003).[6] While normatively the displacement of the material by the symbolic can be dismissed, 'the cultural displacing the material; identity politics displacing class; the politics of constitutional reform displacing the economics of equality' (Phillips 1997, 1) is a phenomenon for which empirical examples abound. Fraser herself makes this clear in expounding the folk paradigms

---

[5] CPSC (2019). All translations from Spanish are my own.

[6] Fraser's theorising (1997, 2003) corresponds to the observations of scholars of Latin America that claims for recognition often cannot easily be separated from those for redistribution, especially when looking at Indigenous movements as a whole (e.g. Yashar 2005). Normatively, Fraser argues that both are needed to achieve social justice (Fraser 2003). This normative dualism does not mean that Fraser is not deeply critical of any theoretical or political attempts to collapse all justice claims into either the politics of recognition or the politics of redistribution. In fact, this is a crucial tenet of her approach.

of justice –widespread ways of understanding social justice underpinned by a certain moral grammar – in which recognition and redistribution can be seen as antithetical (Fraser 2003). These ways of understanding what is just and legitimate are both a crucial arena for – and a crucial subject of – movement struggles. It is a battle about framing; in changing the way that Indigenous rights are framed and legitimated, some demands get privileged while others are side-lined. This creates the 'worthy' claimants of rights that the right against rights can champion.

In Latin America, privileging a certain *kind* of Indigenous rights that are considered less 'threatening' and thus 'permitted' has specifically meant privileging rights containing recognition but not redistribution (Hale 2002; see also Horton 2006; Postero 2007). The notion of 'seeing with both eyes', meaning organising along the axes of *both* class and ethnicity in Bolivia (Albó 2008; Rivera Cusicanqui 1984), does not mean that at other times Indigenous social movement actors cannot struggle with 'one eye closed', nor that their opponents cannot encourage this partial 'blindness'. Paying attention to these classificatory strategies allows us to consider different claims and frames being privileged at different times by different social and political actors. Indigenous movements demanding recognition rather than redistribution have also sometimes been labelled as more 'authentically' Indigenous (Hale 2002; Krausova 2012; Postero 2007); we will see that the Cruceño countermovement engages in such framing too.

However, simply because a right-wing countermovement employs the framing strategy of separating Indigenous activism into 'permitted' and 'non-permitted' does not mean that this framing will have enough resonance to help the countermovement mobilise and maintain momentum. Donna Lee Van Cott's comparative work on multiculturalism and neoliberalism in Latin America suggests that the relative prominence of these two elements in movement demands is determined largely by the relative strength of Indigenous movements, local elites, and the electoral left (Van Cott 2006). Yet this account does not tell the full story either. First, even if the local elites, or rather a regional radical neoliberal countermovement, are the strongest of the three actors, Van Cott's argument seems to assume that they are outright against Indigenous rights. However, the right in Santa Cruz, just like Hale's Guatemalan *ladinos* (Hale 2002), do profess support for Indigenous rights. Yet they do so in a way that is different from how progressive movements define Indigenous rights.

Accordingly, this is not a zero-sum game between neoliberal elites and Indigenous movements. Right-wing countermovements need to cultivate popular support. The right in Santa Cruz draws on membership among all classes in society, supports political parties that continue to win regional elections, and has even boasted the support of some Indigenous leaders. It is also a movement for regional autonomy that cannot be understood simply as the backlash of racist regional elites (Bebbington and Bebbington 2010; Centellas 2016; Perreault and Green 2013). Indeed, between 2004 and 2010, identification with a regional Cruceño identity permeated all sectors of society in the region, even if after 2008 it became more obviously politicised, with an increasing correlation between being conservative and 'feeling Cruceño' (Flesken 2018). What this high level of regional belonging shows is the success of the framing of Cruceño identity and its resonance across Santa Cruz society; this is taken as a measure of the relative 'success' of the movement's framing strategies. While Eaton (2011) shows that the framing of a popular regional identity helped the Santa Cruz autonomy movement, the complexity of its framing strategies remains unexplored. A framing-theory lens looking at *how* the Santa Cruz countermovement frames Cruceño identity and what role indigeneity plays in this these framing strategies has not been applied to this case.

A Mixed-Method Frame Analysis

This chapter analyses the framing strategies used by the countermovement's main actors. Framing refers to the strategic meaning construction that social movements engage in (Benford and Snow 1988, 1992, 2000) and the 'strategic efforts' by activists 'to fashion shared understandings ... that legitimate and motivate collective action' (McAdam *et al.* 1996, 6). It is best understood as 'movement discursive tactics' (McCammon *et al.* 2007, 731). The external resonance of a frame then helps movements mobilise and sustain momentum (Benford and Snow 1992, 2000; Snow 2004; Snow et al. 2014). Frame resonance is affected by the 'discursive opportunity structure', which denotes which constructions of reality are seen as 'realistic' and which claims are held as 'legitimate' (Koopmans and Statham 1999, 228). Social movements strategise about which frames to use both to justify and to amplify the legitimacy of their claims. Indigenous movements and their opponents alike engage in framing battles in terms of both 'realistic' constructions of reality (who is authentically Indigenous) and what claims are legitimate and/or 'permitted'. Both strategies coalesce into a portrayal of a worthy claimant of rights.

This mixed-method chapter employs a sequential design. It analyses qualitative data on framing, collected during field trips in 2011 and 2016,[7] and online in 2021, drawing on semi-structured interviews with regional politicians, members of the Santa Cruz Civic Committee, and pro-autonomy intellectuals, as well as institutional materials, social media, and secondary sources to triangulate the interviews (Brady and Collier 2010; Creswell 2007; Natow 2020).[8] This allowed for an in-depth analysis of the framing strategies used by the Cruceño countermovement. The qualitative data were supplemented by textual data from the CPSC's website from between 2007 and 2020,[9] analysed for the frequency over time of the

[7] Field trips were conducted between 2011 and 2016. This chapter builds on and expands the analysis of my master's and doctoral theses (Krausova 2012, 2018).

[8] Primarily, I used sampling for range to represent different actors within the Cruceño countermovement, complemented by snowball sampling, intended to improve trust within the interview process. I also employed sequential interviewing, which allows for the reconfiguration of theory, until saturation was reached (Small, 2009).

[9] The CPSC website is http://comiteprosantacruz.org.bo/. Textual data between 2007 and 2020 were downloaded in 2020 and 2021 using the online website archiving tool, the Wayback Machine, available at https://web.archive.org/. The year 2007 was the earliest capture of the website on the web archive.

212 *Anna Krausova*

word 'Indigenous' (*indígena*) and its collocations using the online corpora analysis tool Sketch Engine (Allen 2017; Kilgarriff *et al.* 2014).[10] This method shows the patterns of usage of the word, and thus the salience of indigeneity over time. This is compared with the media salience of the term *indígena* during the same period in the regional, right-leaning newspaper *El Deber*, as reported through BBC Monitoring: International Media Reports, and in the Spanish international news agency EFE.[11]

This mixed-method analysis provides evidence of both the framing strategies of the CPSC, the organisation heading the Cruceño countermovement, and the wider resonance of those frames. Such a sequential mixed-method approach (Greene 2008; Small 2011; Teddlie and Tashakkori 2009) presents a novel way to study framing strategies, in terms of both their internal development and their external resonance over time. It finds that we need to pay attention to both longer-term historically and geographically embedded strategies of social movements, and those that are more contingent and responding to changing political opportunities, public opinion, and media cycles. Movement framing strategies have not been analysed in this way before.

Analysis: 'Our Indigenous' and Other Frames

> On a day like today, 460 years ago, the era of *cruceñidad* [Cruceño identity] began ... Our history begins with the founding of Santa Cruz de la Sierra on 26 February 1561, by Spaniards, criollos, mestizos, and Indigenous people who arrived from the mother city, Asunción del Paraguay, as well as by the local Indigenous people. We were a mestizo city, where our origin was forged with the vigour of the old and the new world ... We made the conqueror transform his sword into a plough and fertilise the land with his body and with his dreams. Because the conqueror and the conquered ended up being, in the end, one and the same ... We decided to be part of Bolivia on 6 August 1825. Santa Cruz is a nation 264 years older than Bolivia ... Santa Cruz is today the undisputed *taita*[12] of the republic. Because without Santa Cruz, Bolivia neither lives nor eats.
>
> Rómulo Calvo, president of the CPCS, on the 460th anniversary of the founding of the city of Santa Cruz in Bolivia, 26 February 2021 (Calvo 2021)

In the above speech, the president of the CPCS sums up the two main frames used by the right-wing countermovement in Bolivia's Santa Cruz region in their

[10] I also explored the usage of related words such as 'native' (*originario*) and *indio*, or names of Indigenous nations such as 'Guaraní' and 'Aymara', but *indígena* was the most commonly used term and allowed for the most systematic comparison. Specifically, I analysed collocations (most commonly used words next to the target term) of *indígena* used as an adjective on the website, as well as in the CPSC's institutional documents: in particular which nouns were most frequently modified by it. Sketch Engine is available at https://www.sketchengine.eu/.

[11] Accessed through the LexisNexis database (https://www.lexisnexis.com). This source was used on account of data accessibility, but it also captured the international salience of news about Indigenous people and Indigenous rights, not only in the regional press itself.

[12] *Taita* is a term that tends to be translated as either 'teat' or 'papa'; both translations work in this quote.

opposition to the progressive reforms of the MAS administration. He presents a semi-mythical narrative of the founding of the city of Santa Cruz, in which the conquerors and the conquered mixed unproblematically, quickly forging a seemingly peaceful *mestizaje*. This is where the narrative of a regional Cruceño identity emerges. It feeds into the frame of the uniqueness of Santa Cruz or, first of all, Cruceño *exceptionalism*, now the breadbasket of the country, and home to the Camba Nation, which is portrayed as preceding the foundation of Bolivia by more than 250 years. This is the key frame of the autonomy movement. Second, the speech entails a vision of *authentic indigeneity*, stemming from a folklorisation of Indigenous identities as something belonging squarely in the past. It also contains, however, a devaluing of, and paternalism toward, indigeneity, as it implies that the land was transformed with the bodies and dreams of the conquerors, and that the new mestizo only learned to use land productively from Spanish – rather than Indigenous – ancestors.

Yet while the CPSC heads pro-autonomy and anti-Morales marches and demonstrations, its youth wing, the UJC, was instrumental in instigating the violence against Indigenous peoples and their organisations, as well as state institutions and pro-Indigenous NGOs in 2007 and 2008 (Fabricant 2009; Postero 2017). Several UJC members were also arrested in 2008 in possession of shotguns and ammunition at the Santa Cruz airport prior to the arrival of Evo Morales (FIDH 2008).

Various leaders of Indigenous organisations in Santa Cruz documented the resistance to the struggles of Indigenous movements and the reforms of the Morales government. Celso Padilla, the president of the Consejo Educativo del Pueblo Guaraní (Educational Council of the Guaraní People; CEPOG) in 2008, highlighted the violent backlash experienced by the Guaraníes in Santa Cruz in their attempts to secure land ownership, through the powers granted by the 2009 Constitution (Padilla 2008). Along with the recorded violence (FIDH 2008; Iskenderian Aguilera 2010), this suggests that the right-wing and civic institutions, such as the CPSC, are far from accepting the multicultural nature of Bolivia. Yet, as detailed below, my interviewees were often keen to show just how supportive of Indigenous rights they are. How to make sense of this apparent contradiction? What does this pro-Indigenous framing look like? Has it helped the countermovement maintain momentum, and if so, how?

Cruceño Exceptionalism

In Bolivia, the deployment of strong regional identities in resistance to the central government and its progressive reforms is well documented (Bebbington and Bebbington 2010; Crabtree and Whitehead 2008; Fabricant 2009; Fabricant and Postero 2013, 2014; Gustafson 2006; Kohl 2010; Postero 2017; Webber 2008c). Such studies have focused on the dynamics of the Cruceño regional identity and the different elements and myths it encompasses. This is fascinating in terms of elucidating the ways in which a movement mostly defending elite interests has incorporated popular elements and demands (Peña Claros 2010). The right-wing autonomist movement in Santa Cruz, with the CPSC at its helm, has gained support and legitimacy, partly through 'the appropriation by whites of selective aspects of lowland Bolivian Indigenous culture, that of the Guaraní' (Fabricant 2009, 769). Much of the discourse of Santa Cruz regionalism centres around the particularity of Cruceño and/or Camba identity, which is reflected both in daily references to regional culture, such as 'Camba food' or 'Camba dance', but also in the important, even if not universally accepted, Camba Nation movement (interview with Gustavo Pinto, 1 September 2011). Inextricably linked to the latter is the narrative of *mestizaje*.

As the Cruceño autonomist movement frames its opposition to the Morales administration in the language of unfair exclusion and the right to recognition – using the language of multiculturalism – it also strives to maintain its legitimacy and claim to representativeness for all Cruceños in the face of accusations of racism and the exclusion of Indigenous peoples in an era of state-sponsored multiculturalism. As Kathleen Lowrey posits, 'within Bolivia the embrace of indigeneity has proven universally popular. This is not to say there are no closet racists in Bolivia, but their closeting is important' (2006, 72).

For example, the music group affiliated to the UJC is called Kerembas,[13] from the Guaraní for warrior, *Kereimba*. Moreover, the group celebrates indigeneity – though only insofar as it belongs in the past, or now forms part of the local folklore. For the occasion of the 460th anniversary of the foundation of the city in February 2021, they posted an image on their public Facebook page. This was a copy of a painting by a local artist, Carlos Cirbián Baros, with the founding date and the Kerembas logo superimposed.

This painting, titled *Amanecer del 26 de febrero de 1561* (*Sunrise on 26 February 1561*) was unveiled at an exhibition sponsored by the CPSC on 11 May 2017. The plaque on its right bears the following description):

> This marks the founding by Extremaduran captain Ñuflo de Chaves of the legendary city of Santa Cruz de la Sierra on the banks of the Sutós stream and at the foot of the Riquío mountain range. It is the day that marks the birth of the Cruceño community or Camba Nation, fruit of the biological and cultural fusion between the Spanish explorers and the native ethnic groups of our fertile territory.

This painting is a visual representation of *mestizaje*, depicting an almost peaceful mixing – cultural and physical – of the conquerors and the conquered. It again presents a vision of Indigenous people as historical ancestors of today's Cruceños, rather than acknowledging the lives and struggles of Indigenous people(s) in the region today. Yet as Postero (2017) argues, the Cruceño countermovement was forced to acknowledge the continued existence of Indigenous nations in the region; in the end, the movement used this as an opportunity to improve its framing of ethnicity and equality.

---

[13] In full, the Grupo de Expresión Cultural Kerembas.

Authentic Indigeneity

I first visited the Santa Cruz departmental government, the *gobernación*, in September 2011. The governor, Rubén Costas, was elected on a right-wing conservative pro-autonomy ticket in 2009 and has been in this elected position since 2006 (first as prefect, before the 2009 constitution granted regions greater local governance). Before that, he had served for two years as the president of the CPSC, highlighting the closely knit network of political and civic elites in the region.

The *gobernación* employees, as well as the governor himself, donned uniforms exhibiting a variety of Indigenous symbols. These included the *Patujú* flower, from the *Bandera de Patujú*, the flag that lowland Indigenous organisations have used to represent the lowland Indigenous peoples of Bolivia since the state's plurinationality was recognised in 2009 (the *Wiphala* flag is mainly used by the highland Aymaras and Quechuas). The *Patujú* flag was also flying in the main Santa Cruz square, along with that of Bolivia and the green and white Cruceño flag. Both provide evidence of the symbolic recognition of diversity. Moreover, Oscar Ortiz, secretary of the *gobernación* (and previously the general manager of the *Cámara de Industria y Comercio* (Chamber of Industry and Commerce)) confided that 'our governor is in love with Indigenous culture' (interview with Oscar Ortiz, 7 September 2011).[14]

When I asked him about the *Día de la Tradición Cruceña* (Day of the Cruceño Tradition), celebrated each August and supported by the regional government, Ortiz insisted that 'all the traditions of this land have Indigenous roots ... Indigenous from this area'. This is a multiculturalism that relies on folklorisation of indigeneity into the ('permitted') elements of dress, music, and food. The regional government, representing the institutionalisation of the Cruceño countermovement, has been framing itself as pro-Indigenous – but with a caveat; only the lowland Indigenous groups are officially recognised. And, as we will see below, even the lowland Indigenous nations are recognised as legitimate claimants to certain rights only.

But if it is framing itself as pro-multicultural, what is it about the Morales reforms that the Cruceño right wing openly opposes? Nicolas Ribera, the vice-president of the CPSC in 2011, expressed to me that he does not oppose Evo Morales 'because he is a *cholo*, because he is an *Indio* ... I oppose him because he is a criminal' (interview with Nicolas Ribera, 30 August 2011). Moreover, he described the methods of the Morales government as totalitarian, centralising, and power-grabbing. The use of the word *delincuente* (criminal), if contextualised, is more than a political slur. My interview with Ruth Lozada, Santa Cruz departmental assembly member for the VERDES (Verdad y Democracia Social, or Truth and Social Democracy) political party in 2011 and the former president of the women's wing of the Civic Committee (*Comité Cívico Femenino*), talked about what she saw as the way in which Indigenous peoples from the *occidente*, the Aymaras or the Quechuas, often come to 'beg', or 'make others beg' for them (Ruth Lozada, 8 September 2011). Both are

---

[14] This paternalism is well documented, for example, by Postero in her study of Indigenous political participation in Santa Cruz under the 1994 reforms (Postero 2007, 150).

216   *Anna Krausova*

invoking criminality in relation to Indigenous people, but only to the Aymaras and the Quechuas specifically. This demonstrates a dichotomisation of a non-threatening indigeneity as naive, and the more threatening indigeneity as criminal. Moreover, it is linked to the way in which Indigenous demands are often criticised not for their content, but for the methods that they employ (Bowen 2011, 454).

Ruth Lozada's take on indigeneity overall is an example of the classificatory battles theorised above: 'I believe that this distinction must be made, because the TCOs [*Tierra Comunitaria de Orígen*, Native Community Lands] are the natives, so yes, I believe that they must be respected. Why? Because my natural habitat is what makes me a true *originario*' (Ruth Lozada, 8 September 2011. The notion that one is only 'truly' Indigenous if living in a protected territory is resisted by Indigenous activists themselves (Weber 2013).[15] Lozada continues:

> We are fighting very hard for it to be only the *originarios*, and not ... *originarios-campesinos* [who are recognised], because the *originarios* are the ones that effectively live on from before the colony, and those [ethnic groups] are the ones we should protect ... those types of ethnic groups with all their culture, their way of being, their natural way; and the peasant [*campesino*], the peasant was not an *originario* before the colony.

For Lozada, then, as an elected politician and one of the leaders of the Civic Committee, the 'true' Indigenous people continue a precolonial way of life; this is certainly not the case for the Indigenous leaders and communities of the lowlands to whom she is referring (Grisaffi 2010; Postero 2007). Moreover, in her narrative, they are in need of protection in their 'natural habitat', which is what makes them 'truly Indigenous'. Similarly, during the same 2011 visit to the Santa Cruz *gobernación*, an employee volunteered that 'the Aymaras and Quechuas are not pure Indigenous'.[16] This narrative of 'true', or authentic, indigeneity is a central tenet of the multicultural framing of the Cruceño countermovement.

On the day of the interview with Oscar Ortiz of the Cruceño departmental government, a demonstration took place in the main square of Santa Cruz, right under the windows of the *gobernación* building.[17] This protest concerned land redistribution; in this instance, a community from San Aurelio, on the outskirts of the city of Santa Cruz, were protesting about access to land and were flying *Wiphalas*.[18] In a conversation with one of the *gobernación* employees, I was told that this was simply a problem of private property and respect for the law, as the protestors were

---

[15] In her qualitative research with Chiquitano communities in Bolivia, Katinka Weber notes the contested nature of Indigenous identification. Particularly relevant is one of her interviews highlighting the resistance of many members of these communities to discourses that connect *indígena* or *originario* identities with the need to protect Indigenous 'habitat', as this is seen as a word to be used for 'wild animals' (*animales de monte*), and thus a derogatory slur (Weber 2013).

[16] Talk with an anonymous *gobernación* employee, 7 September 2011, Santa Cruz.

[17] The symbolic centre of the historic white–mestizo power (Postero 2007; Fabricant 2009).

[18] The *Wiphala*, which the 2009 Constitution adopted as a symbol of state, is increasingly being adopted by a variety of Indigenous communities and political causes.

responding to their eviction from land they had previously occupied. Any recourse to invoking an Indigenous identity in claiming these land rights was seen as instrumental, not authentic. However, not only were the protesters Aymara and Quechua, the fact that they were carrying the *Wiphala* suggests that they self-identify – publicly and politically – as Indigenous.

On the topic of protest in Santa Cruz, Oscar Ortiz of the *gobernación* further posited that 'most of the tensions are occurring against Indigenous migrants, or [he corrects himself] peasant [*campesino*] migrants, Quechuas, Aymaras, who come here'. This quote is illuminating, as it implies a certain confusion around which terminology to use, suggesting that Hale is correct in pointing out that 'elites' – or the countermovement – deliberately try to delegitimise certain rights-claimants. When it is a conscious strategy, slips of this kind might be expected.

This insistence on only some Indigenous groups being 'truly' Indigenous makes sense if seen in the wider context of the Cruceño movement's opposition to the redistributive reforms of the MAS government, especially their land redistribution policies. These include the right to land for *indígena-originario-campesino* peoples and nations. The constitutional reform also gave the state far-reaching powers in terms of redistributing even privately owned land if it does not perform a 'social function' (Bolivia 2009, article 393). This extends the agrarian reform introduced by the MAS in 2006, which allows the state to expropriate and redistribute private land if it is found that employment regulations are being broken. This was applied, for example, to the redistribution of privately owned land to Guaraníes in the Santa Cruz region, who had still lived under a system similar to colonial servitude, working for free for large landowners, without recourse to law or access to education and healthcare, among other things (CIDH 2009).

It is in this context that the framing battle takes place in Santa Cruz over what Indigenous rights are and who can legitimately claim them. This framing of 'permitted' Indigenous rights is justified by arguing that those who are demanding the 'non-permitted' rights (i.e. land redistribution) are not 'truly' Indigenous, since the authentically Indigenous person lives in the rainforest, in her natural habitat, and thus does not require the redistribution of privately owned land. These narratives coalesced to create a definition of 'authentic' indigeneity. This awards the legitimacy of multicultural rights claims to those defined as authentically Indigenous, while it rejects the claims of those who claim indigeneity politically but are not, in this narrative, portrayed as 'worthy' enough to do so.

Strategic Framing: Pro-Indigeneity

The Cruceño countermovement thus adopts a language of multiculturalism but in a manner whereby only certain Indigenous groups can actually reap benefits from multicultural reforms. Hale's contribution, discussed above, suggests that elites adapt to the new normal by selectively adopting multicultural language (Hale 2002).

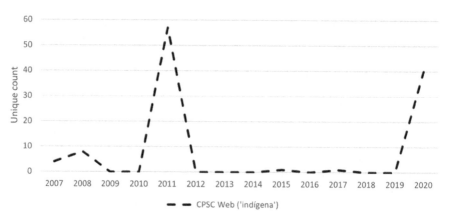

Figure 11.1 CPSC attention to indigeneity. Corpus from the CPSC website, elaborated by the author.

According to such a conceptualisation, we would expect the right-wing countermovement, especially the CPSC, to continue using this pro-Indigenous framing over time. At the same time, Van Cott's argument in reaction to Hale is that the nature of multiculturalism, and thus the content of Indigenous rights, will depend on the relative strength of elites (or the right), the electoral left, and Indigenous movements (Van Cott 2006). This could also be interpreted to mean that when the right is in a stronger position, it has less of a need to adopt a pro-Indigenous language. Is this the case? In order to answer this question, the in-depth snapshot of the framing strategies detailed above is not enough; we need to investigate the evolution, if any, of frames over time.

In order to do so, I turn to a corpora analysis of the CPSC website, looking first at the frequency of mentions of the word *indígena* and then the patterns of its use. Figure 11.1 depicts the frequency of unique mentions of the word *indígena* between 2007 and 2020. This shows that rather than a gradual introduction of the term and/or an increasing usage trend, there are two spikes in the attention paid to Indigenous people and Indigenous rights on the CPSC website. The 2011 spike suggests that the prominent pro-Indigenous narrative within the Cruceño countermovement I encountered in 2011 was, rather than a long-term strategy, a short-term response to a particular political and media context, namely the explosion of the *Territorio Indígena y Parque Nacional Isiboro Sécure* (Isiboro Sécure Indigenous Territory and National Park; TIPNIS) conflict.

This land was recognised as a TCO in 1990. In 2011, the MAS administration announced a project to build a highway between the Cochabamba and Beni departments, which would cut right through the TIPNIS territory. The 2011 March for Territory, Dignity, and Rights of Indigenous Peoples of the East protested the road project and called for respect of the constitutionally recognised rights of self-government and territory of Indigenous peoples, as well as the right to free and prior consultation mandated by the International Labour Organization's Convention 169.

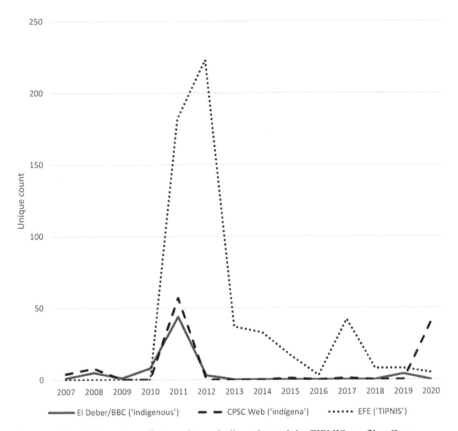

Figure 11.2 CPSC and media attention to indigeneity and the TIPNIS conflict. Corpora from EFE Newswires and the CPSC website, elaborated by the author.

The TIPNIS protests received widespread international attention, given that some of the Indigenous organisations and leaders marching against the Morales government had helped bring this Indigenous president to power five years earlier (Garcés 2010; Krausova 2018; McNeish 2013; Postero 2017). While the conflict has not been resolved, despite a controversial consultation process, it is its dynamics during 2011 that are of interest in this chapter.

Figure 11.2 plots the CPSC's attention to indigeneity over time against the frequency of mentions of the word *indígena* in the regional, right-leaning newspaper *El Deber* (the vast majority of which mention the TIPNIS conflict),[19] and the frequency of articles about the TIPNIS conflict in the Spanish international news agency EFE. This shows that the importance of the topic of Indigenous rights and peoples to the CPSC largely correlates with the salience of indigeneity, and specifically the TIPNIS conflict, in both regional and international media.[20]

[19] As reported in BBC Monitoring: International Reports.
[20] The fact that BBC Monitoring picked up those texts from *El Deber* speaks to both the international salience of the topic and how much attention was paid to the question of indigeneity by the regional press, even if it is an imperfect measure of the latter.

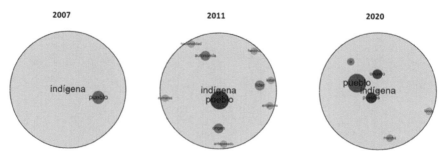

Figure 11.3 Collocations of *indígena*. Corpus from the CPSC website, elaborated by the author.

The authentic indigeneity frame, unlike that of Cruceño exceptionalism, thus emerged as a strategic response to a political and media opportunity. The TIPNIS conflict revealed the contradictory notions of what indigeneity means politically (Krausova 2018; McNeish 2013) and pitted some Indigenous groups in Bolivia against others. This gave the right-wing countermovement in Santa Cruz an opportunity to position itself as supporter of the Indigenous organisations that protested against Morales, but only while this topic was receiving regional, national, and international media attention. The recent spike in attention can be explained by the political instability and polarisation that forced Morales to resign in 2019, and the Cruceño right wing's 2020 general election campaign.

Still, we do not yet know *how* the CPSC talked about Indigenous people and rights on their website, only the *frequency* with which these topics were mentioned. This is shown in the corpora analysis in Figure 11.3, which depicts the collocations of the word *indígena* (specifically modifiers of it used as a noun) in 2007, 2011, and 2020, years in which it was mentioned with at least some degree of frequency.

Since the media attention to the TIPNIS conflict has subsided, references to Indigenous people have not disappeared from the framing repertoire of the CPSC, but their frequency has declined and the ways in which they are talked about has changed as well. The four mentions in 2007 refer to *los indígenas* (Indigenous people). Specifically, they refer to discussions about the representation of Indigenous people on the committee. In 2011, however, the year of the TIPNIS conflict, there were 57 unique mentions of the word *indígena* on the website. While the most common collocation was still 'people', the top five included the neutral but also positive 'leader', 'autonomy', 'origin', and 'heroine'.

Moreover, the CPSC took steps to include Indigenous representatives in its ranks at this time. Posts on its website included the following: 'The Santa Cruz Civic Committee ... began the process of broadening its representativeness with the inclusion of the ... five Indigenous peoples of the region.'[21] At the same time, it

---

[21] 'Nota desde San José de Chiquitos: Comités cívicos provinciales buscan fortalecer el Comité pro Santa Cruz' (CPSC website, posted 09.04.2011). The text can be found on this website: https://web.archive.org/web/20110524143352/https://www.comiteprosantacruz.org.bo/.

was denouncing 'the demagogic Indigenous-originary-peasant autonomy'.[22] This is another example of the CPSC positioning itself as accepting of Indigenous peoples and rights at the height of the TIPNIS media frenzy, but still (a) only for some Indigenous nations, and (b) only for some rights, with the exclusion of the right to autonomy that might require land redistribution.

In 2020, more neutral descriptive words such as 'people' and 'march' returned to the website. Another top collocation was 'fund': this references the corruption scandal within the government's *Fondo Indígena* (Indigenous Fund) (Gustafson 2016) and thus mentions indigeneity in a negative light. There are also positive mentions, however, and the spike in references can be explained by the political conflict in Bolivia between 2019 and 2020 and the need of the Cruceño right wing to seek legitimacy again in the electoral campaign and street battle against the MAS. The use of the term *oriundo*, a synonym for 'native', in the phrase 'indígenas oriundos del departamento de Santa Cruz' (native Indigenous of the Santa Cruz department), seems to be the new expression for *nuestros indígenas* (our Indigenous).[23]

Moreover, since 2011, in general, indigeneity has been relegated to the past again. A good example is the CPSC's development proposal, elaborated in 2014. Titled 'The Santa Cruz Development Model', the 122-page document mentions the word *indígena* four times, and in three instances the reference is to history, such as in this example: 'Among the ancestral influences of the Cruceño culture, we find the Chiquitano Indigenous people, to whom the Jesuits transmitted practices, forms of organisation, customs, and trades during the missionary stage, emphasising their work in music, weaving, cultivation of the land, and religious artistic styles' (CPSC 2014).

Over time, then, the framing of indigeneity by the CPSC, at the helm of the Cruceño countermovement, exhibits two patterns. The first is the framing of indigeneity as something belonging in the past, something that featured only in the historical *mestizaje* that produced today's Cruceño culture. This is part of the Cruceño exceptionalism frame identified in the qualitative part of this study. Temporally, this is a stable frame that builds on a longer history of identity construction in the region. The second frame, that of authentic indigeneity, emerged in response to external political and media pressures and opportunities. Specifically, the TIPNIS conflict brought international attention to the complexity of indigeneity in Bolivia in 2011, allowing the right-wing countermovement to counter the accusations of racism it has battled since the election of Evo Morales in 2005 by pronouncing selective support for some Indigenous groups and types of multicultural rights.

---

[22] 'Persecución a los Autonomistas' (CPSC website, posted 20.12.2010). The text can be found at this website: http://web.archive.org/web/20101227230811/http://www.comiteprosantacruz.org.bo/?paged=2.
[23] This is a phrase used repeatedly on the website. An example of its usage can be found in this document: https://www.comiteprosantacruz.org.bo/asamblea-de-la-crucenidad-aprueba-paro-civico-si-tse-habilita-a-morales/.

This finding emerges from the corpora analysis above. Both the salience and the nature of the pro-Indigenous frame differed in 2011 when compared to the rest of the period under study. While salience was much higher, the framing focused on proclaiming limited rights to some Indigenous groups. This supports the findings of the qualitative analysis, where rights to recognition of difference for the region's Indigenous groups, such as the Guaraní, were publicly supported as legitimate, and their demands as authentic, while the rights to redistribution of Indigenous peoples, especially of the Aymara and Quechua people, were rejected as illegitimate and their claims as instrumental. 'Our Indigenous' people for the Cruceño countermovement are those who are considered conciliatory and pragmatic, rather than conflictual and radical (Lucero 2008), claiming citizenship and respect but not threatening existing relations of production (McNeish 2008).

Yet even this selective pro-Indigenous frame was deployed strategically only when international media paid attention to Indigenous rights in Bolivia. When the pressure not to appear outright anti-Indigenous subsided, the Cruceño countermovement once more paid attention to Indigenous rights only sporadically, and relegated indigeneity to the past rather than recognising it as something that requires political attention now.

Conclusion

The Cruceño exceptionalism framing has remained a stable element of the CPSC's framing repertoire. Conversely, it turns out that the authentic indigeneity frame was reactive to the political context. Federico Rossi's concepts, related to tactics, of the *repertoires of strategies* responding to political opportunities on the one hand and the historically bounded *stock of legacies* (Rossi 2017) on the other, capture this when applied to framing as well. Some frames are embedded in longer histories of struggle (Tarrow 1993) while others involve often rapid innovation in response to changing political opportunities. We need to pay attention to how 'the strategies of social movement actors interact with what constrains them both politically and historically' (Krausova 2020, 842). This helps explain the strategies of the Santa Cruz radical neoliberal countermovement, showing social movement theory's utility in explaining the dynamics and successes of social and political actions that have previously been described mostly as an elite backlash.

In this way, we can see better why the Cruceño countermovement has maintained relatively high levels of popular support and mobilisation capacity. Although the elite backers and contradictions of the MAS governments can also help explain the movement's momentum, this does not tell the full story. These factors alone cannot explain the continued mobilisation strength of the CPSC, nor the electoral victories of the right in the Santa Cruz region. The framing strategies of the movement have also contributed to this. In particular, in combining a frame that drew on broadly accepted historical constructions of Cruceño identity with a politically opportune frame about authentic indigeneity, the movement's framing enjoyed broad popular resonance regionally, and gained recognition internationally. This helped to bolster the legitimacy of its goals and maintain momentum.

The right-wing countermovement in Santa Cruz does not use framing strategies that simply separate redistribution from recognition, class from culture. It does not simply resist redistributive policies while accepting Indigenous rights as legitimate. Instead, it frames certain Indigenous subjects as legitimate, as 'truly Indigenous', and thus worthy of claiming certain multicultural rights. Only some rights can actually be claimed, however; once a political Indigenous subject demands 'non-permitted' rights, in particular land redistribution, they are also labelled as not authentically Indigenous and not worthy. This, in turn, means that any demands for material redistribution are deemed instrumental.

These findings also help make sense of the debate between scholars such as Hale and Van Cott in answer to the question of whether recognition crowds out redistribution (Hale 2002; Van Cott 2006). Examining the ways in which the right in Santa Cruz uses the language of multiculturalism and talks about Indigenous rights shows that neither Hale's top-down elite strategy nor Van Cott's electoral battle position fully explains the relationship between multiculturalism and neo-liberalism within Cruceño politics. A selective and instrumental elite adoption of 'non-threatening' elements of multiculturalism is unlikely to be very successful unless it is able to connect to pre-existing identities. In this case, the Cruceño countermovement builds its version of multiculturalism on a historical regional identity narrative. This is shown above, as narratives of *mestizaje* and Santa Cruz exceptionalism form part and parcel of what is considered 'legitimate' multiculturalism by the Cruceño right. When popular resonance of this limited version of multiculturalism can be achieved in this way, recognition can indeed 'crowd out' redistribution, especially when certain Indigenous groups buy into it themselves (Crabtree and Chaplin 2013; Postero 2017).

Opponents of progressive reforms do not just resist these through the voting booths, or with violent resistance. They also engage in delegitimation attempts and authenticity battles (Luna 2017; Oselin and Corrigall-Brown 2010). In terms of Indigenous movements, insisting on authenticity linked to an assumption of what is traditionally and 'truly' Indigenous is a powerful disempowering strategy (Jackson and Warren 2005). The Cruceño right claims to have its own, acceptable, and democratic form of multiculturalism. This selective adherence to the language of multiculturalism reflects previous research conducted into how right-wing groups can use democratic language for undemocratic ends (Payne 2000). Studying whether and *how* right-wing countermovements adopt progressive language, and how they struggle to achieve wider resonance of this language, is crucial for a better understanding of the interaction between multiculturalism, neoliberalism, and the right in Latin America. We cannot only study Indigenous movements; we must also study the strategies of their opponents. Applying a social movement lens to such opponents elucidates whether and how successful their anti-rights strategies are in specific cases.

References

Albó, X. (2008), *Movimientos y poder indígena en Bolivia, Ecuador y Perú* (La Paz, CIPCA).

Allen, W. (2017), 'Making Corpus Data Visible: Visualising Text with Research Intermediaries', *Corpora*, 12:3, 459–82.

Alvarez, S. E., E. Dagnino, and A. Escobar (1998), *Cultures of Politics, Politics of Cultures: Re-Visioning Latin American Social Movements* (Boulder, CO and Oxford, Westview Press).

Andolina, R., N. Laurie, and S. Radcliffe (2009), *Indigenous Development in the Andes: Culture, Power, and Transnationalism* (Durham, NC, Duke University Press).

Bebbington, D. H. and A. Bebbington (2010), 'Anatomy of a Regional Conflict: Tarija and Resource Grievances in Morales's Bolivia', *Latin American Perspectives*, 37:4, 140–60.

Benford, R. D. and D. A. Snow (1988), 'Ideology, Frame Resonance, and Participant Mobilisation', in *From Structure to Action: Social Movement Participation across Cultures*, ed. B. Klandermans, H. Kriesi, and S. G. Tarrow (Greenwich, JAI Press), pp. 197–218.

Benford, R. D. and D. A. Snow (1992), 'Master Frames and Cycles of Protest', in *Frontiers in Social Movement Theory*, ed. A. Morris and C. M. Mueller (New Haven, Yale University Press), pp. 133–55.

Benford, R. D. and D. A. Snow (2000), 'Framing Processes and Social Movements: An Overview and Assessment', *Annual Review of Sociology*, 26 (August), 611–39.

Bolivia, C. O. (2009), *Constitución Política del Estado* (La Paz: National Congress).

Bowen, J. (2011), 'Multicultural Market Democracy: Elites and Indigenous Movements in Contemporary Ecuador', *Journal of Latin American Studies*, 43, 451–83.

Brady, H. E. and D. Collier (2010), *Rethinking Social Inquiry: Diverse Tools, Shared Standards*, 2nd edn (Lanham, MD, Rowman & Littlefield).

Calvo, R. (2021), 'El presidente del Comité pro Santa Cruz, Rómulo Calvo, en el inicio de los actos por el aniversario 460 de Santa Cruz', video, Facebook, https://www.facebook.com/ComiteProSC/videos/877365922806953/.

Centellas, M. (2016), 'The Santa Cruz Autonomía Movement in Bolivia: A Case of Non-Indigenous Ethnic Popular Mobilisation?', *Ethnopolitics*, 15:2, 245–64.

CIDH (2009), *Comunidades Cautivas: Situactión del Pueblo Indígena Guaraní y Formas Contemporáneas de Esclavitud en el Chaco de Bolivia* (Comisión Interamericana de Derechos Humanos [Interamerican Human Rights Commission]).

CPSC [Santa Cruz Civic Committee] (2014), 'Modelo de Desarrollo Cruceño', https://www.comiteprosantacruz.org.bo/documento/modelo-de-desarrollo-cruceno/.

CPSC [Santa Cruz Civic Committee] (2019), '1950: Fundación del Comité pro Santa Cruz', https://www.comiteprosantacruz.org.bo/announcement/1950-fundacion-del-comite-pro-santa-cruz/.

Crabtree, J. and A. Chaplin (2013), *Bolivia: Processes of Change* (London, Zed Books).

Crabtree, J. and I. Crabtree-Condor (2012), 'The Politics of Extractive Industries in the Central Andes', in *Social Conflict, Economic Development and Extractive Industry: Evidence from South America*, ed. A. Bebbington (London, Routledge), pp. 46–64.

Crabtree, J. and L. Whitehead (2008), *Unresolved Tensions: Bolivia Past and Present* (Pittsburgh, University of Pittsburgh Press).

Creswell, J. W. (2007), *Qualitative Inquiry and Research Design: Choosing among Five Approaches*, 2nd edn (London, Sage).

Dunkerley, J. (2007), *Bolivia: Revolution and the Power of History in the Present* (London, Institute for the Study of the Americas).

Eaton, K. (2007), 'Backlash in Bolivia: Regional Autonomy as a Reaction against Indigenous Mobilisation', *Politics & Society*, 35, 71–102.

Eaton, K. (2011), 'Conservative Autonomy Movements: Territorial Dimensions of Ideological Conflict in Bolivia and Ecuador', *Comparative Politics*, 43:3, 291–310.

Fabricant, N. (2009), 'Performative Politics: The Camba Countermovement in Eastern Bolivia', *American Ethnologist*, 36:4, 768–83.

Fabricant, N. and N. Postero (2013), 'Contested Bodies, Contested States: Performance, Emotions, and New Forms of Regional Governance in Santa Cruz, Bolivia', *Journal of Latin American and Caribbean Anthropology*, 18:2, 187–211.

Fabricant, N. and N. Postero (2014), 'Performing the "Wounded Indian": A New Platform of Democracy and Human Rights in Bolivia's Autonomy Movement', *Identities*, 21:4, 395–411.

Farthing, L. and O. Arigho-Stiles (2019), 'Bolivia's Tragic Turmoil', *NACLA Report on the Americas*, 15 November.

FIDH [International Federation for Human Rights] (2008), *Separatistas y racistas desatan ola de violencia contra autoridades e instituciones del Gobierno de Evo Morales* (Bolivia, FIDH).

Flesken, A. (2018), 'Identity Change in a Context of Intergroup Threat: Regional Identity Mobilisation in Bolivia', *Politics*, 38:1, 51–67.

Fraser, N. (1997), *Justice Interruptus: Critical Reflections on the Postsocialist Condition* (London, Routledge).

Fraser, N. (2003), 'Social Justice in the Age of Identity Politics: Redistribution, Recognition, and Participation', in *Redistribution or Recognition? A Political–Philosophical Exchange*, ed. N. Fraser and A. Honneth (London, Verso), pp. 7–109.

Garcés, F. (2010), *El pacto de unidad y el proceso de construccion de una propuesta de constitucion politica de estado* (La Paz, Centro Cooperativo Sueco).

Greene, J. C. (2008), 'Is Mixed Methods Social Inquiry a Distinctive Methodology?', *Journal of Mixed Methods Research*, 2:1, 7–22.

Grisaffi, T. (2010), 'We Are Originarios ... "We Just Aren't from Here": Coca Leaf and Identity Politics in the Chapare, Bolivia', *Bulletin of Latin American Research*, 29:4, 425–39.

Gustafson, B. (2006), 'Spectacles of Autonomy and Crisis; or, What Bulls and Beauty Queens Have to Do with Regionalism in Eastern Bolivia', *Journal of Latin American Anthropology*, 11:2, 351–79.

Gustafson, B. (2016). 'Bolivia after the "No" Vote', *NACLA Report on the Americas*, 7 March.

Hale, C. (2002), 'Does Multiculturalism Menace? Governance, Cultural Rights and the Politics of Identity in Guatemala', *Journal of Latin American Studies*, 34:3, 485–524.

Hale, C. (2007). 'Rethinking Indigenous Politics in the Era of the "Indio permitido"', *NACLA Report on the Americas*, 38:2, 16–21.

Honneth, A. (2003), 'Redistribution as Recognition: A Response to Nancy Fraser', in *Redistribution or Recognition? A Political–Philosophical Exchange*, ed. N. Fraser and A. Honneth (London, Verso), pp. 110–97.

Horton, L. (2006), 'Contesting State Multiculturalisms: Indigenous Land Struggles in Eastern Panama', *Journal of Latin American Studies*, 38, 829–58.

Iskenderian Aguilera, E. (2010), 'Un Período Defensivo Para La Burguesía Cruceña: Ataques Confirmados o Atribuídos a La Unión Juvenil Cruceñista (Ujc)', *Separata Atículo Primero*.

Jackson, J. E. and K. B. Warren (2005), 'Indigenous Movements in Latin America, 1992–2004: Controversies, Ironies, New Directions', *Annual Review of Anthropology*, 34:1, 549–73.

226 *Anna Krausova*

Kay, C. and M. Urioste (2005), *Latifundios, avasallamientos y autonomías* (Santa Cruz, Fundación Tierra).

Kilgarriff, A., V. Baisa, J. Bušta, *et al.* (2014), 'The Sketch Engine: Ten Years On', *Lexicography*, 1:1, 7–36.

Klein, H. S. (1992), *Bolivia: The Evolution of a Multi-Ethnic Society*, 2nd edn (Oxford, Oxford University Press).

Kohl, B. (2010), 'Bolivia under Morales: A Work in Progress', *Latin American Perspectives*, 37, 107–22.

Koopmans, R. and P. Statham (1999), 'Ethnic and Civic Conceptions of Nationhood and the Differential Success of the Extreme Right in Germany and Italy', in *How Social Movements Matter*, ed. M. Giugni, D. McAdam, and C. Tilly (London, University of Minnesota Press), pp. 225–51.

Krausova, A. (2012), 'Resisting Redistribution with Recognition: Conflicting Multicultural Paradigms in Regional Resistance to Bolivia's State Reforms', M.Phil. dissertation, University of Oxford.

Krausova, A. (2018), *What Social Movements Ask for, and How They Ask for It: Strategic Claiming and Framing, and the Successes and Failures of Indigenous Movements in Latin America*, D.Phil. dissertation, University of Oxford.

Krausova, A. (2020), 'Latin American Social Movements: Bringing Strategy Back In', *Latin American Research Review*, 55:4, 1–11.

Lehoucq, F. (2020), 'Bolivia's Citizen Revolt', *Journal of Democracy*, 3, 130–44.

Lowrey, K. (2006), '*Bolivia multiétnico y pluricultural*, Ten Years Later', *Latin American and Caribbean Ethnic Studies*, 1:1, 63–84.

Lucero, J. A. (2008), *Struggles of Voice: The Politics of Indigenous Representation in the Andes* (Pittsburgh, University of Pittsburgh Press).

Luna, Z. (2017), 'Who Speaks for Whom? (Mis) Representation and Authenticity in Social Movements', *Mobilization* 22:4, 435–50.

McAdam, D., et al. (1996), *Comparative Perspectives on Social Movements: Political Opportunities, Mobilizing Structures, and Cultural Framings* (Cambridge, Cambridge University Press).

McCammon, H. J., H. D. Newman, C. Sanders Muse, C., and T. M. Terrell (2007), 'Movement Framing and Discursive Opportunity Structures: The Political Success of the US Women's Jury Movement', *American Sociological Review*, 72:5, 725–49.

McNeish, J.-A. (2008), 'Beyond the Permitted Indian? Bolivia and Guatemala in an Era of Neoliberal Developmentalism', *Latin American and Caribbean Ethnic Studies*, 3:1, 33–59.

McNeish, J.-A. (2013), 'Extraction, Protest and Indigeneity in Bolivia: The TIPNIS Effect', *Latin American and Caribbean Ethnic Studies*, 8:2, 221–42.

Natow, R. S. (2020), 'The Use of Triangulation in Qualitative Studies Employing Elite Interviews', *Qualitative Research*, 20:2, 160–73.

Oselin, S. S. and C. Corrigall-Brown (2010), 'A Battle for Authenticity: An Examination of the Constraints on Anti-Iraq War and Pro-Invasion Tactics', *Mobilisation*, 15:4, 511–33.

Padilla, C. (2008), 'Interview with Celso Padilla', in *Racismo y discriminación en Bolivia*, ed. Ministerio de la Presidencia (La Paz).

Pairicán, F. (2014), 'Malón: La rebelión del movimiento mapuche 1990–2013' (Santiago, Pehuén Editores).

Payne, L. A. (2000), *Uncivil Movements: The Armed Right Wing and Democracy in Latin America* (Baltimore: Johns Hopkins University Press).

Peña Claros, C. (2010), 'Un pueblo eminente: Autonomist Populism in Santa Cruz', *Latin American Perspectives*, 37:4, 125–39.

Perreault, T. and B. Green (2013), 'Reworking the Spaces of Indigeneity: The Bolivian Ayllu and Lowland Autonomy Movements Compared', *Environment and Planning D: Society and Space*, 31:1, 43–60.

Phillips, A. (1997), 'From Inequality To Difference: A Severe Case Of Displacement?', *New Left Review* I:224, 143–53.

Plata, W. (2008), 'El discurso autonomista de las élites de Santa Cruz', in *Los barones del oriente: El poder en Santa Cruz ayer y hoy*, ed. X. Soruco, W. Plata, and G. Medeiros (Santa Cruz, Fundación Tierra), pp. 101–72.

Postero, N. G. (2007), *Now We Are Citizens: Indigenous Politics in Postmulticultural Bolivia* (Stanford, Stanford University Press).

Postero, N. G. (2017), *The Indigenous State: Race, Politics, and Performance in Plurinational Bolivia* (Oakland, University of California Press).

Razón (2017), 'Presidente: "Tarde o temprano" se construirá la carretera por el TIPNIS', *La Razón*, 26 July.

Rivera Cusicanqui, S. (1984), *Oprimidos pero no vencidos: Luchas del campesinado aymara y qhechwa de Bolivia, 1900–1980* (La Paz, CSUTCB).

Rivera Cusicanqui, S. (1987), *Oppressed but not Defeated: Peasant Struggles among the Aymara and Qhechwa in Bolivia, 1900–1980* (Geneva, United Nations Research Institute for Social Development).

Rochlin, J. (2007), 'Latin America's Left Turn and the New Strategic Landscape: The Case of Bolivia', *Third World Quarterly*, 28:7, 1327–42.

Rossi, F. M. (2017), *The Poor's Struggle for Political Incorporation: The Piquetero Movement in Argentina* (Cambridge, Cambridge University Press).

Small, M. L. (2009), 'How Many Cases Do I Need? On Science and the Logic of Case Selection in Field-Based Research', *Ethnography*, 10:1, 5–38.

Small, M. L. (2011), 'How to Conduct a Mixed Methods Study: Recent Trends in a Rapidly Growing Literature', *Annual Review of Sociology*, 37:1, 57–86.

Snow, D. A. (2004), 'Framing Processes, Ideology, and Discursive Fields', in *The Blackwell Companion to Social Movements*, ed. D. A. Snow, S. A. Soule, and H. Kriesi (Malden, MA, Blackwell), pp. 380–412.

Snow, D. A., R. Benford, H. McCammon, L. Hewitt, and S. Fitzgerald (2014), 'The Emergence, Development, and Future of the Framing Perspective: 25+ Years since "Frame Alignment"', *Mobilisation: An International Quarterly*, 19:1, 23–46.

Soruco, X. (2008), 'De la goma a la soya: El proyecto histórico de la elite cruceña', in *Los barones del oriente: El poder en Santa Cruz ayer y hoy*, ed. D. A. Snow, S. A. Soule, and H. Kriesi (Santa Cruz, Fundación Tierra), pp. 1–100.

Stahler-Sholk, R. and H. E. Vanden (2011), 'A Second Look at Latin American Social Movements: Globalizing Resistance to the Neoliberal Paradigm', *Latin American Perspectives*, 38, 5–13.

Svampa, M. (2017), *Del cambio de época al fin de ciclo: Gobiernos progresistas, extractivismo, y movimientos sociales en América Latina*, 1st edn (Buenos Aires, Edhasa).

Tarrow, S. (1993), 'Cycles of Collective Action: Between Moments of Madness and the Repertoire of Contention', *Social Science History*, 17:2, 281–30.

Teddlie, C. and A. Tashakkori (2009), *Foundations of Mixed Methods Research: Integrating Quantitative and Qualitative Approaches in the Social and Behavioral Sciences* (Thousand Oaks and London, Sage).

228 *Anna Krausova*

Van Cott, D. L. (2006), 'Multiculturalism versus Neoliberalism in Latin America', in *Multiculturalism and the Welfare State: Recognition and Redistribution in Contemporary Democracies*, ed. K. Banting and W. Kymlicka (Oxford, Oxford University Press), pp. 272–96.

Van Cott, D. L. (2010), 'Indigenous Peoples' Politics in Latin America', *Annual Review of Political Science*, 13, 385–405.

Webber, J. R. (2008a), 'Rebellion to Reform in Bolivia Part I: Domestic Class Structure, Latin American Trends, and Capitalist Imperialism', *Historical Materialism*, 16:2, 23–58.

Webber, J. R. (2008b), 'Rebellion to Reform in Bolivia Part II: Revolutionary Epoch, Combined Liberation and the December 2005 Elections', *Historical Materialism*, 16:3, 55–76.

Webber, J. R. (2008c), 'Rebellion to Reform in Bolivia Part III: Neoliberal Continuities, the Autonomist Right, and the Political Economy of Indigenous Struggle', *Historical Materialism*, 16:4, 67–109.

Weber, K. (2013), 'Chiquitano and the Multiple Meanings of Being Indigenous in Bolivia', *Bulletin of Latin American Research*, 32:2, 194–209.

Yashar, D. J. (2005), *Contesting Citizenship in Latin America: The Rise of Indigenous Movements and the Postliberal Challenge* (Cambridge, Cambridge University Press).

12

Righting Rights, Righting Wrongs: Final Reflections

JULIA ZULVER AND LEIGH A. PAYNE

THE CHAPTERS IN this book concur that mobilising on the right against hard-won gains and rights-seekers is a social problem that needs to be addressed. The problem is not the mobilisation on the right itself. Such mobilisation is a healthier democratic alternative to past forms of doing politics on the right in the region: staging authoritarian coups, implanting repressive regimes, and collaborating in terrorist violence against civilians. The right wing in Latin America and elsewhere is not inherently authoritarian or violent, and can be, as Mayka and Smith (2021, 5) note, firmly committed to liberal democracy. Neither does the right have a monopoly on terrorist violence or authoritarian leadership; armed left-wing groups have also engaged in such violence. And not all past right-wing forces have engaged in extra-institutional violence, opting instead to participate democratically within the political system. It could be argued, and some of the chapters in this book do so, that extra-institutional and violent mobilisation by the right occurs when the political system no longer protects the rights of the right.

That is the social problem underlying this volume. After the region's long history of social exclusion – violent, authoritarian, and democratic – a 'rights revolution' began to recognise – to hear and to implement – demands from citizens for change. That these achievements made within democratic systems may be rolled back and replaced with the exclusionary status quo ante is part of the social problem. That those who have promoted rights sometimes face extreme violence by virtue of making demands for equality and inclusion is another part of the social problem. In other words, this struggle for rights and against rights has moved beyond fair and democratic competition. For these reasons, and while acknowledging the value in not conflating rightism with autocracy and populism, we disagree with Mayka and Smith's (2021, 5) assertion that 'the grassroots right might even sometimes be a stabilizing, democratizing force, giving rights actors a stake in the democratic system'.

Proceedings of the British Academy, **255**, 229–247, © The British Academy 2023.

Rights-defenders do not always necessarily face risks of lethal violence; indeed, the right against rights can represent other types of social threat. Even when the risk of extreme violence is less present, the various chapters in this book show that the struggle for rights and against rights rarely operates on an even plane. Those who struggle for more inclusive social, economic, and political rights have had to confront traditional and powerful cultural and political groups within religious, family, and governing institutions. Those who demand redistribution of wealth, land, and power, or who have defended the cultural and environmental rights of Indigenous communities, have fought for those rights against entrenched, landed, and business elites reticent to relinquish their control. And while many of the gains made by rights-seekers were pushed through institutional and legal democratic channels – through the passage of new laws, modifications or rewritings of constitutions, and official recognition of acceptance of difference – the backlash against these gains has taken place within and outside courtrooms, parliaments, and congresses. The struggle has sometimes taken an extrajudicial, extralegal form, often involving violence in the form of threats, attacks, and, in some of the worst cases presented in this volume, assassinations. Even when anti-rights movements do not engage in violence per se – for example in the case of the affirmative action law in Uruguay, or the co-optation of the language of multiculturalism in Santa Cruz in Bolivia – there is a power differential evident in the ways that established mechanisms for progressive change can be ignored, undermined, co-opted, and 'framejacked' by the right against rights. While not all of those who make up the right against rights are historical powerholders – for example, the evangelical blocs who united to back Jair Bolsonaro – the figureheads they support and their preference for a return to 'traditional' values often imply a return to entrenched systems of political and economic power that benefit the elite at the expense of the marginalised.

There is an argument that the right is inherently weak in terms of collective action because individuals within it are accustomed to using personal connections to influence outcomes; they tend not to need or cultivate mobilisational tactics. This could suggest that social movements need not be concerned about rights rollbacks. Yet to remain passive and expect the right against rights to self-implode is not a response any of the authors of these chapters, or the rights-seekers they defend, would advocate. Indeed, for some of those actors who continue to advocate for their rights, sitting and waiting is not an option; without wanting to resort to hyperbole, their cultures, communities, and even lives are at risk so long as the right against rights is actively mobilising – even if weakly – against the gains they have made.

In this concluding chapter, we thus explore what can be done about the social problem created by the right against rights. We first identify the sources of strengths and weaknesses of the right analysed in this volume, the efforts at 'righting rights'. We then suggest a plan of action for 'righting wrongs', that is for the defence of rights against efforts to roll back, reverse, or block rights gains. In the final section of this chapter we situate the right against rights in a broader comparative framework. Specifically, we reinforce the contribution Latin America makes to understanding the right against rights in Europe, North America, and elsewhere. By doing so, we

FINAL REFLECTIONS

contend that the social problem of the right against rights is not a regional one, but global. As such, we suggest that some of the solutions to the right-against-rights social problem could be extended to Latin America and elsewhere. We close by considering the new research agenda this volume inspires.

Righting Rights

The chapters in this book show that while the right has succeeded in mobilising against rights advanced by social movements, it has not always succeeded in actually reversing those rights; it has not always proved capable of 'righting rights'. As Payne (Chapter 2) claims, the rights revolution may be partially protected from the right against rights because of the inherent weaknesses of such movements and mobilisation. She notes that these weaknesses can be categorised into outcomes, internal dynamics, and institutionalisation. In terms of outcomes, when a movement is seen as unable to make gains – or even if the movement is seen as too extreme – it risks losing current and potential members, as gains are not seen to outweigh costs. Paradoxically, victories can also facilitate demobilisation, for example if the movement becomes a political party, or if members experience burn-out after intense action. The movement's internal dynamics may also lead to eventual weakness, particularly in terms of internal and leadership struggles that bring about instability within the movement. These weaknesses can be further compounded when leaders and/or members take steps to institutionalise the movement or transform it into a political party, especially given some members' anti-establishment, anti-system predilections.

Yet, despite its potential for failure or weakness, and the relatively few demonstrable victories over rights, the right against rights has had some successes. In this section, we emphasise when, where, and how the right against rights shows its strength. It has won elections and put candidates into office. It has threatened and killed people, often with relative impunity. It has weakened legislation and, in some cases, it has changed the discourse around rights. It has cut off funding to bodies that champion progressive rights.

The chapters included in this volume show that right-against-rights candidates, campaigning on platforms to roll back or block rights, can count important victories over the past decade or more. They have won democratic elections. Former presidents Jair Bolsonaro in Brazil, and to a lesser extent Iván Duque in Colombia, are notable examples, as is the near win of Fabricio Alvarado in Costa Rica. It is impossible to imagine these candidates winning without strong mobilisation against the rights gains of the LGBT+ community, feminist movements, environmental defenders, and peacebuilders. The capacity of the movements supporting these two leaders successfully framed a 'moral panic' that mobilised the electorate behind them. Thus, these individuals' rises to power can be considered a success of right-against-rights mobilisation, but also, once they were elected, as expanding the sphere of possibilities for ongoing right-against-rights agenda-setting.

The case of Colombia may provide the clearest example of 'righting rights'. As Corredor (Chapter 4) outlined, informal coalitions of the religious right, economic elites, and conservative politicians came together to oppose anti-bullying educational reforms, and then the contents of the country's peace agreement itself, which was framed as promoting a threatening 'gender ideology'. Two years later, these groups once again achieved success when they were able to vote into the presidency Iván Duque, a candidate handpicked by former right-wing president Álvaro Uribe. The 2018 elections saw Duque run against the left-wing Gustavo Petro, a former M-19 guerrilla. During elections, the right against rights framed the potential election of Petro – and what they referred to as his politics of 'Castro-Chavismo' – as a crisis that would effectively turn Colombia into the next Venezuela. And, in 2022, as Petro ran in and successfully won the country's presidential elections, the right against rights continued to accuse both him and his running mate, Afro-Colombian human rights and environmental activist Francia Márquez (Zulver and Piscopo 2022), of representing a threat to the future of the country. While there is reason to be hopeful that Petro and Márquez will move the country toward greater protection of (minority) rights, including the proper implementation of the peace accord, their chances of success will be hampered by the entrenched political and economic elite, who will undoubtedly aim to block progress to protect the status quo.

The 2019 election of Jair Bolsonaro in Brazil could also be seen as the success of right-against-rights mobilisations. As outlined by de Souza Santos (Chapter 6) and Ritholtz and Mesquita (Chapter 5), Bolsonaro coalesced a wide swathe of forces, including evangelicals, not only to vote to oust the Workers' Party (PT), but also to rally in support of his anti-LGBT+ sentiments and violent actions. Behind his election were groups who were previously at odds: evangelicals and Catholics, neoliberal urban elites and rural populists, a democratic right wing and a right wing that continued to endorse the civil-military regime and its human rights violations. Some of these groups overlooked Bolsonaro's extremism, already evident in his years in Congress and his defence of the country's previous authoritarian rule, viewing it as preferable to what they perceived as rampant corruption. Yet corruption in government continued after his election – and within the forces that supported him –and the extremist political and social attitudes and behaviours he fostered escalated.

Where the right against rights has won the presidency, a kind of 'open season' on rights groups has emerged. As Ritholtz and Mesquita (Chapter 5) argue, Bolsonaro's campaign on the far right profited from the public mocking of educational policies designed to promote gender inclusion. By referring to a gender-inclusive programme in schools as the 'gay kit' he emboldened anti-rights organisers and fostered the creation of the 'School without Party' movement, which sought to remove what it understood as 'ideology' from educational institutions in Brazil. The authors also show how conservative politicians such as Álvaro Uribe in Colombia and Keiko Fujimori in Peru rely on different religious groups to increase support for their governments, gain votes, and consolidate power. Despite coming from different religious traditions, these groups unite themselves in opposition to

FINAL REFLECTIONS
233

the so-called 'gender ideology'. In Chapter 9, Tapias Torrado shows how violence against Indigenous human rights and environmental rights defenders occurs in a political context that supports the rights of the right, even when it violates national, regional, and environmental human rights norms and laws. In both of these cases, the consequences of gains made by the right against rights can quite literally be fatal for LGBT+, Indigenous, and environmental rights-seekers. Although the rights remain on the books, the context for implementing those rights on the ground has proved exceedingly difficult.

Even in cases where democratic elections have brought to power less obviously right-against-rights candidates, the right against rights has still made powerful legal gains that have rolled back or blocked victories for the rights of previously marginalised populations. In Bolivia, and despite the 2009 win of Evo Morales and the MAS Party, the economic elite in Santa Cruz was effectively able to co-opt the language of multiculturalism and draw on narratives of Cruceño exceptionalism in order to reject policies that would permit land redistribution and other economic redistribution policies (Krausova (Chapter 11)).

In other countries that boast left-wing governments, we see that subsections of the population are experiencing attacks on their rights to, for example, political participation, as well as the right to live a life free from violence. Juliana Restrepo Sanín highlights the cases of Mexico and Bolivia – two countries with left-wing leaders – where violence against women in politics presents a barrier to political participation (2020). Indeed, Restrepo outlines that these women are sometimes being attacked *as women*, and not necessarily because of their policy positions or ideologies. Rather than frame this as backlash, per se, we argue that this type of de facto prejudice, despite seemingly progressive political leaders, highlights the pervasive undercurrents of discrimination and violence that seek to maintain a patriarchal status quo in politics. The phenomenon of violence against women in politics thus represents a threat to women's hard-won gains to participate politically, even if these rights exist on the books. Cheryl O'Brien and Shannon Walsh's research identifies how opponents (whom they refer to as 'policy rivals') to violence-against-women (VAW) laws in Mexico and Nicaragua were able to frame progressive legislation as 'anti-family'; they leveraged strategic ties between religious elites and allies inside the state to stunt and even reverse progressive VAW laws in these nominally left-wing countries (O'Brien and Walsh 2020, 3).

Winning elections, therefore, is not the only strength of the right against rights, although it is critical to some of the legislative gains that they have made. As Sharnak shows (Chapter 10), powerful political actors mobilising against affirmative action constraints on their freedom in hiring are more likely to achieve success – as they did in Uruguay – when they have helpful representatives in office. Sharnak also describes, however, how this right-against-rights lobby carefully framed the anti-rights project in such a way that moderates – who would not want to be associated with backtracking on race equality – could support. Where the right does not have powerful representation in the legislature, therefore, it is compelled to win over moderates through political crafting.

234 *Julia Zulver and Leigh A. Payne*

The chapters in this book also show that the right against rights does not act only within national borders. Several chapters show how international groups have funded their campaigns in the region. Kane, Moragas, and Stallone (Chapter 7) further demonstrate that national and international groups have attempted to weaken one of the strongest human rights regimes in the world: the Inter-American System (IAS) of Human Rights in the Organization of American States. Indeed, as the IAS has made rights gains for those previously marginalised in the region, the attacks on it have increased. A regional or international right against rights has thus emerged to stymie IAS efforts to expand rights or to bolster rights claims within the region and support rights-seekers. Kane, Moragas, and Stallone show that by mobilising to cut off funding for the IAS, the right against rights has made some gains in reducing the capacity of this institution. They suggest a kind of reverse 'boomerang' model. During the authoritarian period, rights-seekers in the region created transnational advocacy networks (TANs) powerful enough to pressure Latin American states to change. The authors, as well as others in this volume, have suggested that now the 'boomerang' begins in the Global North, where the right against rights targets and empowers local groups in Latin America to fight against feminism, LGBT+, environmental, and other rights, strengthening an anti-rights TAN.

Yet despite what may appear to be the impossible task of regaining rights protections in the region, some chapters have suggested that the right against rights does not always win. As we explore in the next section, this volume aims to present ways to fight to retain rights. In doing so, it offers a glimmer of hope by illustrating the power to block the impact of the right against rights from below and abroad.

Righting Wrongs

The gains made by the right against rights do not go unchecked. Rights-seekers in and outside social movements have undertaken actions to exploit the aforementioned weaknesses and to counter, overpower, and work around the successes of the right against rights.

Righting wrongs, or the efforts to continue to protect the rights gains for excluded individuals and communities, has depended on a set of strategies by rights groups. This has included efforts to make visible – naming and shaming – the outrageous and extremist slurs used by the right against rights, the violent tactics of uncivil movements, and the support for such groups among the political elite. By doing so, rights-seekers can delegitimise the right-against-rights mobilisations, weaken support for them, and attempt to regain the balance of power. A second – and related – strategy is to make these claims internationally, to draw attention to the efforts to undermine rights in Latin American countries, to seek support from abroad to win back those rights, and to discredit those international groups who have funded and supported the anti-rights mobilisations.

We saw this, for example, in the case of Chile's abortion law (Chapter 8). Escoffier and Vivaldi argue that anti-abortion movements were unsuccessful in

FINAL REFLECTIONS

their efforts to block an abortion bill between 2015 and 2017 because their actions and strategies were seen as too extreme and thus unable to build consensus amongst potential political allies in Congress, who did not see the movement as particularly legitimate. Moreover, the pro-choice movement was able to capitalise on these weaknesses to counterbalance the influence of anti-abortion groups effecively. They were able to secure grassroots and institutional support at the level of state (including of former president Michelle Bachelet). They also drew attention to the outrageous and extremist anti-abortion campaign rhetoric that equated abortion with Nazi genocide, thereby delegitimising the right-against-rights movement's demands, alienating its support among moderate constituents, and relegating it to the political fringes.

Indeed, by way of highlighting examples of hope in the region, Chile also represents a case where coalitions of rights-seekers were recently able to engage in large-scale mobilisation, push for a new and democratic political constitution, and elect a young, socialist president who openly supports women's and LGBT+ rights and instated a majority-women cabinet. Again, it was through their strategies of confronting and publicly exposing the right against rights that right-seekers were able to win the vote for a democratic Constitutional Convention that promises to address environmental and Indigenous rights. This coalition has thus far succeeded in blocking the right against rights and ushering Chile into a new political era.

The recent Colombian abortion rights legislation also confronted a highly mobilised right against rights but prevailed. Feminist lawyers built on years of strategic litigation work and demonstrated dogged determination in the face of small setbacks; eventually they were able to take their claims to the Constitutional Court, where they were successful in removing three key restrictions (*causales*) to abortion and extend the gestational limit for the procedure until week 24. Indeed, since the extremely concerning reversal of *Roe v. Wade* by the Supreme Court in 2022, some commentators have suggested that women's movements in the USA should look to Latin America's *marea verde* (green tide) of abortion activists for inspiration when it comes to protecting women's rights to bodily autonomy in the United States (Schmidt 2022; Kitroeff 2022).

Another example of righting wrongs is evident in Salvi's chapter on the anti-human-rights groups in Argentina. Despite the efforts of groups made up of perpetrators' family members to repurpose human rights language and frameworks in favour of imprisoned members of the military junta, as well as to create an imaginary of the family in the same way as, for example, the Madres de Plaza de Mayo do, they have not made significant gains when it comes to preventing the trials for crimes against humanity from advancing. This can perhaps be credited to the counterbalance presented by the families of the disappeared. It is also possible, however, that these groups have been unable to make gains, given a long and robust culture and institutional architecture that promotes human rights in Argentina.

Those rights groups that mobilised during the authoritarian regimes in Argentina and in other parts of the region relied on TANs to name their rights demands, to blame governments for rights violations, shaming them to bring about change.

236 *Julia Zulver and Leigh A. Payne*

Under authoritarian systems, international pressure for rights claims was imperative. As we discussed in the last section, the right-against-rights mobilisations seem to have adopted the same strategies of transnational alliances. And yet, some evidence suggests that the right against rights has not yet won a monopoly over international rights mobilisation. As Sharnak (Chapter 10) shows, pressure from the Black Caucus in the USA played a key role in attempting to implement affirmative-action legislation. Ritholtz and Mesquita (Chapter 5) also consider the transnational LGBT+ mobilisation that has strengthened rights-mobilisation efforts within and across the region. Tapias Torrado (Chapter 9) further reflects on the international attention brought to the killing of Berta Cáceres, Indigenous human rights and environmental rights defender, and the coalition of forces to form an Expert Group (GAIPE) to advance justice, for righting wrongs.

Despite the efforts recognised in the study by Kane, Moragas, and Stallone (Chapter 7) of the right-against-rights mobilisation against the OAS, it continues to play an important role in attempting to right wrongs. A recent example is Colombia's 2021 National Strike, initially a large-scale public mobilisation against a proposed tax reform bill that transformed into a larger set of protests against a proposed health bill, the murder of social leaders, and systematic brutality by the police and armed forces. The Inter-American Commission visited the country to gather testimonies from victims of human rights abuses in the context of protest violence. Such visits, and the recommendations they produce, do not necessarily come with the 'teeth' needed to guarantee change. Nonetheless, these highly visible strategies follow Keck and Sikkink's 'boomerang' logic, whereby citizens are able to bypass blockages and apply pressure on their government through participating in transnational advocacy networks that petition their own (foreign) governments or international bodies to pressure the offending government (Keck and Sikkink 1998). Drawing on a case study in southern Colombia, Zulver's (2021) work on women's mobilisation in the context of patriarchal backlash and armed conflict outlines that one strategy women adopt for their protection is to 'be visible' through similar tactics; they often engage with national and international media, organisations, and donors in order to shine a light on the security risks they face at the hands of uncivil actors in their own communities. This suggests that transnational advocacy networks still play a key role in the balance of power on the side of rights-seekers. In similar contexts of violence, organisations Somos Defensores and INDEPAZ in Colombia publish and disseminate public lists of the social leaders murdered by uncivil movements around the country. While these lists in themselves do not decrease the killings, they denounce the murderous violence against social leaders in the country, opening up the government to uncomfortable questions about what is being done to protect these rights-defenders.

Despite the successes of the right against rights in 'righting rights', as set out above, this section on 'righting wrongs' has outlined the potential sites for resistance to counter those gains in Latin America. In what follows, we put this discussion into comparative perspective, highlighting how the conceptual framework this book presents can 'travel' to other realities, and the ways in which it can complement existing analysis of the right in other global regions.

FINAL REFLECTIONS

Right against Rights in Comparative Perspective

To date, the right against rights in Latin America has not been widely studied in the region or in comparative perspective. Instead, a rather parochial orientation has prevailed in which whole regions of the world seem to be irrelevant to the study of the right-wing movements or the right against rights. In this final section of the volume, we contend that Latin America has much to contribute to comparative frameworks for understanding right-wing movements and mobilisations. We consider how each of the three types of movements discussed in the book with regard to Latin America can enhance analytical tools for understanding right-against-rights mobilisation around the world. In addition, we consider how comparative analysis can move in the opposite direction: Latin America could benefit from a comparative analysis of the strategies adopted in the Global North to monitor and reduce the potential of harm of right-against-rights groups. This final section of the conclusion thus explores 'righting rights' and 'righting wrongs' in a comparative framework.

The Right against Rights outside Latin America

As discussed by Payne (Chapter 2), the notion of countermovements began in the European and United States contexts. Here we have adapted it to Latin America, a region replete with such movements but largely ignored in the scholarship. Looking comparatively, we suggest that a much richer understanding of right-against-rights countermovements that explores how, when, why, and to what impact they mobilise could benefit from going beyond Latin America to other parts of the Global South.

The other two mobilisations – uncivil movements and radical neoliberal mobilisations – have not yet been conceptualised as such in Europe or North America. Instead, groups that would fall into this category are not differentiated from each other and are lumped under a general umbrella category of right-wing mobilisations. In our understanding, these groups are analytically different – and should be studied as such – because of the *ways in which* they attack and aim to undermine rights, and not simply for being part of the right wing, or against rights in general. By focusing on the subset of right-wing movements that involve right-against-rights mobilisations, we suggest that Latin America has much to offer in terms of new ways of conceptualising and analysing the effects of such groups. This section does not attempt to provide that analysis, but aims only to pave the way toward the development of such comparative frameworks.

Countermovements, Uncivil Movements, and Radical Neoliberalism in the Global South

The most obvious place to consider the three categories of right-against-rights movements in the Global South is India. The electoral victories of Narendra Modi and his Hindu nationalist Bharatiya Janata Party occur simultaneously with what

238 *Julia Zulver and Leigh A. Payne*

has been called the 'blue wave' in Latin America: that is the shift to the right after the pink tide, and the subsequent effort to roll back the rights of the excluded. Modi's brand of right-wing nationalism promotes Hindu supremacy, and endeavours to roll back the few rights gained by Muslims, Christians, Dalits, and other subordinate castes. Anti-Muslim and anti-Christian violence has occurred at various moments, as uncivil movements gain ground, acting with impunity. Denial of women's rights and increased violence against women also appear to be part of the right-against-rights mobilisation in India. Indeed, a recent study connects Hindu nationalism to violent attacks against secularists, intellectuals, universities, and non-governmental organisations (NGOs) (Jaffrelot 2021). So too has the right against rights in India reflected a brand of radical neoliberalism: an effort to advance the rights of the private sector against labour rights gains (Chattopadhyay 2019). Can we explain this rise of the right against rights in ways similar to the emergence in Latin America? How do the differences and similarities enrich our understanding of this political and social phenomenon?

Former president Rodrigo Duterte's (2016–22) rise to power in the Philippines also creates a context for the right against rights in that country that resembles the Latin American phenomenon in terms of timing and characteristics. Observers have remarked that 'The populist art of governance is based on nationalism (often with racist overtones), on hijacking the state for the ends of partisan loyalists and, less obviously, on weaponising the economy to secure political power: a combination of culture war, patronage and mass clientelism' (quote by Jan Werner Müller in ANU (2019)). The Duterte government was supported by, and increased the power of, countermovements, violent uncivil movements, and radical neoliberals who aimed to roll back rights claims and eliminate rights-claimants, particularly Diehard Duterte Supporters (DDS). Again, the study of right-wing mobilisations would gain greater analytical power were it to consider how such mobilisations occur in similar ways in different regions and countries around the world. Just as we examined the elections of presidents such as Bolsonaro and Duque, the elections of Modi and Duterte are examples of the success of the right against rights; their rise to power was both catalysed by anti-rights groups and created spaces for these groups to advance their anti-rights agendas.

Anti-gender mobilisations in southern and eastern Africa provide another example of how the study of countermovements can be enriched by moving outside a Global North orientation. Haley McEwen has analysed the spread of such movements as a response to sex education in schools. Analysis of the movements in Kenya and Nigeria reveals the transnational characteristics of this right-against-rights countermovement, particularly the connections to US and European organisations (Dell'Omo 2021). Valentine Moghadam also opens conversations about those women who support right-wing populist or nationalistic movements, particularly focusing on Islamist movements. She reflects on the 54 per cent of Turkish women who voted for Recep Tayyip Erdoğan in 2011 (and indeed suggests that they perhaps are not dissimilar to the 53 per cent of white American women who voted for Donald Trump in 2016), noting that they subscribe to narratives around culture or religion in danger. Their votes may also reflect a certain level of security in traditional household divisions of labour along gender lines (Moghadam 2018).

We are not the first to suggest that there are linkages across the Global North and Global South with regard to the rising power of the right (see, for example, Parfitt (2019)). A 2020 article in *Foreign Policy* suggests that 'the far-right is going global' (Leidig 2020). It documents a 2019 visit by 23 far-right members of the European Parliament to Kashmir – which had recently had its special autonomous status removed by the Modi government. The visit was notable, given that at the time foreign journalists and domestic politicians were denied access to the region, thus suggesting a strengthening of ties between the far right in India and Europe. Trump's former adviser Steven Bannon once referred to Prime Minister Modi as 'a Trump before Trump' (Leidig 2020), and others have linked Modi to French nationalists and anti-Islamic extremism. The article concludes by identifying a new development in Indo-European relations, one that signals a strengthening of the right against rights, in this instance in its manifestation as a countermovement.

What we are calling for is not only the finding of linkages across the right in the Global South and the Global North. While connecting these mobilisations is important, we seek to investigate how those linkages and other factors explain their rise, their appeal, and their threats to rights gains and rights-seekers. We contend that doing so enhances the analytical power behind the study of right-wing mobilisations, and also the development of strategies to reduce those threats.

Uncivil Movements and Radical Neoliberalism in the Global North

The study of countermovements in Europe and North America is well grounded. An understanding of uncivil movements and radical neoliberalism has not formed part of the analysis of right-wing movements in those regions, however. There are a few poignant examples that show evidence of these two types of movements that have been ignored in the scholarship.

The study of contemporary white supremacy in the United States is insufficiently analytically interrogated within research about right-wing movements. Yet, these groups fit neatly within the uncivil movement category of the right-against-rights. The assault on the US Capitol in Washington, DC, in January 2021 is just one example of a coalition of right-wing forces aimed at undermining electoral rights, demonstrating a willingness to use violence to do so, and promoting of a set of rights that these groups perceive to be under threat. These include gun rights, white rights, anti-mask rights, and men's rights. Like the uncivil movements examined in Latin America, these groups use a rights language to justify and legitimise their claims; Alder and Schäublin (2021) refer to these groups as Christian nationalists who both understand the United States to be 'inscribed in a divine plan' and justify the use of violence to defend their vision of Christian America. Their rights orientation, however, targets other rights-bearers, including the Black Lives Matter movement, feminists and women politicians, the LGBT+ community, and what they consider to be a left-wing liberal media (Farivar 2021). Comparative analysis with uncivil movements in Latin America and elsewhere could reveal factors that explain their mobilisation, appeal, and impact. It could further help explain efforts to reduce their threats to rights-bearers and to democracy itself.

An adjacent phenomenon that the storming of the Capitol laid bare is the issue of how social media platforms such as Facebook, YouTube (see Ma (2021)), Instagram, and Twitter are virtually 'unchecked' when it comes to allowing the so-called alt-right to circulate hate speech, rumours, conspiracy theories, and – of utmost concern – open calls for violence (Rohlinger 2021). In the Social Science Research Council's series on Extremism Online, several academics showcase their cutting-edge research and concur that there is a lack of data and information when it comes to understanding the links between online hatred and offline violence. For example, Deana A. Rohlinger and her team at Florida State University are working to systematically assess the characteristics of political expression online, and to see whether 'moderation might affect how individuals express their political identities and views'. Worryingly, they ascertain that individuals will find ways to 'potentially create extremism communities despite outlets' best moderation efforts' (Rohlinger 2021). These findings are consistent with the work of Fenwick McKelvey, who notes that even if platforms such as Facebook agree to remove certain online content, such efforts at automatic moderation ignore 'the structural conditions that instigated these movements' rise over the past decade' (McKelvey 2021). Others, such as Daniel Karell, are investigating how online extremism crosses into the offline world, with initial findings showing that this transition to real-world violence takes place 'more frequently and in more varied ways than widely assumed' (Karell 2021).

A perhaps niche, but nonetheless worrying, example of a burgeoning uncivil movement has an anti-environmentalist, eco-xenophobic agenda. Its infamous proponents include the authors of the mass shooting in El Paso, Texas, and the (self-proclaimed 'eco-fascist') mosque shooting in Christchurch, New Zealand. Rallying under the slogan 'bees, not refugees', these groups use pseudo-science ecological arguments to justify anti-immigrant violence and population control. Departing from a tradition that can be traced to include Madison Grant and John Muir – so-called nature conservationists who promoted white land stewardship – the movement is based in eugenicist thinking and justifies (racist) violence as a method for preventing overpopulation and resource depletion (Cagle 2019). Thus, they use environmental rights claims in a violent attempt to roll back the rights of immigrants. On one hand, such groups seem so fringe as not to demand analysis. And, yet, having seen their violence, and how such previously fringe ideas have gained appeal and won elections for their leaders, beginning to understand them at the initial phase warrants consideration.

Radical neoliberalism also has a strong foothold in both the European and United States contexts. For example, Stubbs and Lendvai-Bainton (2020, 541) refer to the growth of 'authoritarian neoliberalism', where governments employ social, political, and economic means to 'produce targeted and systematic divisions, insecurity

FINAL REFLECTIONS 241

and abandonment resting, *inter alia*, on a renewed heteronormative familialism, repatriarchalisation, national, ethicised demographic renewal, and anti-immigrant sentiments'. They outline this phenomenon particularly in Croatia, Hungary, and Poland, citing, for example, Hungarian president Viktor Orbán's critique of the 'liberal welfare state', which is reminiscent of Margaret Thatcher's decrying of the 'nanny state' in the United Kingdom in the 1980s. In effect, this leads to welfare- and social policy retrenchment. As the authors note: 'the dismantling of older social contracts based on solidarity has contributed, then, to the assembling of new forms of insider–outsider binaries based on mobilisations of anger and systematic dispossessions and foreclosing on the rights of those groups labelled as "undeserving"' (543).

Beginning to analytically disaggregate, identify, and compare not only countermovements, but also uncivil movements and radical neoliberal mobilisations, heightens the analytical power to understand them. In what ways are they similar and different? What factors help explain their emergence, their appeal, and their impact? But also, how can these comparative cases contribute to the reduction of their threats to rights and rights-holders?

Strategies to Limit the Right against Rights

Comparative analysis also contributes to the understanding of how rights-defenders have attempted to reduce the power of anti-rights groups. In this section we look at those efforts outside Latin America to 'right wrongs'. Particularly, how have consolidated democracies in the Global North responded to the threats and other social problems posed by the right against rights to protect the hard-won democratic rights of marginalised people?

What we have found is the creation of organisations that act as 'watchdogs', monitoring the activity of the right against rights. We propose that Latin America could benefit from the creation of organisations similar to the Southern Poverty Law Center (SPLC) in the United States; the Stop Hate UK, Moonshot, and the HateLab in the United Kingdom; and the Centre for Analysis of the Radical Right, run through openDemocracy. A brief review follows of what these organisations have to offer to reduce the threat of the right against rights.

The SPLC is an NGO operating in Montgomery, Alabama, since 1971. Its stated goal is to act as 'a catalyst for racial justice in the [US] South and beyond, working in partnership with communities to dismantle white supremacy, strengthen intersectional movements, and advance the human rights of all people' (SPLC n.d.). It monitors hate groups, defined as those who 'vilify others because of their race, religion, ethnicity, sexual orientation or gender identity' (SPLC n.d.). The groups tracked by SPLC include 'Ku Klux Klan, Neo-Nazi, White Nationalist, Racist Skinhead, Christian Identity, Neo-Confederate, Anti-Immigrant, Anti-LGBTQ, … Anti-Muslim … and radical traditional Catholicism' (SPLC n.d.). The organisation notes that not all groups fall into a single category, and 'many embrace racism and antisemitism as core components' (SPLC n.d.). This list of groups suggests that the SPLC tracks uncivil movements in the United States, yet it is careful to say that having committed violent acts is 'not a requirement for being listed as a hate group'. Instead it focuses on ideology that may catalyse violence, using the case of Dylann Roof's 2015 racist massacre in the Mother Emmanuel Church in Charleston, South Carolina, as an example. Roof had no prior violent activity, and neither did the Council of Conservative Citizens, which inspired his acts.

The SPLC thus monitors groups that have the potential to commit hate crimes. Its monitoring function involves mapping hate groups and creating a measure of the level of hate activity in the United States. The tracking involves: reviewing publications by such groups in social and other forms of media; recording citizens', law enforcement, and news media reports; and engaging in fieldwork and other forms of independent investigations. These data are used in the annually updated 'Hate Map' available on the SPLC website, which visually geo-references the 838 hate groups that the organisation tracked across the United States in 2020, and shows change over time (since 2000). The stated purpose of monitoring these groups is to expose and counter 'fundamentally anti-democratic' activities, to hold law enforcement accountable in recognising the serious harm of such groups, and to combat them. These data are also used by SPLC to produce a blog. The organisation also employs over 100 lawyers and advocates to engage in impact litigation in the areas of 'children's rights, economic justice, immigrant justice, LGBT+ rights, voting rights, and criminal justice reform' (SPLC n.d.) In addition to the monitoring and data-gathering activities to fight hate, the SPLC also has a 'learning for justice' component to work with educators and community activists with the aim of building tolerance, ending hate, and protecting communities. These sorts of activities of tracking and monitoring, exposing, and educating are key to beginning to combat the harm of uncivil movements in ways that would prove useful in other parts of the world.

Stop Hate UK is oriented toward similar goals. Referred to as 'one of the leading national organisations working to challenge all forms of Hate Crime and discrimination, based on any aspect of an individual's identity' (Stop Hate UK n.d.). This NGO began in 1995 'in direct response to the murder of Stephen Lawrence', a Black British teenager who was killed because of his race while waiting for a bus in 1993. The case revealed not only the racist motivation behind the crime, but also how institutional racism within the police investigation unit blocked justice. Stop Hate UK set up a 24-hour-a-day/365-days-a-year helpline as an alternative reporting mechanism for individuals and communities who do not wish to report hate crimes to the police. It created a 'toolkit' to improve local responses to hate crimes. These support mechanisms were expanded to two new areas, but both of these subsequently lost their funding: Stop Learning Disability Hate Crime, and Stop Lesbian, Gay, Bisexual and Transgender Hate Crime. Stop Hate UK is oriented around support for communities facing hate crimes. It has lacked the SPLC's resources in terms of national public visibility and advocacy on behalf of victims and potential victims of hate crimes. Resources, and perhaps the lack of political will behind

FINAL REFLECTIONS

243

the lack of funding, will certainly act as an impediment to organisations that could emerge in other parts of the world.

It is possible that the funding problem could be overcome with the creation of the HateLab: 'a global hub for data and insight into hate speech and crime' (HateLab n.d.) based at Cardiff University in Wales. Although created by the UK Home Secretary in 2017 and funded primarily by UK research councils, the HateLab also receives funding from the US Department of Justice and aims to create a global tracking mechanism. HateLab includes a 'dashboard' that uses 'artificial intelligence to gather data related to hate crime and speech, displaying aggregate trends of hate speech posted on social media around events, such as Brexit and terror attacks' (HateLab n.d.). More recently, HateLab researchers have been referred to as 'hate detectives' for their investigation of pandemic-related hate speech, specifically anti-Chinese, anti-Semitic, and Islamophobic speech (Parkin 2020). 'What we are seeing is a threat to health being weaponised to justify targeting minority groups, no matter how illogical the connections may seem' (Matthew Williams, director HateLab, quoted in Parkin (2020)). Investigation into hate speech, particularly through social media, is seen as one way to anticipate and prevent violent extremists' actions. Using the example of the speech of the gunman in who killed 51 mosquegoers in Christchurch, New Zealand, HateLab's argument is that '[p]erpetrators of terrorist attacks now routinely leave online statements or manifestos to justify their actions, hoping their words might encourage others'. Another finding is that after the killing of 22 people in Walmart in El Paso, Texas, 'there was an 82% rise in the Google search term "how to murder Mexicans"'. In following the Twitter feed before the 2013 murder of Fusilier Lee Rigby by radical Islamists in Woolwich, southeast London, HateLab claims that the evidence gathered from Tweets 'might be possible to predict real world attacks' (Parkin 2020).

Moonshot, founded in 2015, is a for-profit company based in a secret location in London. Its funding depends on private contracts in the UK, the USA, Canada, Australia, and Europe. It is one of the 'clandestine startups … using technology to stem the flow' of hate speech. 'It does not limit its work to any particular strain of radicalism; in addition to the far-right and jihadism, Moonshot's work covers everything from Buddhist extremism in South Asia, to Hindu nationalism and "incel" [involuntary celibate] terrorism in Canada … The company employs 50 people, and uses a mixture of software and human judgment to identify individuals on the internet who … appear interested in extremist propaganda. They then attempt to serve them counter-messaging' (Parkin 2020). Individuals are categorised with 'risk points' depending on their level of activity and engagement on internet sites. Moonshot's strategy is 'redirecting'; it reorients a search for bomb-making, for example, to a site aimed at building tolerance.

OpenDemocracy's Centre for Analysis of the Radical Right (CARR) is also a UK-based 'research centre and pedagogical outreach initiative focused on the study and countering of radical right extremism and intersecting phenomena (e.g. populism, gender, antisemitism, and Islamophobia) that aims to support a variety of mainstream groups, from government agencies to grass-roots charities,

244 *Julia Zulver and Leigh A. Payne*

through podcasts, commentary, research reports, presentations, media interviews and commissioned work' (CARR n.d.). The purpose is to 'counter radical right extremism' around the world, in 'Europe, the US and beyond' (CARR n.d.). The organisation employs experts who prepare 'Research Insight pieces', blogs, vlogs, podcasts, bibliographies, media commentary, consultation materials, and policy formulations. It states that it aims to understand 'the global dynamics of the radical right beyond the Global North, as well as the nature, historicity, and ongoing threat of radical right terrorism in the present moment' (CARR n.d.), but aside from the study of anti-gender mobilisations in Africa discussed in an earlier section of this chapter, the research is almost entirely focused on the Global North. Indeed, even that study in Africa focused primarily on the transnational (United States and Europe) dimensions of the mobilisation. Certainly, however, there are opportunities for CARR to reach out to researchers on right-against-rights movements in Latin America and elsewhere in the Global South. This could be the beginning of 'righting wrongs' in the region and in the world.

On a smaller scale, in 2021 WikiLeaks published its 'Intolerance Network', which contains over 17,000 documents from the right-wing campaigning organisations HazteOir and CitizenGO, as well as affiliates including USA-based organisations such as the Howard Center for Family, Religion and Society, and the 2012 World Congress for Families, which are labelled by the SPLC as hate groups. WikiLeaks released thousands of documents dated between 2001 and 2017 that include internal systems, spreadsheets of donors and members, strategy documents, letters, financial charts, and legal and training documents. WikiLeaks wrote in a press release that they were publishing the dataset with the aim of making visible the instrumental workings of how the right against rights is working to effect change (WikiLeaks, 2021).

In sum, the logic upon which such 'watchdog' organisations premise their actions is that if extremist right-wing groups are tracked, and their activities rendered public and visible, the violence they perpetrate can be identified, exposed, and guarded against before murder or other criminal acts are committed. To date, there is no solidified or systematised organisation that undertakes this exercise in Latin America. We propose that such an approach could contribute to efforts to 'right wrongs' in Latin America and in other areas of the Global South. By creating a monitoring platform that tracks right-against-rights activities across the region, we expect that the more violent expressions of right-against-rights mobilisation could be prevented, thus protecting the lives, rights, and physical integrity of the region's marginalised groups.

Moving Forward

This volume has covered significant ground, in terms of the theorisation of the right against rights as well as the diverse empirical case studies around the region. In concert, the chapters presented in this volume invite thinking about new research agendas and a subsequent set of questions that we insist must be taken seriously and

FINAL REFLECTIONS

245

addressed as a matter of urgency. For example, departing from Payne's (Chapter 2) typology of right-against-rights movements, we suggest that there is value in asking questions about the origins and impacts of these three types of movements, and why they develop as they do in certain contexts and in relation to certain political opportunities. As explored in the above sections, we further assert that studying the right against rights in comparative and global perspective can deepen understandings of both what we can learn about Latin America, and what insights the Latin American experience can bring to other world regions. A form of 'network analysis' could begin to link the right-against-rights mobilisations to similar groups and supporters within and outside countries and regions.

Indeed, global events of recent years have increased the imperative of initiating and expanding this research agenda. Since we began to compile the chapters for this book, the world locked because of the COVID-19 pandemic. Nascent research implies that the impact of this social isolation – and the resulting economic crises that have surged in the wake of the pandemic – has pushed people toward extremism (James and Hardy 2021). Such research implies that the radical right is taking advantage of the pandemic to 'align Covid-19 criticism and conspiracy theories with longstanding right-wing tropes and narratives' that become all the more salient when people are socially isolated or lonely, factors that are known to potentially contribute to radicalisation.

More conclusive research will undoubtedly begin to emerge in the coming months and years. Meanwhile, we do know that COVID-19 has served to exacerbate economic inequalities amongst some of Latin America's most vulnerable, which would appear to strengthen the right in the region. If research does show that the pandemic and its knock-on effects have served to strengthen the right against rights, the insights from this volume, and our above suggestions for a regional rights-monitoring body, become more urgently relevant.

Even if it does not – which we hope is the case – this volume stands as a call for greater academic focus on the threats to the hard-won rights of marginalised peoples around the world. It further calls to use that research to explore how to reduce those threats within a democratic framework. That struggle to protect and expand rights for the excluded should always be urgent.

References

Alder, C. and E. Schäublin (2021), 'Contemporary Christian Nationalism in the US', *CSS Analyses in Security Policy*, 288 (July), https://css.ethz.ch/content/dam/ethz/special-interest/gess/cis/center-for-securities-studies/pdfs/CSSAnalyse288-EN.pdf.

ANU [Australian National University] (2019), 'Duterte's Mid-Term Victory and the Global Shift to the Radical Right', *East Asia Forum*, 3 June, https://www.eastasiaforum.org/2019/06/03/dutertes-mid-term-victory-and-the-global-shift-to-the-radical-right/.

Cagle, S. (2019), '"Bees, Not Refugees": The Environmentalist Roots of Anti-Immigrant Bigotry', *Guardian*, 16 August, https://www.theguardian.com/environment/2019/aug/15/anti.

CARR [Centre for Analysis of the Radical Right (n.d.), 'CARR: Centre for Analysis of the Radical Right', https://www.radicalrightanalysis.com.

Chattopadhyay, K. (2019), 'Why Has India Embraced the Far Right?', *Tribune Magazine*, 30 June, https://tribunemag.co.uk/2019/06/why-has-india-embraced-the-far-right.

Dell'Omo, A. (2021), 'The Anti-Gender Movement', Right Rising,13 April, https://rightrising.fireside.fm/episode21.

Farivar, M. (2021), 'Researchers: More than a Dozen Extremist Groups Took Part in Capitol Riots', *VOA*, 16 January, https://www.voanews.com/2020-usa-votes/researchers-more-dozen-extremist-groups-took-part-capitol-riots.

HateLab (n.d.), website: https://hatelab.net/.

Jaffrelot, C. (2021), *Modi's India: Hindu Nationalism and the Rise of Ethnic Democracy* (Princeton, Princeton University Press).

James, N. and J. Hardy (2021), 'Is Pandemic Isolation Pushing People towards Extremism?', *openDemocracy*, 13 May, https://www.opendemocracy.net/en/countering-radical-right/pandemic-isolation-pushing-people-towards-extremism/.

Karell, D. (2021), 'Online Extremism and Offline Harm', *Social Sciences Research Council*, 1 June, https://items.ssrc.org/extremism-online/online-extremism-and-offline-harm/.

Keck, M. E. and K. Sikkink (1998), *Activists beyond Borders: Advocacy Networks in International Politics* (Ithaca, Cornell University Press).

Kitroeff, N. (2022), 'The Mexican Model of Abortion Rights', *The Daily* (*New York Times* podcast), 17 May, https://www.nytimes.com/2022/05/17/podcasts/the-daily/mexico-abortion-roe-v-wade.html.

Leidig, E. (2020), 'The Far-Right Is Going Global', *Foreign Policy*, 21 January, https://foreignpolicy.com/2020/01/21/india-kashmir-modi-eu-hindu-nationalists-rss-the-far-right-is-going-global/.

Ma, C. (2021), 'Mainstreaming Resentment: YouTube Celebrities and the Rhetoric of White Supremacy', *Social Sciences Research Council*, 13 April, https://items.ssrc.org/extremism-online/mainstreaming-resentment-youtube-celebrities-and-the-rhetoric-of-white-supremacy/.

Mayka, L. and A. E. Smith (2021), 'The Grassroots Right in Latin America: Patterns, Causes, and Consequences', *Latin American Politics and Society*, 63:3, 1–31.

McKelvey, F. (2021). 'Toward Contextualizing Not Just Containing Right-Wing Extremisms on Social Media: The Limits of Walled Strategies', *Social Sciences Research Council*, 13 July, https://items.ssrc.org/extremism-online/toward-contextualizing-not-just-containing-right-wing-extremisms-on-social-media-the-limits-of-walled-strategies/.

Moghadam, V. (2018), 'Gendering the New Right-Wing Populisms: A Research Note', *Journal of World Systems Research*, 24:2, 293–303.

O'Brien, C. and S. D. Walsh (2020), 'Women's Rights and Opposition: Explaining the Stunted Rise and Sudden Reversals of Progressive Violence against Women Policies in Contentious Contexts', *Journal of Latin American Studies*, 52:1, 107–31.

Parfitt, R. (2019), 'Fascism and the International: The Global South, the Far-Right and the International Legal Order', *TWAILR* [*Third World Approaches to International Law Review*], https://twailr.com/series-introduction-fascism-and-the-international-the-global-south-the-far-right-and-the-international-legal-order/.

Parkin, S. (2020), 'Trigger Warning', *Guardian-Weekend*, 2 May.

Restrepo Sanín, J. (2020), 'Violence against Women in Politics: Latin America in an Era of Backlash', *Signs: Journal of Women in Culture and Society*, 45:2, 302–10.

Rohlinger, A. (2021), 'We Cannot Just Moderate Extremism Away', *Social Sciences Research Council*, 9 March, https://items.ssrc.org/extremism-online/we-cannot-just-moderate-extremism-away/.

Schmidt, S. (2022), 'How Green Became the Color of Abortion Rights', *Washington Post*, 3 July, https://www.washingtonpost.com/world/interactive/2022/abortion-green-roe-wade-argentina/.

SPLC [Southern Poverty Law Center] (n.d.), 'SPLC: Southern Poverty Law Center', https://www.splcenter.org/about.

Stop Hate UK (n.d.), 'Stop Hate UK', https://www.stophateuk.org/.

Stubbs, P. and Lendvai-Bainton, N. (2020), 'Authoritarian Neoliberalism, Radical Conservatism and Social Policy within the European Union: Croatia, Hungary and Poland', *Development and Change*, 51: 540–60.

WikiLeaks (2021), 'The Intolerance Network', https://wikileaks.org/intolerancenetwork/press-release?fbclid=IwAR3DjUVwoFTMrzqMtEz1P1o2A7hzfUCTd893xdhGqik6 yf6I5k7Prs70ChA.

Zulver, J. M. (2021), 'The Endurance of Women's Mobilization during "Patriarchal Backlash": A Case from Colombia's Reconfiguring Armed Conflict', *International Feminist Journal of Politics*, 23:3, 440–62.

Zulver, J. and J. M. Piscopo (2022), 'In Colombia, an Activist, Feminist Lawyer Is Running for VP', *The Monkey Cage* (*Washington Post*), 29 April, https://www.washingtonp ost.com/politics/2022/04/29/marquez-petro-colombia-election-may29-afrocolombian/ ?utm_campaign=wp_monkeycage&utm_medium=social&utm_source=twitter.

Bibliography

Adler, J. (2020), 'The Genealogy of "Human Dignity": A New Perspective', *Publications of the English Goethe Society*, 89:1, 17–59.

Agamben, G., A. Badiou, D. Bensaid, *et al.* (2011), *Democracy in What State?* New Directions in Critical Theory, 11 (New York, Columbia University Press).

Alberto, P. L. (2011), *Terms of Inclusion: Black Intellectuals in Twentieth-Century Brazil* (Chapel Hill, University of North Carolina Press).

Albó, X. (2008), *Movimientos y poder indígena en Bolivia, Ecuador y Perú* (La Paz, CIPCA).

Alder, C. and E. Schäublin (2021), 'Contemporary Christian Nationalism in the US', *CSS Analyses in Security Policy*, 288 (July), https://css.ethz.ch/content/dam/ethz/special-interest/gess/cis/center-for-securities-studies/pdfs/CSSAnalyse288-EN.pdf.

Alenda, S. (2020), *Anatomía de la derecha chilena: Nuevos y viejos protagonistas* (Santiago, Fondo de Cultura Económica Chile).

Alenda, S., A. Gartenlaub, and K. Fischer (2019), 'Ganar la batalla de ideas: El rol de los think tanks en la reconfiguración de la centro-derecha chilena', in *Anatomía de la centro-derecha chilena: Nuevos y viejos protagonistas*, ed. S. Alenda (Santiago, Fondo de Cultura Económica Chile), pp. 119–56.

Allen, W. (2017), 'Making Corpus Data Visible: Visualising Text with Research Intermediaries', *Corpora*, 12:3, 459–82.

Alma, A. (2018), '#AbortoLegalYa: Reirse para sacar el aborto del melodrama'. *LATFEM*, 10 May, https://latfem.org/abortolegalya-reirse-para-sacar-el-aborto-del-melodrama/.

Alvarez, S. (1990), *Engendering Democracy in Brazil: Women's Movements in Transition Politics* (Princeton, Princeton University Press).

Alvarez, S. E., E. Dagnino, and A. Escobar (1998), *Cultures of Politics, Politics of Cultures: Re-Visioning Latin American Social Movements* (Boulder, CO and Oxford, Westview Press).

Alzamora Revoredo, B. O. (2003), 'An Ideology of Gender: Dangers and Scope', in *Lexicon: Ambiguous and Debatable Terms Regarding Family Life and Ethical Questions*, ed. Pontifical Council for the Family (Front Royal, VA, Human Life International).

Amnesty International (2013), 'Defending Human Rights in Honduras Is a Crime', https://www.amnesty.org/en/latest/news/2013/11/honduras-human-rights-defenders-under-threat/.

Amnesty International (2013), 'Further Information on UA: 244/13', https://www.amnesty.org/es/wp-content/uploads/2021/06/amr370132013en.pdf.

Amnesty International (2013), 'UA: 244/13. Indigenous Leaders Face Unjust Charges', https://www.amnestyusa.org/files/uaa24413.pdf.

Amnesty International (2022), 'Guatemala: Discriminatory Law Foments Hate and Puts Lives, Rights and Families at Risk', 9 March, https://www.amnesty.org/en/latest/news/2022/03/guatemala-discriminatory-law-lives-rights-families-risk/.

Andolina, R., N. Laurie, and S. Radcliffe (2009), *Indigenous Development in the Andes: Culture, Power, and Transnationalism* (Durham, NC, Duke University Press).

Andrade, E. S. (2010), 'A visão celular no governo dos 12: Estratégias de crescimento, participação e conquista de espaços entre os batistas soteropolitanos de 1998 a 2008', M.Sc. dissertation, Universidade Federal da Bahia.

Bibliography

Andrews, G. R. (2004), *Afro-Latin America 1800–2000* (New York, Oxford University Press).

Andrews, G. R. (2010), 'Afro-World: African-Diaspora Thought and Practice in Montevideo, Uruguay, 1830–2000', *The Americas*, 67:1, 83–107.

Andrews, G. R. (2010), *Blackness in a White Nation: A History of Afro-Uruguay* (Chapel Hill, University of North Carolina Press).

Andrews, G. R. (2011), 'Afro-Uruguay', *Black Past*, http://www.blackpast.org/perspectives/afro-uruguay-brief-history.

Andrews, G. R. (2018), 'Afro-Latin America by the Numbers: The Politics of Census', *ReVista*, 17:2, https://revista.drclas.harvard.edu/afro-latin-america-by-the-numbers/.

ANEP [Administración Nacional de Educación Pública] (2016), 'Guía didáctica: Educación y afrodescendencia', https://www.anep.edu.uy/sites/default/files/images/Archivos/publicaciones-direcciones/DDHH/educacion-afrodescendencia/GuiaDidacticaEducacionyAfrodescendencia.pdf.

Angelo, P. and D. Bocci (2021), 'Are Latin American Nations Turning Their Backs on LGBTQ+ Rights?', *Council on Foreign Relations*, 9 February, https://www.cfr.org/blog/are-latin-american-nations-turning-their-backs-lgbtq-rights.

Angulo, Y. (2019), 'Fabricio Alvarado califica de "feminazis" a las mujeres que promueven el aborto', *El Mundo, Costa Rica*, 30 November, https://www.elmundo.cr/costa-rica/fabricio-alvarado-califica-de-feminazis-a-las-mujeres-que-promueven-el-aborto/.

Anić, J. R. (2015), 'Gender, Gender "Ideology" and Cultural War: Local Consequences of a Global Idea – Croatian Example', *Feminist Theology*, 24:1, 7–22.

ANU [Australian National University] (2019), 'Duterte's Mid-Term Victory and the Global Shift to the Radical Right', *East Asia Forum*, 3 June, https://www.eastasiaforum.org/2019/06/03/dutertes-mid-term-victory-and-the-global-shift-to-the-radical-right/.

AP LLP [Amsterdam & Partners LLP] (2018), 'War on Development: Exposing the COPINH Disinformation Campaign Surrounding the Berta Cáceres Case in Honduras', https://amsterdamandpartners.com/wp-content/uploads/2019/03/War-on-Development-Ver-4.pdf.

Araújo, V. (2019), 'A religião distrai os pobres? Pentecostalismo e voto redistributivo no Brasil', Ph.D. dissertation, São Paulo State University.

Arendt, H. (2007), 'Responsabilidad personal bajo una dictadura', in *Responsabilidad y juicio* (Barcelona, Paidós), pp. 49–74.

Arguedas-Ramírez, G. (2018), 'Gender Ideology, Religious Fundamentalism and the Electoral Campaign (2017–2018) in Costa Rica', *Religion and Global Society*, 6 December, https://blogs.lse.ac.uk/religionglobalsociety/2018/12/gender-ideology-religious-fundamentalism-and-the-electoral-campaign-2017-2018-in-costa-rica/.

Armas Arocena (2013), 'Uruguay: Un país más diverso que su imaginación. Una interpretación a partir del censo de 2011', *Revista de ciencias sociales*, 26:33, 137–58.

Asamblea Nacional Constituyente de Ecuador (2008), 'Constitución de la República del Ecuador', https://www.oas.org/juridico/pdfs/mesicic4_ecu_const.pdf.

Balaguer, M. I., M. L. Baretta, and A. B. Copetti (2021), 'El litigio conservador y su repercusión sobre los derechos sexuales y (no reproductivos desde Córdoba, Argentina', *Derecho y ciencias sociales*, 26, 9–25.

Bale, T. and C. Rovira Kaltwasser (2021), 'The Mainstream Right in Western Europe: Caught between the Silent Revolution and Silent Counter-Revolution', in *Riding the Populist Wave: Europe's Mainstream Right in Crisis*, ed. T. Bale and C. Rovira Kaltwasser (Cambridge, Cambridge University Press).

Barrenechea, R. and E. Dargent (2020), 'Populists and Technocrats in Latin America: Conflict, Cohabitation, and Cooperation', *Politics and Governance*, 8:4, 509–519.

Barros, M. (2017), 'Cambiemos pasado por futuro: Los derechos humanos bajo el gobierno de Mauricio Macri', in *Tensiones en la democracia argentina: Rupturas y continuidades en torno al neoliberalismo*, ed. M. T. Piñero and M. S. Bonetto (Córdoba, Editorial CEA), pp. 47–64.

Bayes, J. and N. Tohidi (2001), 'Introduction', in *Globalization, Gender, and Religion: The Politics of Women's Rights in Catholic and Muslim Contexts*, ed. J. Bayes and N. Tohidi (New York, Palgrave), pp. 1–16.

BBC [British Broadcasting Corporation] (2018), 'El Salvador Court Frees Woman Jailed under Anti-Abortion Laws', *BBC News*, 18 December.

BCN [Biblioteca del Congreso Nacional de Chile] (2017), 'Historia de la Ley N° 21.030', https://www.bcn.cl/historia-de-la-ley/nc/historia-de-la-ley/6701/.

Bebbington, D. H. and A. Bebbington (2010), 'Anatomy of a Regional Conflict: Tarija and Resource Grievances in Morales's Bolivia', *Latin American Perspectives*, 37:4, 140–60.

Beder, S. (1997), *Global Spin: The Corporate Assault on Environmentalism* (Dartington, Green Books).

Beltrán, W. M. and S. Creely (2018), 'Pentecostals, Gender Ideology and the Peace Plebiscite: Colombia 2016', *Religions*, 8, 1–19.

Benford, R. and D. Snow (2000), 'Framing Processes and Social Movements: An Overview and Assessment', *Annual Review of Sociology*, 26:1, 611–39.

Benford, R. D. and D. A. Snow (1988), 'Ideology, Frame Resonance, and Participant Mobilisation', in *From Structure to Action: Social Movement Participation across Cultures*, ed. B. Klandermans, H. Kriesi, and S. G. Tarrow (Greenwich, JAI Press), pp. 197–218.

Benford, R. D. and D. A. Snow (1992), 'Master Frames and Cycles of Protest', in *Frontiers in Social Movement Theory*, ed. A. Morris and C. M. Mueller (New Haven, Yale University Press), pp. 133–55.

Benford, R. D. and D. A. Snow (2000), 'Framing Processes and Social Movements: An Overview and Assessment', *Annual Review of Sociology*, 26 (August), 611–39.

Benjamin, W. (2020), 'Theses on the Philosophy of History', in *Critical Theory and Society: A Reader* (London: Routledge), pp. 255–63.

Benotman, A. (2022), 'Guatemala se declara "capital provida", aumenta penas por aborto y prohíbe el matrimonio igualitario', *France 24*, 10 March, https://www.france24.com/es/américa-latina/20220310-guatemala-aborto-derechos-homosexuales-giammattei.

BHRRC [Business & Human Rights Resource Centre] (2022), 'Human Rights Defenders & Civic Freedoms', https://www.business-humanrights.org/en/big-issues/human-rights-defenders-civic-freedoms/.

Bird, A. (2013), 'The Agua Zarca Dam and Lenca Communities in Honduras: Transnational Investment Leads to Violence against and Criminalization of Indigenous Communities', http://rightsaction.org/sites/default/files/Rpt_131001_RioBlanco_Final.pdf.

Biroli, F. (2019), 'The Crisis of Democracy and the Backlash against Gender', expert paper, UN Women Expert Group Meeting, 25–6 September, https://www.academia.edu/41142806/The_crisis_of_democracy_and_the_backlash_against_gender.

Biroli, F. (2020), 'The Backlash against Gender Equality in Latin America: Temporarility, Religious Patterns, and the Erosion of Democracy', *LASA Forum: The Quarterly Newsletter for the Latin American Studies Association*, 51:2, 22–6.

Biroli, F. and M. Caminotti (2020), 'The Conservative Backlash against Gender in Latin America', *Politics & Gender*, 16, 1–38.

Bibliography

Blabbeando (2013), 'Ecuador: President Rafael Correa Says "Gender Ideology" Threatens Traditional Families', YouTube, 29 December, https://www.youtube.com/watch?v=4J7QMXpUt00&lc=z13hhnjbcsmzi5xtn22viz3b5qqyslzcy.

Blee, K. M. and K. A. Creasap (2010), 'Conservative and Right-Wing Movements', *Annual Review of Sociology*, 36, 269–86.

Blofield, M. (2006), *The Politics of Moral Sin: Abortion and Divorce in Spain, Chile and Argentina* (London, Routledge).

Blofield, M. (2008), 'Women's Choices in Comparative Perspective: Abortion Policies in Late-Developing Catholic Countries', *Comparative Politics*, 40:4, 399–419.

Blofield, M. and C. Ewig (2017), 'The Left Turn and Abortion Politics in Latin America', *Social Politics*, 24:4, 481–510.

Blofield, M. and L. Haas (2005), 'Defining a Democracy: Reforming the Laws on Women's Rights in Chile, 1990–2002', *Latin American Politics and Society*, 47:3, 35–68.

Blofield, M., C. Ewig, and J. M. Piscopo (2017), 'The Reactive Left: Gender Equality and the Latin American Pink Tide', *Social Politics*, 24:4, 345–69.

Bob, C. (2011), *The Global Right Wing and the Clash of World Politics* (Cambridge, Cambridge University Press).

Bolivia, C. O. (2009), *Constitución Política del Estado* (La Paz: National Congress).

Bonilla-Silva, E. (2003), *Racism without Racists: Color-Blind Racism and the Persistence of Inequality in the United States* (New York, Rowman & Littlefield).

Borges, A. (2021), 'The Illusion of Electoral Stability: From Party System Erosion to Right-Wing Populism in Brazil', *Journal of Politics in Latin America*, 13:2, 166–91.

Borucki, A. (2015), *From Shipmates to Soldiers: Emerging Black Identities in the Río de la Plata* (Albuquerque, University of New Mexico Press).

Bosia, M. J. and M. L. Weiss (2013), 'Political Homophobia in Comparative Perspective', in *Global Homophobia: States, Movements, and the Politics of Oppression* (Champaign-Urbana, University of Illinois Press), pp. 1–29.

Bowen, J. (2011), 'Multicultural Market Democracy: Elites and Indigenous Movements in Contemporary Ecuador', *Journal of Latin American Studies*, 43, 451–83.

Bowen, J. D. (2014), 'The Right and Nonparty Forms of Representation and Participation: Bolivia and Ecuador Compared', in *The Resilience of the Latin American Right*, ed. J. P. Luna and C. Rovira Kaltwasser (Baltimore, Johns Hopkins University Press), pp. 94–116.

Brady, H. E. and D. Collier (2010), *Rethinking Social Inquiry: Diverse Tools, Shared Standards*, 2nd edn (Lanham, MD, Rowman & Littlefield).

Braidotti, R. (2011), *Nomadic Subjects: Embodiment and Sexual Difference in Contemporary Feminist Theory* (New York, Columbia University Press).

Brändle, V. K., C. Galpin, and H.-J. Trenz (2022), 'Brexit as "Politics of Division": Social Media Campaigning after the Referendum', *Social Movement Studies*, 21:1–2, 234–53.

Brecha (1985), 'Las dificultades para insertarse en una sociedad blanca', 23 December, 2.

Brecha (1985), '¿Libros que enseñan a ser racistas?', 20 December, 9.

Brustier, G. (2015), 'France', in *Gender as Symbolic Glue: The Position and Role of Conservative and Far Right Parties in the Anti-Gender Mobilization in Europe*, ed. E. Kováts and M. Põim (Brussels, Foundation for European Progressive Studies), pp. 19–39.

Bucheli, M. and R. Porzecanski (2011), 'Racial Inequality in the Uruguayan Labor Market: An Analysis of Wage Differentials between Afro-Descendants and Whites', *Latin American Politics & Society*, 53:2, 113–50.

Buffington, D. and T. Fraley (2011), 'Racetalk and Sport: The Color Consciousness of Contemporary Discourse on Basketball', *Sociological Inquiry*, 81:3, 333–52.

252 *Bibliography*

Bülow, M. von (2018), 'The Empowerment of Conservative Civil Society in Brazil', in *The Mobilization of Conservative Civil Society*, ed. R. Youngs (Washington, DC, Carnegie Endowment for International Peace), pp. 13–18.

Burggraf, J. (2003), 'Gender', in *Lexicon: Ambiguous and Debatable Terms Regarding Family Life and Ethical Questions*, ed. Pontifical Council for the Family (Front Royal, VA, Human Life International), pp. 399–408.

Busby, J. W. (2010), *Moral Movements and Foreign Policy* (Cambridge, Cambridge University Press).

Búsqueda (2022), 'Uruguay está pasando de un "patriarcado a un matriarcado", dice diputado de Cabildo Abierto que critica al "feminismo del 8m"', 9 March, https://www.busqueda.com.uy/Secciones/Uruguay-esta-pasando-de-un-patriarcado-a-un-matriarcado--dice-diputada-de-Cabildo-Abierto-que-critica-al-feminismo-del-8M--uc51446.

Buss, D. E. (1998), 'Robes, Relics and Rights: The Vatican and the Beijing Conference on Women', *Social & Legal Studies*, 7:3, 339–63.

Bustamante, B. (2015), 'Mujeres de blanco denuncian contenido tendencioso en simposio sobre aborto en Chile', *ACI Prensa*, 22 November, https://www.aciprensa.com/noticias/mujeres-de-blanco-denuncian-contenido-tendencioso-en-simposio-sobre-aborto-en-chile-82975.

Butler, J. (2002), 'Is Kinship Always Already Heterosexual?', *Differences*, 13:1, 14–44.

Butler, J. (2017), 'The Phantom of Gender: Reflections on Freedom and Violence', *Folha de São Paulo*, https://www1.folha.uol.com.br/internacional/en/culture/2017/11/1936921-the-phantom-of-gender-reflections-on-freedom-and-violence.shtml.

Cabella, W., M. Nathan, and M. Tenenbaum (2013), 'La población afro-uruguaya en el Censo 2011', *Atlas sociodemográfico y de la desigualdad del Uruguay*, http://www.ine.gub.uy/c/document_library/get_file?uuid=1726c03f-aecd-4c78-b9be-f2c27dafba1d&groupId=10181.

Cagle, S. (2019), '"Bees, Not Refugees": The Environmentalist Roots of Anti-Immigrant Bigotry', *Guardian*, 16 August, https://www.theguardian.com/environment/2019/aug/15/anti.

Caiani, M. and R. Borri (2012), 'Between Violent and Non-Violent Action Strategies: A Study on Extreme-Right Organizations in Italy and Spain', *22nd IPSA World Congress of Political Science*, July, http://aei.pitt.edu/39280/1/pw_130.pdf.

Caiani, M. and D. della Porta (2011), 'The Elitist Populism of the Extreme Right: A Frame Analysis of Extreme Right-Wing Discourses in Italy and Germany', *Acta politica*, 46:2, 180–202.

Caiani, M. and D. della Porta (2018), 'The Radical Right as Social Movement Organizations', in *Oxford Handbook of the Radical Right*, ed. J. Rydgren (Oxford, Oxford University Press), pp. 327–47.

Caiani, M., D. della Porta, and C. Wagemann (2012), *Mobilizing on the Extreme Right: Germany, Italy, and the United States* (Oxford, Oxford University Press).

Calixtre, A. and F. Vaz (2015), 'Nota técnica: PNAD 2014 – breves análises', *IPEA*, 22, 49.

Calvo, R. (2021), 'El presidente del Comité pro Santa Cruz, Rómulo Calvo, en el inicio de los actos por el aniversario 460 de Santa Cruz', video, Facebook, https://www.facebook.com/ComiteProSC/videos/877365922806953/.

Câmara dos Deputados (2019), 'Frente Parlamentar Evangélica do Congresso Nacional', https://www.camara.leg.br/internet/deputado/frenteDetalhe.asp?id=54010.

Campo, A. del (2008), 'El debate médico sobre el aborto en Chile en la década de 1930', in *Por la salud del cuerpo: Historia y políticas sanitarias en Chile*, ed. M. S. Zárate (Santiago de Chile, Universidad Alberto Hurtado), pp. 131–88.

Bibliography

Campos Refosco, H. and M. M. Guida Fernandes (2016), 'Same-Sex Parents and Their Children: Brazilian Case Law and Insights from Psychoanalysis', *William & Mary Journal of Women and the Law*, 23:2, 175–84.

Camus, J.-Y. and N. Lebourg (2017), *Far Right Politics in Europe* (Cambridge, MA, Belknap Press of Harvard University).

Cannon, B. (2016), *The Right in Latin America: Elite Power, Hegemony and the Struggle for the State* (Abingdon, Routledge).

CARR [Centre for Analysis of the Radical Right (n.d.), 'CARR: Centre for Analysis of the Radical Right', https://www.radicalrightanalysis.com.

Carvalho Neto, P. de (1954), 'Temas de la obra afro-uruguaya de Ildefonso Pereda Valdés', *Boletín bibliográfico de antropología americana*, 17:1, 235–8.

Casas, L. and L. Vivaldi (2014), 'Abortion in Chile: The Practice under a Restrictive Regime', *Reproductive Health Matters*, 22:44, 70–81.

Case, M. A. (2011), 'After Gender the Destruction of Man? The Vatican's Nightmare Vision of the "Gender Agenda" for Law', *Pace Law Review*, 31:2, 802–17.

Case, M. A. (2019), 'Trans Formations in the Vatican's War on "Gender Ideology"', *Signs: Journal of Women in Culture and Society*, 44:3, 639–64.

Castañeda, J. G. (2006), 'Latin America's Left Turn', *Foreign Affairs*, 85:3, 28–43.

Castaño Díaz, E., S. L. Palacios, and P. Moreno (2016), 'Propuesta de ajuste de los Acuerdos de Paz entre el Gobierno Nacional y las FARC-EP por parte de la Iglesia Evangélica de Colombia', 13 October, https://docplayer.es/74076357-Ref-propuesta-de-ajuste-de-los-acuerdos-de-paz-entre-el-gobierno-nacional-y-las-farc-ep-por-parte-de-la-iglesia-eva ngelica-de-colombia.html.

Castineiras, M. and T. Urwicz (2016), 'Ser negro en el país de racismo invisible', *Brecha*, 6 July.

Castro Quiroga, L. A. (2016), 'Mensaje de la 101a Asamblea Plenaria de los Obispos de Colombia: Artesanos de la paz "Bienaventurados los que trabajan por la paz" (MT 5, 9)', https://www.cec.org.co/sites/default/files/Comunicado.pdf.

Castro Rea, J. (2018), 'Right-Wing Think Tank Networks in Latin America: The Mexican Connection', *Perspectives on Global Development and Technology*, 17:1–2, 89–102.

Catholic News Agency (2019), 'Efforts Build to Repeal Uruguay's Controversial Transgender Law', 28 March, https://www.catholicnewsagency.com/news/efforts-build-to-repeal-uruguays-controversial-transgender-law-87180.

CEHPRODEC [Honduran Centre for the Promotion of Community Development] (2018), *La producción de energía eléctrica en honduras* (Tegucigalpa, CEHPRODEC).

Centellas, M. (2016), 'The Santa Cruz Autonomía Movement in Bolivia: A Case of Non-Indigenous Ethnic Popular Mobilisation?', *Ethnopolitics*, 15:2, 245–64.

Center for Reproductive Rights (2022), *Center for Reproductive Rights*, https://reproductiv erights.org.

CEPDS [Comisión Especial de Población y Desarrollo Social] (2012), 'Afrodescendientes: Normas para favorecer su participación en las áreas educativa y laboral', Carpetas no. 1288, Anexo I, Repartido no. 761, https://legislativo.parlamento.gub.uy/temporales/D2012100761-01366631.pdf.

CEPDS [Comisión Especial de Población y Desarrollo Social] (2012), 'Versión taquigráfica no. 1030 de 2012', 4 May, https://legislativo.parlamento.gub.uy/temporales/D20120 503-1008-10303160990.HTML.

CEPDS [Comisión Especial de Población y Desarrollo Social] (2012), 'Versión taquigráfica no. 1039 de 2012', 10 May, https://legislativo.parlamento.gub.uy/temporales/D20120 510-1008-10392401713.HTML.

CEPDS [Comisión Especial de Población y Desarrollo Social] (2012), 'Versión taquigráfica no. 1090 de 2012', 7 June, https://legislativo.parlamento.gub.uy/temporales/D20120 607-1008-10909762930.HTML#.

CEPDS [Comisión Especial de Población y Desarrollo Social] (2012), 'Versión taquigráfica no. 1104 de 2012', 14 June, https://legislativo.parlamento.gub.uy/temporales/D20120 614-1008-11044382054.HTML#.

CEPDS [Comisión Especial de Población y Desarrollo Social] (2012), 'Versión taquigráfica no. 1251 de 2012', 13 September, https://legislativo.parlamento.gub.uy/temporales/ D20120913-1008-12512493283.HTML#.

CEPDS [Comisión Especial de Población y Desarrollo Social] (2013), 'Versión taquigráfica no. 2172', 16 June, https://legislativo.parlamento.gub.uy/temporales/S201321723622 273.HTML#.

CEPDS [Comisión Especial de Población y Desarrollo Social] (2013), 'Versión taquigráfica 2126', Carpetas no. 1042/2012, 3 June 2013, https://legislativo.parlamento.gub.uy/tem porales/S20132126939234.HTML#.

Cespedes-Baez, L. M. (2016), 'Gender Panic and the Failure of a Peace Agreement', *AJIL Unbound*, 110, 183–7.

Cháchara (2016), 'The Archidoces of Barranquilla Joins the Rally for the Family', La Cháchara, 8 August, https://lachachara.org/arquidiocesis-de-barranquilla-se-une-a-la-concentracion-por-la-familia/.

Chattopadhyay, K. (2019), 'Why Has India Embraced the Far Right?', *Tribune Magazine*, 30 June, https://tribunemag.co.uk/2019/06/why-has-india-embraced-the-far-right.

CIA [Central Intelligence Agency] (n.d.), 'Ethnic Groups,' *The World Factbook*, https://www.cia.gov/library/publications/the-world-factbook/fields/400.html#BR.

CIDH (2009), *Comunidades Cautivas: Situactión del Pueblo Indígena Guaraní y Formas Contemporáneas de Esclavitud en el Chaco de Bolivia* (Comisión Interamericana de Derechos-Humanos [Interamerican Human Rights Commission]).

Cobos, J. J. (ed.) (2016), 'Marcha abanderados por la familia Bucaramanga', YouTube, 12 August, https://www.youtube.com/watch?v=l3tMzk872rw.

COES [Centre for Social Conflict and Cohesion Studies] (2020), 'Observatory of Conflicts – Cumulative Dataset', Harvard Dataverse, https://doi.org/10.7910/DVN/GKQXBR.

Cohen, A. P. (1985), *The Symbolic Construction of Community* (London, Routledge).

Cohen, S. (2011), *Folk Devils and Moral Panics* (London, Routledge).

Congregation for the Doctrine of the Faith (2002), *Doctrinal Note on Some Questions Regarding the Participation of Catholics in Political Life: Vatican City November 24, 2002* (Vatican, Libreria Editrice Vaticana).

Cooperativa (2015), '"Mujeres de Blanco" marcharon este domingo en contra del aborto', 12 April, https://www.cooperativa.cl/noticias/pais/salud/aborto/mujeres-de-blanco-marcharon-este-domingo-en-contra-del-aborto/2015-04-12/191945_6.html#top-galeria.

COPINH [Council of Popular and Indigenous Organisations of Honduras] (2013), 'COMUNICADO URGENTE: A cuatro días de lucha continuamos firmes en defensa de nuestros ríos exigiendo la salida del proyecto hidroeléctrico Agua Zarca', https://cop inh.org/2013/04/comunicado-urgente-a-cuatro-dias-de-lucha-continuamos-firmes-en-defensa-de-nuestros-rios-exigiendo-la-salida-del-proyecto-hidroelectrico-agua-zarca/.

COPINH [Council of Popular and Indigenous Organisations of Honduras] (2013), 'COPINH – COMUNICADOS URGENTES: ¡A SIETE DÍAS LA LUCHA SIGUE!', https://copinh.org/2013/04/copinh-comunicados-urgentes-a-siete-dias-la-lucha-sigue/.

COPINH [Council of Popular and Indigenous Organisations of Honduras] (2013), 'COPINH toma de carreteras en Rio Blanco', YouTube, https://www.youtube.com/watch?v=Bf9v JyrF894.

Bibliography 255

COPINH [Council of Popular and Indigenous Organisations of Honduras] (2018), 'Alerta! Familia Madrid empleados de la empresa DESA ataca a comunidad de Río Blanco', https://copinh.org/2018/09/alerta-familia-madrid-empleados-de-la-empresa-desa-ataca-a-comunidad-de-rio-blanco/.

Cordero, M., D. Cariboni, and L. Ferreira (2021), 'US "Dark Money" Groups behind Mississippi Abortion Case Spend Millions Overseas', *openDemocracy*, https://www.opendemocracy.net/en/5050/us-rightwing-mississippi-abortion/.

Corrales, J. (2015), 'The Politics of LGBT Rights in Latin America and the Caribbean: Research Agendas', *European Review of Latin American and Caribbean Studies/ Revista Europea de estudios latinoamericanos y del Caribe*, 100, 53–62.

Corrales, J. (2017), 'Understanding the Uneven Spread of LGBT Rights in Latin America and the Caribbean, 1999–2013', *Journal of Research in Gender Studies*, 7:1, 52–82.

Corrales, J. (2020), 'The Expansion of LGBT Rights in Latin America and the Backlash', in *The Oxford Handbook of Global LGBT and Sexual Diversity Politics*, ed. M. J. Bosia, S. M. McEvoy, and M. Rahman (Oxford, Oxford University Press), pp. 184–200.

Corrales, J. (2022), *The Politics of LGBT Rights Expansion in Latin America and the Caribbean* (Cambridge, Cambridge University Press).

Corrales, J. and I. Sagarzazu (2019), 'Not All "Sins" Are Rejected Equally: Resistance to LGBT Rights across Religions in Colombia', *Political Science and Religion Journal*, 12:2, 351–77.

Corredor, E. S. (2019), 'Unpacking "Gender Ideology" and the Global Right's Antigender Countermovement', *Signs: Journal of Women in Culture and Society*, 44:3, 613–38.

Corredor, E. S. (2021), 'On the Strategic Uses of Women's Rights: Backlash, Rights-Based Framing, and Anti-Gender Campaigns in Colombia's 2016 Peace Agreement', *Latin American Politics and Society*, 63:3, 46–68.

Cottrol, R. (2013), *The Long, Lingering Shadow: Slavery, Race, and Law in the American Hemisphere* (Athens, University of Georgia Press).

Cowan, J. K. (2006), 'Culture and Rights after "Culture and Rights"', *American Anthropologist*, 108:1, 9–24.

Cowie, S. (2018), 'Violent Deaths of LGBT People in Brazil Hit All-Time High', *Guardian*, 22 January, https://www.theguardian.com/world/2018/jan/22/brazil-lgbt-violence-deaths-all-time-high-new-research.

CPDI [Comisión de Población, Desarrollo e Inclusión] (2013), 'Carpeta no. 1042/2012, Versión taquigráfica 2126', 3 June, https://legislativo.parlamento.gub.uy/temporales/S20132126939234.HTML#.

CPDI [Comisión de Población, Desarrollo e Inclusión] (2013), 'Distribuido no. 1977', 18 March, https://legislativo.parlamento.gub.uy/temporales/S201319779113111.HTML.

CPDI [Comisión de Población, Desarrollo e Inclusión] (2013), 'Versión taquigráfica no. 2172', 16 June, https://legislativo.parlamento.gub.uy/temporales/S201321723622273.HTML#.

CPDI [Comisión de Población, Desarrollo e Inclusión] (2013), 'Versión taquigráfica 2199', 1 July, https://parlamento.gub.uy/documentosyleyes/ficha-asunto/110651/tramite.

CPSC [Santa Cruz Civic Committee] (2014), 'Modelo de Desarrollo Cruceño', https://www.comiteprosantacruz.org.bo/documento/modelo-de-desarrollo-cruceno/.

CPSC [Santa Cruz Civic Committee] (2019), '1950: Fundación del Comité pro Santa Cruz', https://www.comiteprosantacruz.org.bo/announcement/1950-fundacion-del-comite-pro-santa-cruz/.

Crabtree, J. and A. Chaplin (2013), *Bolivia: Processes of Change* (London, Zed Books).

Crabtree, J. and I. Crabtree-Condor (2012), 'The Politics of Extractive Industries in the Central Andes', in *Social Conflict, Economic Development and Extractive Industry: Evidence from South America*, ed. A. Bebbington (London, Routledge), pp. 46–64.

256   *Bibliography*

Crabtree, J. and L. Whitehead (2008), *Unresolved Tensions: Bolivia Past and Present* (Pittsburgh, University of Pittsburgh Press).

Crenzel, E. (2008), *La historia política del Nunca Más: La memoria de los desaparecidos en la Argentina* (Buenos Aires, Siglo Veintiuno).

Crenzel, E. (2020), 'Four Cases under Examination: Human Rights and Justice in Argentina under the Macri Administration', *Modern Languages Open*, 26:1, 1–13.

Creswell, J. W. (2007), *Qualitative Inquiry and Research Design: Choosing among Five Approaches*, 2nd edn (London, Sage).

CRR [Centro de Derechos Reproductivos] (n.d.), 'FIV en Costa Rica', https://reproductiv erights.org/sites/default/files/documents/FIV-EN-COSTA-RICA_SPN.pdf.

Crumper, P. and T. Lewis (2019), 'Human Rights and Religious Litigation: Faith in the Law?', *Oxford Journal of Law and Religion*, 8, 121–50.

Cruz, T. and M. Lee (2017), 'In Trump Era, It's Time to Reassess Western Hemisphere Alliances', *Houston Chronicle*, 22 June.

Cunha Filho, C. M., A. L. Coelho, and F. I. Perez Flores (2013), 'A Right-to-Left Policy Switch? An Analysis of the Honduran Case under Manuel Zelaya', *International Political Science Review*, 34:5, 519–42.

Cunningham, D. (2004), *There's Something Happening Here: The New Left, the Klan, and FBI Counterintelligence* (London, California University Press).

Curiel, O. (2013), 'La nación heterosexual: Análisis del discurso jurídico y el régimen heterosexual desde la antropología de la dominación', *Maguaré*, 27:1, 310–13.

da Costa, O. B. R. (2020), 'Mais que vencedores: As dinâmicas socioeconômicas nas/das igrejas neopentecostais', *Revista idere*, 12:3, 271–85.

Dada, C. (2016), 'Por aquí pasó Berta Cáceres', *El Faro*, https://elfaro.net/es/201609/centro america/19291/Por-aqui-paso-berta-caceres.htm.

DANE [Departamento Administrativo Nacional de Estadística, Colombia] (2005), 'La visibilización estadística de los grupos étnicos colombianos', https://www.dane.gov.co/ files/censo2005/etnia/sys/visibilidad_estadistica_etnicos.pdf.

Daniels, J. (2009), *Cyber Racism: White Supremacy Online and the New Attack on Civil Rights* (New York, Rowman & Littlefield).

Davis, D. (1999), 'The Power of Distance: Re-Theorizing Social Movements in Latin America', *Theory and Society*, 28:4, 585–638.

Davis, M. (2006), *City of Quartz: Excavating the Future in Los Angeles* (London, Verso).

Davis, S. and J. Straubhaar (2020), 'Producing Antipetismo: Media Activism and the Rise of the Radical, Nationalist Right in Contemporary Brazil', *International Communication Gazette*, 82:1, 82–100.

De la Dehesa, R. (2010), *Queering the Public Sphere in Mexico and Brazil* (Hanover, NH, Duke University Press).

Dell'Omo, A. (2021), 'The Anti-Gender Movement', Right Rising,13 April, https://rightris ing.fireside.fm/episode21.

Detrás de Cámaras DTC (2016), 'Marcha 10/08/16 – Abanderados por la Familia', YouTube, 18 August, https://www.youtube.com/watch?v=iOqlLTfp2uI.

Diani, M. (1992), 'The Concept of Social Movement', *Sociological Review*, 40:1, 1–25.

Diaria (2017), 'Qué pasa con la ley de cuotas para personas afro', *La Diaria*, 27 January, https://ladiaria.com.uy/articulo/2017/1/que-pasa-con-la-ley-de-cuotas-para-perso nas-afro/.

Diario (1978), "Remodelación del Puerto de Montevideo," *El Diario*, 7 December, 4.

Dias, T., M. von Bülow, and D. Gobbi (2021), 'Populist Framing Mechanisms and the Rise of Right-Wing Activism in Brazil', *Latin American Politics and Society*, 63:3, 69–92.

Bibliography

do Nascimento Cunha, M. (2013), 'The Place of Media in the Process of Imaginary Constructions of the "Enemy" in Marco Feliciano Case', *Comunicação, midia e consumo*, 10:29, 51–76.

Domínguez Blanco, M. A. (2020), '"Nosotros también": Sentimientos queer y políticas de odio amoroso hacia la adopción igualitaria en Colombia', *Latin American Studies Association Forum*, 52:1, 37–41.

dos Santos Gonzaga, A. and D. R. Brasil (2020), 'Ativismo judicial: Meio necessário para criação e efetivação dos direitos fundamentais nas relações homoafetivas/Judicial Activism: The Necessary Way for Creating and Enforcing the Fundamental Rights in the Homoaffective Relations', *Brazilian Journal of Development*, 6:1, 1010–28.

dos Santos Sousa, D. D. (2020), 'Das casas ao congresso, igrejas nos lares: Um estudo sobre o modelo de células na igreja do evangelho quadrangular em santarém-pará', *Revista labirinto (unir)*, 32, 167–89.

Dreifuss, R. A. (1981), *1964: A conquista do estado: Ação política, poder e golpe de classe* (Petrópolis, Vozes), https://docero.com.br/doc/nec00vc.

Dunkerley, J. (2007), *Bolivia: Revolution and the Power of History in the Present* (London, Institute for the Study of the Americas).

Eaton, K. (2007), 'Backlash in Bolivia: Regional Autonomy as a Reaction against Indigenous Mobilisation', *Politics & Society*, 35, 71–102.

Eaton, K. (2011), 'Conservative Autonomy Movements: Territorial Dimensions of Ideological Conflict in Bolivia and Ecuador', *Comparative Politics*, 43:3, 291–310.

ECOS Latinamérica (2018), 'La Ley de Afrodescendientes está "en falta" desde su creación', 2 July, http://ecos.la/LA/13/Sociedad/2018/07/02/24734/la-ley-de-afrodescendientes-esta-en-falta-desde-su-creacion/.

Elquintopoder.cl (2016), 'Detenidos desaparecidos y no nacidos: Encuentre las diferencias', https://www.elquintopoder.cl/justicia/detenidos-desaparecidos-y-no-nacidos-encuen tre-las-diferencias/.

Encarnación, O. G. (2016), *Out in the Periphery: Latin America's Gay Rights Revolution* (Oxford, Oxford University Press).

Encyclopedia.com (2018), 'Counter-Movement' (Oxford University Press), https://www. encyclopedia.com/social-sciences/dictionaries-thesauruses-pictures-and-press-relea ses/counter-movement#:~:text=counter%2Dmovement%20An%20organized%20r esponse,or%20fronts%20for%20interest%20groups.

Enloe, C. (1991), 'Womenandchildren: Propaganda Tools of Patriarchy', in *Mobilizing Democracy: Changing the US Role in the Middle East* (Monroe, ME: Common Courage Press), 29–32.

Epicentro (2015), 'Gigantografías que comparan el aborto con torturados en dictadura causan polémica', 3 October, https://www.epicentrochile.com/2015/10/03/gigantograf ias-que-comparan-el-aborto-con-torturados-en-dictadura-causan-polemica/.

Epp, C. R. (1998), *The Rights Revolution: Lawyers, Activists, and Supreme Courts in Comparative Perspective* (Chicago, University of Chicago Press).

Espectador (2016), 'La carta con la que colegios e iglesias se oponen a la Corte por temas LGBTI', *El Espectador*, 5 August, https://www.elespectador.com/colombia/mas-regio nes/la-carta-con-la-que-colegios-e-iglesias-se-oponen-a-la-corte-por-temas-lgbti-arti cle-647547/.

Evangélico Digital (2019), 'Fátima Oliva: En la OEA se promueve destruir la familia', 27 June, https://www.evangelicodigital.com/latinoamerica/8315/fatima-oliva-en-la-oea-promue ven-la-confrontacion-hombre-mujer-y-la-destruccion-de-la-familia.

Fabricant, N. (2009), 'Performative Politics: The Camba Countermovement in Eastern Bolivia', *American Ethnologist*, 36:4, 768–83.

Fabricant, N. and N. Postero (2013), 'Contested Bodies, Contested States: Performance, Emotions, and New Forms of Regional Governance in Santa Cruz, Bolivia', *Journal of Latin American and Caribbean Anthropology*, 18:2, 187–211.

Fabricant, N. and N. Postero (2014), 'Performing the "Wounded Indian": A New Platform of Democracy and Human Rights in Bolivia's Autonomy Movement', *Identities*, 21:4, 395–411.

Fang, L. (2017), 'Sphere of Influence: How American Libertarians are Remaking Latin American Politics', *The Intercept*, August.

FARC-EP [Fuerzas Armadas Revolucionarias de Colombia – Ejército del Pueblo] (2016), 'Comunicado conjunto #82', 24 July, https://www.cancilleria.gov.co/sites/default/files/comunicadoconjunto82.pdf.

Farivar, M. (2021), 'Researchers: More than a Dozen Extremist Groups Took Part in Capitol Riots', *VOA*, 16 January, https://www.voanews.com/2020-usa-votes/researchers-more-dozen-extremist-groups-took-part-capitol-riots.

Farthing, L. and O. Arigho-Stiles (2019), 'Bolivia's Tragic Turmoil', *NACLA Report on the Americas*, 15 November.

Fassin, D. (2016), *La razón humanitaria: Una historia moral en el tiempo presente* (Buenos Aires, Prometeo).

Fassin, D. and R. Rechtman (2009), *The Empire of Trauma: An Inquiry into the Condition of Victimhood* (Princeton, Princeton University Press).

Fassin, E. (2016), 'Gender and the Problem of Universals: Catholic Mobilizations and Sexual Democracy in France' *Religion & Gender*, 6:2, 173–86.

Fassin, E. (2020), 'Anti-Gender Campaigns, Populism, and Neoliberalism in Europe and Latin America', *LASA Forum: The Quarterly Newsletter of the Latin American Studies Association*, 51:2, 67–71.

Faúndes, A. and J. Barzelatto (2006), *The Human Drama of Abortion: A Global Search for Consensus* (Nashville, Vanderbilt University Press).

Feldman, M. (2019), 'On Radical Right Mainstreaming in Europe and the US', in *Europe at the Crossroads: Confronting Populist, Nationalist, and Global Challenges*, ed. P. Bevelander and Ruth Wodak (Lund, Nordic Academic Press).

Feldmann, A. E. (2019), 'Colombia's Polarizing Peace Efforts', in *Democracies Divided: The Global Challenge of Political Polarization*, ed. T. Carothers and A. O'Donehue (Washington, DC, Brookings Institute).

Ferreira, M. G. M. and M. Fuks (2021), 'O hábito de frequentar cultos como mecanismo de mobilização eleitoral: O voto evangélico em Bolsonaro em 2018', *Revista brasileira de ciência política*, 34, 1–27.

FIDH [International Federation for Human Rights] (2008), *Separatistas y racistas desatan ola de violencia contra autoridades e instituciones del Gobierno de Evo Morales* (Bolivia, FIDH).

FLACSO-Chile [Facultad Latinoamericana de Ciencias Sociales Chile] (2001), *Percepciones y actitudes de las y los chilenos a principios del siglo XXI: Encuesta nacional de opinión pública FLACSO 2001* (Santiago de Chile, FLACSO-Chile).

Flesken, A. (2018), 'Identity Change in a Context of Intergroup Threat: Regional Identity Mobilisation in Bolivia', *Politics*, 38:1, 51–67.

FMO [Netherlands Development Finance Institution] (2016), 'FMO Suspends All Activities in Honduras Effective Immediately', https://www.fmo.nl/news-detail/9483b943-4b56-487e-b392-a1464c781a2b/fmo-suspends-all-activities-in-honduras-effective-immediately.

FMO [Netherlands Development Finance Institution] (2017), 'FMO and Finnfund Finalize Exit Agua Zarca', https://www.fmo.nl/news-detail/21a7c615-a32b-471c-9378-60317196daf6/fmo-and-finnfund-finalize-exit-agua-zarca.

Bibliography 259

Fraser, N. (1997), *Justice Interruptus: Critical Reflections on the Postsocialist Condition* (London, Routledge).

Fraser, N. (2003), 'Social Justice in the Age of Identity Politics: Redistribution, Recognition, and Participation', in *Redistribution or Recognition? A Political–Philosophical Exchange*, ed. N. Fraser and A. Honneth (London, Verso), pp. 7–109.

Friedman, E. J. (2003), 'Gendering the Agenda: The Impact of the Transnational Women's Rights Movement at the UN Conferences of the 1990s', *Women's Studies International Forum*, 26:4, 313–31.

Friedman, E. J. and C. Tabbush (2018), 'Contesting the Pink Tide', in *Seeking Rights from the Left*, ed. E. J. Friedman (Durham, NC, Duke University Press), 1–47.

Front Line Defenders (2021), 'Global Analysis', https://www.frontlinedefenders.org/sites/default/files/2021_global_analysis_-_final.pdf.

GAIPE [Grupo Asesor Internacional de Personas Expertas] (2017), 'Dam Violence: The Plan that Killed Berta Cáceres', November, https://www.gaipe.net/wp-content/uploads/2017/10/GAIPE-Report-English.pdf.

Galeano, E. (1987), *Memory of Fire*, Vol. II, *Faces and Masks* (New York, Pantheon Books).

Galeano, E. (2013), *Soccer in Sun and Shadows* (New York, Nation Books).

Galston, W. A. (2022), 'What Are Americans Thinking about the January 6 Hearings?', *FixGov* (Brookings Institution), 23 June, https://www.brookings.edu/blog/fixgov/2022/06/23/what-are-americans-thinking-about-the-january-6-hearings/.

Garbagnoli, S. (2016), 'Against the Heresy of Immanence: Vatican's "Gender" as a New Rhetorical Device against the Denaturalization of the Sexual Order', *Religion & Gender*, 6:2, 187–204.

Garcés, F. (2010), *El pacto de unidad y el proceso de construccion de una propuesta de constitucion politica de estado* (La Paz, Centro Cooperativo Sueco).

Garretón, M., A. Joignat, N. Somma, and T. Campos (2018), *Informe annual observatorio de conflictos 2018*, Notas COES de política pública, 17 (Santiago de Chile, Centro de Estudios de Conflicto y Cohesión Social).

Gatti, G. (2011), 'De un continente al otro: El desaparecido transnacional, la cultura humanitaria y las víctimas totales en tiempos de guerra global', *Política y sociedad*, 3, 519–36.

Gibson, E. (1992), 'Conservative Electoral Movements and Democratic Politics: Core Constituencies, Coalition-Building, and the Latin American Electoral Right', in *The Right and Democracy in Latin America*, ed. D. A. Chalmers, M. do C. C. de Souza, and A. A. Boron (New York, Praeger-Greenwood), pp. 13–42.

Glendon, M. A. (1995), 'Declaración de interpretación del término "género" por la santa sede', *L'Osservatore Romano*, 38, 1.

Global Witness (2017), 'Honduras: The Deadliest Country in the World for Environmental Activism', https://www.globalwitness.org/en/campaigns/environmental-activists/honduras-el-país-más-peligroso-del-mundo-para-el-activismo-ambiental/.

Gold, T. and A. M. Peña (2021), 'The Rise of the Contentious Right: Digitally Intermediated Linkage Strategies in Argentina and Brazil', *Latin American Politics and Society*, 63:3, 93–118.

Goldentul, A. (2016), 'De "hijos y nietos de presos políticos" a "puentes para la legalidad": La conformación de una nueva agrupación de familiares de agentes de represión en Argentina (2008–2016)', paper presented at the seminar on *La investigación en proceso*, GESHAL, 24 November.

Goldstein, A. A. (2019), 'The New Far-Right in Brazil and the Construction of a Right-Wing Order', *Latin American Perspectives*, 46:4, 245–62.

Gómez-Suárez, A. (2016), *El triunfo del No: La paradoja emocional detrás del plebiscito* (Bogotá, Icono).

260 *Bibliography*

Gould, D. B. (2009), *Moving Politics: Emotion and ACT UP's Fight against AIDS* (Chicago, University of Chicago Press).

Government of Guatemala (2022), 'Guatemala es oficialmente reconocida como Capital Provida de Iberoamérica', https://www.maga.gob.gt/guatemala-es-oficialmente-reconocida-como-capital-provida-de-iberoamerica/.

Goyena, P. V. and E. Canstatt (1874), 'Ley declarando que no hay esclavos en todo el territorio de la Republica', Law no. 242, 12 December, in P. V. Goyena and E. Canstatt, *La legislación vigente de la República Oriental del Uruguay*, Vol. I (Montevideo, Imprenta de el Uruguay).

GPO [US Government Publishing Office] (2018), 'Advancing US Interests through the Organization of American States: Hearing before the Subcommittee on the Western Hemisphere of the Committee on Foreign Affairs House of Representatives. One Hundred Fifteenth Congress, Second Session', https://www.govinfo.gov/content/pkg/CHRG-115hhrg28645/html/CHRG-115hhrg28645.htm.

Graff, A. (2014), 'Report from the Gender Trenches: War against "Genderism" in Poland', *European Journal of Women's Studies*, 21:4, 431–6.

Graff, A. and E. Korolczuk (2017), ' "Worse than Communism and Nazism Put Together": War on Gender in Poland', in *Anti-Gender Campaigns in Europe: Mobilizing against Equality*, ed. R. Kuhar and D. Paternotte (London, Rowman & Littlefield), pp. 175–94.

Graff, A., R. Kapur, and S. D. Walters (2019), 'Introduction: Gender and the Rise of the Global Right', *Signs*, 44:3, 1–22.

Greene, J. C. (2008), 'Is Mixed Methods Social Inquiry a Distinctive Methodology?', *Journal of Mixed Methods Research*, 2:1, 7–22.

Greenspan, B. (2018), *The Greenspan Report*, https://casocaceres.com/en/el-informe-greenspan/.

Griffin, R. (2017), 'Interregnum or Endgame? The Radical Right in the "Post-Fascist" Era', in *The Populist Radical Right: A Reader* (New York, Routledge), pp. 15–27.

Grisaffi, T. (2010), 'We Are Originarios ... "We Just Aren't from Here": Coca Leaf and Identity Politics in the Chapare, Bolivia', *Bulletin of Latin American Research*, 29:4, 425–39.

Grugel, J. and L. B. Fontana (2019), 'Human Rights and the Pink Tide in Latin America: Which Rights Matter?', *Development and Change*, 50:3, 707–34.

Guilhot, N. (2011), '¿Limitando la soberanía o produciendo gubernamentalidad? Dos modelos de derechos humanos en el discurso político de Estados Unidos', *Revista política*, 49:1, 219–41.

Gustafson, B. (2006), 'Spectacles of Autonomy and Crisis; or, What Bulls and Beauty Queens Have to Do with Regionalism in Eastern Bolivia', *Journal of Latin American Anthropology*, 11:2, 351–79.

Gustafson, B. (2016). 'Bolivia after the "No" Vote', *NACLA Report on the Americas*, 7 March.

Hale, C. (2002), 'Does Multiculturalism Menace? Governance, Cultural Rights, and the Politics of Identity in Guatemala', *Journal of Latin American Studies*, 34:3, 485–524.

Hale, C. (2005), 'Neoliberal Multiculturalism: The Remaking of Cultural Rights and Racial Dominance in Central America', *PoLAR: Political and Legal Anthropology Review*, 28:1, 10–28.

Hale, C. (2006), *Más que un Indio: Racial Ambivalence and Neoliberal Multiculturalism in Guatemala* (New Mexico, School of American Research Press).

Hale, C. (2007). 'Rethinking Indigenous Politics in the Era of the "Indio permitido" ', *NACLA Report on the Americas*, 38:2, 16–21.

Bibliography

Hale, C. R. (2011), 'Resistencia para que? Territory, Autonomy and Neoliberal Entanglements in the "Empty Spaces" of Central America', *Economy and Society*, 40:2, 184–210.

Harvey, D. (2003), *The New Imperialism* (Oxford, Oxford University Press).

HateLab (n.d.), website, https://hatelab.net/.

Hedström, P. and P. Bearman (2017), *The Oxford Handbook of Analytical Sociology* (Oxford, Oxford University Press).

Hedström, P. and R. Swedberg (1998), *Social Mechanisms: An Analytical Approach to Social Theory* (Cambridge, Cambridge University Press).

Heinz, J. P., A. Paik, and A. Southworth (2003), 'Lawyers for Conservative Causes: Clients, Ideology, and Social Distance', *Law and Society Review*, 37:1, 5–50.

Heraldo (2016), '"La ministra Parody miente", dice Alejandro Ordóñez', *El Heraldo*, 9 August, https://www.elheraldo.co/nacional/la-ministra-parody-miente-dice-alejandro-ordonez-277191.

Hernández, Á. ['@AngelaHer'] (2016), 'Nos querian imponer la IDEOLOGIA DE GENERO en los colegios', Twitter, 27 August, https://twitter.com/angelaher/status/76963876949 4491136.

Hernández, T. K. (2012), 'Affirmative Action in the Americas', *Americas Quarterly*, July 24, https://www.americasquarterly.org/fulltextarticle/affirmative-action-in-the-americas/.

Hernández, T. K. (2013), *Racial Subordination in Latin America: The Role of the State, Customary Law, and the New Civil Rights Response* (New York, Cambridge University Press).

Hess, D. and B. Martin (2006), 'Repression, Backfire, and the Theory of Transformative Events', *Mobilization*, 11:2, 249–67.

Heumann, S. (2014), 'Gender, Sexuality, and Politics: Rethinking the Relationship between Feminism and Sandinismo in Nicaragua', *Social Politics: International Studies in Gender, State & Society*, 21:2, 290–314.

Hirabahasi, G. and Cury, T. (2022), Justiça confirma prisão de pastores suspeitos de esquema de corrupção no MEC', CNN Brasil, 22 June, https://www.cnnbrasil.com.br/politica/justica-confirma-prisao-de-pastores-suspeitos-de-esquema-de-corrupcao-no-mec/.

Hirsch-Hoefler, S. and C. Mudde (2013), 'Right-Wing Movements', in *The Wiley-Blackwell Encyclopedia of Social and Political Movements*, ed. D. Snow, D. della Porta, B. Klandermans, and D. McAdam (Hoboken, NJ, Wiley-Blackwell), pp. 1–8.

Holmes, H. A. (1944), 'Ildefonso Pereda Valdés y su libro "Negro esclavos y negros libres"', *Revista Iberoamericana*, 8:15, 21–30.

Honneth, A. (2003), 'Redistribution as Recognition: A Response to Nancy Fraser', in *Redistribution or Recognition? A Political–Philosophical Exchange*, ed. N. Fraser and A. Honneth (London, Verso), pp. 110–97.

Hooker, J. (2005), 'Indigenous Inclusion/Black Exclusion: Race, Ethnicity and Multicultural Citizenship in Latin America', *Journal of Latin American Studies*, 37, 285–310.

Horton, L. (2006), 'Contesting State Multiculturalisms: Indigenous Land Struggles in Eastern Panama', *Journal of Latin American Studies*, 38, 829–58.

Hoyos Castañeda, I. M. (2016), 'El "Enfoque de género" en el acuerdo final para la terminación del conflicto y la construcción de una paz estable y duradera', https://www.las2orillas.co/wp-content/uploads/2016/10/ENFOQUE-DE-GE%CC%81NERO-EN-ACUERDO-FINAL-LA-HABANA.pdf.

HRP [UNDP/UNFPA/UNICEF/WHO/World Bank Special Programme of Research, Development and Research Training in Human Reproduction] (2022), *Global Abortion Policies Database*, https://abortion-policies.srhr.org.

Htun, M. (2003), *Sex and the State: Abortion, Divorce, and the Family under Latin American Dictatorships and Democracies* (Cambridge, Cambridge University Press).

262 *Bibliography*

Htun, M. (2004), 'From "Racial Democracy" to Affirmative Action: Changing State Policy on Race in Brazil', *Latin American Research Review*, 39:1, 60–89.

Htun, M. (2016), *Inclusion without Representation: Gender Quotas and Ethnic Reservations in Latin America* (Cambridge, Cambridge University Press).

Hunter, W. (1997), *Eroding Military Influence in Brazil: Politicians against Soldiers* (Chapel Hill, University of North Carolina Press).

Hunter, W. and T. J. Power (2019), 'Bolsonaro and Brazil's Illiberal Backlash', *Journal of Democracy*, 30:1, 68–82.

IACHR [Inter-American Commission on Human Rights] (2013), 'Annual Report, Chapter IV, Honduras', http://www.oas.org/en/iachr/docs/annual/2013/TOC.asp.

IACHR [Inter-American Commission on Human Rights] (2017), 'IACHR Regrets Ban on Gender Education in Paraguay', 15 December, https://www.oas.org/en/iachr/media_center/PReleases/2017/208.asp.

IACHR [Inter-American Commission on Human Rights] (2018), 'Advances and Challenges towards the Recognition of the Rights ofLGBT+ Persons in the Americas', OEA/Ser. L/V/II. 170 Doc. 184, December, https://www.oas.org/en/iachr/reports/pdfs/LGBT+-RecognitionRights2019.pdf.

IACHR [Inter-American Commission on Human Rights] (2022), 'CIDH Saluda anuncio de veto presidencial a proyecto de ley "Protección de la vida y la familia" en Guatemala', March, http://www.oas.org/es/CIDH/jsForm/?File=/es/cidh/prensa/comunicados/2022/052.asp.

IACHR [Inter-American Commission on Human Rights] and OHCHR [Office of the High Commissioner for Human Rights] (2017), 'IACHR and OHCHR Express Concern over Post-Election Violence in Honduras', http://www.oas.org/en/iachr/media_center/PReleases/2017/197.asp.

IBGE [Institute Brasileiro de Geografia e Estatistica] (2010), 'Censo demográfico. Principais resultados: Caracteristicas da populaçao e dos domicilios', https://www.ibge.gov.br/estatisticas/sociais/populacao/9662-censo-demografico-2010.html?edicao=10503&t=destaques.

IBGE [Institute Brasileiro de Geografia e Estatistica] (2010), 'Censo demográfico. Principais resultados: Sinopse', https://www.ibge.gov.br/estatisticas/sociais/populacao/9662-censo-demografico-2010.html?edicao=9673&t=destaques.

ICSO-UDP [Instituto de Investigación en Ciencias Sociales, Universidad Diego Portales] (2015), 'Encuesta Nacional UDP 2015', https://www.duna.cl/media/2015/11/Todos-los-Resultados-Encuesta-UDP-2015-1.pdf.

Ideaspaz (2016), 'El termómetro de la paz', http://www.ideaspaz.org/especiales/termometro/.

Idler, A. (2016), 'Why the Real Test for Colombia's Peace Process Begins after the Demobilisation Process', *Monkey Cage*, 8 September.

Ignazi, P. (2003), *Extreme Right Parties in Western Europe* (Oxford, Oxford University Press).

ILO [International Labour Organization] (1989), 'C169: Indigenous and Tribal Peoples Convention', https://www.ilo.org/dyn/normlex/en/f?p=NORMLEXPUB:55:0::NO::P55_TYPE,P55_LANG,P55_DOCUMENT,P55_NODE:REV,en,C169,/Document.

ILO [International Labour Organization] (1989), 'Indigenous and Tribal Peoples Convention (no. 169), https://www.ilo.org/dyn/normlex/en/f?p=NORMLEXPUB:12100:0::NO:12100:P12100_INSTRUMENT_ID:312314:NO.

INE [Insituto Nacional de Estadística Uruguay] (2011), 'Census 2011: Manual del Censista', http://www3.ine.gub.uy/c/document_library/get_file?uuid=0025b663-abc5-4ab4-8517-e3302eb1f090&groupId=10181.

Bibliography 263

InformAborto (2014), 'Camión de InformAborto sigue mostrando la realidad del #Aborto en el centro de Santiago!', Facebook, https://www.facebook.com/informaborto/photos/835562923161176.

InformAborto (2015), 'Aborto es matar a un niño fruto de una violación', Facebook, https://www.facebook.com/informaborto/photos/1023363127714487.

InformAborto (2016), 'InformAborto en el Congreso mostrando la realidad de un aborto legal y seguro', Facebook, https://www.facebook.com/informaborto/photos/1112769368773862.

International Justice Resource Center (2019), 'US Resists International Oversight, Reduces IACHR Funding over Reproductive Rights', 8 April, https://ijrcenter.org/2019/04/08/u-s-resists-international-oversight-reduces-iachr-funding-over-reproductive-rights/.

Isgleas, D. (2019), 'El Estado sigue lejos de cumplir la cuota de empleados "afro"', *El País*, July, https://www.elpfdiariaais.com.uy/informacion/politica/sigue-lejos-cumplir-cuota-empleados-afro.html.

ISHR [International Service for Human Rights] (2015), 'Human Rights Defenders and Corporate Accountability', http://www.ishr.ch/sites/default/files/documents/business_and_human_rights_monitor_-_english_november_2015-final_last_version-2.pdf.

Iskenderian Aguilera, E. (2010), 'Un Período Defensivo Para La Burguesía Cruceña: Ataques Confirmados o Atribuídos a La Unión Juvenil Cruceñista (Ujc)', *Separata Atrículo Primero*.

Jackson, J. E. and K. B. Warren (2005), 'Indigenous Movements in Latin America, 1992–2004: Controversies, Ironies, New Directions', *Annual Review of Anthropology*, 34:1, 549–73.

Jaffrelot, C. (2021), *Modi's India: Hindu Nationalism and the Rise of Ethnic Democracy* (Princeton, Princeton University Press).

James, N. and J. Hardy (2021), 'Is Pandemic Isolation Pushing People towards Extremism?', *openDemocracy*, 13 May, https://www.opendemocracy.net/en/countering-radical-right/pandemic-isolation-pushing-people-towards-extremism/.

Jaspers, J. M. (1997), *The Art of Moral Protest: Culture, Biography, and Creativity in Social Movements* (Chicago, University of Chicago Press).

Jelin, E. (2010), '¿Victimas, familiares o ciudadanos/as? Las luchas por la legitimidad de la palabra', in *Los desaparecidos en la Argentina: Memorias, representaciones e ideas (1983–2008)*, ed. E. Crenzel (Buenos Aires, Editorial Biblos), pp. 227–49.

Jelin, E. and P. de Azcárate (1991), 'Memoria y política: Movimientos de derechos humanos y construcción democrática', *América Latina hoy*, 1, 29–38.

Kajsiu, B. (2019), 'The Colombian Right: The Political Ideology and Mobilization of Uribismo', *Canadian Journal of Latin American and Caribbean Studies*, 44:2, 204–24.

Kampwirth, K. (2008), 'Neither Left nor Right: Sandinismo in the Anti-Feminist Era', *NACLA Report on the Americas*, 41:1, 30–4.

Kane, G. (2008), 'Abortion Law Reform in Latin America: Lessons for Advocacy', *Gender and Development*, 16:2, 361–75.

Karell, D. (2021), 'Online Extremism and Offline Harm', *Social Sciences Research Council*, 1 June, https://items.ssrc.org/extremism-online/online-extremism-and-offline-harm/.

Kay, C. and M. Urioste (2005), *Latifundios, avasallamientos y autonomías* (Santa Cruz, Fundación Tierra).

Keane, J. T. (2020), 'Explainer: Can a Priest or a Member of a Religious Order Publicly Endorse a Political Candidate?', *America: The Jesuit Review*, 3 September.

Bibliography

Keck, M. and K. Sikkink (1998), *Activists beyond Borders: Advocacy Networks in International Politics* (Ithaca, Cornell University Press).

Kenny, M. L. (2018), *Deeply Rooted in the Present: Heritage, Memory, and Identity in Brazilian Quilombos* (Toronto, University of Toronto Press).

Kibuuka, B. G. L. (2020), 'Complicity and Synergy between Bolsonaro and Brazilian Evangelicals in COVID-19 Times: Adherence to Scientific Negationism for Political Religious Reasons', *International Journal of Latin American Religions*, 4, 288–317.

Kilgarriff, A., V. Baisa, J. Bušta, *et al.* (2014), 'The Sketch Engine: Ten Years On', *Lexicography*, 1:1, 7–36.

Kitroeff, N. (2022), 'The Mexican Model of Abortion Rights', *The Daily* (*New York Times* podcast), 17 May, https://www.nytimes.com/2022/05/17/podcasts/the-daily/mexico-abortion-roe-v-wade.html.

Klein, H. S. (1992), *Bolivia: The Evolution of a Multi-Ethnic Society*, 2nd edn (Oxford, Oxford University Press).

Kohl, B. (2010), 'Bolivia under Morales: A Work in Progress', *Latin American Perspectives*, 37, 107–22.

Koopmans, R. and S. Olzak (2004), 'Discursive Opportunities and the Evolution of Right-Wing Violence in Germany', *American Journal of Sociology* 110:1, 198–230.

Koopmans, R. and P. Statham (1999), 'Ethnic and Civic Conceptions of Nationhood and the Differential Success of the Extreme Right in Germany and Italy', in *How Social Movements Matter*, ed. M. Giugni, D. McAdam, and C. Tilly (London, University of Minnesota Press), pp. 225–51.

Kopecky, P. and C. Mudde (2003), *Uncivil Society? Contentious Politics in Post-Communist Europe* (London, Routledge).

Korol, C. (2018), *Las revoluciones de Berta* (Buenos Aires, América Libre).

Korolczuk, E. and A. Graff (2018), 'Gender as "Ebola from Brussels": The Anticolonial Frame and the Rise of Illiberal Populism', *Signs: Journal of Women in Culture and Society*, 43:4, 797–821.

Kováts, E. and A. Pető (2017), 'Anti-Gender Discourse in Hungary: A Discourse without a Movement?', in *Anti-Gender Campaigns in Europe*, ed. D. Paternotte and R. Kuhar (London, Rowman & Littlefield), pp. 117–31.

Krausova, A. (2012), 'Resisting Redistribution with Recognition: Conflicting Multicultural Paradigms in Regional Resistance to Bolivia's State Reforms', M.Phil. dissertation, University of Oxford.

Krausova, A. (2018), *What Social Movements Ask for, and How They Ask for It: Strategic Claiming and Framing, and the Successes and Failures of Indigenous Movements in Latin America*, D.Phil. dissertation, University of Oxford.

Krausova, A. (2020), 'Latin American Social Movements: Bringing Strategy Back In', *Latin American Research Review*, 55:4, 1–11.

Krystalli, R. and K. Theidon (2016), 'Here's How Attention to Gender Affected Colombia's Peace Process', *Washington Post*, 9 October, https://www.washingtonpost.com/news/monkey-cage/wp/2016/10/09/heres-how-attention-to-gender-affected-colombias-peace-process/.

La Tercera (2015), 'Diputada UDI Marisol Turres: "Hay violaciones que no son violentas"', *La Tercera*, 16 September, https://www.latercera.com/noticia/diputada-udi-marisol-turres-hay-violaciones-que-no-son-violentas/.

La Tercera (2016), 'Las polémicas frases que marcaron el debate de la despenalización del aborto', *La Tercera*, 16 March, http://www.t13.cl/noticia/politica/las-frases-marcaron-discusion-despenalizacion-del-aborto.

Bibliography

La Tercera (2017), 'Elisa Walker: "Este proyecto es un gesto de humanidad y creo que el Catolicismo es parte de eso"', *La Tercera*, 27 August, https://www.latercera.com/noti cia/elisa-walker-este-proyecto-gesto-humanidad-creo-catolicismo-parte/.

Lakhani, N. (2020), *Who Killed Berta Cáceres? Dams, Death Squads, and an Indigenous Defender's Battle for the Planet* (New York, Verso).

Lamas, M. (2015), *El largo camino hacia la ILE: Mi versión de los hechos* (Mexico City, Universidad Nacional Autónoma de México).

Lancaster, R. N. (1992), *Life Is Hard: Machismo, Danger and the Intimacy of Power in Nicaragua* (Berkeley, University of California Press).

Lancaster, R. N. (2011), *Sex Panic and the Punitive State* (Berkeley, University of California Press).

Lankford, J. (2018), 'Senator Lankford Leads Letter to Secretary Pompeo', 21 December, https://www.lankford.senate.gov/news/press-releases/senator-lankford-leads-letter-to-secretary-pompeo.

Laqueur, T. (1989), 'Bodies, Details, and the Humanitarian Narrative', in *The New Cultural History*, ed. L. Hunt (Berkeley, University of California Press), pp. 176–204.

Las2orillas (2016), 'Las cartillas de orientación sexual que Parody le sacó en la cara a Uribe', 16 August, https://www.las2orillas.co/las-cartillas-de-orientacion-sexual-que-parody-le-saco-en-la-cara-a-uribe/#.

Leão, D. (2012), 'Cotidiano – Ser especial', *Folha de São Paulo*, 25 December, https://www1.folha.uol.com.br/paywall/login.shtml?https://www1.folha.uol.com.br/fsp/cotidi ano/80046-ser-especial.shtml.

Lehmann, D. (2021), 'Ritual, Text and Politics: The Evangelical Mindset and Political Polarisation', in *A Horizon of (Im)possibilities*, ed. K. Hatzikidi and E. Dullo (London, University of London Press), pp. 103–20.

Lehoucq, F. (2020), 'Bolivia's Citizen Revolt', *Journal of Democracy*, 3, 130–44.

Leidig, E. (2020), 'The Far-Right Is Going Global', *Foreign Policy*, 21 January, https://foreignpolicy.com/2020/01/21/india-kashmir-modi-eu-hindu-nationalists-rss-the-far-right-is-going-global/.

Lemaitre, J. (2009), 'Love in the Time of Cholera: LGBT Rights in Colombia', *Sur: International Journal on Human Rights*, 6:11, 73–90.

Lemaitre, J. (2012), 'By Reason Alone: Catholicism, Constitutions, and Sex in the Americas', *International Journal of Constitutional Law*, 10:2, 493–511.

Lessa, F. (2022), *The Condor Trials: Transnational Repression and Human Rights in South America* (New Haven, Yale University Press).

Levitsky, S. and K. M. Roberts (2011), *The Resurgence of the Latin American Left* (Baltimore, Johns Hopkins University Press).

Loiola, J. R. A. (2020), 'Neopentecostalismo e a "teologia de gestão": Uma leitura sociológica do "ethos" religioso da Igreja Sara Nossa Terra no Distrito Federal (1992–2018)', Ph.D. dissertation, Universidad Estadual Paulista, São Paulo.

Londoño, F. (2016), 'Intervención en Comisión de Constitución, Legislación, Justicia y Reglamento del Senado de la República de Chile', 6 January, https://www.bcn.cl/historiadelaley/nc/historia-de-la-ley/6701/.

Loveman, M. (2014), *National Colors: Racial Classification and the State in Latin America* (New York, Oxford University Press).

Lowrey, K. (2006), '*Bolivia multiétnico y pluricultural*, Ten Years Later', *Latin American and Caribbean Ethnic Studies*, 1:1, 63–84.

Loxton, J. (2014), 'The Authoritarian Roots of New Right Party Success in Latin America', in *The Resilience of the Latin American Right*, ed. J. P. Luna and C. Rovira Kaltwasser (Baltimore, Johns Hopkins University Press), pp. 117–40.

266 *Bibliography*

Loxton, J. (2021), *Conservative Party-Building in Latin America: Authoritarian Inheritance and Counterrevolutionary Struggle* (Oxford, Oxford University Press).

Lucero, J. A. (2008), *Struggles of Voice: The Politics of Indigenous Representation in the Andes* (Pittsburgh, University of Pittsburgh Press).

Luna, Z. (2017), 'Who Speaks for Whom? (Mis) Representation and Authenticity in Social Movements', *Mobilization* 22:4, 435–50.

Luna, J. P. and C. Rovira Kaltwasser (2014), *The Resilience of the Latin American Right* (Baltimore, Johns Hopkins University Press).

Luz, J. de la (2013), interview in *Triunfadores: Negros Profesionales en el Uruguay*, ed. Pamela Laviña (Montevideo, Editorial Psicolibros Universitario, 2013), 109–15.

Ma, C. (2021), 'Mainstreaming Resentment: YouTube Celebrities and the Rhetoric of White Supremacy', *Social Sciences Research Council*, 13 April, https://items.ssrc.org/extrem ism-online/mainstreaming-resentment-youtube-celebrities-and-the-rhetoric-of-white-supremacy/.

Machado, M. D. D. C. (2012), 'Evangelicals and Politics in Brazil: The Case of Rio de Janeiro', *Religion, State and Society*, 40:1, 69–91.

MADR [Ministero de Agricultura y Desarrollo Rural] (1993), 'Ley 70 de 1993', 27 August, minagricultura.gov.co/Normatividad/Leyes/Ley%2070%20de%201993.pdf

Maira, G. and C. Carrera (2019), 'Estrategias feministas para la despenalización del aborto en Chile: La experiencia de la mesa acción por el aborto', in *Aborto en tres causales en Chile: Lecturas del proceso de despenalización*, ed. L. Casas and G. Maira Vargas (Santiago de Chile, Centro de Derechos Humanos UDP), pp. 181–202.

Malkin, E. (2018), 'They Were Jailed for Miscarriages: Now Campaign Aims to End Abortion Ban', *New York Times*, 9 April.

Marcos, A. (2016), 'Unas falsas cartillas sobre educación sexual culminan en marchas en defensa de la familia en Colombia', *El Pais*, 10 August, https://elpais.com/internacio nal/2016/08/10/colombia/1470835286_954924.html.

Markarian, V. (2004), 'De la lógica revolucionaria a las razones humanitarias: La izquierda uruguaya en el exilio y las redes transnacionales de derechos humanos (1972–1976)', *Cuadernos del CLAEH*, 89:2, 85–108.

Martin, L. (2013), *Rich People's Movements: Grassroots Campaigns to Untax the One Percent* (Oxford and New York, Oxford University Press).

Masci, D. (2014), 'Why Has Pentecostalism Grown So Dramatically in Latin America?', Pew Research Center, 14 November, https://www.pewresearch.org/fact-tank/2014/11/ 14/why-has-pentecostalism-grown-so-dramatically-in-latin-america/#:~:text=In%20 the%20early%2020th%20century,which%20resonated%20with%20many%20people.

Mason, C. (2019), 'Opposing Abortion to Protect Women: Transnational Strategy since the 1990s', *Signs*, 44:3, 665–92.

Matamala, M. I. (2014), 'Aborto en Chile: Cuerpos, derechos y libertades', in *Voces sobre el aborto: Ciudadanía de las mujeres, cuerpo y autonomía*, ed. Articulación Feminista por la Libertad de Decidir (AFLD) (Santiago de Chile, AFLD; Escuela de Salud Pública 'Dr. Salvador Allende G.', Facultad de Medicina, Universidad de Chile), pp. 7–20.

Mayka, L. and A. E. Smith (2021), 'The Grassroots Right in Latin America: Patterns, Causes, and Consequences', *Latin American Politics and Society*, 63:3, 1–31.

McAdam, D. (1982), *Political Process and the Development of Black Insurgency, 1930– 1970* (Chicago, University of Chicago Press).

McAdam, D., et al. (1996), *Comparative Perspectives on Social Movements: Political Opportunities, Mobilizing Structures, and Cultural Framings* (Cambridge, Cambridge University Press).

McCammon, H. J., H. D. Newman, C. Sanders Muse, C., and T. M. Terrell (2007), 'Movement Framing and Discursive Opportunity Structures: The Political Success of the US Women's Jury Movement', *American Sociological Review*, 72:5, 725–49.

McCrudden, C. (2008), 'Human Dignity and Judicial Interpretation of Human Rights', *European Journal of International Law*, 19:4, 655–724.

McCrudden, C. (2015), 'Transnational Culture Wars', *International Journal of Constitutional Law*, 13:2, 434–62.

McKelvey, F. (2021), 'Toward Contextualizing Not Just Containing Right-Wing Extremisms on Social Media: The Limits of Walled Strategies', *Social Sciences Research Council*, 13 July, https://items.ssrc.org/extremism-online/toward-contextualizing-not-just-con taining-right-wing-extremisms-on-social-media-the-limits-of-walled-strategies/.

McNeish, J.-A. (2008), 'Beyond the Permitted Indian? Bolivia and Guatemala in an Era of Neoliberal Developmentalism', *Latin American and Caribbean Ethnic Studies*, 3:1, 33–59.

McNeish, J.-A. (2013), 'Extraction, Protest and Indigeneity in Bolivia: The TIPNIS Effect', *Latin American and Caribbean Ethnic Studies*, 8:2, 221–42.

McPhate, M. (2016), 'Pope Francis' Remarks Disappoint Gay and Transgender Groups', *New York Times*, 3 August, https://nyti.ms/2aNN0uR.

McVeigh, R. (2009), *The Rise of the Ku Klux Klan: Right-Wing Movements and National Politics* (London, University of Minnesota Press).

Meneses, D. (2019), 'Con Mis Hijos No Te Metas: Un estudio de discurso y poder en un grupo de Facebook peruano opuesto a la "ideología de género"', *Anthropologica*, 37:42, 129–54.

Meyer, D. S. and S. Staggenborg (1996), 'Movements, Countermovements, and the Structure of Political Opportunity', *American Journal of Sociology*, 101:6, 1628–60.

Meyer, P. J. (2018), 'Organization of American States: Background and Issues for Congress', 14 March, https://fas.org/sgp/crs/row/R42639.pdf.

Middlebrook, K. J. (2000), *Conservative Parties, the Right, and Democracy in Latin America* (London, Johns Hopkins University Press).

Mills, C. W. (1956), *The Power Elite* (Oxford and New York, Oxford University Press).

Ministerio de Educación de Colombia, Fondo de Población de las Naciones Unidas, Programa de las Naciones Unidas para el Desarrollo, and Fondo para la Infancia de las Naciones Unidas (2016), *Ambientes escolares libres de discriminación: 1. Orientaciones sexuales e identidades de género no hegemónicas en la escuela. Aspectos para la reflexión* (Bogotá, Ministerio de Educación Nacional).

Moghadam, V. (2018), 'Gendering the New Right-Wing Populisms: A Research Note', *Journal of World Systems Research*, 24:2, 293–303.

Monte, M. E. and J. M. Vaggione (2018), 'Cortes irrumpidas: La judicialización conservadora del aborto en Argentina', *Revista rupturas*, 9:1, 107–25.

Montgomery, P. (2019), 'Hispanic Evangelicals and Allies Hold "Justice Summit", Cheer Mike Pence', *Right Wing Watch*, 20 March, https://www.rightwingwatch.org/post/hispa nic-evangelicals-allies-hold-justice-summit-cheer-mike-pence/.

Morán, J. M. (2015), 'El desarrollo del activismo autodenominado "pro-vida" en Argentina, 1980–2014', *Revista mexicana de sociología*, 77:3, 407–36.

Moreira, A. J. (2012), 'We Are Family! Legal Recognition of Same-Sex Unions in Brazil', *American Journal of Comparative Law*, 60:4, 1003–42.

Moreno, P. (2016), 'Colombian Evangelicals and the Debate after the Peace Agreement', Evangelical Focus, 4 November, https://evangelicalfocus.com/features/2055/pablo- moreno-colombian-evangelicals-and-the-debate-after-the-peace-agreement.

268   *Bibliography*

Morgan, L. M. (2014), 'Claiming Rosa Parks: Conservative Catholic Bids for "Rights" in Contemporary Latin America', *Culture, Health and Sexuality*, 16:10, 1245–59.

Motta, S. C. (2014), 'Militarized Neoliberalism in Colombia: Disarticulating Dissent and Articulating Consent to Neoliberal Epistemologies, Pedagogies, and Ways of Life', in *Constructing Twenty-First Century Socialism in Latin America*, ed. S. C. Motta and M. Cole (Basingstoke, Palgrave Macmillan).

Mottl, T. L. (1980), 'The Analysis of Countermovements', *Social Problems*, 27:5, 620–35.

Mouffe, C. (2004), 'Le politique et la dynamique des passions', *Rue Descartes*, 3:3–4, 179–92.

Mudde, C. (2017), *The Populist Radical Right: A Reader* (New York, Routledge).

Mudde, C. (2022), 'The Far-Right Threat in the United States: A European Perspective', *Annals of the American Academy of Political and Social Science*, 699:1, 101–15.

Mujica, J. (2010), 'La tradición y la vida: Sobre los grupos conservadores y la democracia contemporánea', in *El activismo religioso conservador en Latinoamérica*, ed. J. M. Vaggione (Córdoba, Ferreyra/CIECS), pp. 171–91.

Mujica, V. (2018), 'Gerentes afrodescendientes son casos atípicos en las empresas uruguayas', *El Observador*, 14 February, https://www.elobservador.com.uy/nota/gerentes-afrode scendientes-son-casos-atipicos-en-las-empresas-uruguayas-2018214500.

Nadel, J. H. (2014), *Fútbol: Why Soccer Matters in Latin America* (Gainesville, University of Florida Press).

Natow, R. S. (2020), 'The Use of Triangulation in Qualitative Studies Employing Elite Interviews', *Qualitative Research*, 20:2, 160–73.

Nemer, D. (2021), 'The Human Infrastructure of Fake News in Brazil', *Item*, 6 July, https://items.ssrc.org/extremism-online/the-human-infrastructure-of-fake-news-in-brazil/.

Ng'weno, B. (2007), 'Can Ethnicity Replace Race? Afro-Colombians, Indigeneity and the Colombian Multicultural State', *Journal of Latin American and Caribbean Anthropology*, 12:2, 414–40.

Nicholasen, M. (2018), 'Mothers of Stillborns Face Prison in El Salvador', *Harvard Gazette*, 31 October, https://news.harvard.edu/gazette/story/2018/10/how-the-pro-life-movem ent-became-entrenched-in-el-salvador/.

Nogueira, C. (2015), 'Intervención en Comisión de Salud de la Cámara de Diputados de la República de Chile', Boletín no. 9895-11: *Sesiones Comisión Salud, Cámara de Diputados* (March–July), 'Discusión de la Ley N° 21.030 que regula la despenalización voluntaria del embarazo en tres causales', transcribed by I. Palma, Programma de Investigación sobre el Aborto en Chile (Universidad de Chile), 13 July.

Norris, S. (2019), 'International Anti-Feminist Network Organises Rally in Spain', *Open Democracy*, 8 March, https://www.opendemocracy.net/en/5050/international-anti-feminist-network-organises-rally-spain/.

Nuevo Siglo (2016), 'Iglesia pide al Gobierno despejar dudas sobre acuerdos de paz', 4 July, https://www.elnuevosiglo.com.co/articulos/7-2016-iglesia-pide-al-gobierno-despejar-dudas-sobre-acuerdos-de-paz.

OAS [Organization of American States] (2013), 'Inter-American Convention against All Forms of Discrimination and Intolerance', https://www.oas.org/en/sla/dil/inter_amer ican_treaties_A-69_discrimination_intolerance.asp.

OAS [Organization of American States] (2013), 'Inter-American Convention against Racism, Racial Discrimination and Related Forms of Intolerance', https://www.oas.org/en/sla/dil/inter_american_treaties_A-68_racism.asp.

OAS [Organization of American States] (2016), 'American Declaration on the Rights of Indigenous Peoples', AG/RES. 2888 (XLVI-O/16)), https://www.oas.org/en/sare/documents/DecAmIND.pdf.

Bibliography

269

OAS [Organization of American States] (2017), 'Declaration of the OAS General Secretariat Regarding the Presidential Elections in Honduras', http://www.oas.org/en/media_cen ter/press_release.asp?sCodigo=E-090/17.

OAS [Organization of American States] (2018), 'Resumen de presentaciones de coaliciones de la sociedad civil y de actores sociales, 26 June, http://www.oas.org/es/49ag/docs/pre sentaciones-coaliciones/Insumos-de-Coalicion-49-Asamblea-General-OEA.pdf.

O'Brien, C. and S. D. Walsh (2020), 'Women's Rights and Opposition: Explaining the Stunted Rise and Sudden Reversals of Progressive Violence against Women Policies in Contentious Contexts', *Journal of Latin American Studies*, 52:1, 107–31.

Observador (2015), 'Institución de Derechos Humanos investigará denuncia de racismo en boliche del Cordón', *El Observador*, 22 September, https://www.elobservador.com.uy/ nota/institucion-de-derechos-humanos-investigara-denuncia-de-racismo-en-boliche-del-cordon-201592212490.

O'Donnell, G. (1973), *Modernization and Bureaucratic-Authoritarianism: Studies in South American Politics* (Berkeley, Institute of International Studies, University of California).

Oficina del Alto Comisionado para la Paz (2016), 'Humberto de la Calle habla sobre la inclusión del enfoque de género en los acuerdos de paz', YouTube, 24 July, https:// www.youtube.com/watch?v=SG8X50uyz2w.

Oficina del Alto Comisionado para la Paz (2016), *Sistematización opciones y propuestas voceros del No y lo acordado en el nuevo acuerdo*, 29 November, Bogotá, https:// www.jep.gov.co/Sala-de-Prensa/Documents/tomo-8-proceso-paz-farc-refrendacion-plebiscito-.pdf.

Oficina Nacional del Servicio Civil (2019), *Ingresos de personas afrodescendientes en el Estado*, Ley no. 19.122, https://www.gub.uy/oficina-nacional-servicio-civil/sites/ofic ina-nacional-servicio-civil/files/documentos/publicaciones/Informe%20Afro%202 019.pdf.

OhMyGeek! (2018), '¿De dónde proviene el meme del "feto ingeniero"?', https://ohmyg eek.net/2018/04/19/meme-feto-ingeniero/.

Olaza, M. (2017), 'Afrodescendencia y restauración democrática en Uruguay: ¿Una nueva visión de ciudadanía?', *Revista de ciencias sociales*, 30:40 (January–June), 63–82.

Olaza, M. (2017), *Afrodescendientes en Uruguay: Debates sobre políticas de acción afirmativas* (Montevideo, Doble Clic Editoras).

Ordóñez Maldonado, A. (2016), '"Acuerdo Santos/Timochenko es una imposición de la ideología de género": Alejandro Ordóñez', YouTube, 24 September, https://www.yout ube.com/watch?v=gh3Gd4gv0mM&t=86s.

Oro, A. P. (2005), 'The Politics of the Universal Church and Its Consequences on Religion and Politics in Brazil', trans. E. J. Romera, from *Revista brasileira de ciências sociais*, 18:53, 53–69, http://socialsciences.scielo.org/pdf/s_rbcsoc/v1nse/scs_a05.pdf.

Oselin, S. S. and C. Corrigall-Brown (2010), 'A Battle for Authenticity: An Examination of the Constraints on Anti-Iraq War and Pro-Invasion Tactics', *Mobilisation*, 15:4, 511–33.

Ossandón, M. (2016), 'Intervención en Comisión de Constitución, Legislación, Justicia y Reglamento de la Cámara de Diputados de la República de Chile', 9 March, https:// www.bcn.cl/historiadelaley/nc/historia-de-la-ley/6701/.

Padgett, D. (2021), 'Honduras Makes Overturning Same-Sex Marriage Ban Near Impossible', *Out Magazine*, https://www.out.com/news/2021/1/28/honduras-makes-overturning-same-sex-marriage-ban-near-impossible.

Pairicán, F. (2014), 'Malón: La rebelión del movimiento mapuche 1990–2013' (Santiago, Pehuén Editores).

270 *Bibliography*

Pais (2019), 'Fracasó el prereferéndum para habilitar consulta por la ley trans', *El País*, 5 August, https://www.elpais.com.uy/informacion/politica/fracaso-prerreferendum-habilitar-consulta-ley-trans.html.

Paiva, F. and M. Nicolau (2013), '"… e o Marco Feliciano não me Representa": As múltiplas formas de um meme no Instagram', in *XV Congresso de Ciências da Comunicação na Região Nordeste* (São Paulo, Sociedade Brasileira de Estudos Interdisciplinares da Comunicação), https://www.portalintercom.org.br/anais/nordeste2013/resumos/R37-0207-1.pdf.

Panotto, N. (2020), 'Incidencia religiosa en clave multilateral: La presencia de redes políticas evangélicas en las asambleas de la OEA', *Revista cultura y religión*, 14:1, 100–20.

Parfitt, R. (2019), 'Fascism and the International: The Global South, the Far-Right and the International Legal Order', *TWAILR* [*Third World Approaches to International Law Review*], https://twailr.com/series-introduction-fascism-and-the-international-the-global-south-the-far-right-and-the-international-legal-order/.

Parke, C. (2018), 'The Right's "Gender Ideology" Menace Rolls to Africa', *Political Research Associates*, 4 May, https://politicalresearch.org/2018/05/04/the-rights-gender-ideology-menace-rolls-to-africa.

Parkin, S. (2020), 'Trigger Warning', *Guardian-Weekend*, 2 May.

Parlamento del Uruguay (2013), 'Ficha asunto Afrodescendencia', https://parlamento.gub.uy/documentosyleyes/ficha-asunto/110651/ficha_completa.

Paternotte, D. and R. Kuhar (2017), '"Gender Ideology" in Movement: Introduction', in *Anti-Gender Campaigns in Europe*, ed. D. Paternotte and R. Kuhar (London, Rowman & Littlefield), pp. 1–22.

Payne, L. A. (1994), *Brazilian Industrialists and Democratic Change* (Baltimore, Johns Hopkins University Press).

Payne, L. A. (2000), *Uncivil Movements: The Armed Right Wing and Democracy in Latin America* (Baltimore, Johns Hopkins University Press).

Payne, L. A. (2023), 'Right-Wing Movements in Latin America', in *The Oxford Handbook of Latin American Social Movements*, ed. F. M. Rossi (Oxford, Oxford University Press), Chapter 32.

Payne, L. A. (Forthcoming) 'Right-Wing Movements (Latin America)', in *The Wiley-Blackwell Encyclopedia of Social and Political Movements*, ed. D. Snow, D. della Porta, B. Klandermans, and D. McAdam (Hoboken, NJ, Wiley-Blackwell).

Payne, L. A. and A. A. de Souza Santos (2020), 'The Right-Wing Backlash in Brazil and Beyond', *Politics & Gender*, 16:1 (*Special Symposium on Women's Parties*), 32–8.

Payne, L. A., G. Pereira, and L. Bernal-Bermúdez (2020), *Transitional Justice and Corporate Accountability from Below: Deploying Archimedes' Lever* (Cambridge, Cambridge University Press).

PCCMM [Predicadores Católicos Comunidad María Mediadora] (2016), 'Abanderados por la Familia – Marcha en Manizales', YouTube, 10 August, https://www.youtube.com/watch?v=t1Vxjon7M7k.

Peña Claros, C. (2010), 'Un pueblo eminente: Autonomist Populism in Santa Cruz', *Latin American Perspectives*, 37:4, 125–39.

Peñas, M. A. and J. M. Morán (2014), 'Conservative Litigation against Sexual and Reproductive Health Policies in Argentina', *Reproductive Health Matters*, 22:44, 82–90.

Pentin, E. (2015), 'Cardinal Sarah: ISIS and Gender Ideology Are like "Apocalyptic Beasts"', *National Catholic Register*, http://www.ncregister.com/blog/edward-pentin/cardinal-sarahs-intervention-isis-and-gender-ideology-are-like-apocalyptic-.

Bibliography

Pereda Valdés, I. (1941), *Negros esclavos y negros libres: Esquema de una sociedad esclavista y aporte del negro en nuestra formación nacional* (Montevideo, Imprenta Gaceta Comercial).

Pereda Valdés, I. (1965), *El negro en el Uruguay: Pasado y presente* (Montevideo, Instituto Histórico y Geográfico del Uruguay).

Pérez Bentacur, V. and C. Rocha-Carpiuc (2020), 'The Postreform Stage: Understanding Backlash against Sexual Policies in Latin America', *Politics and Gender*, 16:1, 11–18.

Pérez Guadalupe, J. L. (2019), *Evangelicals and Political Power in Latin America* (Lima, Konrad Adenauer Stiftung; Instituto de Estudios Sociales Cristianos de Perú).

Pérez Guadalupe, J. L. and S. Grundberger (2018), 'Evangélicos y poder en América Latina', https://www.kas.de/c/document_library/get_file?uuid=35e0675a-5108-856c-c821-c5e1725a64b7&groupId=269552.

Perreault, T. and B. Green (2013), 'Reworking the Spaces of Indigeneity: The Bolivian Ayllu and Lowland Autonomy Movements Compared', *Environment and Planning D: Society and Space*, 31:1, 43–60.

Persico, M. M. (2015), 'Afro-Uruguayan Culture and Legitimation: Candombe and Poetry', in *Black Writing, Culture, and the State in Latin America*, ed. J. C. Branche (Nashville, Vanderbilt University Press).

Petras, J. and H. Veltmeyer (2001), *Globalization Unmasked: Imperialisms in the 21st Century* (Halifax, NS, Fernwood).

Phillips, A. (1997), 'From Inequality To Difference: A Severe Case Of Displacement?', *New Left Review* I:224, 143–53.

Phillips, T. (2018), 'Brazil's Fearful LGBT Community Prepares for a 'Proud Homophobe', *Guardian*, 27 October.

Pinker, S. (2011), *The Better Angels of Our Nature: Why Violence Has Declined* (London, Penguin Random House).

Piscopo, J. M. (2020), 'Women Leaders and Pandemic Performance: A Spurious Correlation', *Politics and Gender*, 16:4, 951–9.

Plata, W. (2008), 'El discurso autonomista de las élites de Santa Cruz', in *Los barones del oriente: El poder en Santa Cruz ayer y hoy*, ed. X. Soruco, W. Plata, and G. Medeiros (Santa Cruz, Fundación Tierra), pp. 101–72.

Postero, N. G. (2007), *Now We Are Citizens: Indigenous Politics in Postmulticultural Bolivia* (Stanford, Stanford University Press).

Postero, N. G. (2017), *The Indigenous State: Race, Politics, and Performance in Plurinational Bolivia* (Oakland, University of California Press).

Power, T. J. (2000), *The Political Right in Postauthoritarian Brazil: Elites, Institutions, and Democratization* (University Park, Pennsylvania State University Press).

Power, T. J. and W. Hunter (2019), 'Bolsonaro and Brazil's Illiberal Backlash', *Journal of Democracy*, 30:1, 68–82.

Pontificia Universidad Católica de Chile [PUC] (2021), *Encuesta Nacional Bicentenario*, Santiago de Chile, https://encuestabicentenario.uc.cl.

Quijano, A. (2000), 'Coloniality of Power, Eurocentrism, and Latin America', *Nepantla: Views from the South*, 1:3, 533–80.

Quintero Garzón, C. J. (2019), *Discursos acerca de la infancia y el acuerdo de paz en Colombia: Un relato de los lugares de visibilidad e invisibilidad de los niños en la prensa (2012–2016)* (Bogotá, Universidad Pedagógica Nacional).

Radio Católica Metropolitana 1450AM (2016), 'Marcha Abanderados por la Familia, Iglesia Católica presente', YouTube, 11 August, https://www.youtube.com/watch?v=5S0x onjxl7Q.

272 *Bibliography*

Rainey, C. (2014), 'A US Diplomat in Uruguay Alleges She Was Denied Entry to a Restaurant because of Her Race', *New York*, 9 December, http://www.grubstreet.com/2014/12/cir cus-restauant-uruguay-allegedly-turned-away-black-diplomat.html.

Ramírez, M. F. ['@7MarcoFidelR'] (2016), 'Acabo de votar NO en plebescito de Farc-Santos', Twitter, 2 October, https://twitter.com/7MarcoFidelR/status/782607295125549056.

Razón (2017), 'Presidente: "Tarde o temprano" se construirá la carretera por el TIPNIS', *La Razón*, 26 July.

Recagno, V. (2016), 'Ubunto', *La Diaria*, 18 August, https://ladiaria.com.uy/articulo/2016/8/ubuntu/.

Red Nacional de Defensoras de Honduras (2018), *Informe sobre la situación de defensoras*, http://im-defensoras.org/wp-content/uploads/2018/05/Informe-de-Agresiones-a-def ensoras-2016-2017.pdf.

Reich, G. and P. dos Santos (2013), 'The Rise (and Frequent Fall) of Evangelical Politicians: Organization, Theology, and Church Politics', *Latin American Politics and Society*, 55:4, 1–22.

Rennó, L. R. (2020), 'The Bolsonaro Voter: Issue Positions and Vote Choice in the 2018 Brazilian Presidential Elections', *Latin American Politics and Society*, 62:4, 1–23.

Restrepo Sanín, J. (2020), 'Violence against Women in Politics: Latin America in an Era of Backlash', *Signs: Journal of Women in Culture and Society*, 45:2, 302–10.

Reuters (2019), 'Pompeo Launches Commission to Study Human Rights Role', 8 July, https://www.reuters.com/article/us-usa-rights-pompeo-idUSKCN1U31SA.

Reuterswärd, C. (2021), 'Pro-Life and Feminist Mobilization in the Struggle over Abortion in Mexico: Church Networks, Elite Alliances, and Partisan Context', *Latin American Politics and Society*, 63:3, 21–45.

Reuterswärd, C., P. Zetterberg, S. Thapar-Björkert, and M. Molyneux (2011), 'Abortion Law Reforms in Colombia and Nicaragua: Issue Networks and Opportunity Contexts', *Development and Change*, 42:3, 805–31.

Ribeiro, L. M. P. and D. da Silva Cunha (2012), '"Bola de Neve": Um fenômeno pentecostal contemporâneo', *Horizonte: Revista de estudos de teologia e ciências da religião*, 10:26, 500–21.

Rice Hasson, M. (2019), 'Gender Ideology: Ideological Aggression against Women and Girls', Commission on the Status of Women 2019, New York, 20 March, http://webtv.un.org/search/gender-equality-and-gender-ideology-protecting-women-and-girls-csw63-side-event/6016177611001/?term=Gender%20ideology&sort=date&page=2.

Richard, N. (2001), 'La problemática del feminismo en los años de la transición en Chile', in *Estudios latinoamericanos sobre cultura y transformaciones sociales en tiempos de globalización* (Buenos Aires, CLACSO), pp. 227–39.

Riguetti, B. (2019), 'Gloria Rodríguez: La población negra no está representada en Parlamento', *La Diaria*, 2 January.

Rivera Cusicanqui, S. (1984), *Oprimidos pero no vencidos: Luchas del campesinado aymara y qhechwa de Bolivia, 1900–1980* (La Paz, CSUTCB).

Rivera Cusicanqui, S. (1987), *Oppressed but not Defeated: Peasant Struggles among the Aymara and Qhechwa in Bolivia, 1900–1980* (Geneva, United Nations Research Institute for Social Development).

Roberts, K. M. (2014), 'Democracy, Free Markets, and the Rightist Dilemma in Latin America', in *The Resilience of the Latin American Right*, ed. J. P. Luna and C. Rovira Kaltwasser (Durham and London, Johns Hopkins University Press).

Rochlin, J. (2007), 'Latin America's Left Turn and the New Strategic Landscape: The Case of Bolivia', *Third World Quarterly*, 28:7, 1327–42.

Bibliography

273

Rodrigues-Silveira, R. and E. U. Cervi (2019), 'Evangélicos e voto legislativo: Diversidade confessional e voto em deputados da bancada evangélica no Brasil', *Latin American Research Review*, 54:3, 560–73.

Rodríguez, C., E. Canas, H. Pardo, and J. M. Rodríguez (2016), 'Peace Agreement', YouTube, 21 November, https://misionpaz.org/acuerdo-de-paz/?lang=en.

Rodriguez, D. (2016), 'Abanderados por la familia', https://www.youtube.com/watch?v=O8SG-LWDlKc.

Rodríguez, R. J. (1988), 'Carta de Director', *Mundo Afro*, 1:1 (August), 3.

Rodríguez, R. J. (2003), *Racismo y derechos humanos en Uruguay* (Montevideo, Ediciones Étnicas).

Rodríguez Rondón, M. (2016), 'La infancia como símbolo y moneda de cambio', Centro Latinoamericano de Sexualidad y Derechos Humanos, http://www.clam.org.br/busca/conteudo.asp?cod=12437.

Rodríguez Rondón, M. A. (2017), 'La ideología de género como exceso: Pánico moral y decisión ética en la política colombiana', *Sexualidad, salud y sociedad*, 27, 128–48.

Rohlinger, A. (2021), 'We Cannot Just Moderate Extremism Away', *Social Sciences Research Council*, 9 March, https://items.ssrc.org/extremism-online/we-cannot-just-moderate-extremism-away/.

Rojas Herrera, J. E. (2016), 'Comunicado de prensa', https://www.cec.org.co/sites/default/files/Comunicado%20de%20prensa.pdf.

Romancini, R. (2018) 'From "Gay Kit" to "Indoctrination Monitor": The Conservative Reaction in Brazil', *Contracampo*, 37:2, 85–106.

Romero, J. (2015), '"Mujeres de Blanco" en Roma: El grito de las mujeres que busca defender la vida de los chilenos por nacer', InfoCatólica, https://www.infocatolica.com/blog/delapsis.php/1506040935-mujeres-de-blanco-en-roma-lel.

Romero, S. (2012), 'Brazil Enacts Affirmative Action Law for Universities', *New York Times*, 30 August, https://www.nytimes.com/2012/08/31/world/americas/brazil-enacts-affirmative-action-law-for-universities.html.

Rosenblatt, F. (2018), *Party Vibrancy and Democracy in Latin America* (New York, Oxford University Press).

Rossi, F. M. (2017), *The Poor's Struggle for Political Incorporation: The Piquetero Movement in Argentina* (Cambridge, Cambridge University Press).

ROU (2006), 'Ley no. 18.059: Día nacional del candombe, la cultura afrouruguaya y la equidad racial', 20 November, https://www.gub.uy/ministerio-desarrollo-social/sites/ministerio-desarrollo-social/files/documentos/publicaciones/1775.pdf.

ROU [República Oriental del Uruguay] (2004), 'Ley no. 17.817: Lucha contra el racismo, la xenofobia y la discriminación', 6 September, https://www.gub.uy/ministerio-desarrollo-social/sites/ministerio-desarrollo-social/files/documentos/publicaciones/1774.pdf.

ROU [República Oriental del Uruguay] (2011), 'Diario de sesiones de la Cámara de representantes," 2nd session, 2 March, https://legislativo.parlamento.gub.uy/temporales/20110302D0002_SSN6162605.html.

ROU [República Oriental del Uruguay] (2011), 'Diario de Sesiones de la Cámara de representantes', 60th session, 6 December, https://parlamento.gub.uy/documentosleyes/ficha-asunto/110651/tramite.

ROU [República Oriental del Uruguay] (2012), 'Diario de Sesiones de la Cámara de representantes', 59th session, 17 October, https://legislativo.parlamento.gub.uy/temporales/70784335268641.PDF#pagina18.

ROU [República Oriental del Uruguay] (2013), "Diario de Sesiones de la Cámara de senadores', 31st ordinary session, no. 229, Vol. 509, 16 July, https://parlamento.gub.uy/documentosyleyes/ficha-asunto/110651/tramite.

274 *Bibliography*

ROU [República Oriental del Uruguay] (2013), "Diario de Sesiones de la Cámara de representantes', 36th extraordinary session, 8 August, https://legislativo.parlamento.gub.uy/temporales/98357126751753.PDF#pagina126.

ROU [República Oriental del Uruguay] (2013), 'Ley no. 19.122: Afrodescendientes. Normas para favorecer su participación en las áreas educativa y laboral' (2013), https://www.gub.uy/ministerio-desarrollo-social/sites/ministerio-desarrollo-social/files/documentos/publicaciones/1781.pdf.

ROU [República Oriental del Uruguay] (2018), 'Ley no. 19.684: Ley integral para personas trans', 7 November, https://www.gub.uy/ministerio-desarrollo-social/sites/ministerio-desarrollo-social/files/documentos/publicaciones/1922.pdf.

Rousseau, S. (2020), 'Antigender Activism in Peru and Its Impact on State Policy', *Politics and Gender*, 16:1, 25–32.

Rovira Kaltwasser, C. (2014), 'From Right Populism in the 1990s to Left Populism in the 2000s – and Back Again?', in *The Resilience of the Latin American Right*, ed. J. P. Luna and C. Rovira Kaltwasser (Baltimore, Johns Hopkins University Press), pp. 143–66.

Rovira Kaltwasser, C. and S. M. Van Hauwaert (2020), 'The Populist Citizen: Empirical Evidence from Europe and Latin America', *European Political Science Review*, 12:1, 1–18.

Rowell, A. (1996), *Green Backlash: Global Subversion of the Environmental Movement* (London, Routledge).

Rubio, M. and M. Lee (2016), 'Rubio, Lee Call Out "Cultural Imperialism" of OAS', press release, 3 October, https://www.rubio.senate.gov/public/index.cfm/2016/10/rubio-lee-call-out-cultural-imperialism-of-oas.

Ruetalo, V. (2008), 'From Penal Institution to Shopping Mecca: The Economics of Memory and the Case of Punta Carretas', *Cultural Critique*, 68 (Winter), 38–65.

Rupar, A. (2022), 'Mike Lee's Texts and the Coup in Search of a Legal Theory', 18 April, https://aaronrupar.substack.com/p/mike-lee-texts-mark-meadows-chip-roy?s=r.

Saad-Filho, A. (2013). 'Mass Protests under "Left Neoliberalism": Brazil, June–July 2013', *Critical Sociology*, 39:5, 657–69.

Sahgal, N. (2017), '500 Years after the Reformation, 5 Facts about Protestants around the world', Pew Research Center, 27 October, https://www.pewresearch.org/fact-tank/2017/10/27/500-years-after-the-reformation-5-facts-about-protestants-around-the-world/.

Salvi, V. (2011), 'The Slogan "Complete Memory": A Reactive (Re)Signification of the Memory of the Disappeared in Argentina', in *The Memory of State Terrorism in the Southern Cone*, ed. F. Lessa and V. Druliolle (New York, Palgrave Macmillan), pp. 43–61.

Salvi, V. (2012), *De vencedores a víctimas: Memorias militares sobre el pasado reciente en la Argentina* (Buenos Aires, Biblos).

Salvi, V. (2020), 'Tayectoria, capital e ideología: Las declaraciones de los perpetradores en los juicios por crímenes de lesa humanidad en Argentina', *Kamchatka revista de análisis cultural*, 15, 193–215.

Sans, M. (2011), 'National Identity, Census Data, and Genetics in Uruguay', in *Racial Identities, Genetic Ancestry, and Health in South America*, ed. S. Gibbon, R. Ventura Santos, and M. Sans (New York, Palgrave Macmillan).

Sanserevino, B. (2013), '2013: Aprobamos Leyes', https://www.facebook.com/notes/bertha-sanseverino/2013-aprobamos-leyes-que-consolidan-derechos/10151988482259351/.

Santos, J. M. (2016), 'Alocución del Presidente Juan Manuel Santos sobre nuevo acuerdo de paz', 12 November, https://www.cancilleria.gov.co/en/newsroom/news/alocucion-presidente-juan-manuel-santos-nuevo-acuerdo-paz.

Bibliography

Santos, J. M. (2016), 'Declaración sobre el nuevo Acuerdo de Paz tras reunirse con el Jefe del Equipo Negociador y con el Ministro del Interior', in *Biblioteca del proceso de paz entre el Gobierno Nacional y las FARC-EP*, ed. Oficina del Alto Comisionado para la Paz (Bogotá, Presidencia de la República de Colombia), pp. 204–6.

Saroglou, V. (2011), 'Believing, Bonding, Behaving, and Belonging: The Big Four Religious Dimensions and Cultural Variation', *Journal of Cross-Cultural Psychology*, 42:8, 1320–40.

Sarti, C. A. (2004), 'O feminismo brasileiro desde os anos 1970: Revisitando uma trajetória', *Revista estudos feministas*, 12:2, 35–50.

Schmidt, S. (2022), 'How Green Became the Color of Abortion Rights', *Washington Post*, 3 July, https://www.washingtonpost.com/world/interactive/2022/abortion-green-roe-wade-argentina/.

Schmitt, C. (2008), *The Concept of the Political* (Chicago: University of Chicago Press).

Scott, J. C. (1985), *Weapons of the Weak: Everyday Forms of Peasant Resistance* (New Haven: Yale University Press).

Scott, J. and G. Marshall (2015), *A Dictionary of Sociology* (Oxford, Oxford University Press).

Semana (2016), 'Ideología de género: Una estrategia para ganar adeptos por el "No" al plebiscito', https://www.semana.com/nacion/articulo/ideologia-de-genero-una-estrate gia-para-ganar-adeptos-por-el-no-al-plebiscito/488260/.

Semana (2016), ' "Lo que he tratado es de abrirles los ojos a los colombianos": Alejandro Ordóñez', 25 September, https://www.semana.com/nacion/articulo/alejandro-ordonez-habla-del-proceso-de-paz-el-gobierno-santos-la-ideologia-de-genero-y-el-plebiscito/ 495287/.

Semana (2016), 'Plebiscito por la paz: El decisivo voto de los evangélicos', 17 September, https://www.semana.com/nacion/articulo/plebiscito-por-la-paz-el-voto-de-los-evangeli cos-es-decisivo-para-la-campana/494042.

Serrano-Amaya, J. F. (2017), 'La tormenta perfecta: Ideología de género y articulación de públicos', *Sexualidad, salud y sociedad*, 27, 149–71.

Sharnak, D. (2022), 'The Road to Recognition: Afro-Uruguayan Activism and the Struggle for Visibility', in *Narratives of Mass Atrocity: Victims and Perpetrators in the Aftermath*, ed. S. Federman and R. Niezen (New York: Cambridge).

Sharnak, D. (2023), *Of Light and Struggle: Social Justice, Human Rights, and Accountability in Uruguay* (Philadelphia, University of Pennsylvania Press).

Sikkink, K. (1997), 'The Emergence, Evolution, and Effectiveness of the Latin American Human Rights Network', in *Constructing Democracy: Human Rights, Citizenship and Society in Latin America*, ed. E. Jelin and E. Hershberg (Boulder, Westview), pp. 59–84.

Sikkink, K. (2011), *The Justice Cascade: How Human Rights Prosecutions Are Changing World Politics* (London, W. W. Norton).

Sikkink, K. and Booth Walling, C. (2006), 'Argentina's Contribution to Global Trends in Transitional Justice', in *Transitional Justice in the Twenty-First Century: Beyond Truth and Justice*, ed. N. Roht-Arriaza and J. Mariezcurrena (New York, Cambridge University Press).

Simi, P. and R. Futrell (2011), *American Swastika: Inside the White Power Movement's Hidden Spaces of Hate* (Toronto, Rowman & Littlefield).

Simmel, G. (1994), 'Bridge and Door', *Theory, Culture & Society*, 11:1, 5–10.

Simmons, E. (2014), 'Grievances Do Matter in Mobilization', *Theory and Society*, 43, 513–46.

Bibliography

Sinohydro Group (2013), 'Response to Report by Rights Action about Alleged Violence & Intimidation against Lenca Indigenous Communities Related to the Constructions of Agua Zarca Dam, Honduras', Business & Human Rights Resource Centre, https://www.business-humanrights.org/en/latest-news/sinohydro-group-response-to-report-by-rights-action-about-alleged-violence-intimidation-against-lenca-Indigenous-communities-related-to-the-constructions-of-agua-zarca-dam-honduras/.

Sistema Informativo del Gobierno (2016), 'Más de 100 líderes religiosos de todo el país le dicen sí a la paz', 4 July, http://es.presidencia.gov.co/noticia/160704-Mas-de-100-lideres-religiosos-de-todo-el-pais-le-dicen-si-a-la-paz.

Small, M. L. (2009), 'How Many Cases Do I Need? On Science and the Logic of Case Selection in Field-Based Research', *Ethnography*, 10:1, 5–38.

Small, M. L. (2011), 'How to Conduct a Mixed Methods Study: Recent Trends in a Rapidly Growing Literature', *Annual Review of Sociology*, 37:1, 57–86.

Smith, A. E. (2019), *Religion and Brazilian Democracy: Mobilizing the People of God* (Cambridge, Cambridge University Press).

Snow, D. A. (2004), 'Framing Processes, Ideology, and Discursive Fields', in *The Blackwell Companion to Social Movements*, ed. D. A. Snow, S. A. Soule, and H. Kriesi (Malden, MA, Blackwell), pp. 380–412.

Snow, D. A., R. Benford, H. McCammon, L. Hewitt, and S. Fitzgerald (2014), 'The Emergence, Development, and Future of the Framing Perspective: 25+ Years since "Frame Alignment"', *Mobilisation: An International Quarterly*, 19:1, 23–46.

Soares, F. B. (2020), 'As estratégias de argumentação e as formas de desinformação nas mensagens de Jair Bolsonaro no Twitter durante o segundo turno das eleições presidenciais de 2018', *Mediação*, 22:30, 8–22, http://revista.fumec.br/index.php/mediacao/article/view/7424.

Soley, X. and S. Steininger (2018), 'Parting Ways or Lashing Back? Withdrawals, Backlash and the Inter-American Court of Human Rights', *International Journal of Law in Context*, 14, 237–57.

Soruco, X. (2008), 'De la goma a la soya: El proyecto histórico de la elite cruceña', in *Los barones del oriente: El poder en Santa Cruz ayer y hoy*, ed. D. A. Snow, S. A. Soule, and H. Kriesi (Santa Cruz, Fundación Tierra), pp. 1–100.

SoyChile (2015), 'Lorenzini: "Hay mujeres que tienen violaciones porque, a lo mejor, tomaron un traguito de más"', 6 February, https://www.soychile.cl/Santiago/Politica/2015/02/06/303544/Lorenzini-Hay-mujeres-que-tienen-violaciones-porque-a-lo-mejor-tomaron-un-traguito-de-mas.aspx.

SPLC [Southern Poverty Law Center] (n.d.), 'SPLC: Southern Poverty Law Center', https://www.splcenter.org/about.

Spring, M. and L. Webster (2019), 'A Web of Abuse: How the Far Right Disproportionately Targets Female Politicians', *BBC Newsnight*, 15 July, https://www.bbc.com/news/blogs-trending-48871400.

Stahler-Sholk, R. and H. E. Vanden (2011), 'A Second Look at Latin American Social Movements: Globalizing Resistance to the Neoliberal Paradigm', *Latin American Perspectives*, 38, 5–13.

Stedman, S. J. (1997), 'Spoiler Problems in Peace Processes', *International Security*, 22:2, 5–53.

Stop Hate UK (n.d.), 'Stop Hate UK', https://www.stophateuk.org/.

Stubbs, P. and Lendvai-Bainton, N. (2020), 'Authoritarian Neoliberalism, Radical Conservatism and Social Policy within the European Union: Croatia, Hungary and Poland', *Development and Change*, 51: 540–60.

Stull, M. (2018), 'State Department Emails between Mari Stull and White House,' 1 June, https://www.documentcloud.org/documents/6309201-State-Department-Emails-Betw een-Mari-Stull-and.html#document/p137/a569058.

Subercaseaux, F. (2015), 'Intervención en Comisión de Salud de la Cámara de Diputados de la República de Chile', Boletín no. 9895-11: *Sesiones Comisión Salud, Cámara de Diputados* (March–July), transcribed by I. Palma, Programma de Investigación sobre el Aborto en Chile (Universidad de Chile), 8 June.

Sutton, B. and E. Borland (2013), 'Framing Abortion Rights in Argentina's Encuentros Nacionales de Mujeres', *Feminist Studies*, 39:1, 194–234.

Svampa, M. (2017), *Del cambio de época al fin de ciclo: Gobiernos progresistas, extractivismo, y movimientos sociales en América Latina*, 1st edn (Buenos Aires, Edhasa).

Switzer, J. V. (1997), *Green Backlash: The History and Politics of the Environmental Opposition in the US* (Boulder, CO, Lynn Rienner).

Sztainbok, V. (2009), 'Imagining the Afro-Uruguayan Conventillo: Belonging and the Fetish of Place and Blackness', Ph.D. dissertation, University of Toronto.

Tabbush, C. and M. Caminotti (2020), 'Más allá del sexo: La ampliación de la oposición conservadora a las políticas de igualdad de género en América Latin', *LASA Forum: The Quarterly Newsletter of the Latin American Studies Association*, 51:2, 27–31.

Tabbush, C., M. C. Díaz, C. Trebisacce, and V. Keller (2016), 'Matrimonio igualitario, identidad de género y disputas por el derecho al aborto en Argentina: La política sexual durante el kirchnerismo (2003–2015)', *Sexualidad, salud y sociedad*, 22 (April): 22–55.

Tabosa, F. J. S., P. U. de Carvalho Castelar, and G. Irffi (2016), 'Brazil, 1981–2013: The Effects of Economic Growth and Income Inequality on Poverty', *CEPAL Review*, 120, 153–70.

Tapias Torrado, N. R. (2020), 'Indigenous Women Leading the Defence of Human Rights from the Abuses by Mega-Projects in Latin America, in the Face of Extreme Violence', D.Phil. dissertation, University of Oxford, https://ora.ox.ac.uk/objects/uuid:3a1393b3-1a8b-4341-bb6e-7a33897db5c7.

Tapias Torrado, N. R. (2022), 'Honduras: ¡Berta vive, la lucha sigue! Corporate Accountability for Attacks against Human Rights Defenders', in *Economic Actors and the Limits of Transitional Justice: Truth and Justice for Past Business Complicity in Human Rights*, ed. L. A. Payne, G. Pereira, and L. Bernal-Bermúdez (Oxford, Oxford University Press), pp. 214–35.

Tapias Torrado, N. R. (2022), 'Overcoming Silencing Practices: Indigenous Women Defending Human Rights from Abuses Committed in Connection to Mega-Projects: A Case in Colombia', *Business and Human Rights Journal*, 7:1, 9–44.

Tarrow, S. (1993), 'Cycles of Collective Action: Between Moments of Madness and the Repertoire of Contention', *Social Science History*, 17:2, 281–30.

Teddlie, C. and A. Tashakkori (2009), *Foundations of Mixed Methods Research: Integrating Quantitative and Qualitative Approaches in the Social and Behavioral Sciences* (Thousand Oaks and London, Sage).

Teichman, J. (2019), 'Inequality in Twentieth-Century Latin America: Path Dependence, Countermovements, and Reactive Sequences', *Social Science History*, 43:1, 131–57.

Tele13 (2016), 'Soledad Alvear: "El aborto es lo más machista que hay"', 26 October, https://www.t13.cl/noticia/politica/soledad-alvear-aborto-es-mas-machista-hay.

Thompson, C. (2005), *Making Parents: The Ontological Choreography of Reproductive Technologies* (Cambridge, MA, MIT Press).

278 *Bibliography*

Tiempo (2016), 'Cartilla sobre discriminación sexual en colegios dividió al país', *El Tiempo*, 14 August, https://www.eltiempo.com/vida/educacion/cartillas-sobre-diversidad-sex ual-en-colegios-genera-debate-en-colombia-39931.

Tiempo (2016), '"Gina Parody trata de imponer sus creencias en la educación": Diputada', *El Tiempo*, 20 August, http://www.eltiempo.com/colombia/otras-ciudades/debate-entre-diputada-angela-hernandez-y-gina-parody-por-educacion-lgbt-31465.

Tiempo (2016), 'Iglesia apoya rechazo a ideología de género en manuales de convivencia', *El Tiempo*, 9 August, https://www.eltiempo.com/archivo/documento/CMS-16668897.

Tilly, C. (1978), *From Mobilization to Revolution* (Reading, MA, Addison-Wesley).

Tilly, C. (1984), *Big Structures, Large Processes, Huge Comparisons* (New York, Russell Sage Foundation Publications).

Tilly, C. (2003), *The Politics of Collective Violence* (Cambridge, Cambridge University Press).

Todorov, T. (2000), *Los abusos de la memoria* (Buenos Aires, Paidós Asterisco).

Torres-Parodi, C. (2003), *Acciones afirmativas para lograr la equidad de salud para los grupos étnicos/raciales* (Washington, DC, Organización Panamericana de la Salud).

Townsend-Bell, E. (2021), '"We entered as blacks and we left as Afro-descendants": Tracing the Path to Affirmative Action in Uruguay', *Latin American and Caribbean Ethnic Studies*, 16:3, 237–58.

Turek, L. F. (2020), *To Bring the Good News to All Nations: Evangelical Influence on Human Rights and US Foreign Policy* (Ithaca, Cornell University Press).

UN [United Nations] (1998), 'Declaración sobre las defensoras y los defensores de los derechos humanos, Asamblea General', http://www.ohchr.org/Documents/Issues/Defenders/Declaration/declaration_sp.pdf.

UN [United Nations] (2011), 'Guiding Principles on Business and Human Rights: Implementing the United Nations "Protect, Respect and Remedy" Framework' (New York, United Nations Office of the High Commissioner for Human Rights), https://www.ohchr.org/sites/default/files/documents/publications/guidingprinciplesbusinesshr_en.pdf.

UN [United Nations] (2018), 'Free, Prior and Informed Consent: A Human Rights-Based Approach – Study of the Expert Mechanism on the Rights of Indigenous Peoples', 10 August, A/HRC/39/62, https://www.ohchr.org/en/documents/thematic-reports/free-prior-and-informed-consent-human-rights-based-approach-study-expert.

UNGA [United Nations General Assembly] (2017), 'Report of the Special Rapporteur on the Situation of Human Rights Defenders', A/72/170, https://undocs.org/en/A/72/170.

Urbina Ortega, O. (2016), 'Comunicado sobre las orientaciones del ministerio de educación respecto a los manuales de convivencia de los colegios', 8 August, https://diocesisd ecucuta.com/diocesis2/comunicado-sobre-las-orientaciones-del-ministerio-de-educac ion-respecto-a-los-manuales-de-convivencia-de-los-colegios/.

Uribe Vélez, A. (2016), 'Frente al resultado del Plebiscito: Expresidente Álvaro Uribe Vélez', 3 October, https://alvarouribevelez.com.co/uribe-hoy/frente-al-resultado-del-plebiscito-expresidente-alvaro-uribe-velez/.

Urueña, R. (2019), 'Evangelicals at the Inter-American Court of Human Rights', *AJIL Unbound*, 113, 360–4.

Uruguay Presidencia (2019), 'Becas estatales son recibidas por 20% de adolescentes y jóvenes afrodescendientes de Uruguay', 1 July, https://www.presidencia.gub.uy/comun icacion/comunicacionnoticias/lanzamiento-mes-afrodescendencia-aumento-num ero-de-becas.

Vaggione, J. M. (2005), 'Reactive Politicization and Religious Dissidence: The Political Mutations of the Religious', *Social Theory and Practice*, 31:2, 233–55.

Bibliography

Vaggione, J. M. (2014), 'La politización de la sexualidad y los sentidos de lo religioso', *Sociedad y religión: Sociología, antropología e historia de la religión en el Cono Sur*, 24:42, 209–26.

Vaggione, J. M. (2017), 'La Iglesia Católica frente a la política sexual: La configuración de una ciudadanía religiosa', *Cadernos Pagu*, https://www.academia.edu/41142806/The_crisis_of_democracy_and_the_backlash_against_gender.

Vaggione, J. M. (2018) 'Sexuality, Law and Religion in Latin America: Frameworks in Tension', *Religion and Gender*, 8:1, 14–31.

Vaggione, J. M. and M. das Dores Campos Machado (2020), 'Religious Patterns of Neoconservatism in Latin America', *Politics and Gender*, 16:1, 6–10.

Van Cott, D. L. (2006), 'Multiculturalism versus Neoliberalism in Latin America', in *Multiculturalism and the Welfare State: Recognition and Redistribution in Contemporary Democracies*, ed. K. Banting and W. Kymlicka (Oxford, Oxford University Press), pp. 272–96.

Van Cott, D. L. (2010), 'Indigenous Peoples' Politics in Latin America', *Annual Review of Political Science*, 13, 385–405.

Van Roeckel, E. and V. Salvi (2019), 'Unbecoming Veteranship: Convicted Military Officers in Post-Authoritarian Argentina', *Conflict and Society*, 5, 115–31.

Vecchioli, V. (2001), 'Políticas de la memoria y formas de clasificación social: ¿Quiénes son las "víctimas del terrorismo de estado" en la Argentina?', in *La imposibilidad del olvido*, ed. B. Groppo and P. Flier (La Plata, Ediciones Al Margen).

Vecchioli, V. (2005), 'La nación como familia: Metáforas políticas del movimiento argentino de derechos humanos', in *Cultura y política en etnografías sobre la Argentina* (Quilmes, Universidad Nacional de Quilmes), pp. 241–69.

Vecchioli, V. (2013), 'Las víctimas del terrorismo de Estado y la gestión del pasado reciente en la Argentina', *Papeles del CEIC: International Journal on Collective Identity Research*, 90, 1–26.

Velasco, K. (forthcoming), 'Transnational Backlash and the Deinstitutionalization of Liberal Norms: LGBT+ Rights in a Contested World', *American Journal of Sociology*, preprint available at https://osf.io/preprints/socarxiv/3rtje/.

Veltmeyer, H. and J. Petras (2015), *El neoextractivismo: ¿Un modelo posneoliberal de desarrollo o el imperialismo del siglo XXI?* (Mexico, Crítica).

Verma, P. (2020), 'Pompeo's Quest to Redefine Human Rights Draws Concern at UN', *New York Times*, 22 September.

Vinal, S. (dir.) (2021), *La lucha sigue (The Struggle Continues)*, documentary film (Mutual Aid Media).

Viterna, J. (2012), 'The Left and "Life" in El Salvador', *Politics and Gender*, 8:2, 248–54.

Vivaldi, L. and V. Stutzin (2017), 'Mujeres víctimas, fetos públicos, uteros aislados: Tecnologías de género, tensiones y desplazamientos en las representaciones visuales sobre aborto en Chile', *Zona franca*, 25:25, 126–60.

Wade, P. (1993), *Blackness and Race Mixture: The Dynamics of Racial Identity in Colombia* (Baltimore, Johns Hopkins University Press).

Webber, J. R. (2008), 'Rebellion to Reform in Bolivia Part I: Domestic Class Structure, Latin American Trends, and Capitalist Imperialism', *Historical Materialism*, 16:2, 23–58.

Webber, J. R. (2008), 'Rebellion to Reform in Bolivia Part II: Revolutionary Epoch, Combined Liberation and the December 2005 Elections', *Historical Materialism*, 16:3, 55–76.

Webber, J. R. (2008), 'Rebellion to Reform in Bolivia Part III: Neoliberal Continuities, the Autonomist Right, and the Political Economy of Indigenous Struggle', *Historical Materialism*, 16:4, 67–109.

Weber, K. (2013), 'Chiquitano and the Multiple Meanings of Being Indigenous in Bolivia', *Bulletin of Latin American Research*, 32:2, 194–209.

Bibliography

Whyte, L. (2017), '"They are coming for your children": The Rise of CitizenGo', *Open Democracy*, 9 August, https://www.opendemocracy.net/en/5050/the-rise-of-citizengo/.

Wibisono, S., W. R. Louis, and J. Jetten (2019), 'A Multi-Dimensional Analysis of Religious Extremism', *Frontiers in Psychology*, 10, article 2560.

Wibisono, S., W. Louis, and J. Jetten (2019), 'The Role of Religious Fundamentalism in the Intersection of National and Religious Identities', *Journal of Pacific Rim Psychology*, 13.

Wiesehomeier, N. and D. Doyle (2014), 'Profiling the Electorate: Ideology and Attitudes of Right Wing Voters', in *The Resilience of the Latin American Right*, ed. J. P. Luna and C. Rovira Kaltwasser (Baltimore, Johns Hopkins University Press), pp. 48–72.

WikiLeaks (2021), 'The Intolerance Network', https://wikileaks.org/intolerancenetwork/press-release?fbclid=IwAR3DjUVwoFTMrzqMtEz1P1o2A7hzfUCTd893xdhGqik6yf6I5k7Prs70ChA.

WikiLeaks (n.d.), 'The Intolerance Network', https://wikileaks.org/intolerancenetwork/press-release?fbclid=IwAR3DjUVwoFTMrzqMtEz1P1o2A7hzfUCTd893xdhGqik6yf6I5k7Prs70ChA.

Wills-Otero, L. (2014), 'Colombia: Analyzing the Strategies for Political Action of Álvaro Uribe's Government, 2002–10', in *The Resilience of the Latin American Right*, ed. J. P. Luna and C. Rovira Kaltwasser (Baltimore, Johns Hopkins University Press), pp. 194–215.

Wodak, R. (2015), *The Politics of Fear: What Right-Wing Populist Discourses Mean* (London, Sage Publications).

Wodak, R. (2019), 'Analysing the Micropolitics of the Populist Far Right in the "Post-Shame Era"', in *Europe at the Crossroads: Confronting Populist, Nationalist, and Global Challenges*, ed. P. Bevelander and R. Wodak (Lund, Nordic Academic Press), pp. 63–92.

Yashar, D. J. (2005), *Contesting Citizenship in Latin America: The Rise of Indigenous Movements and the Postliberal Challenge* (Cambridge, Cambridge University Press).

Yong, A. (2012), 'A Typology of Prosperity Theology: A Religious Economy of Global Renewal or a Renewal Economics?', in *Pentecostalism and Prosperity: The Socio-Economics of the Global Charismatic Movement*, ed. K. Attanasi and A. Yong (New York, Palgrave Macmillan), pp. 15–33.

Zaremberg, G. (2020), 'Feminism and Conservatism in Mexico', *Politics and Gender*, 16:1, 19–25.

Zavatti, F. (2021), 'Making and Contesting Far Right Sites of Memory: A Case Study on Romania', *Memory Studies*, 14:5, 949–70.

Zilla, C. (2018), Evangelicals and politics in Latin America: Religious switching and its growing political relevance (No. 46/2018). SWP Comment, Stiftung Wissenschaft und Politik (SWP), Berlin.

Žižek, S. (2008), *Violence: Six Sideways Reflections* (New York, Picador).

Zucco, C. and T. J. Power (2020), 'Fragmentation without Cleavages? Endogenous Fractionalization in the Brazilian Party System', *Comparative Politics*, 53:3, 477–500.

Zulver, J. and J. M. Piscopo (2022), 'In Colombia, an Activist, Feminist Lawyer Is Running for VP', *The Monkey Cage (Washington Post)*, 29 April, https://www.washingtonpost.com/politics/2022/04/29/marquez-petro-colombia-election-may29-afrocolombian/?utm_campaign=wp_monkeycage&utm_medium=social&utm_source=twitter

Zulver, J. M. (2021), 'The Endurance of Women's Mobilization during "Patriarchal Backlash": A Case from Colombia's Reconfiguring Armed Conflict', *International Feminist Journal of Politics*, 23:3, 440–62.

Zúñiga, A. (2016), 'Intervención en Comisión de Constitución, Legislación, Justicia y Reglamento del Senado de la República de Chile', 2 November, https://www.bcn.cl/historiadelaley/nc/historia-de-la-ley/6701/.

Index

2016 Peace Referendum 16, 20, 103;
background 85–8; 'No' Campaign 16, 86,
88, 89, 92

Abanderados por la Familia *see* Champions
of the Family
abortion 1, 14; Argentina 14, 144; Brazil
118, 144; Chile 44, 145–7; Colombia 14,
144, 235; Cuba 14; Dominican Republic
144; El Salvador 39, 42; emergency
contraception 141, 146, 148; Mexico City
14, 144; support for decriminalisation
143; Uruguay 14, 144, 189, 190, 196;
vilification of 38
adoption 118, 120, 122, 123, 124
affirmative action 1, 15, 23, 34, 47,
233; Brazil 188; Colombia 15, 188;
United States 236; Uruguay 15, 23,
41, 44, 48, 181–99, 230; *see also*
Law 122
Afro-Brazilians 18, 188
Afro-Colombians 188, 232
Afro-Latinx 1, 14, 15
Afro-Uruguayans: blanqueamiento 184,
185; history of 184–8; *see also* affirmative
action
AFyAPPA 61–3, 70
Agua Zarca 22, 162, 166, 168, 169, 170, 171
Aguilar, Alfonso 136
Alcantara, Lucio 123
Alianza Cambiemos Party 61
Alvarado, Fabricio 231
Alvear, Soledad 155
Andrews, George Reid 186
anti-abortion countermovements: Argentina
9, 157–8; Brazil 122; Catholic Church
143, 157; Chile 20, 22, 39, 48, 51, 52,
145–7, 235; Colombia 22; Dominican
Republic 14; El Salvador 14, 22, 42, 183;
evangelical church 143; failures 143–5;
feminist mobilisation 48, 143, 144, 148;
Guatemala 14; Nicaragua 14; United
States 136; Women in White 153, 155
anti-environmental countermovements 35,
240; *see also* Agua Zarca; DESA
anti-genderism 44, 92, 104, 238, 244;
Catholic Church 44, 78, 80, 92; definition
of 78; evangelical church 44, 78; in
schools 83–5; overview 80–1; *see also*

gender ideology; evangelical church; 2016
Peace Referendum
anti-LGBT+ countermovements: Brazil 17,
32–3, 36, 100, 102, 108, 121, 124, 183,
232; Catholic Church 46; Colombia 103,
107; Costa Rica 103; educational manuals
83, 88, 89; evangelical church 46; gay kit
102, 113, 232; Guatemala 108; Honduras
108; Peru 103, 108; transnational backlash
107–8; transnational networks 98–109
Araújo, Victor 125
Archimedes' Lever 52, 164–5
Argentina *see* human rights; humanitarian
rhetoric
Asociación de Familiares y Amigos de Presos
Políticos en Argentina *see* AFyAPPA
assisted reproduction 123, 124, 135
authoritarianism 1, 11, 13
Aymaras 215, 216, 217, 222

Bachelet, Michelle 142, 143, 146, 153,
156, 235
Barneix, Pedro 17
Barros, Mercedes 75
Benjamin, Walter 98, 109
BIPOC 3, 4, 32, 33, 46
Biroli, Flávia 40
Black Lives Matter 33, 239
Blanco Party 190, 192, 197
Blee, Kathleen 12
Bob, Clifford 7, 129
Bolivia *see* Cruceño countermovements;
radicial neoliberal movements
Bolsonaro, Jair 17, 32, 119, 231, 232
Borucki, Alex 184
braided action framework 163–6; *see also*
Council of Popular and Indigenous
Organisations of Honduras (COPINH)
Brazil *see* anti-LGBT+ countermovements;
evangelical church
Bucheli, Marisa 185
Butler, Judith 41, 105

Cabildo Abierto 197
Cáceres, Berta 18, 34, 41, 49, 51, 162–7,
170, 171
Caiani, Manuela 5
Calle, Humberto de la 88
Caminotti, Mariana 40

282 *Index*

Camus, Jean-Yves 12
castrochavismo 101
Catholic Church: 2016 Peace Referendum 31, 87, 88, 91; anti-genderism 37, 78, 83–5, 88; Brazil 232; size of 82; transnational advocacy networks on the right 21; *see also* right against rights
Centre for Analysis of the Radical Right (CARR) 241, 243
Centre for Justice and International Law (CEJIL) 174
Cersósimo, Gustavo 191
Chamorro, Jimmy 85
Champions of the Family 84
childfamilynation 99, 109
Chile *see* anti-abortion countermovements
Chiquitanos 221
church-in-cells 21, 112, 113, 114, 117
Colombia *see* anti-genderism; 2016 Peace Referendum
colonialism 1, 81, 108, 136, 173
Colorado Party 190, 191, 192
Con Mis Hijos No Te Metas (Don't Mess with My Kids) 134
Condor Trials 17
Corrales, Javier 104
Correa, Rafael: pink tide 13
Costas, Rubén 215
Council of Popular and Indigenous Organisations of Honduras (COPINH) 162, 164, 169, 170, 173–4; braided action 166–7, 176; *see also* Cáceres, Berta
Creasap, Kimberley 12
Cruceño countermovement 23, 35, 207, 210, 211, 212, 214, 217, 221
Cruceño identity 213; exceptionalism 213–14
Cruz, Ted 136
cultural imperialism 21, 45, 134–7
Cunha, Eduardo 121, 124
Cusicanqui, Silvia Rivera 209

da Silva, Lula: pink tide 13
Dehesa, Rafael de la 104
della Porta, Donatella 5
Desarrollo Energéticos S.A. (DESA) 169–70, 172, 173, 174; *see also* Agua Zarca
Diani, Mario 5
divorce 122
domestic violence 122, 124
Duque, Iván 82, 231, 232
Duterte, Rodrigo 238

economic actors 168, 177
elite interests 2, 5; *see also* radical neoliberal movements
elite political dynamics 8
enfoque de género (gender perspective) 79, 87, 90

Enloe, Cynthia 107
environmental movements 4, 14, 18, 32; *see also* COPINH; Cáceres, Berta
Escola sem Partido (School without Party) 103
euthanasia 11
evangelical church 7, 9, 31, 230; anti-genderism 37, 83–5, 89, 93; Brazil 21, 48, 51, 118–19, 120, 232; growth of 82; political penetration of 114–15; transnational advocacy networks on the right 21, 132; voting behaviour 125; World Revival Centre Church 84, 89; *see also* anti-abortion countermovements; anti-LGBT+ countermovements; church-in-cells; right against rights

Farabundo Martí Liberation Front (FMLN) 37
FARC 16, 92; anti-genderism 79; *see also* 2016 Peace Referendum
Fassin, Didier 65, 67
Feliciano, Marco 118–19, 121
feminist movements 9, 14, 17, 18, 21, 78, 80, 88, 105, 118, 119, 132, 142, 144, 145, 231, 235
Fortenberry, Jeff 137
framejacking 41, 107, 230; abortion 153; women's empowerment 40
Franco, Marielle 18
Fraser, Nancy 209
Free Brazil Movement (MBL) 34
Frei, Eduardo 145
Frente Amplio 181, 183, 186, 188, 189, 190, 193, 197
Fujimori, Alberto 8
Fujimori, Keiko 108, 232

Galeano, Eduardo 184
García, Allan 170
García, Tomás 170
gender ideology 16, 81, 83, 90, 91, 100, 103–5, 113; *see also* anti-genderism
Goldentul, Analía 67
grassroots right 10
Griffin, Roger 11
Grupo Gay da Bahia 36, 124
Guaraníes 213, 214, 217, 222

Hale, Charles 192, 209, 217, 223
hate speech 11, 243
HateLab 241, 243
Hernández, Ángela 85
Hijos y Nietos de Presos Políticos (HNPP) *see* Puentes para la Legalidad (Bridges to Legality)
Honduran Broad Movement for Dignity and Justice (MADJ) 174
Honduras *see* Cáceres, Berta Agua Zarca; DESA

Index

human rights: defenders in Honduras
175; trials in Argentina 59–75; *see also*
OAS–IAS
humanitarian rhetoric 67–71

ILO Convention 169 on Indigenous and
Tribal Peoples 15, 165, 166, 169, 171, 219
imperialism 108
impunity laws: Argentina 60, 61
Indigenous movements 205, 210, 211, 213,
218; *see also* environmental movements
Indigenous peoples 15, 131, 163; identity
215–17; permitted vs non-permitted rights
206, 207, 209, 210, 211, 215, 217, 223;
Wiphala 205, 215, 216; *see also* Lenca
people; Quechuas; Aymaras; Guaraníes
instutitional rights 8
Inter-American Commission on Human
Rights (IACHR) *see* OAS–IAS
Inter-American Court of Human Rights
(IACtHR) *see* OAS–IAS
International Advisory Group of Experts
(GAIPE) 174, 236
in-vitro fertilisation *see* assisted reproduction
Isiboro Sécure Indigenous Territory and
National Park (Territorio Indígena y
Parque Nacional Isiboro Sécure, TIPNIS)
218, 219, 220, 221
Islamic fundamentalism 12, 80, 81, 239, 243

Jaime Guzmán Foundation (FJG) 151
Justa Libres 84, 87, 89

Karell, Daniel 240
Kerry, John 135
Kirchner, Cristina 62
Kirchner, Néstor 61
Kirchnerism 61, 75
Kokay, Erika 121
Kopecky, Petr 11

Lakhani, Nina 18
Lancaster, Roger 106
Laqueur, Thomas 68
Law 19.122, 181, 182; implementation
of 193–6; passage of 189–93; *see also*
affirmative action
Lawrence, Stephen 242
Lebourg, Nicolas 12
Lee, Mike 135
Lemaitre, Julieta 44
Lenca people 162, 166, 169, 171
LGBT+ rights: 2016 Peace Referendum 91;
adoption 15, 80, 90, 106, 118; same-sex
marriage 123, 196; vilification of 38; *see
also* anti-LGBT+ countermovements
Lobo, Porfirio 169
Loiola, J. R. A. 116

Lorenzini, Pablo 155
Lowrey, Kathleen 214
Lozada, Ruth 215, 216

Macri, Mauricio 49, 61, 70
Madres de la Plaza de Mayo 20, 60, 62, 66,
68, 235
Márquez, Francia 232
Marshall, Gordon 6, 10
Mayka, Lindsay 9, 229
McCrudden, Christopher 11
McEwen, Haley 238
McKelvey, Fenwick 240
Memoria Completa 63–4, 73
mestizos 23, 41, 212, 213, 214, 221,
223
Meyer, David 12
Micheletti, Roberto 168
Ministry of Women and Gender Equality
(MMEG) 148, 149, 154, 155, 158
Modi, Narendra 237, 238, 239
Moghadam, Valentine 36
Monzillo, Inés 197
Moonshot 241, 243
moral panic 20, 36, 38, 51, 100, 104, 106,
113, 142, 157, 231
Morales, Evo 205, 208, 209, 213, 215, 220,
233; pink tide 13
Mothers of the Plaza de Mayo *see* Madres de
la Plaza de Mayo
Motta, Sarah 34
Mouffe, Chantal 102
Movimento Brasil Livre (MBL) 17
Mudde, Cas 11, 13
multiculturalism 15, 23, 207, 209–11,
215, 223

nativism 13
Nogueira, Claudia 155
Nunca Más (Never Again) 64–5

OAS–IAS 21; abortion 131; background
130–3; framejacking 133–7; General
Assembly 131–3; LGBT+ rights 131;
transational anti-rights mobilisation
134–7; United States 134–5,
136, 137
O'Brien, Cheryl 6, 233
Oliva, Fátima 133
Orbán, Victor 241
Ordoñez, Alejandro 84, 89
Ortiz, Oscar 215, 216, 217
Ortuño, Edgardo 186, 195

Pacha Mama 15
Paiva, Eleuses 123
Pardo, Hector 87
Parody, Gina 83, 85

Index

Payne, Leigh A., 63, 183; Uncivil Movements 10, 19, 98
Pentecostal Church *see* evangelical church
pink tide 13–14, 101; Brazil 13–14
Pinker, Steven 18
Pinochet, Augusto 22, 39, 146
Pompeo, Mike 4, 136, 138
populism 2, 8, 10, 13, 229
Porzecanski, Rafael 185
Power, Tim 8
pro-choice mobilisation 22, 52, 142, 143, 145, 147–51, 154
Proud Boys 33
Puentes para la Legalidad (Bridges to Legality) 61–3, 67, 68, 71

Quechuas 215, 216, 217, 222
Quintero Garzón, Cindy Johana 106
Quiroga, Castro 87

radical neoliberal movements: Bolivia 205–22; Global North 239–41
Rea, Castro 4, 5, 31, 32, 36
Rechtman, Richard 67
Restrepo Sanín, Juliana 233
Rigby, Lee 243
right against rights: analytical framework 30; Catholic Church 7, 31, 43–4, 92; Christianophobia 124; coded discourse 23, 41, 198; countermovements 6, 19, 31, 46, 53; crisis-building 144; definition of 7; evangelical church 31, 92; failures 48–9; far right 11; Global South 237–9; heterophobia 124; impact of 18–19; Latin American context 7–13, 53; legitimating myths 153; mobilisation of 3, 5–7; moderate factions 11; proliferation of 19; radical neoliberal mobilisations 19, 22, 23, 33–5, 46, 53, 162–3, 206, 207–9, 222; rejection of Indigenous identity 171, 172; religious formations 82; strategies to limit 241–4; successes 47–8; uncivil movements 19, 32–3, 46, 53, 99–100, 166
right-against-rights mobilisation tactics: double militancy 43–4; framing 37, 53; impact of 46–7; leadership and organisation 42–3; legitimating myths 39–42; reducing impact of 49–53; threat, historical symbols, and cultural cues 38–9; transnational advocacy networks on the right 44–5; visibility and disruption 45–6
'righting rights' 24, 230, 231–4
'righting wrongs' 24, 230
rights: backlash against 16–18; definition of 3–5; of nature 15

Roblón, El 169
Rodríguez, Romero Jorge 187
Roe v. Wade 235
Rohlinger, Deana A., 240
Rubio, Marco 135
Rueda Sierra, Ismael 84
Rule of Law 1983, 64

Salazar Gómez, Rubén 83
Sanseverino, Bertha 181, 198
Santa Cruz 206, 208; Civic Committee 209, 211, 212, 215, 220, 221, 222; *see also* radical neoliberal movements
Santos, Juan Manuel 86, 90, 106
Sarmiento, Claudia 156
Saroglou, Vassilis 115
Scott, John 6, 10
Serrano-Amaya, Fernando 104
Sikkink, Kathryn 18, 59, 236
Silva, Néstor 195
Simmel, Georg 125
Smith, Amy Erica 9, 229
Smith, Chris 137
social media: right-wing use 9, 89, 91, 173, 240
social movements 6, 207; as right-wing movements 5; competing definitions of 5–6
Southern Poverty Law Centre (SPLC) 241, 242
Staggenborg, Suzanne 12
Stop Hate UK 241, 242
Suplicy, Marta 121
swing conservative allies 143, 144, 151, 156

Thatcher, Margaret 241
Tilly, Charles 5, 105
Townsend-Bell, Erica 189
transgender people 99, 121, 141, 197; gender-affirming surgeries 102
transgender rights 196; *see also* LGBT+ rights
transnational advocacy networks on the right 2, 20, 44, 234, 235; anti-LGBT+ 98–109; *see also* right against rights
Trujillo, Carlos 136
Trump, Donald 18, 135, 136, 238
Turres, Marisol 155

U Party 83, 84, 86
uncivil movements 10–11, 19, 171; Global North 239–41; United States 33; *see also* right against rights
Unión Juvenil Cruceñista (UJC) 209, 213, 214

Urbina Ortega, Oscar 84
Uribe, Álvaro 34, 44, 82, 232; *see also* 2016 Peace Referendum
Uruguay *see* affirmative action
US Capitol insurrection 33, 51, 239

Vaggione, Juan Marco 40, 43, 153
Valdés, Ildefonso Pereda 185
Vamos Uruguay 190
Van Cott, Donna Lee 210, 218, 223
Vargas, Yolanda 85
Vázquez, Tabaré, 186

Velasco, Kristopher 105
Vida SV ('Si a la Vida' (Yes to Life)) 42
Viterna, Jocelyn 38

Walker, Elisa 156
Walsh, Shannon Drysdale 6
WikiLeaks 244
Wyllys, Jean 33, 119, 121

Zaremberg, Gisela 52
Zelaya, Manuel 168
Zúñiga, Alejandra 154